Creole Identity in the French Caribbean Novel

Florida A&M University, Tallahassee
Florida Atlantic University, Boca Raton
Florida Gulf Coast University, Ft. Myers
Florida International University, Miami
Florida State University, Tallahassee
University of Central Florida, Orlando
University of Florida, Gainesville
University of North Florida, Jacksonville
University of South Florida, Tampa
University of West Florida, Pensacola

Creole Identity in
the French Caribbean Novel

❧ *H. Adlai Murdoch*

University Press of Florida

Gainesville · Tallahassee · Tampa · Boca Raton

Pensacola · Orlando · Miami · Jacksonville · Ft. Myers

06 05 04 03 02 01   6 5 4 3 2 1

Library of Congress Cataloging-in-Publication Data
Murdoch, H. Adlai.
Creole identity in the French Caribbean novel / H. Adlai Murdoch.
p. cm.
Includes bibliographical references and index.
ISBN 0-8130-1835-8 (cloth: alk. paper)
1. Caribbean fiction (French)–History and criticism. 2. Creoles in
literature. I. Title.
PQ3944.M87 2001
843.009'9729–dc21   00-064908

The University Press of Florida is the scholarly publishing agency for
the State University System of Florida, comprising Florida A&M
University, Florida Atlantic University, Florida Gulf Coast University,
Florida International University, Florida State University, University
of Central Florida, University of Florida, University of North Florida,
University of South Florida, and University of West Florida.

University Press of Florida
15 Northwest 15th Street
Gainesville, FL 32611-2079
http://www.upf.com

To my parents
To my wife, Judy
And to the people of the Caribbean

Know yourself, before they tell you who you are.
—African proverb

Contents

Acknowledgments

While it has long been a commonplace in projects such as these to point out that those to be thanked are legion, in this case the axiom is literally an accurate one. I would like to begin by thanking my dissertation committee at Cornell University—Nelly Furman, Jonathan Culler, Henry Louis Gates, Jr., and N. Gregson Davis—who taught me the practice and value of close reading and interpretation. At Wellesley College, I'd like to thank Margaret Cezair-Thompson, Selwyn Cudjoe, Venita Datta, Salem Mekuria, Jean Stanley, AmyNoel Wyman, and the late Michel Grimaud for stalwart company along the way. Friends and colleagues, including Françoise Lionnet, Kwame Anthony Appiah, Michael Dash, Josephine Diamond, Anne Donadey, Tony Hurley, Biodun Jeyifo, Renée Larrier, Edris Makward, Mireille Rosello, Dominic Thomas, Keith Warner, Pascale DeSouza, and Claire Andrade-Watkins have provided critical moments of support, encouragement, and intellectual exchange over the years. My participation in the summer seminar at the School of Criticism and Theory in 1993 and my intersections with Homi Bhabha and my fellow participants proved a momentous turning point in the gestation and development of this project.

The French Department at the University of Illinois at Urbana-Champaign has since 1996 provided me with a safe and supportive home base from which to complete this project, and in this regard I'd like to thank Evelyne Accad, Doug Kibbee, Emile Talbot, and Yvette-M. Smith for critical help and guidance. The secretarial staff, especially Barb Oehlschlaeger-Garvey and Ann Preisel, as well as Mustapha Hamil, Jane Kuntz, Elizabeth Zahnd, and other members of my graduate seminars, played key roles in helping the book itself, as well as the ideas in it, to see the light of day. Friends and colleagues in other departments, particularly Kwaku Korang, Robert Dale Parker, and Zohreh Sullivan of the English Department, know only too well the ways in which their generosity of time and spirit helped shape the manuscript. I'd also like to thank the Illinois Program for Research in the Humanities for the semester's leave that afforded me valuable writing time and space at a critical juncture. My exchanges with the other IPRH Fellows served to hone a number of ideas and concepts. Also, the conversations I held with Suzanne Dracius during her visit to the campus in April 1998 were of inestimable help in shaping my reading of her work. I also offer my sincere thanks to Susan Fernandez and Deidre Bryan of the University Press of Florida, who carefully shepherded the manuscript through the different stages of production and demonstrated great patience and understanding with a first-time author.

Portions of chapter 1 originally appeared as "(Re)Figuring Colonialism: Narratological and Ideological Resistance in the Work of Edouard Glissant," *Callaloo* 15, 1 (Winter 1992):2–11, copyright 1992 by Charles H. Rowell, reprinted by permission of the Johns Hopkins University Press.

Portions of chapter 2 originally appeared as "Divided Desire: Biculturality and the Representation of Identity in *En attendant le bonheur*," *Callaloo* 18, 3 (Summer 1995):579–92, copyright 1995 by Charles H. Rowell, reprinted by permission of the Johns Hopkins University Press.

Portions of chapter 3 originally appeared as "(Dis)Placing Marginality: Cultural Identity and Creole Resistance in Glissant and Maximin," *Research in African Literatures* 25, 2 (1994):81–101, reprinted by permission of Indiana University Press.

Portions of chapters 3 and 4 originally appeared as "Exploring the Margin: Models of Cultural Identity in the Postcolonial French Caribbean," *Journal of Commonwealth and Postcolonial Studies* 6, 1 (Spring 1999), reprinted by permission of the journal.

Portions of chapter 5 originally appeared as "Re-Siting Resistance: Chamoiseau's Articulation of Creole Identity," *Sites* 3, 2 (Fall 1999), 315–21. I am grateful to the publishers, Gordon and Breach, for permission to reprint.

Portions of chapter 5 also appeared as "Inscribing Caribbean *Oraliture*: The Polysemic Discourse of Patrick Chamoiseau," in *Multiculturalism and Hybridity in African Literatures*, edited by Hal Wylie and Bernth Lindfors, copyright African Literature Association, 2000. Permission to reprint has been granted by the publisher, Africa World Press.

Portions of chapters 1 and 5 also appeared as "Narrating Creole Culture: Strategies of Selfhood in the Francophone Caribbean Novel," in *Migrating Words and Worlds: Pan-Africanism Updated*, edited by E. Anthony Hurley, Renée Larrier, and Joseph McLaren, copyright African Literature Association

1999. Permission to reprint has been granted by the publisher, Africa World Press.

The translations used in this book are taken from the following editions:

Edouard Glissant, *The Ripening*, translated by J. Michael Dash, reprinted by permission of Heinemann Educational Publishers, a division of Reed Educational and Professional Publishing Ltd.

Maryse Condé, *Hérémakhonon*, translated by Richard Philcox, reprinted by permission of Lynne Rienner Publishers Ltd.

Daniel Maximin, *Lone Sun*, translated by Clarisse Zimra, reprinted by permission of the University Press of Virginia.

Patrick Chamoiseau, *Solibo Magnificent*, translation copyright 1997 by Rose-Myriam Réjouis and Val Vinokurov. Afterword copyright 1997 by Rose-Myriam Réjouis. Reprinted by permission of Pantheon Books, a division of Random House, Inc.

All other translations are the work of John Garvey. Where double page citations appear in parentheses, the first number refers to the English translation and the second to the French edition.

Finally, I would like to express my appreciation to my parents, Hilson and Sylvia Murdoch, for the pride in West Indian culture and history and the devotion to intellectual endeavor that they instilled in me so long ago in our native Antigua. This book is in large part a product of their early encouragement. To my wife, Judy, who lived with the ups, downs, and periodic small triumphs that ultimately produced this volume, I owe more than I can ever say or show.

Introduction

Conceptualizing Creoleness
French Caribbean "Postcolonial" Discourse

I have Dutch, nigger, and English in me,
   and either I'm nobody, or I'm a nation
Derek Walcott, *"The Schooner Flight"*

In *The Conquest of America*, Tzvetan Todorov proposes Christopher Columbus's arrival in the New World as the political and temporal site establishing the modernity of our contemporary identities: "Even if every date that permits us to separate any two periods is arbitrary, none is more suitable, in order to mark the beginning of the modern era, than the year 1492. . . . We are all the direct descendants of Columbus, it is with him that our genealogy begins, insofar as the word *beginning* has a meaning" (5). In a similar vein, Paul Gilroy posits in *The Black Atlantic* the notion of ethnic and cultural exchange with Africa as the primary symbol of our era's emerging modernity. For the peoples of the Caribbean, the inheritors of the traces of these twin historical trajectories, the ambiguities implicit in this post-Columbian era encapsulate the doubleness that lies at the core of any identitarian framework through which their interests might be discursively articulated. By joining the specific patterns of slavery, colonialism, and racism engendered in the region with the complexities of ethnic and cultural admixture brought about by the sugar-driven tensions of the colonial encounter, it becomes increasingly evident that the beginnings of Caribbean modernity are mediated, inter alia, by the destruction of the early Amerindian population, the transportation and enslavement of an African labor force, the subsequent insertion of hundreds of thousands of Indian and Chinese immigrants as indentured servants, and the integration of British, French, Spanish, Dutch, and Portuguese cultures that are the ineradicable trace of the colonial period.

More specifically, the story and trajectory of French Caribbean modernity are simultaneously the story of a cycle of violence inseparable from the colonial project—one present, indeed, from the very moment of its inception—and the related story of the making and breaking of divided metropolitan loyalties. As Gordon K. Lewis points out, "Colonialism generated in the Caribbean mentality a divisive loyalty to the metropolitan culture that explains the historical tardiness of the final arrival of national independence . . . and . . . that perverse attachment to the governing colonial power explains why . . . the French Antilles remain politically tied to . . . France" (239–40). The cultural and discursive implications of this division form the core of this book, for as a result of the complex contradictions that emerge from the colonial period, any vision of Caribbean modernity must take into account not only these intrinsic patterns of domination, destruction, and death that are part of the region's post-Columbian history, but the tensions and teleologies of an ethnocultural heterogeneity whose particularization of global patterns of creolization was recognized and celebrated by the awarding of the Goncourt and the Nobel Literature prizes to regional authors Patrick Chamoiseau and Derek Walcott, respectively, in 1992.

But this heterogeneity is not in and of itself a monolithic construct. Indeed, it is the specifics of the sociopolitical pluralism brought about by departmentalizing the overseas French Caribbean colonies of Guadeloupe and Martinique in 1946, and their authors' subsequent attempts to explore alternate discursive parameters for articulating a cultural identity read as creole through its elaboration of a complex yet unlocalizable set of differences—indeed, from a postcoloniality that is not yet one—that this book seeks to explore.

In theoretical terms, French Caribbean postcolonialism is itself the locus of yet another level of paradoxical doubling. Typically, postcolonialism defines the period when links of domination and subservience with the colonizing country have been severed, when the subject territory can exercise that freedom of action and of expression inhibited by the colonial framework. But one of the hallmarks of contemporary French Caribbean discourse is the very fact that the pressing sociocultural and geopolitical paradoxes of its ties to the French mainland have led its thinkers to explore alternative models of discursive self-articulation that can mine the terrain of difference that sets the imagined community against the metropole. As a result, the narrative strategies and discursive patterns of these novels are necessarily varied; adopting and adapting varying attitudes toward the genesis and implications of Caribbean creolization, they address alternative postcolonial possibilities, a repositioning of the axis of the periphery and its other that retains the ambiguities of an alterity both intrinsically different and yet not quite. Importantly, this is also the site of a critical conjunction, for this doubling of postcolonialism's discursive boundaries is echoed in the complexities of the creole figure, a construct which, as I shall show, is itself imbued with crucial characteristics of doubling, disjuncture, and difference. Within this creole postcoloniality, then, lies the articulative framework of an identitarian strategy that is both ambivalent and differential; the true resonance of these creole fictions emerges in the discursive space within which alternative sites and strategies of inscription rewrite accepted notions of subjectivity, otherness, and modernity.

While the doubleness of the creole figure is one facet of the sociocultural phenomenon of Caribbean modernity, creolization as a process is by no means restricted to the Caribbean region. Much of the history of the modern period is characterized by patterns of migratory movement and population inflows and outflows that have effectively creolized the structure of many ethnic groups and national communities. As a result, racial and cultural interaction have long been integral aspects of the growth of nations in the modern era. Ultimately, these culminations of a historical interpenetration of cultures would produce what Michael Dash, in *The Other America*, calls "a growing acknowledgement of plurality and creolization as a global phenomenon"; for if, in Dash's words, the Caribbean is seen as "the vanguard in the process of cross-culturality" (6), this conclusion compels us to seek out the specifics of Caribbean difference, to examine these differential boundaries of hybridization and creolization and the ways in which they were shaped by the complexities of the Caribbean experience. For the French Caribbean in particular, notions of Caribbeanness and creoleness would form the discursive core of a strategy of creative hybridity that sought to articulate identity through the exploration and exploitation of pluralism, ambiguity, and instability.

How, then, can we approach the specific difference(s) that creoleness has wrought in the Caribbean? And further, how is this creolization to be differentiated from its related phenomena of hybridity and *métissage*? The in-betweenness of French Caribbean postcolonialism generates a sense of group identity that functions outside, and in spite of, the political ties to the metropole that produce what Richard Burton has called an "unrequited longing for fusion, either by possession or by absorption, with a valorized French Other" (1993: 83), producing a critical ambivalence that gestures toward the unhyphenated use of the term "postcolonial" within the context of this study. Such issues of alienation and of national and cultural group identity also impact questions of exclusion and inclusion, of cultural intersection and ethnic heterogeneity as they occur in a Caribbean context. Indeed, as Stephen Slemon suggests, "Post-colonial nation-states develop new forms of international relations and self-constitution as they proceed . . . in the process developing new structures for group identification and collectivity" (180). As we shall see, it is the constitution of the group in a differential identitarian context, and its capacity for shaping and articulating the intersections and ambiguities of regional geopolitics, that will be the chief concern not only of this work's critical framework but of its authorial discourses as well.

With these caveats, we can now look at the parameters of the term "creole," where close examination will show a corresponding association with the discourse of colonialism. Indeed, it is an inherently unstable category, shot through with the ambiguities and essentialisms of its origins in the colonial period. The OED standard definition inscribes the creole in terms of instability and alterity, figuring a European *or* an African subject linked to displacements of place rather than race, stressing the otherness of any specific origins and the absence of any reference to skin color: "In the West Indies and other parts of America, Mauritius, etc.: *orig.* A person born and naturalized in the country, but of European (usually Spanish or French) or of African Negro race: the name having no connotation of colour, and in its reference to origin being distinguished on the one hand from born in Europe (or Africa), and on the other hand from aboriginal."[1] In this way, a creole person can be either white or black, colonizer or colonized, articulating an essential ambiguity that both mediates and ruptures the strategies of containment that have circumscribed and determined the dominant designations of difference that have been the traditional corollary of the colonial encounter. What emerges from such a definition is primarily the play of difference that the term implies, for indeed a creole subject or culture may be black or white, African, Caucasian, or East Asian, colonial or metropolitan, or, for that matter, the product of myriad ethnic and linguistic influences and origins. In other words, if the creole figure can be located only as one among several possibilities, or even, in some cases, several possibilities at once, then the discursive creoleness I am elaborating here may be engaged through similarly multiple sites and strategies of doubling, difference, and dislocation. It is the undecidability of this shifting signifier, then, upon which I am drawing, in its most creative sense, to posit a continuum of discursive division and doubleness as the basic framework upon which these variant fictions of the creole are constructed. Every choice in this selection of novels, then, will be seen to be similar to its others yet different, each being a specific instantiation of a complex, unlocalizable social and cultural discourse.

But the importance of articulating a so-called third space, particularly where it serves to locate a postcolonial position, must also be the simultaneous recognition of how this space functions in discursive terms. Homi Bhabha's useful formulation is of interest here: "The importance of hybridity is not to be able to trace two original moments from which the third emerges, rather hybridity . . . is the 'third space' which enables other positions to emerge. This third space displaces the histories that constitute it, and sets up new structures of authority" (1990:211). It is thus hybridity's role in formulating alternative discursive positions, rather than the binary framework driving hybridity itself, that becomes crucial in formulating an enabling framework for the Caribbean process of creolization, marking the division between a globalizing cultural hybridity and the specific difference grounding its regional instantiation.

In a certain sense, the importance of patterns of creole interaction as a sort of structural foundation for Caribbean societies was established through the work of the poet and historian Edward Brathwaite. In *The Development of Creole Society in Jamaica, 1770–1820*, Brathwaite proposed that the principle of cultural distinctness upon which much of the historical definition of the region was drawn be abandoned in favor of an increasing recognition of the intrinsic sociocultural pluralism of the islands. Drawing on this notion, the editors of the recent volume *Caribbean Creolizations* have suggested a current definition of this cultural process, rooted in transformation and shaped by the region's syncretism: "Creolization is thus defined as a syncretic process of transverse dynamics that endlessly reworks and transforms the cultural patterns of varied social and historical experiences and identities" (3). What is foregrounded here is the notion of change; in conjunction with the multiplicities of history, culture, and identity, the resulting juxtapositions and interactions give rise to associative strategies of adaptability, re-presentation, and relationality: indeed, in its capacity for creative contestation, Balutansky and Sourieau claim that "creolization becomes a power for reversing the processes of acculturation (or assimilation), deculturation, discontinuity, and marginalization that have affected the entire Caribbean" (5). With increasingly few groups left untouched by this process of exchange, defining the specifics of difference becomes an even more pressing question; as Stuart Hall argues in

"When Was 'the Post-colonial'?": "Understood in its global and transcultural context, colonisation has made ethnic absolutism an increasingly untenable cultural strategy. It made the 'colonies' themselves, and even more, large tracts of the 'post-colonial' world, always-already 'diasporic' in relation to what might be thought of as their cultures of origin" (1996:250). If "Caribbeanness" as a cultural/discursive framework is to be adequately addressed and defined, it must be thought of not simply in terms of a binary relationship between the Other and the Same—where these nonspecific patterns of ethnocultural inter-penetration are pluralized through colonial repetition—but through a set of commonalities and practices that engage difference even as they diverge from the geopolitical patterns governing the hierarchical relations between metro-pole and colony. In stressing this point, Hall opens the door to the infinite possibilities of an interstitial postcolonial praxis that operates against the grain of nations and borders.

Each of these fictions, then, by interrogating the complex creole network of language, history, politics, and ethnic and cultural admixture that are at work in the French Caribbean territories of Guadeloupe and Martinique, addresses the core issues of Caribbean creole identity, albeit in significantly different ways. They do so by tapping the traces of confrontation, contradiction, and ambivalence to reveal varying aspects of the tensions and textures of interac-tion, coexistence, and cultural interpenetration that (re)define the terms of an ongoing Caribbean pluralism. The discursive practices framed by these works articulate differential figures of openness, multiplicity, and modernity that resonate with polysemic pluralism, constructing new categories of a relational, postcolonial identity from the interstices of cultural signification.

Inhabitants neither of colonies nor independent countries, French West Indians must enact a daily double gesture that splits their subjectivity between metropole and department, extending additional patterns of complexity to a region already subtended by traces of alienation, displacement, and double-ness. Indeed, as if to underscore the ironies and paradoxes that limn the terrain of this relationship, the fiftieth anniversary of the departmentalization law was feted in both department and metropole; first in Paris, through an exposition at the Palais de Chaillot from 16 November through 15 December 1996, under the theme *Les départements d'outre-mer: quatre siècles d'histoire commune*. This event was then restaged in the Antilles, installed in the Salle Osenat in Schoelcher, Martinique, from 9 to 26 April 1997. While a more sober-minded view of the deleterious overall effect of departmentalization on these territories in areas like unemployment and exports could be easily articulated, this example of the double vision of the DOMs (*département d'outre- mer*, or French overseas department) sums up quite effectively the paradoxes and inconsistencies of the overseas departmental relationship.

If the works of the five authors studied here embody a sense of Caribbean creoleness, then, they do so as much because of their variety of character and milieu as because of the dissimilar approaches they take to discourse and representation. These works seek to trace and transform the tensions of alienation and displacement that shape the postcolonial pluralisms of ethnicity, culture, and politics at work in the French Caribbean. Here the concept of ethnicity will be of particular importance, given its multivalent postcolonial resonances as Stuart Hall has articulated them in "New Ethnicities": "Ethnicity acknowledges the place of history, language and culture in the construction of subjectivity and identity, as well as the fact that all discourse is placed, positioned, situated, and all knowledge is contextual" (1996:446). From this perspective, ethnicity is no longer simply a corollary of reductive and destructive forms of nationalism but is integral to the construction of differential discourses of identitarianism within a postcolonial context.

La Lézarde, the subject of chapter 1, was Edouard Glissant's first novel. Published in 1958, it received the prestigious Prix Charles Renaudot in France, paradoxically appearing at a time when the very survival of the French republic appeared to be in jeopardy. The novel's interrogation of the subjective and social implications for his native Martinique of the decade-old departmental relation with France inaugurated a fresh look at the terms and conditions that had brought this relationship into being. By engaging in fictional terms with an event that was progressively reshaping both Martinican politics and its national psyche, and by recasting the decision in terms of a pivotal election, Glissant was able to critique the genesis of the Césaire-sponsored *loi de départmentalisation* of 1946. As Gregson Davis points out in *Aimé Césaire*, this law "required two years of unflagging advocacy in the face of opposition from the Right before it was eventually successful" (95). The novel would be a discursive examination of the repercussions of a decision that, arguably, had wrought as momentous a change in Martinican life as the Act of Emancipation that had preceded it by exactly one hundred years.

The discursive and structural complexity of *La Lézarde* is an initial move, the beginning of his effort, as Celia Britton puts it in her recent book *Edouard Glissant and Postcolonial Theory*, "to grasp the whole of the complex, multiply interrelated and overdetermined cultural reality of Martinique in its relation to France and to the rest of the Caribbean" (8). But where the primary focus of Britton's study is to place Glissant's use of language in a postcolonial frame, my own aim is to reveal the extent to which, from a Glissantian perspective, the intrinsic doubleness and ambiguity already innate in the departmental moment had overdetermined the multiple levels of intra-island social and subjective relations. It is this fracturing of the already colonized Martinican psyche, its simultaneous repetition and dissolution of self and Other, metropole and periphery, that is ultimately the subject of *La Lézarde*.

In Maryse Condé's *En attendant le bonheur*, on the other hand, I examine the ways in which Condé's autobigraphical novel manipulates the key issues of ethnicity, politics, and place to interrogate the location of a space for Caribbean women's identity. As I shall argue, Condé does this principally by merging unorthodox discursive patterns with the re-presentation of a fragmentary subjectivity, in order to analyze more closely what Leah Hewitt, in her *Autobiographical Tightropes*, terms the protagonist's "search for a 'place' of her own, a sense of roots, belonging, and worth" (163). In contrast to Hewitt's focus on the autobiographical, however, my study stresses Condé's conflation of fragmented voice, place, and perspective as a means of engaging the elusive core of an undefinable creoleness that provides the underpinning for concepts of Caribbean womanhood. The deliberate polyphony of Condé's prose elides the divisions between oral exchange, discursive aside, and interior monologue, so that the multiple pasts and dislocated present of Véronica, her protagonist, become figures for the pluralized discourses that re-present the creolization of her Guadeloupean origins. By pursuing her identity quest through a series of sexual relationships—the first with a Guadeloupean mulatto, then with a white French professional, and lastly with a black African politician with claims to nobility—Véronica's complexities reflect and embody the multiple axes and alliances that continue to determine any framework for collective identity that can be constructed in the Caribbean context. The intrinsic patterns of alienation that arise from any and all of Véronica's associations underscore the complex, multipartite space(s) of Caribbean creolization, while the author's innovative turn with a narrative discourse whose displacements mediate between alienation and liberation demonstrates, as Condé herself put it in a recent article, that "language for the West Indian writer is the only way of shaping the future" (1993:127). The difference and diversity of creoleness in the Caribbean are the elements ultimately valorized by her writing.

By contrast, Daniel Maximin's *L'Isolé Soleil* takes an almost purely discursive approach to its (re)articulation of the principal axes of historical and cultural identity in the French Caribbean. While, on the one hand, this might be read as a response to the historic instantiation of colonialism through discourse, such critics as Benita Parry have long since shown that, in a postcolonial context, simply negating a framework of oppression does nothing to alter the established tenor of its terms. Rather, Maximin's goal is the (re)writing of the historical and psychocultural experience in the French Caribbean, exposing and articulating an occulted history from the perspective of its people. He accomplishes this by deploying an astonishing array of metafictional techniques and devices, constructing a polyphonic panoply that ranges across two centuries of Caribbeanness. His work thus reveals the historic inscription of a people's identity through a series of critical *lieux de mémoire* that both demonstrates and defines their spirit of cultural resistance. This paradigm of literary marooning takes as its point of departure its protagonist's desire to discursively (re)construct the *grandes étapes* of her family's history. By constantly shifting voices, positionalities, and perspectives, inscribing an insistent self-reflexivity that meditates on patterns of discursive doubleness even as it erects and erases them, Maximin's novel writes *about* writing the Caribbean into being. Maximin thus puts into play a self-sustaining interrogation of difference and pluralism that embodies the very idea of Caribbean multiplicity that is the subject of his novel.

In my approach to Suzanne Dracius's *L'Autre qui danse*, I take as my point of departure the conflation of ethnocultural métissage and geocultural exile that the author inscribes through the tensions traced by the contradictory characteristics of the two sisters who are her novel's protagonists. By interrogating the very basis of what it means to be both French and West Indian — by tracing the psychocultural displacements intrinsic to the journey from Martinique to France and its inevitable return — Dracius highlights the challenges and difficulties posed by the inability to locate a space of social and cultural belonging for the subject. Also, her choice of mixed-race, or *métises*, Caribbean women as icons of this complex category of disjunctures allows the author to re-present the plurality of ethnicity, culture, and place that undergirds the creolization of the Martinican subject even as she explores the importance of these implications for a feminine component always already dominated and displaced. Dracius is able to incorporate and interrogate key issues of language use, cul-

tural authenticity, and exile and belonging—particularly for the new generation of *négropolitains*—as she traces the opposing parameters of her fraternal
protagonists through a shifting canvas of narrative techniques.

Finally, my reading of Patrick Chamoiseau's *Solibo Magnifique*—a novel
that appeared some four years before the publication of *Texaco* brought him
such critical acclaim—takes as its point of departure the cultural and linguistic polyphony that is such an integral part of the Martinican experience. The
novel's concentration on the underrepresented and disappearing class of *djobeurs* allows for both parody and metafictional play, providing insights into the
metropolitan constructions of alienation that rend both the social whole and
its speech patterns into fragments of an ethnocultural ensemble whose actions
enlighten even as they entertain. Ultimately, it is this cultural unrepresentability whose polyvalence Chamoiseau both champions and turns to discursive advantage, deriving a critical discourse of difference from its intersections
of language and culture, ethnicity and class.

Each of these texts inscribes its own instantiation of cultural difference,
reading and writing key concepts of Caribbean creolization from a variety of
positions and perspectives. Writing the poetics of Caribbean creole performance, then, calls for a disjunctural literary discourse, generating sites and
strategies whereby the inscription of narrative dislocation and linguistic ex-
perimentation in the very fabric of the narrative figures the negotiation of sociocultural identity and empowerment through pluralism and difference.

Articulating Antillanité

The principles of *antillanité*, or Caribbeanness, that Glissant elaborates most
fully in *Le Discours antillais* (translated as *Caribbean Discourse* [CD]) form
a complete epistemological break with the tensions and teleologies of negritude. Realizing that a simple response to the hierarchies of a colonial discourse does nothing to negate its essential properties, Glissant seeks to specify
the terms and conditions of a creole culture that he locates beyond the boundaries of (neo)colonialism, within a Caribbean context of constant creative
flux and an insistent, multiple modernity. Thus the core of antillanité is inscribed between the articulative axes of uprooting and transformation—perhaps the two principal elements that have informed strategies of subaltern
survival: "I feel that what makes this difference between a people that survives
elsewhere, *that maintains its original nature*, and a population that is trans-

formed elsewhere *into another people* . . . and that thus enters the constantly shifting and variable process of creolization (of relationship, of relativity), is that the latter has not brought with it, not collectively continued, the methods of existence and survival, both material and spiritual, which it practiced before being uprooted" (CD 15; emphasis in the original). Within this critical context of transformation the initial instantiation of Caribbean creolization takes shape; through a curious concatenation of change and pluralism, of *becoming* less than self or Other but simultaneously more than the sum of both, the creative instabilities and undecidabilities of racial and cultural admixture eventually spawn the multipartite core of French West Indian subjectivity.

By inscribing and analyzing destructive regional tendencies toward what he terms "Reversion"—the misplaced obsession with a single origin—and "Diversion"—the neocolonial concealment of an ongoing domination—Glissant illuminates the disturbing facets of cultural and historical dispossession to frame the latent possibilities of an alternative, emergent creolization.[2] This generative framework turns the ambivalence and incessant slippage of the Caribbean condition into a discursive redefinition of the what and the how of French West Indian being and becoming. As Glissant puts it, "Today the French Caribbean individual . . . understands that from all this history . . . *another reality* has come about. . . . He can conceive that synthesis is not a process of bastardization as he used to be told, but a productive activity through which each element is enriched. He has *become* Caribbean (CD 8; emphasis in the original). Functioning through displacement, relocation, and transformation, patterns of mutation and metamorphosis replace notions of pure origin with the fertile imaginativeness of the cross-cultural imagination.

What Glissant stresses, in other words, is the creativity of the composite, a construct founded in hybridity but one that also surpasses it, a productive multiplicity that continually transforms and reinvents itself. The historical and geopolitical specificities of the French Caribbean, the cultural pluralisms engendered by ethnic admixture, and the dualities of departmental dependence make this a scene of creolization that displaces negative notions of braiding, binarism, and sterility. "Creolization as an idea is not primarily the glorification of the composite nature of a people: indeed, no people has been spared the crosscultural process. . . . To assert peoples are creolized, that creolization has value, is to deconstruct in this way the category of 'creolized' that is considered as halfway between two 'pure' extremes" (CD 140).

Glissant would continue to valorize the relative aspects of this notion of

Caribbean creolization in the *Poétique de la relation* (translated as *Poetics of Relation* [PR]): "Creolization seems to be a limitless *métissage*, its elements diffracted and its consequences unforeseeable. Creolization diffracts, whereas certain forms of *métissage* can concentrate one more time" (34). Here, by emphasizing the phenomenon of diffraction, Glissant valorizes the ethnic and cultural interpenetration germane to the Caribbean experience; within this context of multiple, interrelated cultures, notions of purity were quickly erased, the islands' history as sites of contact and exchange being facilitated by the very openness of the Caribbean Sea that now embodies a new configuration of those traces of both self and Other that departmentalism re-cites and rewrites. However, departmental realities should not impede the inscription of cultural identity. "The hope for a Caribbean cultural identity must not be hampered by our people not achieving independence, so that . . . our threatened but vital Caribbeanness . . . would disappear before taking root" (PR 224). Here, the artist's role is crucial; since s/he both "articulates this threatened reality but also explores the often hidden workings of this fragmenting process" (PR 235), this joining of culture with geopolitics lays the discursive groundwork for Caribbean creolization.

While Glissant's vision of creolization has apparently adapted to the burgeoning globalization of hybridity between the publication of *Le Discours antillais* in 1981 and the appearance of *Poétique de la relation* some nine years later, my own reading of his theoretical position is grounded in his nationalistic inscription of the Caribbean as an intense, specific paradigm of a more global, generalized phenomenon of creolization. This groundbreaking vision, most clearly articulated in the *Discours*, positions the French Caribbean squarely in the forefront of a field of discourse that insists upon the unfixed, relational nature of contemporary cultural identity in general and of its Caribbean paradigm in particular, generating a network of difference that inscribes a new framework for identitarianism through the paradoxical ambiguity of an interstitial geopolitics. However, contrary to Dash's position that "Glissant provides a way out of the temptation to relapse into identitarian thought" (1995:148), I contend that it is precisely the category of identitarianism that largely subtends Glissant's work; the cultural and geopolitical dilemma of departmentalization supplies not only the impetus for isolating a viable postcolonial alternative to departmentalism, but the catalyst for transforming this intrinsic doubleness into the forms and formulas that will mediate the complexities of French Caribbean cultural identity in a discourse all its own. For in this project to fully articulate the Caribbean as "a multiple series of relation-ships" (*CD* 139), Glissant's vision of antillanité, shaped and spawned by textu-ality, is but a partner with poetics.

Toward a "Poetics of Relation"

Glissant's *Poetics of Relation* is an expansion and elucidation of the ideas es-poused in his earlier *Caribbean Discourse*, drawing on the parameters and particularities of the region's historical experience to map the boundaries of a world in constant cultural flux. Here, while noting the extent to which geopo-litical events and movements have made creolization a global phenomenon, Glissant inscribes regional realities as framing a unique and intense transac-tional space: "The Caribbean . . . may be held up as one of the places in the world where Relation presents itself most visibly. . . . the Caribbean . . . ap-proximates the idea of Relation for us as much as possible" (*PR* 33–34/46). For him, the region is a microcosmic paradigm of multiple, multiform historical and cultural transformation.

By stressing patterns of fluctuation and circularity, Glissant insists that rela-tional poetics must be deliberately and yet creatively unstable. It is a form of discourse that "remains forever conjectural and presupposes no ideological stability. . . . A poetics that is latent, open, multilingual in intention, directly in contact with everything possible" (*PR* 32/44). This is a perspective, then, that prizes openness and doubleness, an "unrootedness" that functions through diffraction and what he terms "errantry." There is no question, however, that, for Glissant, the case of Caribbean creolization is the paradigmatic form of this cultural interconnectedness: "What took place in the Caribbean, which could be summed up in the word *creolization*, approximates the idea of Relation for us as much as possible. It is not merely an encounter, a shock . . . a *métissage*, but a new and original dimension allowing each person to be there and else-where, rooted and open" (*PR* 34; emphasis in the original). Grounded in si-multaneity and paradox, in the interlectal space between being and becoming, a relational poetics is the discursive re-presentation of these multiple traces of affiliation and synthesis.

If an intrinsic openness and lack of boundaries are necessarily what is stressed here, these elements point to a process and a poetics of infinite possi-bility. This notion of pluralism, transformation, and exchange is made more explicit in the *Introduction à une poétique du divers*: "In order for relation to exist, there must be two or more self-contained identities or entities that accept both change and exchange" (42; my translation). These ideas were first elaborated in a critical section of *Poétique de la relation*; drawing on the distinction made by Gilles Deleuze and Félix Guattari in their *Mille Plateaux*, Glissant constructed two contrasting sets of characteristics to differentiate between root and relation identity, underlining the inscription in origin, filiation, and singularity of the one and the insistence on contact and chaos, community and connection of the other (*PR* 157–58). The figure of the rhizome, the product of this intersection of differences, became the metaphor for the articulation of identity in a creolized culture: "Root identity therefore rooted the thought of self and of territory and set in motion the thought of the other and of voyage. . . . Relation identity exults the thought of errantry and of totality" (*PR* 144). Through his framing of a composite construct whose core characteristics verge on the re-citation and repetition of cultural intersections, Glissant emphasizes the polyvalence and simultaneity of a cultural inscription that deliberately crosses boundaries of politics and temporality, history and aesthetics.

Charting Créolité

As a set of cultural principles, *créolité* insists upon the openness and complexity of the identitarian experience in the (French) Caribbean context but establishes its difference from antillanité's geopolitical concerns by concentrating on developing patterns of creative expression that would reflect the multiplicity of the creole mosaic. Thus the creole language serves as a fundamental metaphor for créolité's *prise de position*, not only in its structural amalgamation and transformation of various strands of both African and European lexical and grammatical patterns, but in its generative history as an icon of plantation resistance and cultural communication that continues into the contemporary period. While relatively broad in scope, then, créolité does emphasize the conflation of cultural pluralism and artistic expression as a means of re-presenting Caribbean creoleness. Both global and local, it aims at demarginalizing the departments' link to the metropole and at valorizing the expression of diversity over the implicit oneness of Western universalism.

It is here, then, that the theoretical divergence between antillanité and créolité is initially inscribed; rather than a framework for geopolitical identitarianism, creoleness, as it is articulated in the manifesto *In Praise of Creoleness* by Jean Bernabé, Patrick Chamoiseau, and Raphael Confiant, seeks to mediate the cultural expression of a heterogeneous human experience. "That is why it seems that, for the moment, *full knowledge of Creoleness will be reserved for Art*, for Art absolutely. That will be the precondition of our identity's strengthening" (90; emphasis in the original). In other words, créolité sets itself up as a broad-based aesthetic framework meant to catalyze the inscription of hybrid ethnocultural contact.

Now it would be no exaggeration to point out that the *créolistes* have been increasingly and vociferously attacked on precisely these grounds in recent years, both by critics and by other French Caribbean novelists.[3] But while these critical perspectives by authors like Maryse Condé incorporate an acknowledgment of the artistic achievement of an author like Chamoiseau, the critical reception of créolité does remain problematic to a certain extent, since its apparent insistence upon a sort of creole plenitude located among the *djobeurs* and lower classes and in an idyllic, predepartmental past lays it open to the dreaded charge of essentialism.[4] Here, the narrow world of the storyteller, the folktale, and the country market is pitted against an increasingly interactive and circulatory relation between department, metropole, and the world at large. As Richard Burton puts it, "Prospective and progressive in theory, Créolité is in practice often retrospective, even regressive, in character. . . . There is a danger, in short, that Créolité may itself fall prey to the trap of universalism and essentialism so vigorously denounced in the *Eloge*" (NAC 156). It is precisely this paradox of an apparently regressive interculturality that is perhaps the greatest challenge posed by créolité.

But such discursive excavations into the past are far from unknown in the postcolonial context. As Françoise Lionnet points out in her article "Logiques métisses," a typical response on the part of subaltern groups to modernization efforts read as assimilationist and undertaken by a dominant culture is "to retain a sense of its own cultural authenticity by advocating a return to [precolonial] traditions . . . mythifying its own original ethnic or cultural purity" (105). And in fact, such a reading echoes, perhaps not coincidentally, a position enunciated by Frantz Fanon in *The Wretched of the Earth*: "The claim to a national culture in the past . . . rehabilitate[s] that nation and serve[s] as a justification for the hope of a future national culture" (210). By drawing up cultural paradigms for the present and future based on occulted patterns and principles of the past, then, postcolonial discourses in general, and their Caribbean creolizations in particular, are engaging in a program of contestation with implied constructive and transformative potential for their subjects.

In his admittedly oedipal reading of the life, times, and work of Aimé Césaire, Raphaël Confiant seeks to refine the definition of creolization by enlarging its discursive and geopolitical context. By simultaneously stressing the key roles of "multiplicity" and "identity," he invests the creolization process with global importance through its modernist mediation of the interpenetration of peoples and cultures: "The term 'creole' is thus eminently modern . . . even post-modern, in the sense that it signals the emergence of a new model of identity that might be termed 'multiple' or 'mosaic,' and that appears to be establishing itself almost everywhere" (1993:266; my translation). For Confiant, creolization thus becomes a process that assumes specific sites and strategies when articulated in a Caribbean context.

Most recently, in a landmark and wide-ranging interview, published in the journal *Transition*—probably not coincidentally—almost exactly ten years after the pronouncement and publication of *Eloge de la créolité*, all three créolistes buttress and flesh out the discursive positions they had elaborated earlier. Here they point out that créolité is intrinsically a plural concept—"our position is that there are several Créolités" (142)—valorize the role of disjuncture in its articulation of identity—"Créolité is all about understanding mosaic, multiple identities" (153)—and suggest that creolization is more than a simple synthesis, more than métissage. "There's *métissage* in creolization, but creolization is chaos—shock, mixture, combination, alchemy" (136). Not simply conflict, then, but a conjoining, the interaction of the many in a context of difference.

A creolized Caribbean discursive framework such as we have discussed remaps the literary terrain, an enunciatory positioning of contestation over the canonical. The relocation of the frictions of cultural fragmentation and colonial subjection to a doubled, heterogeneous space of collective identification crystallizes in the double-voiced narratives by Maryse Condé and Daniel Maximin of Guadeloupe, and by Martinique's Edouard Glissant, Patrick Chamoiseau, and Suzanne Dracius-Pinalie. Their work bridges the binaries besetting the regional condition, emphasizing a simultaneous slippage and proliferation of enunciatory positions to inscribe an ideology of indeterminate interconnection as the generative ground of French West Indian postcolonial subjectivity. Neither specific adherents nor opponents of Glissant's theory of antillanité, or Caribbeanness, or of the créolité, or creoleness, articulated by Bernabé, Chamoiseau, and Confiant, these discourses draw on the creative conflation of discourse and subjectivity to articulate their interrogation and illumination of indigenous identitarian patterns and pluralisms, manipulating the antinomies of a dis-membered historical heritage into the generative ground of a nationness that writes the myriad ethnic, cultural, and linguistic patterns of the region into the warp and woof of a creole Caribbean difference. The resulting patterns of interstitial identity rewrite and reframe reductive notions of postcolonialism that either articulate only a negativized response to colonial domination on its own terms or insist upon a completeness of temporal and political disjuncture that would be beyond the capacity of the DOMs to articulate. These several novelistic discourses envisage new sites of cultural difference and subjective contestation that derive alternative strategies of representation and empowerment from the multiplicities of ethnic and cultural pluralism and historical displacement.

In a recent refinement—however necessary such an evolutionary step might be deemed—of the spirit and practice of créolité, Ernest Pepin and Raphaël Confiant choose to stress the problematics of coexistence and heterogeneity that, in contrast to the linear universalisms of the metropole, form the core of Caribbean creoleness: "An identity of coexistence is necessary and is an imperative to reject the exclusiveness of the One and its militant isolation. It is from this fertile ground that Créolité stems, not as an antinegritude but as a broadening of the initial breakthrough of our world as it actually is, as a light revealing our heterogeneous reality" (SC 98). Further, the role of language is reinscribed as a mediating metaphor for an open, modernist framework of intercultural multiplicity: "Créolité is immersed within the 'creolized' modernity of the world and thus supports the creativity of the Creole language . . . Through this relationship to languages, which also applies to cultural relations, créolité rediscovers another history of the world—the history of its multiplicity" (SC 98). By reasserting these principles of pluralism, within a context framed by modernity, language, and multiplicity, créolité as a concept abandons perhaps to some degree those programmatic strictures and structures that implied its limitation to the narrow confines of folk art. Indeed, by valorizing its literariness, créolité redefines its primacy as a form of cultural poetics: "The fundamental literary stakes of créolité are to re-vision language, narrative aesthetics, orchestration of events and places from a plural conception of identity . . . validating and developing all the strategies crafted by our people in response to the requirements of their specific history" (SC 99–100). By mapping plural identities through pluralized discourses, the specificities of the Caribbean context inscribe their difference, part of an overall framework through which these selected works forge new poetic paths and parameters for a discursive identitarianism that is both more than antillanité or créolité, yet neither simply the one nor the other.

These intrinsic ambiguities and anxieties of the departmental moment in the Caribbean illuminate the thematics and teleologies of a dynamic and transformative culture whose interrogation of the temporalities and paradoxes of postcoloniality refigure the very terms in which postcoloniality itself may be defined. In tandem with these plurivalent, decentered discourses, whose very openness, as we shall see, interrogates and exploits the ambiguities of the word "creole" itself, the formal constituents of narrative can further the articulation of a differential creole perspective, enacting emblems of pluralism and heterogeneity embedded in and reflected through narrative form, theme, and discourse.

The five works studied here occupy a particular place in the articulation of French Caribbean discursive identity. Given that the large majority are first novels, they form a definitive yet divergent thematic cluster that frames the range of approaches and practices that simultaneously define and designate the creole experience in the French Caribbean. Finally, as we try to come to terms with the sites and strategies of the creole inscribed in these novels, their discourses should perhaps be read more as variants than as models of antillanité, créolité, or a specific historicity. Discursively, they re-cite and reframe plural paradigms of Caribbeanness in order to explore and extend the contours and possibilities of a creole cultural framework that would be a functional sign of regional difference. The narratives examined here, then, interrogate creole issues through the prism of a composite Caribbean pluralism that both incorporates and surpasses the theoretical concepts of antillanité and créolité.

La Lézarde

Alienation and the Poetics of Antillanité

Le Divers n'est donné á chacun que comme
une relation, non comme un absolu pouvoir ni
une unique possession. . . . L'Autre est en moi,
parce que je suis moi. De même, le Je périt,
dont l'Autre est absent (abstrait).
Edouard Glissant, *L'Intention poétique*

Glissant's Martinique: Antillanité and Literature

The structures and strategies of creole doubling that I have outlined in the introduction are established in the work of the Martinican author Edouard Glissant. Through the deliberate recuperation of the dualities and disjunctures of a forgotten colonial history, his novels interrogate the shape and substance of an interstitial identity grounded in the Caribbean experience. A poet and essayist as well as a novelist, he has produced since the 1950s several books of poetry, a half-dozen novels, and four books of essays, in which he has discursively explored the myriad oppositional phenomena produced by colonialism and, more important, departmentalization in the region. Glissant's work stages the poetics of identity in the Caribbean context, the influence of his work so far-reaching that he is now acknowledged by later authors, like Chamoiseau and Confiant, as having made it possible for them to articulate their vision of a creolized Caribbean culture. For Glissant, as we have seen, antillanité, or Caribbeanness, and a *poétique de la relation*, or cross-cultural poetics, embody the cornerstones of a discursive practice whose deliberate disjunctures of language and linearity reflect the tensions and teleologies of the colonial encounter. It is the particular significance of the departmental moment, the presumption of its capacity to divide the regional experience into a sort of ethereal "before" and "after" while concealing its preservation of colonial realities, that provides Glissant with a context for his exploration of the paradoxes and parameters of French Caribbean identity.

In a certain sense, Glissant's own trajectory placed him in close proximity to Martinique's transition from colony to department. Born in 1928, he attended the Lycée Schoelcher in Fort-de-France, the prestigious school also frequented by Césaire and Fanon. Although he left to pursue his studies in the metropole in 1946, the year of departmentalization, he would have been eighteen years old at this pivotal moment in Martinican history. Thus it can be claimed that the transition of the French Caribbean colonies to departmental status in 1946 provided the impetus for his interrogation of the new relationship, its form as re-presentative as it is relational. The presumption of equality that accompanied the new regime, the idea that Guadeloupe and Martinique were now departments no different from, say, the Cantal or the Puy-de-Dôme, spoke to the need to explore and elaborate the contradictions of cultural perspective and erasure of historical experience that were insistently mediated by issues of distance and difference, the *mer* and the metropole that still separated the Antillais from the *mère-patrie*. The recognition of the presence of a new temporality produced expectations that would supposedly wipe clean the slate of history, tending to ignore realities of cultural and political difference; this persistent ambiguity would become the hallmark and defining sign of the region, even as it reflected the larger patterns of the periphery.

The seeds of this hybrid inscription had been sown over time on a number of levels: the remarkable and persistent oscillations of island history since their official colonization by France in 1635 not only demonstrate the extent of the metropole's double vision with regard to its overseas Others but also reinforce the importance in this relationship of the colonial intersection of politics and language. Martinique was first, if only briefly, declared to be a department of France as a result of the Revolutionary Constitution of 1793, and slavery was abolished the following year. This panacea was quickly brought to an end by the British occupation of 1794–1802, with slavery being officially reinstated with the island's return to French control, lasting until the official emancipation decree of 27 April 1848. The changes of regime in France between 1848 and 1880, with their concomitant conferral and retraction of universal male suffrage, free education, and the dispersal of the labor force from the plantations, resulted in a globally assimilationalist policy that successive generations have alternately confirmed or denied. The culmination of this flux and reflux was the integration act of 1946, a transformative moment upon which, following a bill proposed by Aimé Césaire, the French Caribbean's full assimilation into the political structure of the metropolitan power may be profitably contrasted with an Anglophone Caribbean that was on the verge of implementing its movement toward independence. If, then, the legacy of this process, as Richard Burton points out, is "to possess a double consciousness as both a West Indian and, since the departmentalization law of 1946, an integral citizen of France" (1992:186), the tensions of these twin allegiances would, appropriately, be progressively articulated in the very domains of politics and language which had mediated the inscription of metropolitan codes of domination and hegemony.

For, as we shall see, it is primarily in the field of language that the ongoing contestation of the colonial encounter takes place; it is through the nuances and the mastery of language that both colonizer and colonized refract and demarcate the intersection of the issues of culture and politics that both define and divide their cultures. As Frantz Fanon points out, "To speak . . . means above all to assume a culture, to support the weight of a civilization. . . . Every colonized people—in other words, every people in whose soul an inferiority complex has been created by the death and burial of its local cultural originality—finds itself face to face with the language of the civilizing nation; that is, with the culture of the mother country" (1968a:17–18). The ordeal of being forbidden to speak creole at school—and, among the burgeoning middle classes, even at home—on pain of punishment creates a situation in which the colonial subject is forced to develop a psycholinguistic "double consciousness," in which he or she adopts a language determined by the social context or even, in some cases, by the interlocutor. The internalization of these cultural and political dichotomies that are the product of the metropolitan relationship splits the DOM-TOM subject into a bipolar construct that simultaneously reflects the terms of the Other and the Same. This struggle for identity is inscribed in the diffuse dualities of cultural doubleness. As Richard Burton agues, "He therefore confronts the metropolitan power . . . both as 'other'— since, its departmental status notwithstanding, Martinique is still ultimately a *possession* of France—and as 'same'" (1992:186). And it is at this juncture, in the interstices of an alienation that makes such critical distinctions increasingly impossible, within a hybrid framework located precisely at the intersection of colonialism and discourse, that the discursive articulation of regional issues of identity politics and ethnocultural pluralism begins to assume an overarching importance.

If the concept of representation as an underpinning of discourse was what allowed colonialism to advance and impose the terms of its authoritarian system of knowledge, and to appropriate the world of the colonized as a representable system both fixed and knowable, then the terms of its contestation would have to be both subversive and deliberately nonlinear, framed as a discourse that would interrogate and explode the binary assumptions of metropolitan mastery. The discursive context with which writers like Glissant would now have to contend had articulated an intentionality linked to colonial power which had allowed Europe to reduce its Others to a fixed reality, erecting stereotypes of race and class meant to rationalize the need for the reductive hierarchies of the colonial relation. Yet the primary paradox of this discursive system was its simultaneous elaboration of a duplicitous double standard, one in which principles of civility—and civilization—were applicable only to the world of the metropole. By exploiting this authoritarian ambivalence, an ambiguity which is the corollary of the binary discourses of the colonial encounter, novelists like Glissant were ultimately able to construct their own discourse of creolization, of antillanité, articulating an alternative rather than a response to colonial authority, and mapping an innovative site of discursive and cultural re-presentation which would counter colonial hegemony by exploiting, assimilating, and transforming the gaps and antitheses inherent in what was ultimately a plural colonial project.

Glissant's theory of antillanité forms a loose framework within which the fictional context of his work is situated; his novels explore and interrogate the fragmented trajectory and multiple subject positions of Martinican history, seeking to identify various points at which the disjunctures of the past can be assimilated into the complex cultural pluralisms of the present. In his four books of essays, Glissant consistently articulates pluralistic notions of writing and culture as a means of elucidating and contextualizing the historical experience of the region. Leveling the diversity and heterogeneity of Le Divers against the universalist claims of Le Même, Glissant seeks to inscribe the multiple paths that have eventuated the complexities of contemporary Caribbean culture. This he accomplishes, in part, by undertaking a close reading of what he calls Le Détour, revealing a construct whose very heterogeneity functions in direct contrast to the hegemonic unicity of what he terms "Reversion . . . the obsession with a single origin . . . 'to negate contact'" (CD 16/30).

These univocal impositions are subverted and transformed, however, when confronted with the complexities of forced exile, the principles of cultural transformation and adaptation, and the identitarian contestations of a creolized, departmentalized population: "Diversion is the final recourse of a population whose domination by an Other is concealed: one must look for the principle of domination *elsewhere*, when it is not obvious in the country itself. For the means of domination (assimilation) is the best of camouflage, as the physical manifestation of domination . . . is not directly visible. The creole language is the first area of Diversion" (CD 20/32). His concept of the *Détour* is thus manifestly and unalterably linked here not only to colonial domination but to the specifically Martinican issues of departmentalization, assimilation, neocolonialism, and the viability of an indigenous *lingua franca*.

In later sections of *Le Discours antillais*,[1] a massive work synthesizing notions of Caribbean history, society, literature, and culture, he articulates and expands more fully upon his concept of the political and performative aspects of the creolization of the Caribbean. As we have seen in the introduction, it is here that Glissant constructs the cornerstones of a discourse of difference that can mediate the staging of identity's discursive and ethnocultural complexities in the Caribbean context: *antillanité*, or Caribbeanness, and a *poétique de la relation*, or a cross-cultural poetics. These two interrelated and interdependent concepts form the basis of Glissant's account of the specificity of the Caribbean experience, distilling the core concepts of his theoretical and narrative discourses to weave a relational, even complicitous, identitarianism that will undergird the form of his fiction: "The concept of Caribbeaness springs from a reality which we will have to question, but one which also corresponds to a vow whose legitimacy we will have to establish. . . . Reality is undeniable: cultures derived from the plantation system, insular civilisations . . . social pyramids with . . . African or Hindu at its foundation, European at the peak, with compromised languages; a general cultural phenomenon of creolisation" (CD 221–22/422).

Only by affirming the specificity of this culture and the values it articulates through the process of creolization will the formulation and maintenance of the Caribbean identity be assured. Between the desire and the alienation of antillanité, what undergirds Glissant's discursive undertaking is the translation of the double experience of integration and exclusion engaged by departmentalization, of the fragmentation and cultural pluralism of borderlines, into a collective experience of nation*ness* that is inscribed by a new Caribbean textual poetics of difference. By exposing the ambiguity grounding not only the hierarchical patterns of authoritarianism on which colonialism was based, but also a DOM-TOM system that simultaneously seduces the Antillais into believing in the value of a relationship with the metropole while concealing the geopolitical realities of an ongoing colonial relationship, Glissant constructs a counterdiscourse that goes beyond a simple response to colonial discourse on its own terms. It confronts and masters the fractured past by rewriting the ruptures and disjunctures, the hierarchies and contradictions, of the colonial experience into a cross-cultural poetics that locates new sites of contestation and community through alternative strategies of discursive exploration.[2] For if the slippage opened up within its framework allows us to suggest that colonialism in fact articulated a crisis of confidence in imposing stereotypes of race and culture on the Other—a process that occurs, in Benita Parry's words, when "the civil discourse of a culturally cohesive community is mutated into the text of a civilizing mission," so that "its enunciatory assumptions are revealed to be in conflict with its means of social control" (1987:41)—then the core ambivalence of this hegemonic script is in fact that which permits a postcolonial creole discourse to establish itself by staging the negotiation and resiting of a strategic gap.

By revealing that both colonizer and colonized are implicated in the labyrinth of colonial positionality, Glissant compels us to rethink the traditional paradigms of colonialism and postcolonialism, and to recognize the necessity of constructing a creole discourse that will reflect the ongoing complicities of the colonial encounter. A postcolonial discourse that responds to the fixed realities of colonial hegemony on their own terms, and fails to take this imbrication into account, runs the risk of relegitimizing the very hierarchies it seeks to overturn. Glissant's discourse evades these polarities by tracing oppositionality through a site of contestation whose ground is neither the ambivalent authority of a colonial discourse nor the rigidified responses of its Other. As we have seen, Glissant contrasts the figures of root and rhizome as oppositional spatiocultural perspectives on the Caribbean heritage of creolization; in his view, the latter framework assumes the plural, protean properties of its hybrid culture, as its insistence on fragmentation and doubling subverts metropolitan concepts of rootedness and monoculture through the intrinsic pluralities of its construction. By interrogating the assumptions of hierarchy and assymetry assigned to roles in the colonial script, Glissant is able to evade the linear logic of what he terms "root-identity," drawing rather on the disjunctive, multidimensional, polyvalent temporalities of the "relation-identity" to create a series of ruptures that dis-locate a metropolitan legacy of universalism and exclusion. For if a textual poetics of difference is to be forged from the disparate dissonances of the creole, then the translation of patterns of ambiguity into repeatable categories of meaning, into a hybrid transdisciplinarity which goes beyond the binarisms of the colonial canon, must also address the cultural complexities of the society it seeks to represent.

La Lézarde: The Politics of Colonial Ambiguity

Glissant's first novel, *La Lézarde*,[3] won the Prix Renaudot upon its publication in 1958 and has since been recognized as one of the seminal works in the francophone Caribbean literary canon. Set in the fictional community of Lambrianne, the novel may be read as a thinly disguised re-presentation of the author's homeland of Martinique. The plot revolves around the elections of September 1945, marking a historical and cultural turning point for the French colony which would lead ultimately to departmentalization. Essentially, the intrigue concerns a group of young political activists who, seeing the desired outcome of the elections threatened by the presence of a notorious political henchman of the opposition, decide on his elimination. Fearing discovery, exposure, and their party's subsequent defeat if they carry out the deed themselves, however, they suborn a young peasant from the countryside and induce him to commit the murder for them. Both this ploy and the peasant's efforts prove dramatically successful, but the novel ends with an election victory followed by a final, symbolic act of retribution visited upon the companion of the unwary instrument of this electoral success.

In this novel Glissant makes use of the plethora of ambiguities attending the politics of post/colonial liminality to address the relative positionality of both colonizer and colonized in a context of social and political flux. The novel thus becomes both means and point of interrogation, an ever-expanding network of ambivalences that ultimately implodes and collapses upon itself. Its characters, and the issues they embody and explore, appear to regress rather than to progress, and their inability to properly address the complex issues that frame this moment of transition will eventually doom them to an ending that is anything but a point of resolution. The pressing issues of disjuncture and duality that are presaged by the plot allow these facets of post/colonial identity to be formulated as a series of questions. Key patterns and parameters of the novel are made subject to a number of signs and codes in order to reflect and refract the ambiguous structures engendered by the presumptive mastery of a colonial discourse. His vision of a poetics of cultural creolization interrogates the factitious basis of colonial binarisms as it simultaneously exposes the extent to which their necessary imbrication constructs an alternative discursive space, mapping a geopolitics grounded in the signifying system of the creole. It is difficult, however, to echo the sentiment of thematic optimism some recent critics have apparently been able to cull from their reading of *La Lézarde*; in my own view, the novel tends much more toward a darker, more pessimistic, and conflictual trajectory, with an absence of any really positive sense of resolution or accomplishment in either subjective or political terms.[4]

Protean patterns of positionality and oppositionality are set in train by the conflictual economy of the colonial encounter, producing a society whose internal contradictions and covert parallels may reasonably be read in terms of race, ethnicity, and class. However, Glissant specifically inscribes nonlinear forms of narrative address in order to further contextualize the desire for a discourse that does not retrace the boundaries of colonial oppression. The ethnic and cultural fragmentation of the Martinican experience and its historical subjection to the doubling and dispersal of a colonial discourse tend to translate this pluralism into hybrid signs of postcolonial possibility. Through Glissant's reading of the reflexive relationship of self and Other as they are constituted in the conflictual confines of colonialism, the political possibilities of a nascent postcolonialism can be reinscribed by opening up the latent complexities of Martinican departmentalism. As Richard Burton suggests, "The great strength of Glissant's historical vision . . . lies precisely in his determination to understand, espouse and assume the Martinican reality in all its multifaceted contradictoriness" (1984:305). In other words, Glissant's idea of a cultural poetics of difference culls the authoritarian ambiguities that have shaped the Martinican experience into a discourse that re-presents its overwhelming cultural realities of doubling and hybridity.

Perhaps the narrative's most effective figure for these polarities is that of the novel's title. For while in its feminine form in the novel the substantive *lézarde* refers primarily to the Lézarde river, a figure, as we shall see, for the complex divisions and pluralities that mark the community of Lambrianne, in its masculine, referential connotation the substantive also signifies a crack, or fissure. This double resonance of a literal and figurative splitting effectively encapsulates the discontinuities that define the community, generating an initiatory ambiguity of ideology and perspective which is maintained and amplified throughout the novel. Snaking down from the mountains through the town to finally expire in the sea, the river is thus a primary marker not only of the critical disjunctions that are the corollary of the colonial encounter but also of the intersubjective experience of the community at large. The entirety of chapter 6 is given over to the personification of the river and to the tracing of its protean, pluralistic evocation of the community it both divides and defines. Characterized variously as "a people in revolt" (32/30), "a factory owner inspecting his boilers closely" (32/30), "a naked girl, heedless of passers-by on the banks" (32/30–31)" and "like a woman fulfilled and ripe with pleasure" (32/31), the ever-changing river seems to personify the complex nature both of the people and of their geopolitical context, the diversity and difference that colonialism paradoxically produces through its appropriation of peoples and cultures and the assumption of its authority to differentiate. These plural possibilities disturb the simple binaries instantiating the colonial as a knowable, fixed reality; the very title of the novel suggests from the outset the unrelieved uncertainties awaiting Lambrianne in its moment of decision.

Discursive notions of post/colonial intersubjectivity converge through the persistent parallels that the narrative establishes between the peasant, Thaël, and Mathieu, the leader of the group of activists, and, perhaps even more important, between Thaël and Garin, the henchman of the opposition he agrees to kill, and through the larger possibilities of protean transformation signified by the Lézarde; the people, both individually and as the subjective categories they represent, as well as the compelling collaborative and conflictual intricacies of their politics, combine to inscribe the complex, liminal, contradictory culture of Lambrianne. Embodying as he does the compound parallels and contradictions of the colonial relationship, Thaël is the crux of doubling and difference; as a multiple site of post/colonial signification, he functions in the plot to chart the ambivalent progress of the novel's basic armature, an urgent call for the recognition of the complex temporalities of colonial authority and the differential categories it imposes upon the colonized. By dispersing and realigning the fixed positionality of the colonial stereotype, Glissant's complex elaboration of the multiple location of subjective sites produced by a colonial discourse ultimately underlines the role of the interstice in the negotiation of the periphery.

From the outset, markers of the double nature of the colonial condition abound, serving to alert the reader to situational complexities and challenges of which the characters remain unaware. One of the most striking aspects of *La Lézarde*'s narration is its insistence on protean, fragmented changes in perspective. The address constantly alternates between *je, ils, vous,* and *nous;* it appears to be constantly contradicting and metamorphosing itself as it shifts to accommodate changes in ideological and expository perspective. The entire sixth chapter of the third section is narrated in the second person singular, drawing on deliberate strategies of doubling and disjuncture that simultaneously trace and displace the triangle mapped by reader, character, and narrator. Even at the beginning of the novel, issues of division and parallelism are clearly at work, identifying the various sites at which colonialism has rendered the basic binarisms of this society creatively unstable.

The fragmentation of the colonial population signified through the plural characterization of the Lézarde is recuperated by the world of distance separating Mathieu and Thaël, the two protagonists. Mathieu is a town dweller, a bourgeois—as are the rest of the activists—concerned, it seems, more with the nuances of political ideology than with the conflicts and compromises of its actual praxis. Thaël is a peasant from the countryside, a man of the soil closer to the realities of struggle and survival than Mathieu and his cohorts ever will be. Yet somehow the complexities of this liminal moment, in their capacity to define the past as well as the future, seem to summarize all that both binds and separates them, a capacity reflected in the political act whose resonances and consequences they will both come to share.

The uncertainties produced by the colonial discourse that determines both their worlds are deepened further by the deliberate obscurantism of the narrator's repeated references to himself in the third person. The most direct result of such a narrative strategy is to defeat the possibility of ascertaining his or her other identity with any sense of certainty, a goal whose origins may perhaps be traced back to a refusal to accept an implicit identification with any one ideological position. However, this does not prevent the narrator from repeatedly referring to him/herself in the first person, pointing to the multivalency of his own role in the text: "I heard these words, but I was still a child, and they echoed within me. *I was both witness and object: the one who sees and the one who must endure, who is called and who is shaped. I knew Thaël and Mathieu*" (22/16; emphasis mine). In fact, the narrator is represented as being also subject to the undecidabilities of the discourse itself: "And I, as a child (child of this story, growing with each word . . .)" (33/22; parentheses in original). In this strategy, which also reflects the disjunctures and ambiguities of colonialism through the form of the narration itself, the negotiation of the space that separates self and Other challenges and rewrites the traditional boundary between individual and community, colonizer and colonized. Indeed, reading *La Lézarde* involves an intricate process of cross-referencing and elimination, aided by duplications of important narrative sequences, whole chapters enclosed in parentheses, and the elusive, doubled re-presentation of the simultaneity of key events—all aimed at undermining the fixed polarities of the colonial encounter and exposing the double subjection of colonizer and colonized to the uncommon ruptures and resemblances imposed by a colonial discourse.

Thaël, the primary protagonist of *La Lézarde* and, as we shall see, the primary counterpart of Garin, his intended victim, is a character whose social identity may be said to embody the indeterminacy and dispersal that are inscribed by the attempt to read the polarities of a colonial discourse through patterns of alterity drawn from the psychoanalytic paradigm.[5] While we should take care not to impose Westernized norms blindly upon the uncertainties of the colonial script, at the same time such readings are valuable for the insights they can add to an understanding of the tensions and pluralities at work in the scene. Thaël, we recall, is a peasant, leading an uncomplicated existence in the hills of the Lambrianne landscape when we first encounter him. Indeed, the first words of the first chapter, which will eventually be ironically recuperated by the opening words of the last, draw on these patterns of departure and discovery: "Thaël left his house in the mountains, and there was already a sprinkle of sunlight on the dew-covered rust spots of the roof. Primeval warmth of man's first dawn!" (18/11)." Drawn from the countryside to the political and interpellative structures of the city, he is, significantly, still marked by the geographical extremes of the country, just able to perceive "the boundary of known and unknown" (18/11–12); further, the liminality of his situation is emphasized: "His journey had only just begun" (19/12).

Importantly, not only is his psychological ambiguity marked from the outset, "as Thaël descends . . . everything gradually comes apart" (19/12), but his dogs, which will have a key role to play in the resolution of the plot and whose importance is linked to their master's ambivalent attitude toward and tenuous control over them, are immediately given pride of place. "Then he heard the dogs. Sillon! Mandolée! They had been named, since he had grown up in a world of legend and mystery . . . inspiring Thaël with admiration as well as the desire to escape. These dogs knew their master's feeling of repulsion, a feeling he had always suppressed" (19/12). This tenuousness of the master's voice, the oppositional fear and favor in which these animals are held by him, will assume ever-increasing importance as it parallels Thaël's progress toward the definitive encounter with the Other; he is positioned, literally, in the middle ground, situated between "the black angry rocks of the ocean . . . and the gentle murmuring of the beaches of the sea" (51/59). But Thaël has an unshakeable attachment to both Mathieu and Garin; indeed, his double attachment to them both places him as colonial subject marking a moment of transition in an undecidable, interstitial space, and the narrative draws on these multiple conflicts and collusions to rewrite the implications of traditional colonial tropes of alienation and duality.

Insistently, the parallelisms and conflicts of Thaël and Mathieu continue to determine the dialectical development of the narrative: "'But I come from the mountains. . . .I am driven by a passion I do not understand. I wish to understand this passion!' Mathieu smiled but he was a victim of the same passion" (31–32/29). It is increasingly clear that each is both overdetermined by a colonial discourse and already alienated as the object of desire of the other. Indeed, Mathieu speaks to Valérie of Thaël as "my best friend," and says of him that "I am his brother" (83–84/107); significantly, Thaël, in turn, also speaks to Garin of Mathieu as "my brother" (98/127).

This subjective interpenetration that they share is also written on Valérie's mediating body, as the passion for her which both men share comes to signify their passion for a free Lambrianne and the blindness and contestation that simultaneously separate them and subordinate them to colonial misprision. This inscription of Valérie as symbolic object of desire may be profitably contrasted with the figure of Mycéa, whom Beverley Ormerod, in a recent article, sees as "an emblem of integrity and revolutionary ardour. . . . she is an idealized, abstract figure, proud and reserved, in contrast to the more sensual girls around her." If, however, as Ormerod argues, Mycéa is indeed a figure who "stands for the Caribbean landscape, pregnant with half-lost memories that hint at Martinique's unrealized need for self-discovery" (1999:111), one conclusion that may plausibly be drawn here suggests the subjugation of female characters and female desire, at least in the early Glissant, to a dominant, overarching masculinity. For if Valérie may also be read as a figure for a Lambrianne possessed by the Other, then, as we shall see, the killing of Valérie by Thaël's dogs, which closes the novel, the uncanny return of the colonial repressed, is a firm foreclosure of feminine desire, as well as a remarkable rendition of the uncommon, unrecognized persistence of colonial discourses in the construction of strategies of liberation. The narrative's annulment of this mutual object of desire becomes a powerful indictment of the blind acceptance of authoritarian linearities in a colonial context of uncertainty.

The incessant (re)doubling of character and situation through which Glissant maps the heterotopia of postcolonial subjectivity is thus put into place early in the intrigue. By implicitly comparing Thaël's inscription in the land and his implicit separation from the world of secular politics with the bourgeois vision and strategic fragmentation of the activists, Glissant quickly conveys the various voices and positions of the colonial experience. The double nature of life in Lambrianne, soon to become a figure for the alienated subjectivity inherent in the intragroup relationships, is what Thaël discovers when he descends from the mountains, only to find in himself the same duality: "Thaël finally got to know the plain, with its heavy, dazzling light . . . and *silence explosive enough* to take hold of a man's strength. He was most dazzled by the impalpable, mysterious unrelieved intoxication . . . the ceaseless struggle between the *principle of drought and the accident of water*" (27/24; emphasis mine). The underlying principle of existence in Lambrianne is this conflictual duality—extending from the liminal, oppositional relationship between land and water, hill and plain, to the intersubjectivity that overdetermines the inhabitants—whose relationships, as we shall observe, draw on patterns that are the product of the multilayered structures of their individual existences.

The activists themselves, as Frederick I. Case suggests, are cut off, both socially and politically, from the community whose interests they claim to protect: "Glissant's group of young intellectuals is somewhat removed from the socioeconomic ills of their society insofar as the group is comprised of a number of relatively privileged individuals" (1985:70). But what needs to be emphasized here, in my view, is the extent to which this internal socioeconomic separation serves to erect a doubly symbolic state of blindness; by attempting to eliminate their compatriot Garin, and in accomplishing this task through the third-party proxy of Thaël, they repeat and exacerbate the already complex set of contradictions through which the colonial script locates and overdetermines both the narrative and its subjects. The initial, mysterious meeting between Mathieu and Thaël, for example, suggests the existence of a series of subconscious links between them whose boundaries encompass more than the merely tangible.

These schisms and parallels recur discursively at several critical junctures in the narrative, especially at the moment when the group decides to kill Garin, the political agitator. The critical imbalance represented by his presence is clearly put by the text: "They had learnt that a government official had been authorized to put down the political movement in Lambrianne. It was to be expected. But the man chosen happened to be an old inhabitant of the country, a renegade and hence doubly guilty. He had to be rendered harmless. Everyone knew that, renegade that he was, he was prepared to commit the worst acts of violence; our friends decided that it was up to them to muzzle this beast" (24/18–19). Garin's very status, then, is problematic on a number of levels; criminal, renegade, and social outcast though he may be, not only is he a member of the community, a colonial subject to the same degree as Thaël, Mathieu, and the others, but, at the same time, his criminal role separates him from this community just as his governmental role inscribes him in the colonizer's domain.

The complexity that attends this ambiguous character and the coming event of his death takes place in a doubling of discourses and positions whose deliberate disjunctures mark the impossibility of locating the simple polar opposites that are the supposed corollary of colonialism. For the group, their own reluctance to perform this political murder themselves separates them not only from their intended victim but also from their chosen agent, Thaël. "Soon the group of friends found itself alone, feverish and impatient. They all knew they would have to prove their worth. They decided therefore to eliminate the official. 'But,' thought Mathieu, 'we cannot do it ourselves, we are too well-known, too easily located.' . . .That was the nature of the land and its first suppression of injustice. The land which was learning the new and violent way of the world, after so much forgotten violence; and it made its cry heard" (25/19–20). Indeed, perhaps the largest irony in the decision to eliminate Garin is the unspoken fact that he is a fellow national, a colonial subject, despite his questionable political loyalties. So political victory for the group of bourgeois activists depends upon defeating colonial oppression through the proxy of a member of the peasant class, chosen to eliminate yet another colonial subject working to ensure the survival of the colonial status quo. Such contradictions work to underline further the positional fragmentation of the forces of liberation symbolized by their leader, Mathieu. His realization that "we cannot do it ourselves" not only presents him as speaking, or thinking, for the others of the group—an act which preserves sociopolitical hierarchies even as it serves to underline his own sense of superiority and distance—but presents him through a sort of discursive twilight that is neither direct speech—for it remains an unspoken thought—nor free indirect discourse nor, for that matter, reported speech. This sort of discursive displacement has the effect not only of separating the group from the larger social whole in whose name, or for whose benefit, it purports to act, but also separates Mathieu, in his role as leader, from the rest of the group for whom he appears to think and speak.

Further complicating the discourse is the immediate jump from Mathieu's internalized utterances to an omniscient form of narrative commentary, one which tends to blur the lines separating both narrative moments: "'We cannot do it ourselves, we are too well-known, too easily located.' . . . That was the nature of the land.' " Such a sequence of diversified discursive positions serves to problematize the multiform subjectivity of the activists and their various roles, and to underline the pluralisms of a colonial society seeking to translate its uncertainties into a site of contestation. Far from being a positive attempt to "write into existence" a "transcend[ent] . . . deed," then, as Chris Bongie argues (1998:146), the complex intersections of plot and discourse in *La Lézarde* may be said to be putting into place a framework for interrogating and illuminating the complexities and contradictions attending the post/colonial site through the complications and resonances of the assassination deed itself.

More globally, the narrative discourse of *La Lézarde* goes to peculiar lengths to reflect the plural sites and perspectives of this liminal post/colonial moment. In the last scene, for example, by virtue of its double representation as a sort of direct thought enclosed within quotation marks, the form of Mathieu's discourse reflects the extent to which the situation reflects the undecidabilities of the colonial script, inscribing the pains that the narrative must take in order to re-present the infinite economy of exchange which this scene enacts. Indeed, the entire novel is also strikingly marked by the persistent, unremitting use of free indirect discourse (FID) across the narrative spectrum,[6] a style with implications that seem particularly appropriate to the representation of specific patterns of colonial subjectivity. While FID has been critically defined by Shlomith Rimmon-Kenan as "contributing or being analogous to the governing thematic principle(s) of the work under consideration . . . convey[ing] the theme of the discontinuous, developing self"

(1983:113), it is a form that is also intrinsically reflective of the alienation and insufficiency of colonial roles. From its initial identification of a subject unable to adequately express itself as "I," FID also effectively articulates the partial presence and identitarian displacement of those rendered subject to the discursive dislocations of the colonial encounter. The ever-increasing use of FID by postcolonial authors bears witness to their recognition of the potential of this narrative code to re-present the overlapping, oppositional, and fragmented formulations of identity that emerge in the negotiation of the post/colonial moment.

From this perspective, then, the repeated re-presentation of the group of conspirators through the prism of FID specifically articulates the fragmentation of any fixed, unitary colonial positions, a splitting whose traces mark both colonizer and colonized. By staging their ambivalence through a narrative perspective that specifically suggests an incomplete discursive subject, Glissant shows both colonialism's deleterious disjunctures and the latent possibilities for resiting colonial re-presentation in a narrative context he would ultimately define as *antillanité*. As we shall see, in the period immediately following Garin's death, at what is perhaps the novel's most critical stage of doubling and disjuncture, the entire community is ultimately figured by these patterns of subjective displacement.

The intrinsic pluralities and polarities that produce the divisions of a colonial perspective are also effectively shown at that key moment in the text when Thaël agrees to kill Garin for the activists. Here, a wealth of subjective signification is incorporated into the interstices of the narrative: "He did not hesitate because of moral scruples, he would tell them that. It was not the prospect of bloodshed that made him reluctant. . . . The sacrifice of a human life is highly regarded in mythology. Is this also true of stark reality? Was one man the key to the order and the balance that were his ultimate goals? . . . Of course, this renegade was capable of ordering even more suffering on the people. And misery thicker than a dense fog approaching from the sea would darken the land. That had to be prevented. That was the essential thing. . . . (Before a dumbfounded Thaël stands Pablo. He had known from ever since that Thaël would accept. . . . He was calm, gentle, in command of the situation)" (49–50/56–57).

By re-presenting Thaël's pained rationalization of his acquiescence to the murder in FID, the narrative conveys both his sense of internal division and his simultaneous distance from the rest of the activists with whom he has thrown in his lot. This use of free indirect discourse, underlined by the presence of parentheses and the stark contrast of Pablo's demeanor, signifies the fragmentation that is already ingrained in this liminal community, the uneven perspectives and positions at work in the society whose axes are symbolized by Mathieu, Thaël, and Garin. For the tensions that both bind and separate the inhabitants are also those translated by the narrator into the plural resonances of his discursive act. While the inability of the subject to express himself as "I," which is implied by FID's joining of narrator and character, tends to suggest Thaël's simultaneous placement in a number of positions, this idea is consolidated by the really intriguing presence of the commentary accompanying Pablo's distanced, calm acceptance of Thaël's stupefaction, a narrative gloss whose placement in parentheses underscores the marginal role of the average character in this context. Glissant will again make use of parentheses in the text, at a more intriguing moment and on a much more significant scale, but the bracketing of this fragment reinforces the sense of marginality raised by these discursive positions, and questions the very structures of separation recuperated by the divisions implicit within a colonial discourse.

The creolization that is at work in Glissant's narrative is one that operates simultaneously on several levels. Since his goal is the re-presentation of the conflictual forces that have split both the colonial subject and its cultural memory, he accomplishes this by problematizing both the content and the form of the narrative framework. In other words, the constant regression, doubling, and discursive reversal that recur throughout the novel determine not only the ideological positions assumed by the characters but also the discourse that provides the terrain for their actions. Thus, in contradistinction to Chris Bongie's astonishing assertion that "*La Lézarde* moves forward in a relatively straight line" (1998:146), it seems to me that the deliberate doubling and fragmentation of the work's narrative line and perspective appear incontestable, forming an integral part of the author's discursive articulation of the antinomies undergirding the intersection of departmentalism and postcolonialism. Indeed, I would argue that it is in such complex ambiguities and undecidabilities that Glissant's modernity is primarily inscribed.

From this perspective, perhaps the most remarkable, and certainly the most critical, scene in the novel is the one recounted in chapter 16 of part 1. It represents a meeting held by the activists in which questions of means and method are discussed, and already we are forewarned of the deliberate displacements and disequilibrium that the discourse will undergo; the narrative tells us that "there they held a strange conversation, terse, impulsive, crazy, with crosscurrents and alluvial deposits which swirled under the surface of what they said, bearing their secret passions" (53/62). The scene is striking more from the perspective of its form than from that of its content; indeed, the conversation is rather enigmatic and elliptical. But not only is the scene introduced through the use of the first-person plural, it effectively occurs twice. In the first instance, the dialogue is presented without mediation or commentary, in a "theatrical" format in which each speaker is designated simply by name, followed by a colon and his or her respective "lines." But then, as if this disturbance of previously established patterns of narrative modality were insufficient, the scene is immediately recuperated and reproduced, this time in italics but now through a first-person narrative introduced as "minutes of the last meeting," and contravening the linear sequences of its previous re-presentation to the extent that every utterance is now displaced from its original position relative to the other utterances in the scene.

The striking manner in which the presentation of this scene stages its own double difference from the novel's already alternative temporalities of post/colonial displacement—for it is the singular occurrence of its kind—compels us to consider its deliberate construction of an ambiguous space of oppositional discursive "otherness." For Glissant is very clearly putting into place structures that will ground the very terms in which the novel will articulate the temporal dislocation and identificatory substitutions that are the corollaries of an Antillean imaginary of the creole; indeed, the chapter is a paradigm of the doubling and displacement upon which the novel's pluralities of character and plot are largely based. Integral to a reading of the first scene is the fact that the theatrical format upon which it draws articulates the nuances of *role-playing*, the mimetic re-presentation of the already written. By implicitly defining the activists as role-players, he constructs an important relation between the duality of the self-image and the alienation of an attenuated identity, colonial cultural subjects caught in the interstices of discursive disjuncture. In other words, each role-player occupies a paradoxical subjective space, serving as an ambivalent agent of colonialism's inevitable rhetoric of repetition, and this complex re-iteration constitutes the first level of the doubling by which the chapter recuperates the complex cultural connections and political contradictions that form the basis of a creole community. The ostensible reason for the meeting, the sanctioning of Mathieu's increasingly high-handed behavior, serves only to underline the perceptible subjective dispersal that attends it.

"*Margarita:* You are the one responsible. *Thaël:* Yes. Yes. It's me. *Gilles:* Mathieu had made up his mind a long time ago. *Michel:* What are we doing? *Luc:* Mathieu must redeem himself. I propose excluding him from the group for two months. *Thaël:* You are a good Catholic? " (54/63). But further, its astonishing departure from preestablished patterns of narration marks a deliberate discursive attempt to inscribe the traces of an interstitial intersubjectivity in the very fabric of the narrative, creolizing the discourse through the implied alienation and doubling of these sociopolitical/dramatic roles and emphasizing the alluvial slippages and metonymies of a latent, emerging antillanité.

Along similar lines, the chapter's second level of doubling or second moment of re-presentation, in which the content of the primary scene is simultaneously glossed and displaced, effectively problematizes further the entire narrative structure of the novel, vacating paradigms of textual authority and placing the entire site under the sign of erasure. By rearticulating the intrinsic ambivalence of both of these subjects and of the foundational framework in which they are forced to act, the *narrative/dédoublement* disperses the situational space, interrogating the dialectical assumptions underlying colonial practice and undermining the symbolic certitude of its signifying system. "Minutes of the last meeting; Mathieu under discussion. Pablo as recording secretary . . . there is a discussion as to who is the leader. I don't say a word. Mathieu is our leader and yet we have no leader: both things are true . . . as if any anyone can be helped. . . . There is only the tumult, the savage call, the burning flame, but I am sure that we are on the verge of finding something" (56/65–66). As the rapport is made to serve double duty as a functional secondary level of commentary to which only reader and reporter are privy, the constant, repeated redoubling of the discursive framework, combined with the insistent (under)mining of uncertainty (*Matthew is our leader and yet we have no leader: both things are true. . . . There is only the tumult*), inscribe the undecidabilities and disseminations of postcolonial positionality in the insistent liminalities of meaning of the region's contemporary context.

This reflexive turn transforms the "imagined community" of the colonial French Caribbean from inhabitants of a confined symbolic space to one engaging hybrid communal possibilities, accomplishing a resiting of the boundaries of national narratives and, implicitly, of discursive paradigms of the postcolonial. The complex, staggered evolution of the plot conveys the performance of difference by opening up new spaces of contestation and translation by articulating the supplementary ideological turns and reciprocities of both situation and character. This peripatetic quality attaching to the narration underlines the elaborate nature of the pervasive intersubjectivity in the creole economy of exchange governing both narrative structure and colonial subject.

The event that perhaps best symbolizes the interpenetrative instability of the positions at work in the community of Lambrianne follows Thaël's conquest of his own hesitations: "He is not as prepared as he thought to plunge a knife into the chest of another man" (71/89–90). He then goes back into the hills to find, in what Maria do Nascimento calls a "voyage initiatique et . . . une complicité avec le mystère des origines (416)," the source of the Lézarde river, the figure for the oppositional orientations of the entire community, bottled up beneath Garin's house.

Garin, along with Thaël and Mathieu, represents the third node in the complex triad of subjective signification that governs the text. Both a colonial and a well-known henchman of the opposition, Garin has a history of violence and subversion; he is described as "the renegade Garin. (A man who grew up without care; first a waiter, then chauffeur to an important plantation owner and soon a man capable of anything: he has killed for money. . . . He had left the country when there were threats against his life. He came back with new authority, on an official mission!) This rough creature now gives orders, throws his weight about" (71/89). These negative characteristics aside, this strategic location of Garin's identity structure within parentheses serves to draw attention to the fact that it is indeed his positionality, rather than his personal attributes, that will ultimately influence and determine his meeting with Thaël and the direction of the plot. Further, we are told that he is engaged in a somewhat questionable affair with the very planter with whom he used to work; while the disposition of land on the eve of such a momentous election can certainly redound to the profit of the unscrupulous, Garin simultaneously appears to be in the deal for his own ends: "'I represent the law. And you cannot accuse me without implicating yourself as well. . . . Not as a personal favour. Those days are gone.' . . . The slight man is at the mercy of his former chauffeur " (75/95). Garin's task is to follow the Lézarde to the sea, a journey of three days, but it is deliberately left unclear whether his disingenuous agenda is ultimately meant to bring enrichment to his former employer or to himself. Either action, however, will only disperse and deepen further the oppositions at work in the plot that render Garin an indeterminate signifier of colonial instability; ultimately, the ambivalent ideological perspective that underwrites his alterity will parallel the problematic trajectory signified by Thaël's attempt on his life, making possible an extraorinary subjective transformation that will, through their respective roles, firmly link the double subjection of these two protagonists to the overlapping temporalities of this liminal moment in Caribbean geopolitics.

The house that Garin has built over the source of the Lézarde, then, possesses an unsurpassed importance in the development of the narrative. The revelatory character of Thaël's moment of discovery is represented quite clearly in the text.

> Then he discovers the house. Heavy, shuttered. . . . This house fascinates him. He cannot figure out why, but it seems somehow monstrous. Yet it was like any other, closed in on itself, silent. Thaël prowls around all day. . . . The front is most impressive: the paint fresh, the walls cared for. The wind and rain come from the north, he thinks. It is the other side that protects the house really. . . . [He] goes back to look more closely at the extraordinary stream of water, he could hear the murmur of the spring coming from inside the house. . . . the middle of the room is empty, a yawning emptiness. . . . Empty and lifeless. That is until Thaël, guided by the noise, arrives at the spring from which the water is flowing. The imprisoned source of the Lézarde, guarded by thick walls, surrounded by marble tiles, like an idol bedecked with ornaments. . . . It all begins here. 72–74/ 91–93.

From its closed shutters to its monstrous appearance, the house is an enigma. Indeed, its hybrid centrality, significantly offset by the emptiness at its center, generates a double metonymic link both to Garin's authoritarian association with the colonizer and to the sheltered source of the Lézarde that makes it a perfect figure for the power and inscrutable ambiguity of the colonial site. Its enigmatic quality also draws metonymically on Garin's contradictory social position. On the one hand, as a native of Lambrianne, he is as much a member, and a product, of this colonial society as Thaël, Mathieu, and the other activists; he is subject to the same pattern of discursive strictures as they are. On the other hand, his decision to place himself at the disposal of those working against the interests of independence and autonomy also inscribes him in the field of the Other, immediately rendering him an intrinsically complex and ambivalent figure. The extraordinary ambiguity of this position makes his house a perfect figure for the doubled inscriptions attending the colonial encounter and places him in a similarly indeterminate position to that taken by Thaël with regard to the activists.

Both Thaël and Garin, then, are caught up in the interstices of an identity crisis, neither completely colonial subjects nor wholly representative of the Other in whose desire they are both already inscribed. Thus Thaël's statement that "it all begins here" suggests his own implicit recognition of the forces joining them both and of the joint role that Thaël, Garin, and his control of the source of the Lézarde in its role as cultural signifier have to play in the articulation of a field of signification from this creole temporality of difference.

Given the importance of the Lézarde to the cultural cohesion of Lambrianne, then, the location of its source under the control of the colonizer's double agent suggests a recognition of the protean nature of colonial authority. In other words, because the complex figure of the source—both symbol of the past and starting point of the future—signifies the oppositions of the colonial condition for both colonizer and colonized, this ambivalence produces in turn a space within which all who are subject to colonial intervention become imbricated in this attempt to trace a differential line of descent for the imminent postcolonial moment. Interestingly, this space is not only controlled by Garin; its center remains empty until Thaël enters it, and the latter's realization that "I discover the source at the same time that I find the man" (74/92) is indicative of the paradoxically central relationship that he is about to form with his elusive quarry.

In what is perhaps the most significant sequence in the narrative, Garin and Thaël proceed to descend the Lézarde together, both aware that Garin knows that Thaël's ultimate task is to kill him. Together, they function as an articulated sign of the undecidability of the colonial site, their reciprocal affiliation an ineluctable, strategic symbiosis immediately made overt at the beginning of chapter 3 of part 2: "They begin their descent, one following the other, *bound by an invisible thread. . . . they turn with no alternative to the mocking complicity of the streaming waters*" (77/98; emphasis mine). Yet at the same time, it is this very imbrication that must be surpassed so that an alternative, tertiary pattern of postcolonial antillanité may supplant it: "At such moments they both pulled at the invisible bonds that held them together. . . . they both grow weak in the oppressive silence that . . . condemn[s] and oppress[es] them. . . . Garin is affected (disturbed, overcome) by this waiting for Thaël, by the wish which will only be fulfilled by his, Garin's, death. But he is not conscious of all this"

(78–79/100). The river whose traces they follow downstream now inhabits that unnameable place of slippage and of doubling that is produced as the colonial site re-presents the unsettling anxieties and affiliations that are its hallmark.

The ineluctable conflict and consensus that governs this interaction between Thaël and Garin will ultimately shape new sites of resistance and contestation. Given that each is simultaneously interpellated both as a postcolonial inhabitant of Lambrianne and as the colonial Other in whose discourse the subject is always already alienated—Garin's link to the opposition is matched by Thaël's acceptance of his murderous task—the desire for recognition from this Other that governs the indeterminacy of their discursive subjection will force them to sink, or swim, together.

Importantly, the narrator leaves no doubt as to the complicity of both characters in the trajectory of events limned by their descent of the river. They are joined not only by the geopolitical discourse that shapes their specific subjectivity but also by a sort of destiny that draws them increasingly closer together: "So Thaël and Garin follow fate, along the course of the river. . . They are together now. The obstacles along the way are less trouble now. Thaël helps Garin out of the mud, Garin carries Thaël from one embankment to another. . . . So, little by little, they become closer" (86/111). Yet at the same time, their rhetoric remains ensnared in the ambivalent indeterminacies of the colonial encounter. Glissant's vision of the construction of a creole cultural community that must prevail against the grain of an overarching discourse of domination stages the symbolic formation of this body politic, mediated by the hybrid creativity of a liminal moment of displacement and disjuncture.

This Glissantian perspective on Caribbean realities, which Beverley Ormerod describes in her book *An Introduction to the French Caribbean Novel* as "an attempt to acquire a sense of the continuous flow of time which lies dormant in the Caribbean landscape" (36), deliberately establishes a specific discursive temporality of difference in order to reflect and convey the contradictions and discontinuities that have determined the regional experience. In terms of the liminal moment of transition symbolized by the impending elections, the repetitions, obscurities, and parallels that emerge from the ideological interaction centering on Garin's death signify a re-presentation of the complex undercurrents that together create the imaginary of this people. The pluralities of the past, present, and the imminent future, re-presented through the affinities and antitheses of identity and ideology, converge in these heterotopic lines of character and plot whose insistent inversions mark the impossibility of a linear narrative logic. These relational aspects of the discursive space of *La Lézarde* operate within a larger framework of colonial undecidability that forces the recuperation of its tensions through the temporal ruptures and identitarian rifts of the narrative. The discursive "double signification" that permeates *La Lézarde* links these protean alluvial traces of colonial division to the interstitial inscription of an impending departmentalization. This synthesis of narrative, cultural, and ideological patterns limns the impossibility of a unitary logic and prefigures the ineluctable collision of interests and positions that attend the redefinition of colonial teleologies. In the tangential intersections of Thaël and Garin, and their encounter with the chiaroscuro world of the Lézarde river, colonialism's binary boundaries of origin and identity will be contested, reformulated, and relocated.

In journeying down the river, the two men form a paradoxical bond; their mediation by the symbolic resonances of the Lézarde leads to "their strange, almost unconscious friendship, the fraternity that they were in spite of themselves about to share" (94/122). If the river transforms and unites them, it simultaneously disturbs the oppositions that they represent to the extent that the approaching sea must now contain this combination of unity and irreconcilability. This critical juncture between river and sea, as Beverley Ormerod suggests, becomes "a transition from flux and mutability to a timeless immobility, an infinite spaciousness, and induces in both men a surrender to the inevitable" (1985:48). What is inescapable, however, is the presence of that symbolic, relational reciprocity that implicitly mediates their functional intersection within the text, and that ultimately determines both the moment and the manner of Garin's death.

For significantly, Garin's demise by drowning, when it does occur, does not take place in the waters of the Lézarde; this event occurs just beyond the point where the river joins and becomes one with the sea. This site of transition is marked by a sandbar, and it is Garin's attempt to traverse this bar that precipitates his death. The Rubicon-like symbolic importance of the bar is indicated early on in the narrative, when in a prefigurative moment of discussion among the activists, the intricacies and dualities of the impending transition are inscribed in symbolic terms: "'The sea is a little like politics,' Pablo was saying. . . . there was a sand bar feared even by accomplished swimmers, and which was approached with extreme caution by sailing boats on their return from fishing. . . . 'Politics is a serious matter, neither romantic nor mysterious. Let's go beyond the sand bar, but let's guard against any eventuality'. . . . 'No one has ever drowned, not so?'" (40–41/43). Notwithstanding the debatable and paradoxical means adopted by the group to arrive—through Thaël—at the bar, it is Garin's vain attempt to cross the bar and the implications of this symbolic transition from the discursive space of the river to that of the sea that define this act as a symbolic moment of performative modernity for them both, a transition supplemented by the crucial fact that Thaël is never shown to be directly responsible for Garin's death except for his role in overturning their boat.

Indeed, the text clearly shows Thaël's ongoing hesitation with regard to the actuality of murder and, significantly, conveys this through free indirect discourse: "Why all this noise, all these words? He cannot do it. He could never in cold blood, kill a man" (100/129–30). Importantly, we also see Thaël's subordinate stance in this schema, and the predominant role played by the sea in articulating these final axes of association and antithesis:

> The sea weighs these things and takes the life of one and the death of the other! Look. Look again. . . . Garin cries out (his entire body leaning into the wall, *he wants to overcome the sand bar*, to laugh in the sunlight on the other side, he wants to mock Thaël, he is mocking the sea where all plans are undone. . . . Then at last he leaps on Garin. . . . The canoe against the sea, and Thaël against Garin. *When the sea wages war, nothing is left but foam.* . . . The water breaks the fragile bond between them. Garin struggles against the blue maelstrom. . . . Thaël swims. . . . He does not know that *the sea has overcome Garin.* . . . Where is the river, the Lézarde. . . . Valérie is swimming with him. (113–14/146–47; emphasis mine)

Here, it is effectively the sea that takes Garin's life; and indeed, for a moment, Thaël remains quite unaware of this eventuality. Subjected as they are to the symbolic script of the sea, which, paradoxically, condemns one of them to death and, as we shall see, the other to life in a deliberate dialectic of ongoing colonial duality, the tortuous complexities of their mutual condition, one now also mediated by Valérie but over which both Thaël and Garin had little if any control, are now resited by this passage of translation, significantly inscribed from the outset as the terminal point in the Lézarde's figurative passage through the community of Lambrianne.

The water and the land have always marked the ineluctable boundaries of this discursive economy—in a critical referential gesture, the sea signifies both the horrors of the Middle Passage in a slavery-dominated past and the umbilical tie of the Antilles to the metropolitan *mère-patrie*, the very tie placed in question by the imminent departmental election—and now also mark indelibly the manner of Garin's demise. For whereas the stated goal of Thaël's encounter with Garin was always his death, it was also a goal that, given the parallelism of their ideological inscription in the text, Thaël could not be allowed to carry out personally, since such an act would imply the creation of an unbridgeable chiasmus of subjective signification. The manner and moment of Garin's death thus simultaneously set the stage for the remarkable identitarian revelation that follows, the scene marking both an end and a beginning for Thaël's double existence in the community of Lambrianne, and preparing his entry into the symbolic realm of patriarchal culture. Water itself plays a critical role here, undermining any illusions of subjective mastery or control. As Michael Dash appositely remarks in his reading of the forces at work in this scene, "The water does not perform a cleansing role here but indeed quite an opposed function, that of challenging the certitude of a pure consciousness" (1992:80). Ultimately, as we shall see, it is precisely these patterns of certitude and purity that are placed in question—and left unresolved—by this critical encounter between Garin and Thaël. Garin, then, mediating the axes of this passage in one of the most critical moments in the novel, dies attempting to "overcome the sandbar," to accomplish, in effect, a discursive metastasis from the dualities of the river to the infinite timelessness of the sea. But the interstices of the very colonial discourse by which he is overdetermined also tend to conceal the fact that this attempted transition is in fact an unmediated leap from a binary colonial past to a plural postcolonial future, from overdetermination to liberation without taking care to negotiate the traces and modalities of an interstitial, implicit difference which is almost absolute but not quite—and that Garin's attempt was therefore doomed from the very outset. It is through the flux and fluidity of such an interstitial moment—one whose tensions underwrite the construction of the migrant collaborative consciousness of the creole—that the connections and contestations of a new cultural identification will be charted and defined.

Indeed, the symbolic significance of the bar should not be understated. We recall Jacques Lacan's reformulation of Ferdinand de Saussure's construction of the bar separating signifier and signified. Lacan's rereading of Saussure posits the bar as a "barrier resisting signification . . . the irreducibility in which the relations between signifier and signified, the resistance to signification is constituted" (1977:149, 164). He further points out the importance of "the crossing of the bar—and the constitutive value of this crossing for the emergence of signification" (1977:164). Now if we return to the text to reread Garin's attempt to cross the bar from the perspective of this liminal moment of postcolonial transition, it becomes clear that, notwithstanding this postcolonial paradigm's intrinsic subversion of the binary bases of Western theory, such a crossing would have implied the accomplishment of an alternative paradigm of signification rewriting and overdetermining the entire symbolic structure of the narrative economy, immediately risking its imminent closure. In other words, given the creole constraints that must continue to shape the form of the narrative and the positionality of its characters, not only was it literally and figuratively impossible for Garin to cross the bar, he could not have been *allowed* to do so, for such an action would have implied the retroactive joining of figure to ground, of signifier to signified, erasing the pervasive duality of metropolitan hierarchies and displacing the compulsive disjunctures of departmentalization whose appropriation and institution create these contestatory sites of sociopolitical identity. The novel's initial insistence on a radical relocation and revision of the implicit divisions at work in an encounter between the discursive linearities of colonialism and the perpetual dislocations of departmentalization compels the foreclosure of any eventuality that would recuperate the very dichotomies whose revision and recognition are necessary to the differential praxis of a new cultural community where values would be grounded in the diverse affiliations of antillanité.

But perhaps the most remarkable aspect of this critical moment in the narrative is the way in which it allows a new articulation of Thaël as a postcolonial subject who is arguably less than one—neither entirely colonizer nor colonized—but now recognizably double. As the death of Garin is reported and the local representative of colonial authority, the policeman Alphonse Tigamba—who by virtue of his social role, his ineluctable colonial inscription, and his close knowledge of the group's members embodies perhaps the ultimate compromise—begins the interrogation, the discourse incorporates a series of italicized responses whose double register—as both narrative commentary and internal monologue by Tigamba—simultaneously conveys Tigamba's anguish at his foreknowledge of a plot now apparently come to fruition, and reinforces the sudden transformation of Thaël's identitarian position: "'What happened?' 'We went out in a boat. . . . We overturned, he did not come back.' The starkness of words. *You killed him, but what to do? Be careful what you say, this man is powerful*" (118/153). For, in a sudden and astonishing reversal, we discover that in the wake of these events the protagonist suddenly no longer calls himself by the name with which we have become familiar. In response to Tigamba's question, "What is your name?" (118/153), he identifies himself for the first time by his full name, "Raphaël Targin." In other words, not only has this subject, given his involvement in rather than his responsibility for Garin's death, instantiated a new identity, but the inextricable link between the demise of Garin and this new nomenclature is signaled by the striking fact that "Targin" constitutes an almost exact anagram of "Garin," with the name of the Other preserved in the supplement of the initial "t" and in the final four letters that close both "Thaël" and "Raphaël." Indeed, the significance of this nominative and positional exchange is reinforced by the next line of narrative commentary/monologue, which appears in italics following Thaël's identificatory speech act: *"Raphaël Targin, and no longer Thaël"* (118/154).

By literally writing his performance with the letters of ambiguity, Thaël signals his dual inscription as both self and Other, his ineluctable inscriptive isolation from the group of activists simultaneously rendering him the contradictory counterpart of an already overdetermined Garin. Given his unconscious subjection to these parameters of Otherness, by virtue of which he forgoes the necessary step of explicitly acknowledging the affiliative ambiguity by which he is shaped, the constitutive imbrication of his identity with the field of the Other through which the nascent postcolonial community must be written unknowingly sets up the ultimate return of the colonial repressed, the uncanny reinscription of the very elusive enunciative modalities that beset the terrain of the colonial encounter.

The Discourse of Antillanité

The sweeping interrogation and re-placement of colonial positionalities that are at the heart of Glissant's narrative practice involve both the discourse and the subjects of the colonial encounter. Indeed, the narrative sets up a doubled framework within which binary patterns appear to persist within the relationship between the colony and the metropole, while these patterns and their corollaries of fragmentation are simultaneously subverted, undermining any attendant assumptions of chronology and coherence. This Glissantian doubleness, as we have seen, extends both from colony to metropole and along the twin trajectories traced by Mathieu and Thaël and Thaël and Garin, shaping the patterns and paradigms of the pervasive complicity that defines this post-colonial condition.

Glissant makes use of a variety of innovative techniques to mark and measure the contingent nature of coincidence and event in the narrative, inscribing as he does so a deliberate deferral of narrative resolution whose symbolic implications are revealed only at the end of the novel. For example, chapter 6 of part 3, titled "L'Election," is narrated in the second-person singular, a deliberately self-reflexive turn that implicates both author and reader even as it inscribes revolving patterns of discursive and subjective alienation, reinforcing the notion, as Michael Dash suggests, that "the subject in Glissant has a shaping effect on and is shaped by the object of its attention" (1995:64). Other innovations abound, all contributing to an overall narrative discourse that instantiates the very fragmentation, dislocation, and pluralism that constitute the subject of the narration.

In this regard, chapter 11 of part 2, titled "L'Acte," represents an extraordinary attempt at conveying both the inexorability of impending events and the simultaneity of a multitude of narrative situations. "Four journeys. Four directions. . . . Four clear furrows in the surrounding confusion" (104/136). The discourse slips imperceptibly from one character and situation to another, from a conversation between Mathieu and Papa Longoué, the *quimboiseur*, to one between Luc and Gilles, who are elsewhere but in the same moment: "'I cannot hear you, Mister Mathieu. Ah! My sight is going, and my hearing too. . . .' 'The sea!' Luc exclaims (but they, Luc and Michel, are near the railings around the square, waiting for those who set out—Where to? . . .)" (107/139). Glissant's deliberate attempts to subvert the authoritative linearities of omniscient, chronological narration are grounded in his conviction, clearly articulated later in the *Discours antillais* (105/198), that realist narrative is not inscribed in the cultural topography of Antilleans since its attendant binaries and linearities are not reflective of the Antillean experience; by contrast, the discontinuities and disjunctures of his fictive discourse recuperate the discordant doubling of Caribbean history and geopolitics.

Yet, most remarkable is probably the fact that all of chapter 10 of part 2, articulating an event paralleling in importance that critical moment in the intrigue when Garin and Thaël are on the verge of undertaking their momentous river descent, is enclosed in parentheses. This chapter recounts a large, nighttime political meeting held on the market square of Lambrianne. Tension is high and the event is highly significant, for the election of which it is the harbinger cannot be far off. It might be expected that this would be the point where declarations would be made, sides taken, denouncements carried out, and political platforms established. However, while the text rhetorically enacts these gestures, it simultaneously undermines and marginalizes them through the presence of parentheses and by rendering the entire scene in free indirect discourse. The inherent ambiguity and fragmentation of FID succeed in erasing the name and the space of identity, since the protean nature of the narrative voice effectively prohibits any attempt to recuperate a tangible positionality from the narrative, recuperating the inherent ambivalence of a liminal postcoloniality that reinscribes the binaries of the very authority it seeks to displace.

The parentheses, then, are discursively resonant in several ways. They point, for example, to the hierarchical relationship between political activity and the descent of the river by Garin and Thaël, implicitly interrogating the efficacy of the former. They also address the overall discursive status of this extract and the moment it articulates; since the totality of the chapter, almost five pages long, is entirely located within parentheses, this may be read as a primary sign of its status as a narrative within a narrative, and of the significance of its embedded status. If, as Tzvetan Todorov points out in his *Introduction to Poetics*, an embedded narrative establishes "a relation of causal explanation [or] a relation of thematic juxtaposition" (1981:53), then the narrative characteristics of this sequence may be taken as a microcosmic re-representation of the thematics of the main text. The alterity that FID conveys joins with the embedded narrative to produce an incessant dis-figuring of both narrative and subjective cohesion.

Once the meeting opens, these tendencies toward the erasure of linearity are immediately extended. Not only does the narrative avoid stable origins, it is linked to a specific speaker only through the most tenuous of metonymic associations: "The meeting was opened by a party speaker. He spoke of the importance of the country, not of the pettiness of its exploiters. The time had come to cast aside fear. They had trapped *us* like caged rats within the encircling sea. But *we* have made their barren prison fertile with our blood and sweat, and made it *our own*. Poverty was an old friend. The question was as clear as water pouring from the rock. Nothing could be clearer: this is a purely feudal relationship. How long could *we* tolerate the sight of our oppressors, unpunished and unworthy? *We* must all fight for what we believe in" (102/132;

emphasis mine). Since this passage incorporates several paradoxical stages of discursive slippage, it calls for a close, nuanced reading of its patterns.

If we begin to reread this passage from the point where the political discourse itself begins, the first thing that strikes us is its opening in medias res, and the absence of the article in the original French: "Importance of the country." This lack of a semantic grounding tends to displace the words from the context of the speaker; its effect is to erase any temporal or subjective contextualization from the enunciation of this discourse. Its tone, content, and orientation tend to suggest the existence of a specific point of ideological or geopolitical reference, but the rule of subversion engaged by the absence of the article simultaneously works along with the mode of free indirect discourse to prohibit any precision of attribution, and thus to pluralize the discursive voice. Already textual ambiguity and polyphony are inscribed as the primary terms of representation, with pluralism and dispersal already in place as over-determinants of the text.

Through the multiple, protean resonances of the pronoun *nous* (we, us), the rest of the passage continually undergoes further displacement, re-presenting a colonial condition of subjection and embodying the contestation of the marginal, the displaced, the (under)represented. Just as the possession of the *cagibi* (cage) does not erase its presence nor alter its linear lines of colonial descent, so the assumption of self-determination on a national scale will not alter the duality of this liminal moment of transition as postcolonial subjects assuming limited control of an environment whose history and temporality differ radically from the metropole. The polyvalency of subject positions that marks this postcolonial society is continually figured by its own intrinsic oppositions and contradictions. And so even the final exhortation of "we must all fight for what we believe in," a plural address to a plural subject which implies a speaker at one with his audience, suggests rhetorically a unity in contestation, but upon closer examination it is in fact delimited by the suggestion of social fragmentation and disjuncture which may be inferred from the fact that the exhortation has to be made at all.

In sum, then, the entire chapter embodies a subversive subtext, a subjective liminality that is perpetually reinforced and recuperated by the rhetorical structure of its own discourse. By further enclosing these communal contradictions within parentheses, the contingent nature of the meeting itself is underlined, the uselessness of conventional politics within a context of unknowable and unfathomable ambiguity reinforced. Given the symbolically important and ineluctable trajectory about to be traced by Thaël and Garin, and its implicit effect upon the community whose complexities they purport to represent, the entire meeting may just as well never have occurred. The whole chapter, therefore, traces an intrinsic reiterative doubling of subjectivity which is perpetually reinforced and recuperated by the unstable rhetorical operations of the colonial encounter. Its remapping of a supposedly central politics into a peripheral praxis still inscribed in the margin provides a striking structural echo of the extent to which the traditional approaches of a colonial hierarchy, and an inscription in its attendant authority, are made to verge on the irrelevant, by ignoring the multiple perspectives and protean relationships intrinsic to a burgeoning antillanité. The multiplicities and undecidabilities of place generate an interstitial incalculability that localizes the inscription of Caribbeanness even as it interrogates the subjective and discursive modalities of the metropolitan binary.

Perhaps the primary way in which the associative ambiguities and parallels by which this text resites and reframes both its colonial characters and the discourse that determines their sense of community is through the deliberate decentering of identity and perspective through free indirect discourse. While its primary function is typically the transmission of thought and commentary through its merging of character and narrator, FID has found increasingly common use among postcolonial authors as an effective means of conveying issues of alienation and displacement, through the appropriation of the inherent dualities germane to this form. Pointing to its role as a narrative device for simultaneously conveying thought and commentary, Wallace Martin succinctly defines FID as "a mixture or merging of narrator and character" (1986:138). This merging of perspectives intrinsically joins subjects as well, rendering it impossible to distinguish between them, to set them apart. It may be said to signify a split in the ego of the discursive subject; the subject so signified does not, and cannot, affirm itself as "I," for only direct discourse possesses the capacity to mediate this inscription. Such a subject does not speak but is *spoken for*, relinquishing both the ability to fully engage in discourse and the characteristics of a fully constituted discursive subject. When FID is placed at the service of a narrative that translates and refigures the contradictions of the colonial situation and its attendant discourses, it becomes the mark of a pluralist and substitutive framework, decentering the fixity of meaning and of identity. If FID is then assimilated as the discursive sign of the divided and fragmented colonial subject, it can reflect and recuperate the intrinsic multiplicity and dispersal of the colonial subjective space. As we shall see, Glissant's use of this discursive form extends and enhances his narrativization of the problematics of postcolonial pluralism.

Glissant's extensive and varied use of FID as a referential framework for the alienation and ambiguity of his characters constitutes an important and innovative inscription of this narrative device within a context of postcolonial discourse. The subtle shifts in tone and perspective that presage the inscription of FID underline the perpetual slippage signified by its constant resurgence. For example, the entire speech conveying Thaël's acceptance of his murderous task is written in FID, suggesting not only the speaker's intrinsic indecision but his simultaneous separation and alienation from the perspective of his counterparts: "But what is the nature of the link between myth and reality? The sacrifice of a human life is highly regarded in mythology. Is this also true of stark reality? Was one man the key to the order and the balance that were his ultimate goals? Was this one man's death enough to attain peace of mind? " (49/56). Here, Thaël appears ready to commit this political act as much for himself as for the others (connaître la sérénité); interestingly, the important role played by legend and sacrifice in Thaël's subconscious, quite visible in this extract, will return to revise his future at the end of the novel.

But perhaps the most striking instance of FID in *La Lézarde* occurs following the death of the political henchman Garin, during the inquest presided over by Judge Parel. This episode, which opens part 3 of the novel, titled "L'Election," significantly contains not a single line of direct discourse pertaining to the events under investigation. The few lines of attributable direct speech serve to contextualize the colonial community through the courtroom proceedings, and concern reminiscences of petty larceny, or the bribes that the judge would accept for a reduction or revocation of sentence. Turning the proceedings to Garin's case immediately engenders FID and its concomitant alienation, as our narrative access to the judge's consciousness, for all practical purposes, is couched in its disjunctures: "There was now this case of a drowning! . . . Why did these people always want to go to the sea; did he, Parel, High Court judge, go down there? . . . He had been ordered to make a full investigation, to show no mercy to this boy; the Garin fellow was important" (123/161). By textually subjecting the judge, symbol of colonial authority, to the divisions and dualities of a colonial discourse, Glissant's recognition of his authority within a colonial framework is simultaneously placed under erasure. An alternation between the dualities that mediate between "the Garin fellow" and the judge himself takes place, reinforcing the double slippage that occurs between sign and act and between discourse and subject, and resiting these multiple misprisions of colonial authority: "But the judge hated important people. What right had they to tell a judge what decision to make? Just because some idiot did not know how to swim!" (123/161). By switching imperceptibly from omniscient reporting to internal monologue, Glissant makes ambiguity and dislocation the ground of this scene's representative economy, exacerbating the imbrication of the judge and of the community at large in the fragmentation of identity generated by the colonial project.

The high point of the scene, Thaël's testimony, is also marked in its turn by this nonattributability and plurality of the discourse. In the space of three short sentences, the narrative enacts a remarkable sequence of variations in perspective, which, while retaining Thaël as the focalizer, decenters and disperses the narrative center even farther: "Thaël was amazed, so many people had turned up, all this ritual. The young man was not afraid, he simply waited for things to run their course. His statement before the court made an impression because it was so simply delivered and so precise in its details; this young man could not have invented these things, he was sincere" (124/162). In the first sentence, the use of the demonstrative adjectives *ce* and *cette* (this) marks the shift from the third-person omniscient narration with which the sentence began (Thaël was amazed), to the internal monologue of Thaël's own perception. But this shift is only temporary, for the following sentence, introduced by "the young man," immediately reverts to an omniscient third-person narrative, the change in perspective suggesting a subjective division within Thaël and, paradoxically, the simultaneous participation of narrator and community in this symbolic ritual of resurgence. The final sentence, however, is perhaps the most noteworthy, for while it picks up where its predecessor leaves off, the introductory "His statement" stemming rhetorically from "the young man," and the sudden reappearance of the demonstrative "this young man" in the middle of the sentence, without the semblance of any sort of transition, reinscribe the discourse into a free indirect mode, conveying the sentiments of the narrator, the judge, and the community at large, and thus the progressively protean perspective both of the population and of the discursive strategy that represents them. More important, the metonymic relation between community and free indirect discourse within the same discursive space tends to demonstrate the pervasive subjective slippage attending both Thaël and, by implication, Garin, his principal counterpart, as they are reinscribed in this colonial site. These oppositions and contradictions, the subtle shifts in subjective and in discursive perspective, mark the displacement effected by a colonial discourse and figure its re-presentation of a subjective category whose peripatetic excursions mark it as incontrovertibly interstitial.

In the end, Judge Parel even sums up the proceedings and pronounces the verdict in free indirect discourse, determining that "it was implausible that this young fellow could have killed Garin, you needed a lot of imagination to come up with that. And this Garin fellow was during his lifetime supposedly on the judge's side, but to no avail; the latter felt no remorse at his death" (125/163). While these intersections of identity seem the natural culmination of the fragmentation and doubling produced by the colonial script, the affiliative indeterminacy re-presented and appropriated in this narrative by the incessant slippages of FID appear to generate no discursive differentiation between Thaël, the judge, and the community at large. From a symbolic perspective, the judge's pronouncement, couched as it is in FID, allows him to speak in the name of the entire community that he represents, but each element here speaks with, for, and in place of the other, extending the alterities of the postcolonial perspective both to the narrative structure and to the fractured forms of identity that are the corollary of its figures.

Following the election victory, however, somehow a hollowness seems to remain. Interestingly, despite this death by remote control, the indecision and uncertainty that have pervaded the narrative scene extend, ironically, to the very question of the vote; the following exchange between the peasant Lomé and Mathieu emphasizes the ideological ignorance and instability that are at the heart of this community: "Brother Mathieu, who will get our vote?" "The people, of course." "Who are the people, friend?" (128/166). The explosion of joy that greets the election result—the activists have backed the winning party—in reality does nothing either to effect a new communal temporality or to dislocate teleologies already at work on the sociocultural level. In other words, the fact that the death of Garin and the election it precedes do not effectively warn of the dangerous dualities that are the implicit corollary of an impending departmentalization places the entire ideological project—method and means, victor and vanquished—at risk of dissolution. And in this poetics of a disconcerted collectivity, both narrator and narration have consistently displayed a telling combination of self-reflexivity and ambivalence that underscores the novel's deliberate structural re-vision of the very issues it interrogates.

Ultimately, what Glissant puts into practice is a metafictional approach to the narration of antillanité. His conflation of the multiplicities of image, discourse, and subjectivity creates a narrative economy that constantly reflects on the means and terms of its production, and that consistently interrogates and subverts its implicit chronologies of cause and effect, subject and object to displace any linear assumptions of discursive and identitarian production. At the level of discourse, for example, the reader cannot help but be struck by the consciously tentative tone of the narrative voice. Indeed, the narrator, who remains eternally unnamed, repeatedly blurs the lines of continuity between self, community, and reader; the demarcations of division that simultaneously establish patterns of affiliation and separation between the major characters extend to engender major dualities of narrative perspective. For example, early on, a clear distinction is made between the adult who narrates and the child who witnesses, emphasizing, through a series of repetitions and double registers, the duality that mediates between temporalities of then and now. "And I, as a child (the child of this story, growing with each word) accompany these women, I roll around on the sand. . . . I do not know (I will grow with this story) that the river symbolized the true nature of everyday toil. . . . I do not yet know that a man only fulfils himself when he savours the meaning of the land in his own story (in its moments of passion and joy)" (33/31–32). His extraordinary morcelization of the progress of growth and awareness not only problematizes the status of the subject, it suggests that the narrator who is "the child of this story, growing with each word" does so almost as a fragmented corollary of the discourse, the disjuncture and signification of the story generating and imparting a reflected, relative meaning to his own life. Here, the impossibility of designating precisely a singular subjective space is testimony once again to the ineluctable fragmentation of subjectivity and its alienation within the sign.

Similarly, the multiplicity of perspectives and of peripeteia in the narrative is intentionally present to undermine any intimation of a possible authority, through the metonymic relation to the notoriously false linearity of the discursively constructed existence—as, for example, in autobiography, as contemporary literary theory has demonstrated[7]—where the effect of retrospective narration is to engender from random events seemingly apparent connections of cause and effect. As Hayden White points out, "This value attached to narrativity in the representation of real events arises out of a desire to have real events display the coherence, fullness, and closure of an image of life that is and can only be imaginary" (1981:23).[8] In other words, the multiplicity of displacements, positions, and parallels that the narrative successively puts into place deliberately interrogates narrative assumptions, reducing the role of the subject in the construction of meaning and simultaneously valorizing the indeterminacy of the narrative act.

In his book *Edouard Glissant*, Michael Dash reads these narrative disjunctures as a means toward the emergence of "individual awareness, whether political, emotional, or spiritual; it is not only the narrator who grows within the story, but several of the others do so as well, measurably and at times painfully" (62). As early as chapter 2, the narrator insists upon the mutability of his status, his perspective in fact positioned midway between agency and submission: "I heard these words, but I was still a child, and they echoed within me. I was both witness and object: the one who sees and who must endure, who is called and who is shaped. I knew Thaël and Mathieu and all their friends; here is how" (22/16). It is the very interstitial nature of the narrator's predicament that engenders its value, shaping and being shaped by a desire to merge both past and present, criticism and creativity, from his position in the middle. As Dash points out in his book, "He confesses desperately to the desire both to remember and understand the past and to be a witness and participant . . . both a witness and a recorder, the incompatibility of omniscience and direct experience, objectivity and subjectivity" (63). The protean mutability of the narrative voice, which slips repeatedly from "I" to "we," and indeed to "you," mimes this deliberate indeterminacy in order to further reinscribe the plural perspectives and creative instability of this creole community.

The community itself is ultimately defined in one of those passages inscribed in the second person: "You suddenly understood that this entire history had been nothing but a fierce collective effort to escape the mean destiny that had been imposed on this world, the petty provincialism that overwhelmed this country, as well as feelings of shame and self-disgust" (168–69/216). As the narrative nears its end, it falls to the exhausted Mathieu to proffer a definition of the uniquely plural nature of this nascent creole community: "Almost all the peoples of the world coming together here. Not for a day; for centuries. And what comes out of it? The Caribbean people. The Africans our ancestors, indentured Breton servants, Hindu coolies, Chinese shop-keepers. All together and we were expected to forget Africa. And what happens? We have not forgotten. Very well" (173/222). It is from the transformative encounters of this ethnocultural melting pot that the specificity of Antillean culture took shape, and this many-sidedness is, at bottom, what informs Glissant's complex construction of character, plot, and voice, enabling his discourse to reflect both the birth pangs of the Franco-Caribbean experience, and the latent but protean possibilities of its diasporic transnationalism. It will be the novel's explosive end, however, that will ultimately bring into perspective the implicit, simultaneous parallels and contradictions that any consideration of the full complexities of geopolitical creolization must embrace.

While the narrator's transition from child to man recuperates the liminal nature of the narrative events, it is the indeterminacy of the narrative itself that remains the heart of the matter: "The child that I was and the man that I am have this in common: they confuse legend and history" (82/105). The network of signification traced by the narrator and his narrative, persistent and pervasive throughout the novel, eventually provides a coda of commentary that demands a new vision from the doubleness it insistently reiterates, even as it appears to valorize the disjunctures of the past: "I am a child in the street and a man in my memory. . . . Yes, I feel I am two people, a sensation frozen in time. I still hear echoes of the last celebration, I still hear the wild rejoicing of bygone days" (180/230). It is this narrative subtext of instability, then, a creole carnival of doubleness and masking, parallelism and slippage, that overdetermines both text and character even as it insists upon the ineluctability of its own disjunction, whose interrogation of an incomplete departmental vision ultimately permits the final, most explosive encounter of the novel to take place.

Glissant closes the narrative with a convulsive episode, choosing the moment of her postelection return to Thaël's cottage on the eve of their wedding to immolate Valérie—textual symbol of a liberated Lambrianne doubly desired by both Thaël and Mathieu—by Thaël's dogs, Sillon and Mandolée. From the beginning these animals have been defined by their *noms de légende* and by the fact that they "seemed to have concentrated in themselves the explosive force of the highlands." There is also the important corollary that their vicious nature is only tenuously controlled by Thaël; indeed, in a gesture that underlines the figural duality that is to come, we can credit this force with "inspiring Thaël with admiration as well as the desire to escape" (12/19). If they answer only to him, the interaction of both is but an involuted one at best. In one gesture, by insisting on the exception that proves the rule, Glissant puts the paradoxes undergirding the entire narrative into focus, bringing the novel's binarisms full circle and demonstrating the destructive capacity of rejected colonial desire by underlining the consequence of such misrecognition. He accomplishes this while implicitly criticizing and condemning the pervasive blindness that continues to plague the necessary construction of a creole context of politics and performance as a legitimate backdrop for a postcolonial praxis of Caribbean creolization.

It is of more than passing interest that the entirety of chapter 20 of part 1, in which Valérie's future is foretold by Papa Longoué, is enclosed in parentheses in the narrative. We have already noted Glissant's strategic use of such techniques to signal contexts of doubling and simultaneity, as well as supposedly elided or marginalized events; significantly, here, Papa Longoué's prediction, warning of an encounter with dogs on a dark mountain, prefigures the exact circumstances of Valérie's ultimate death. Also, both Valérie, who is also Mathieu's cousin, and Thaël are orphans; while Mathieu has lost his father, and finds a surrogate one in Papa Longoué, the sense of exile that binds this pair renders them a symbolic mirror image of each other. Thaël's physical and psychological exile grounds the dualities of a young man who, ironically, is "too young to vote" (148/191), and this in turn mimics Valérie's symbolic recuperation of the forces that have overdetermined Thaël and that also define the larger community: "Yes, Valérie had with her both the grandeur of the mountains and the endurance of the plains" (141/182).

Importantly, her symbolic complicity in Garin's death, culminating in the relationship that develops during the election process, is symbolically prefigured by the *absence* of the bar: "and they found each other, finally free to love each other (*and not for one moment were they disturbed by thoughts of the sand bar*, and not once did they remember the terrifying swim, neither Thaël who had experienced it nor Valérie who had imagined it), finally delivered to each other in this moment of calm and shared confidence" (161/207; emphasis mine). Sharing this state of calm certainty, they forget the symbolic function of the barrier to signification and the assumption of linearity between past and future that its absence re-presents, which are precisely the issues that are about to be put to the test in the alternative crossing that awaits them.

Given her own symbolic, symbiotic, yet differential relationship to Thaël, then, Valérie's death represents the painful but necessary exposure of the inevitable conjunction of colonizer and colonized to Thaël's eyes. Their ascent of the mountain symbolically retraces Thaël's captious descent of the Lézarde with Garin and designates their own mutual subconscious implication within a misplaced authority that must be ruptured in order for it to be ultimately supplanted by the complex liberative ideologies of a cultural and political creolization. The figures that accompany the ascent seem to surge threateningly about them; Valérie seems to see "terrible shadows rise up on either side, waiting to pounce on her, already closing in, lying in wait, pressing in on her" (190/246). The beasts, whom Thaël greets by "the legendary names he had given to his dogs, names from that tale which terrified him as a child," seem to perceive an imminent attack upon their master, and "they rushed out so quickly that there was no hope of escape" (192–93/248–49). The suddenness and viciousness of this overwhelming attack, which Thaël is powerless to stop, puts an end to the multiple symbolic resonances that attach to their expectations of conjugal association, and punctuates the simple linearity of the denouement by exposing the incompatibility of the colonial desire within which both Thaël and Valérie are confined. The symbolic function of her death at the hands of the dogs seems to make possible this confrontation with accepted but inadequate colonial binaries of self and Other, and to compel their appropriation and relocation to an alternative site of difference, a moment of recognition which ultimately allows the contestation and pluralism of an incipient antillanité to take hold.

This event also marks the textual return of the repressed, the inevitable reappearance of the master's discourse when its authoritarian modalities are accepted but their implications ignored. For in the shocking, symbolic ending of La Lézarde may be traced the culmination of a submission to colonial control and a simultaneous refusal to countenance the contradictions engendered by the desire for a dialectics of difference. Glissant's deliberately intertextual ending entails a veiled rereading of the Greek myth of Actaeon and Artemis, the goddess of hunting, in which the hunter Actaeon, having been turned into a stag, was attacked and killed by his own dogs for having secretly watched Artemis bathing. Indeed, so attached were Actaeon's dogs said to be to him that they were completely inconsolable following his death until Chiron, Actaeon's centaur-mentor, made them a likeness of their master.[9] This substitutive doubling of one of the seminal myths of Western culture—generating a new myth which is both a displacement and a replacement of the Greek original—holds important implications for the transition to a differential perspective on writing and authority, and marks a discursive act of appropriation that objectively reveals the necessity of constructing a differential mode of resistance which operates from a resiting rather than a simple reversal of binary colonial roles. In a sense, through Valérie, Lambrianne is destroyed by that very Western discourse with which Thaël, the hunter, had sought too readily to

assimilate, the attack reflecting the final traces of his subconscious acquiescence to a colonial culture that is inscribed both through his love of myth and
attachment to these *noms de légende*. This sense of double jeopardy emerges
from the unavowed but indisputable submission to the dominant strictures of
colonial control implicit in his acceptance of his murderous task and his blindness to the attendant subjective ambivalence that it entailed. As Targin takes
the place of Garin, his own colonial mentor and counterpart, the return to
engagement that closes the novel, with the dogs licking Thaël's feet with their
bloody muzzles while he makes plans to starve them into death on the site of
the source, tropes Chiron's construction of Actaeon's likeness in that his return
to the origins of the Lézarde—and, by implication, of the community it represents—with these murderous beasts marks symbolically a new beginning for
subject and community that operates simultaneously on several levels, as a
belated but necessary recognition of the symbolic significance of an un-
articulated submission to colonial authority, and the ineluctable resurgence of
the displaced desire it engenders. The repetition and difference framing
Thaël's act together mark this location in the present as a space of creolization
from which this hybrid culture will ultimately derive its true legitimacy.

This symbolic (re)source to which Thaël (re)turns, in what Dominique
Lecloux calls a "progression . . . dans l'univers de l'ombre, vers une connais-
sance plus approfondie de ses racines (407)," assumes greater imoportance
when the reductive resonances of his primary identity pattern, an uncomplicated confrontation with the patrons of power, are attacked and erased. His
decision to destroy the dogs upon this site through this starvation-induced
madness symbolically unravels the false oppositions and secret desires upon
which the colonial framework is constituted, simultaneously articulating
through its fissures a social and textual poetics of difference that negotiates the
interstices of pluralism to herald a new basis for an ethics of postcolonial identity.

Yet the critical nature of certain events that are key to the outcome of the
plot refuses an easy dismissal, in this early exposition of creole cultural performance as an articulative archetype for a postcolonial Caribbean paradigm of
antillanité. It is interesting to note that Papa Longoué, the community's *quimboiseur* and thus its primary material link with the iterability of the past, dies at
almost the exact moment that the election result is announced, suggesting a
post/colonial future umbilically—and therefore dangerously—separate and
distinct from the colonial and indeed the ancestral past. Indeed, each of the

novel's three deaths enacts a symbolic engagement with the discontinuities and dualities of this encounter between past and future. Yet if, in this context of contestation, patterns of pluralism tend to mark a sort of communal discontinuity, then Garin, himself a principal site of post/colonial ambivalence, must perish within the sphere of this very landscape in order for his doubled counterpart to have the possibility of escaping the confines of a linear authority, a set of confines he is ultimately forced to confront. With both Thaël and Garin linked to patterns of hybrid signification, Thaël's eventual acceptance of the material implications of geopolitical creolization through Valérie's death is ultimately dependent upon his symbolic separation from Garin and from the profound paradoxes of the post/colonial moment his activities re-present. These three doomed characters, then, as Michael Dash rightly argues, "share a common refusal or inability to grasp the significance of the changes taking place around them or of the values of the Lézarde river" (1995:72). Together, they trace the complex, common teleology of an interjacent, postcolonial past and future that figures the community of Lambrianne.

Each of these protagonists—Thaël, Mathieu, and Garin—must articulate with his Others if the full complexities of this liminal moment are to be elaborated and addressed. But through their devotion to the development of the supposedly differential discourse of departmentalism, and their simultaneous, unwitting submission to the name of an outmoded but still tellingly capable pattern of colonial authority, they locate—albeit inadvertently—the divergent undercurrents and strategies by which colonialism can continue to influence the societies in which it has been implanted.

The pervasive nature of this force is ultimately figured by Valérie's violent and apparently inexplicable death at the hands of Thaël's dogs. With the martyred Valérie the object of desire of both Thaël and Mathieu, the eventual effects of these parallels and disjunctures destroy the nascent nationalism she ultimately comes to represent. Her death disrupts the axis of postcolonial revolt, effectively maintaining the circulation of contradictory discourses on which the novel's symbolic structure is based. But while the proleptic character of Glissant's conclusion proposes an effective awakening to alternative possibilities, both narrative and discourse suggest that any substantive change in the hierarchies generated by contesting colonialism must be carried out on the articulative ground of an immanent, interstitial ambivalence.

The narrative thus effectively installs alterity and ambiguity as inalterable features of the postcolonial identity structure; such a subject is shown to be mediated both by a pluralized fragmentation of desire and by an ineluctable inscription in the field of the Other. This double gesture re-figures the traditional desire of the postcolonial subject to achieve recognition from the colonizing Other by displacing and usurping the Other's subjective space through persistent acts of mimetic replication. Interpellated into an imaginary recognition of the real conditions of existence, this subject seems historically and culturally doomed to the perpetual recuperation of the terms of its own misrecognition, contributing materially to the ongoing dislocation of its own discursive space. From this perspective, Mathieu's exhortation to the narrator of *La Lézarde* regarding the specific style and substance of the narrative discourse are particularly apposite here: "Write a story. . . . Write it like a river. Slow. Like the Lézarde. With rushing water, meanders, sometimes sluggish, sometimes running freely, slowly gathering the earth from either bank" (174–75, 224). Thus the narrative form can be seen to reflect the deliberate disjunctures and articulative ambivalences of a fragmented post/colonial Lambrianne and its subjects, made to face the creative uncertainties of approaching departmentalization. The discontinuous, fragmented nature of the historical and cultural experience of colonization produces specificities of splitting and parallels of opposition in this French Caribbean context, patterns which must be appropriated and resited in order to inscribe new terms for an alternate subjectivity. Ultimately, if, in Thaël's words, "we turn to the past in order to know the future" (144/186), then the complex characterizations and structured ambivalences of *La Lézarde* substantiate the assertion that the hierarchical assumptions persistently underguiding post/colonial authority in the French Caribbean can be effectively contested and countered only through the pluralities and positionalities of a deliberately doubled discourse of difference.

En attendant le bonheur
Creole Conjunctions and Cultural Survival

Tout ce qui touche à la femme noire est
objet de controverse.
Maryse Condé, *La Parole des femmes*

Deriving a Discourse

In the case of feminine-centered narrative, the forces at work in the field of postcolonial discourse assume a different character, reflecting the need to generate definitions different from a preexistent, overarching, masculine discourse which, particularly in a colonial context, had historically arrogated to itself the primary role of defining parameters of signification, appropriation, and cultural inscription. As far as a feminine Caribbean discourse is concerned, the task of delineating a specific discursive space becomes doubly difficult, since the discourse must take into account issues of gender and culture, as well as the double subjection by which colonialism exacerbates for women the repressive hierarchies of its authoritarian patriarchal structures.

In "Writing Like a Woman," Peggy Kamuf addresses the troubled terrain that binds language, gender, and the re-presentation of identity. She states: "Using language . . . we are all, more or less, in the position of a father, the parent of mediation. . . . If, on the other hand, by 'feminist' one understands a way of reading texts that points to the masks of truth with which phallocentrism hides its fictions, then one place to begin such a reading is by looking behind the mask of the proper name, the sign that secures our patriarchal heritage: the father's name and the index of sexuality" (284, 286). This strategy of reading articulated by Kamuf necessarily suggests the exposure of the implicit norms and stereotypes engendered by an adherence to a patriarchal discursive system. Assumptions of stability and agency tend to be subverted by such a reading, as the analysis seeks not to accept or repeat predetermined authoritarian roles, but rather to displace these assumptions by revealing the prejudices of their underlying premises. From the point of view of a feminized postcolonial discourse, the articulation of a narrative strategy that will, in differential terms, effectively contest the assumptions of authority already inherent in traditional narration and exacerbated by the masculinist assertions of the colonial encounter will be the primary challenge faced by any elaboration of a hybrid cultural identity. As Nelly Furman explains: "If the function of the feminist endeavor is to unveil the workings of the patriarchal system of values and display the structures which control the social and cultural order, then we must begin . . . by confronting the politics of language. . . . Language, from a poststructuralist position, is not an empirical object but a structuring process; and questions concerning women and literature will be broached differently according to whether we apprehend language as a stable medium or a continuous process" (1985:59–60, 64). As we shall see, it is by appropriating the ambiguity inherent in the relation between language and subjectivity that Maryse Condé's narratives initiate a subversion of the precepts of cultural, colonial, and discursive patriarchy.

Traditionally, the role of language in male-dominated discourses has been to convey a certain "universality" of human experience and the transmutation of this experience into literary representation. By overtly recognizing that the colonial project was chiefly enabled by oral performance and written discourse, we can interrogate the points of conjunction between language and colonialism, annexing new terms for a postcolonial feminine subjectivity at precisely the point where its double difference demands recognition. This task requires the simultaneous recognition and reformulation of habitual textual inscriptions of both gender and language; as Furman continues, "The literary works of male authors reflect chiefly a male view of life which is not necessarily women's experience. . . . When literature is viewed as a representational art whose function is to 'picture' life, what is ignored or pushed aside is the part played by language" (1985:63). The problem of establishing the cultural pluralities of creole subjectivity through a nonauthoritarian discourse of difference implies a site of multiple modernities, especially where language and subjectivity encounter a postcolonial feminine-centered discourse that seeks *not* to define itself in relation to male. A narrative strategy that paradoxically emphasizes the anxieties that lie in establishing points of difference rather than of similitude can translate the task of finding a place from which to speak into the cultivation of sites of ongoing ambivalence and negotiation. It is through such a consciously articulated discursive strategy, one that continuously restages these issues of difference and hybridity, that a creolized culture will seek to inscribe a specifically Caribbean sense of identity within the textual economy. By displacing authoritarian singularities of expression and intention, these notions of cultural and subjective hybridity can be reflected in the structure of the text.

These conjunctions of language and difference, then, reflect both the authoritarian assertions of the postcolonial encounter and the disjunctive dissonances of a doubled, creolized vision of regional realities, and ground the complex colonization of the Caribbean woman. Initiating such a discourse of difference necessarily interrogates questions of gender, history, and culture as they are inscribed within a discursive framework; if language is the ground upon which issues of identity construct the parameters of their operation, then difference in language can become a primary arena for the inscription of cultural identity. As Bill Ashcroft, Gareth Griffiths, and Helen Tiffin point out in *The Empire Writes Back*: "All post-colonial societies realize their identity in difference rather than in essence. They are constituted by their difference from the metropolitan and it is in this relationship that identity both as a distancing from the centre and as a means of self-assertion comes into being. . . . The discourse of the post-colonial is therefore grounded on a struggle for power—that power focused in the control of the metropolitan language" (167). This contestation of authority, focusing as it does on binary language and difference, inaugurates the terms and tensions of the problematic inscription of the creative undecidabilities and disjunctural patterns of Caribbean identity. In a Caribbean context of creole creativity, then, the interconnectedness of language, culture, and colonialism can determine the patterns of a postcolonial narrative strategy that synthesizes key issues of contestation and ambivalence.

Culturally speaking, this interconnectedness of the creole draws on a persistent preoccupation with place and with origins that functions as a catalyst in the search for Caribbean identity. The discussion of the regional history of hybridity and erasure in *Empire* suggests a tendency to generate patterns of desire and alienation grounded in fields of alterity that seek to establish a relationship of dependence with a mythical, unitary cultural (m)Other: "In a society which bore the permanent traces of conflict, repression, immigration, and forced migration . . . it has in some cases been seen to be necessary to revive that lost ancestral link before the Caribbean present can be understood, before the islands become 'home'" (146–47). This insistent search for home, a nostalgic quest for the patterns and parallels of an elusive, long-lost linearity and unicity—but one which must become an identity and a discourse grounded in the creole authenticity of the Caribbean region—will lead Condé's Véronica Mercier on a circuitous journey of nostalgia and discovery through Europe and Africa before she comes to terms with the innate potential of her own cultural ambiguity.

This notion of doubling disturbs traditional teleologies, engendering radical narrative and discursive strategies that inaugurate an identity structure rooted in difference. The merging of the postcolonial dialectic with a feminist perspective engenders doubled strategies of narrative emancipation, a determination to create a space that will permit and enhance the elaboration of a paradigmatic postcolonial female "voice." This voice will be as strategic as it is specific, conveying the modernities of the margin as it seeks, in Rachel Blau DuPlessis's phrase, to "write beyond the ending": "Writing beyond the ending means the transgressive invention of narrative strategies, strategies that express critical dissent from dominant narrative. . . . [It] . . . produces a narrative that denies or reconstructs seductive patterns of feeling that are culturally mandated, internally policed, hegemonically poised" (1985:5). These discursive strategies ultimately write disjuncture into difference, ambiguity and anxiety into a dialectic that renegotiates a subtle subversion of authoritarian patriarchal codes. The critical fusion of discourse, gender, and postcolonialism disturbs the traditional boundaries of subjectivity and marginalization; the effective elaboration of a female Caribbean subject in all its postcolonial complexity necessitates a multidimensional, interrogative narrative strategy that will capture the nuances of ambiguity and fragmentation that frame this doubly dislocated identity. Traditional narrative practice is shot through with patriarchal attributes and assumptions; as Evelyn O'Callaghan explains, "The practice of fiction is inevitably loaded, often related to an epistemology that justifies patriarchal and imperial assumptions" (1993:74). Thus the role of a differential form and function in articulating a creolized feminocentric postcolonial voice is rendered even more more important; its intervocality facilitates a vision of Caribbean woman as Other whose relational interaction with her several communities both shapes the structure of Condé's narrative project and, ultimately, determines the cultural identity of her protagonist.

En attendant le bonheur: **Happiness In-between**

Born in Guadeloupe in 1937, Maryse Condé has long been recognized as perhaps the foremost contemporary woman writer of the francophone Caribbean. With an *oeuvre* that includes ten novels, six plays, and assorted short stories, she has also edited several critical collections and authored several volumes of crticism. She has held prestigious professorships in the United States, won numerous literary awards on both sides of the Atlantic, and a number of journals have published special issues devoted to her work. In her groundbreaking career, Condé appears to have attained the sort of literary stature previously reserved, perhaps, for writers like Césaire and Glissant.

A number of themes run consistently through Condé's work, and it is specifically her treatment of issues of identity given the hybrid nature of creole culture that I wish to explore here. The regional vision that Condé has articulated in several novels clearly imbricates discursive form with issues of identity, using the past to interrogate the present and to choose future paths.

Condé's first novel, *En attendant le bonheur,*[1] remains one of the earliest works to interrogate, in both thematic and discursive terms, the complex questions underlying the ambiguities of exile, identity, and cultural displacement that mark the disparate material realities encountered by the francophone Caribbean female subject. Adversely reviewed and roundly criticized upon its first publication, the novel has been the subject of a fierce amount of controversy, not least because of the apparent primacy accorded to sexual liberation by the novel's activist protagonist, as well as the seemingly ambivalent position taken by this protagonist toward both her ancestral homeland of Africa and the culture of her own Caribbean. As Condé herself has stated in an interview with Ann Armstrong Scarboro: "The Guadeloupeans and the Martinicans did not like the picture of their society. The Africans objected to the image of Africa. The Marxists did not like the denunciation of the evils of so-called African Socialism. The militants objected to Veronica, the central character, as a negative heroine, and the feminists hated her because she looked for her liberation through men" (205). Yet it can be claimed that such a plethora of criticism pointed, paradoxically perhaps, precisely toward the pluralities and oppositions that create the creole conditions of possibility that are in fact the novel's hallmark.

The novel was recently reissued under the new title of *En attendant le bonheur. Hérémakhonon,* the novel's original title, and, paradoxically, the corollary of its African resonances, has now been relegated to the status of a subtitle. This revision of the binary cultural and subjective geopolitics framing the novel's plot and protagonist appears to give new primacy to the problematics of inscribing a pluralized, differential feminine identity within a context of *francophonie* and departmentalization. As Condé herself points out in the preface, her narrative strategy entails deliberate discursive choices: "It occurred to me to have the story narrated by a negative heroine. As the narrator, Véronica is narcisisstic, selfish, indecisive, sometimes even spineless, but she presents the drama. Her perspective is at first indifferent, but little by little she finds herself drawn to the center of the action" (12). Similarly, the novel's analysis of sociocultural alienation is also the product of the protagonist's *mal à l'aise:* "By reducing the Caribbean, and especially Guadeloupe, to its 'negrobourgeois' circle, Veronica is committing a gross injustice regarding its people" (13).

This deceptively linear plot, then—one in reality constantly subverted and undermined by the traces of an ongoing discursive displacement—traces the concerns of a young Guadeloupean woman, Véronica Mercier,[2] who, suffering the angst of physical and psychological displacement, leaves France to undertake a three-month sojourn in an unnamed African country in order to "find herself." When this period, marked by both personal and political turmoil, comes to a close, she leaves Africa to return to Paris. From the outset, the structure of the narrative is interesting on two levels. First, the very theme of the novel underlines the common Caribbean issue of alienation, the ambivalence of departmental subjects who must come to terms with the twin geocultural poles of France and the West Indies. While the subjective dilemma of the Antillean caught between competing allegiances has long been a central narrative theme in both the anglophone and francophone Caribbean, it is the cultural and political fact of departmentalization that gives Véronica's situation its particular specificities. On the most immediate level, we are confronted with a female protagonist who, caught up in the double disjuncture that history has imposed upon the women of the region, is split between the inability to recognize herself as a Caribbean subject and the desire for subjective valorization which she hopes the sojourn to, and in, the African (m)other will engender. She is re-presented as a subject who has internalized colonially driven stereotypes of race and class, just as her family has, on a larger scale, internalized metropolitan discourses of racial superiority and domination in their own bid for social advancement and recognition. Indeed, it is in the conjunction of her position as a Guadeloupean bourgeoise and her familial inscription as a *négresse rouge* that Véronica's inability to achieve social inscription and recognition may be said to find their patterns of origin.

These patterns of alienation and misrecognition are produced through subjection to the authoritarian linearities of a metropolitan discourse of colonialism, as this subject, torn between Africa and the Caribbean, between self and Other, race and place, seeks to surpass the binary paradoxes and ambiguities undergirding the identity she is attempting to construct. Thus Véronica inscribes an alternative paradigm to the pattern of legitimacy through lactification that Frantz Fanon elaborates for the French Caribbean female subject in *Black Skin, White Masks:* "For, in a word, the race must be whitened; every woman in Martinique knows this, says it, repeats it. Whiten the race, save the race" (47). In her turn, Véronica will run a gamut of ethnic possibilities, ultimately seeking perhaps a symbolic corollary of whiteness through the achievement of social recognition for her bourgeois interstitiality, a pattern of desire and alienation that colonialism and departmentalization have imposed on the region. Indeed, it is her indecisiveness as a postcolonial female subject that will determine both the pattern of her displacement in the domain of the Other and the means by which she ultimately reappropriates her identity from the field of its misprision.

Second, and perhaps even more important, the fragmentation and ambiguity that mark the subjectivity of this female Caribbean subject are inscribed in the very discourse of the narrative. For in fact this work is marked by the somewhat unusual phenomenon of a nonspeaking protagonist. That is, the protagonist restricts her utterances to a continuous internal monologue; her discourse never appears within the formal structures signifying direct speech.[3] We will address the parameters and implications of the choice of this construct shortly, but for the moment we should note that the narrator, who must be seen as a subject *different* from Véronica, never stops speaking, thereby emphasizing the simultaneity of presence that paradoxically links her own inscription to that of her counterpart. The internal monologue is a powerful narrative strategy, carrying implications for the structure of the subject as well as that of the discourse itself. This absence of direct dialogue that marks the text signifies an interpellative framework that is symptomatic of alienation, since its implied foreclosure of the *rapport à l'autre* tends to reinscribe the subject into the field of the imaginary. The resulting map of misrecognition defines Véronica through an ambivalent discursive site that incrementally retraces the triangular trajectory of her attempts at subjective inscription, from Guadeloupe to France, then from France to Africa and back. Importantly, however, whereas the *form* of her communication is similar to dialogized speech, its *function* is different, in that its aim is purely self-referential, and articulation with the other remains ambiguous and unresolved.

The disjunctive simultaneity that both joins and separates these two discursive moments is of crucial importance in tracing Véronica's ultimate coming to terms with the nature of her alienation. Her search for ancestors, her determination to re-place the past with the present, the Caribbean with Africa, address a complex sense of otherness and lack-in-being which is re-presented by her refusal of dialogue. Such a narrative strategy—one clearly grounded in ambiguity and doubleness—holds particular implications for the question of perspective; as Christopher Miller suggests in his reading of the novel, "On the level of explicitly represented actions, everyone speaks but her; meanwhile she alone *thinks*, and her internal reflections constitute the dominant point of view" (1996:176). Miller, on the one hand, rightly reads this conjunction of discourse with subjectivity as one empowering the narrator: "Her position is one of power, a means of critique that allows the narrator to present Africa in a certain light" (1996:178). On the other hand, as I shall argue, while indeed "the reader can often infer what she has said" (1996:176), Véronica does not in fact speak, thus casting light upon the displaced pluralities of her Caribbeanness. Miller's incomplete accounting of the novelistic discourse tends to elide the deliberate dualities undergirding both French Caribbean society as well as the complex inscription of narrative voice(s). The indeterminacy and lack figuring these voices mime the complex indeterminacy of the subject's interpellative position, torn as she is between the conflicting subjective positions signified by the interstitiality of the internal monologue and its implied fragmentation of cultures; ultimately, when compelled to confront her alterity and to choose a discursive position, Véronica, in a critical (non)move, opts for continuing this internalized, dual-voiced form of narrative re-presentation.

In *En attendant le bonheur*, then, the phenomenon of internal monologue is clearly linked to creating definitions of cultural identity. In *Transparent Minds*, Dorrit Cohn examines the contradictory structure of similar first-person narratives and demonstrates that the form to which that adopted by Condé may be most closely assimilated, essentially an audience-directed discourse combined with a silent self-address, points to a protagonist who "writes as if [s]he were thinking, but thinks as if [s]he were addressing others . . . a form filled with significance" (177). In the context of Condé's narrative, the presence of internal monologue and the recurring inscription of its effect of communicative foreclosure upon the protagonist is made to signify the articulation of a pervasive cultural ambivalence, her fragmented but simultaneous inscription between France, the Caribbean, and Africa. In other words, re-presenting the protagonist through internal monologue amounts to a conscious reflection of her sense of displacement and duality, as her cultural fragmentation is figured by the ambiguity of her discursive position. Given what Cohn calls "the other-directedness of [t]his thought" (177), the resulting inability to discern the origin or addressee, or even the temporality of the protagonist's double discourse, inscribes this subject into a sort of discursive neutrality in which a subjective strategy that both denies and desires recognition of/by the Other is made an integral element of the novel's discursive structure. This overdetermination of subject and text by regional anxieties of cultural influence becomes a hallmark of the narrative discourse of *En attendant le bonheur*.

This initial refusal of cultural hybridity, reflective of the protagonist's need to find *African* roots and ancestors to augment the absence of a sense of antillanité, or Caribbeanness, produces a conflict of subjectivity and culture that is simultaneously mediated and measured by the multicultural origins underlying the configuration of Caribbean social and cultural forms. The ambiguity of the subjective discourse in *En attendant le bonheur*, the refusal of dialogic self-affirmation combined with the "other-directedness" of the discourse, together represent the paradox of the *absence* of a firm interpellative position, the critical instability of a protagonist caught *between* cultures, *between* discourses, as she searches for a means of mediating her double displacement from both her French and West Indian axes through the complexities of this subjective division that drives her into a referential and symbolic union with Africa. In its attempt to represent her doubly colonized position as a Caribbean woman, exacerbated by the departmental doubleness that makes her a light-skinned, rootless bourgeoise from a DOM in which the fragmented population's sociopolitical allegiance—though as a group they are made up mainly of the descendants of African blacks—is astygmatically split between metropole and island home, this interweaving of identity, class, gender, and culture effectively problematizes the primary issues of pluralism and hybridity in the search for identity that impacts and overdetermines the French Caribbean region. Condé has succeeded in re-presenting the myriad ambiguities of Caribbean subjectivity through a complex signifying chain, embodying through the subordinated female subject the cultural conflict that has marked the region's history and the fragmenting effects of a colonial discourse of displacement that persists in a variety of guises.

Condé's deliberate narrative strategy, then, suggests a pattern defined by the authors of *The Empire Writes Back* as "a radical subversion of the meanings of the master's tongue" (146); her protagonist's inability to communicate with her interlocutors re-presents her feminine Caribbean subjectivity through a dislocated discursive system whose inherent uncertainties and ambivalences subvert preconceived notions of patriarchy and position. The representative possibilities opened up by this constant renegotiation of the indices and registers of identity suggest what Peggy Kamuf calls the textual "signature"; what she defines, in her book *Signature Pieces*, as "a device repeatedly associated with a subject" (3). By figuring this protagonist through the interstices of internal monologue, the very form of the text becomes the emblem of her emerging identity structure, rewriting the hybridities of her cultural alienation and division by unceasingly interrogating the implications of their root context of neo-colonialism.

Véronica's nine-month stay in Africa—she describes her *séjour* as lasting "nine months . . . a pregnancy" (20/42)—takes her through several stages of subjective awareness. From her desire for recognition by the Other, through her recognition of the futility of this synthesis and its eventual repudiation, she grows increasingly aware of the untenability of her own position, of the multiple conflicts between her and the society through which she is seeking self-affirmation. As Françoise Lionnet points out in her chapter on this novel in her book *Autobiographical Voices*, "The narrator's failure to act upon the insights she gleans points to a passivity and a lack of will symptomatic of her colonial background and ambiguous situation" (175). In the end, as we shall see, it is this very ambiguity that figures not only her stay and her discourse but, ultimately, her departure, the final act in this process of self-realization.

This ambiguity is recuperated in the very oppositions that are inscribed in the novel's title. For not only is this two-part structure—*En attendant le bonheur (Hérémakhonon)*—made up of a juxtaposition of French and West African languages that underlines the paradoxical relationship between the subject and the object of her desire, but the present participle form of the verb in the French title tends to stress the interminable, impossible aspect of the quest itself, buttressed by the corollary of parentheses that symbolically marginalize the field of the African Other. Such a reading suggests not only the problematics of cultural duality, but also the protagonist's ineluctable ambivalence, signified by the implicit hierarchies of these dual languages.

The novel opens with the protagonist's problematization of her own decentered subjectivity. Through the device of the flashback, she succeeds in merging the ambiguity of her own subject position into the temporal and communicative uncertainty engendered by the internal monologue. Her ambiguity relative to issues of history, culture, and her own cultural context emerges as any fixity of locution is progressively eroded and made inconstant:

> Honestly! You'd think I'm going because it is the in thing to do. Africa is very much the thing to do lately. . . . Why am I doing this?
> "Purpose of visit?"
> The police officer really hits the nail on the head. . . . Surely from that part of the coast that produced my father's ancestors. . . . Purpose of visit? No, I'm not a trader. Not a missionary. Not even a tourist. Well, perhaps a tourist, but one of a new breed, searching out herself, not landscapes. (3/ 19–20)

Here, the protagonist succeeds in elaborating the main preoccupations of her narrative: the special, personal nature of her voyage to Africa, the preponderance of issues of cultural difference, her problematic relationship to her parents and to her father in particular, and the prevalence of her own narcissism. Further, with the significant absence of diacritical marks of communication made clear from the outset, it is inarguable that this deliberately ambiguous discourse is meant to reflect the iconoclastic ambiguity of the protagonist herself. Indeed, this symbolic cultural alienation is simultaneously recuperated on the subjective level; as Susan Andrade points out: "Alienated both politically and sexually, she is able to perceive herself only through someone else" (1993:222). As the narrator's point of view alternates between Africa and the Caribbean, past and present, the self and the increasingly multivalent sites of the Other, the instability of the narrative perspective constantly illuminates both her own ambivalence and the recuperation of this indeterminacy by the narrative voice.

Indeed, the protagonist continually states and restates her lack of rootedness, her sense of division and abandonment, and her need for a valid group of ancestors who will generate a sense of self and of cultural particularity that will give meaning and direction to her wandering. For example, early attempts at self-definition take place through the displaced signifier of the African society to which she aspires, defining the Caribbean self through the African Other while addressing its function as mediator of her hybrid subjectivity: "Don't they know I don't care a damn for their town? I am not an ordinary tourist. I am looking. . . . What am I looking for in this land of Africa?" (9/27). Interestingly, it is through this figure of negative self-definition that the protagonist tacitly avows Africa's mediatory role in defining her hybridity. It is this alterity that, as Andrade suggests, grounds analeptically and proleptically her sense of exclusion from both the Caribbean and the African spheres: "This obsession with available and lost history, particularly with the void into which her Caribbean ancestors have disappeared, dominates Véronica's thinking and prevents her from understanding the specific condition of the African nation" (217–8). Exterior to the society while yet appearing to be part of it, drawing from Africa without giving anything in return, her relationship with *la mère Afrique* which will ultimately undergo a radical change, permitting her to come to terms with that which she had so long sought to escape.

Shortly after her initial encounter with the minister of the interior, Ibrahima Sory—whose responsibility for internal state security will assume increasing importance—with whom she will have a prolonged and pivotal affair during her stay in Africa, the protagonist reinscribes the intersection of her lack of local involvement both with his political recuperation of patriarchal authority and with his additional role as mediator of her search for identity:

> He would never understand that the political person of Ibrahima Sory leaves me cold. And his role in the nation. And his family's. I didn't come to get mixed up in their quarrels and take sides. *I came to find a cure. Ibrahima Sory, I know, will be the marabout's gree-gree.* We'll exchange our childhoods and our past. *Through him I shall at last be proud to be what I am.* . . . I have already resumed hope. (42/71–72; emphasis mine)

These insistent denials of her involvement in the culture and politics of the African milieu in which she finds herself become ever more frequent and vehement, implying, as Freud has suggested in his essay "Negation," that the true reality of the situation lies elsewhere, in the absolute necessity to the subject of that which is being denied: "The subject matter of a repressed image or thought can make its way into consciousness on condition that it is *denied*. Negation is a way of taking account of what is repressed" (1963:213–14). As Sory's double role encounters the patriarchal authority implied by his recuperation of the father's role, he symbolically fetishizes her repressed object of desire, and she already sees her future through him. Here, the simultaneity of Véronica's denial and acknowledgment of her desire inexorably overdetermines the increasing ambiguity of her position.

By repeatedly characterizating herself as a tourist, a foreigner, Véronica emphasizes that sense of division separating her, psychologically and culturally, from the suggestive parallels of Africa's immensity; she seeks the resolution of her apparently ambiguous cultural hybridity through the mediation of Ibrahima Sory as the personification of an already consolidated African Other. The outsider's desire for a historical sense of unity achieved through Sory recurs repeatedly throughout the text: "I got it into my head that this man would reconcile my two selves. . . . He must help me find a cure. . . . I came to seek a land inhabited by Blacks, not Negroes, even spiritual ones. In other words, I'm looking for what remains of the past. I'm not interested in the present" (50, 51, 56/83, 84, 89). What this protagonist seeks through the conflation of past and present, self and Other, Africa and the Caribbean, is a new subjective structure that combines the elements from her succession of binary existences to produce a new hybridity. In an interview with Françoise Pfaff, Maryse Condé herself emphasized her deliberate definition of this Caribbean protagonist through signifiers of cultural division and ambiguity: "I had decided to draw a negative character, my opposite: a person lacking will, energy and vitality, a character who does not know exactly who she/he is. This was a self-portrait and yet not a portrait. Some readers were shocked because they wanted to believe . . . the myth that we, the people of the black world, were all one" (1993:88). The diversity and cross-culturality of the Caribbean region, and the implicit historical, social, and cultural differences between Africa and the Caribbean, mark the boundaries of Véronica's trajectory of alienation. Resolving these dualities is of critical importance to the discursive resolution of her dilemma; Françoise Lionnet calls her "the stereotypical *métis*, the one who embodies the maledictions of miscegenation: the boundary crosser. She is the third term, the excluded middle and the voice of the Antillean double bind" (1989:176). What, then, in this complex cultural dialectic of continually intersecting doubleness, is the underlying nature of the alterity through which she ultimately constructs her identity?

Ibrahima Sory, or Nègres avec aïeux

Sory, the minister of the interior, the "nigger with ancestors," object of Véronica's dual desire, functions as a sort of mediator and catalyst in the delineation of Véronica's identity construction. The trajectory of their relationship more or less parallels that of her growing recognition of the structures that overdetermine her existence. He is a paradoxical personification of the figure of Africa, a signifier that mediates both the subject's twin traces of exile and her desire for unification through the African Other. Nor is it insignificant that Africa's traditionally maternal role is marked in the novel through a masculine figure. Indeed, Sory may be said to embody a subversion of Africa's traditional discursive representation as "la mère Afrique," a symbolic structure that reductively assimilates Africa to stereotypes of nurturing domesticity. The hierarchical assumptions grounding this construct are now foreclosed as a result of the shift in gender ascription occurring within the sign. Further, through the power and authority that devolve from his political standing, Sory also re-presents the dominant paternalism that has figured Véronica's development thus far and from whose delimiting grasp she must free herself. In other words, Sory inscribes a critical doubling of the place of the Other, in that he is an other whose desire cannot be appropriated; the double sign of his political and personal masculinity distorts and subverts the supposed plenitude and unity of Africa's alterity, which is in turn opposed to the African signifier's traditionally nurturing articulation and generates a chiasmus that refigures the intrinsic ambiguity of Véronica's desire.

In addition, by elaborating the authoritarian discourses from which Véronica remains alienated but yet demands recognition, he mediates the paradoxical polyvalence and fragmentation of her desire. Any desire ascribed to him, then, is in fact a displacement of the protagonist's desire, especially since the narrative discourse always, and only, re-presents Sory from Véronica's point of view. He is thus an irreducibly plural signifier, embodying vastly complex cultural and psychological structures; Françoise Lionnet describes him as a figure in whom "are bound up complex unconscious processes in which the split between Real and Symbolic is confirmed and binary Manichean positions prevail" (1989:172). This capacity of Sory's to oscillate between symbolic and subjective re-presentations of "Africa" tends to reinforce his own role as a mediator of desire and cultural alienation. In fact, it is virtually impossible not to note the primary English homonym for his name (Sorry) that comes to mind, which is certainly no coincidence, serving to underline the contradictory authoritarianism through which he is inscribed, one that discursively reproduces his position as a dis-placed signifier of colonial assimilation. As he mediates Véronica's desire for cultural integration, these polysemic patterns grounding Sory as subject provide a contrapuntal foil for Véronica's desire, represented through the carnal exhibitions—denoting a parallel desire to appropriate and re-cite the legitimacy of Sory's ethnic past as well—that link metonymically Véronica to Sory himself. It is by recognizing the paradoxes, pluralisms, and limitations of this desire that Véronica finally comes to terms with her latent, interpellative hybridity.

Upon closer examination, the trajectory of the Mercier-Sory relationship is revealed as one inscribed not only in self-awareness but in constant self-criticism and self-questioning. While Véronica appears from the outset to be aware of the limitations and paradoxes of the sexual relationship, this ongoing process of self-interrogation signals her growing recognition of her own interstitiality, functioning in tandem with the foreclosure of dialogic communication to reframe the subject's cultural ambivalence in both narrative and discursive terms. For example, as their first physical encounter is on the point of consummation, Véronica demonstrates her awareness of the extent to which this act will problematize her position: "I'm going to bed with a perfect stranger. . . . This man who is about to take me does not know that I am a virgin of sorts. . . . I now realize why he fascinates me. He hasn't been branded. . . . Tell me that you understand me, my nigger with ancestors. . . . Am I talking? Or do I think I'm talking?" (36, 37, 38/64, 65, 66).

This passage is an excellent example of the difference between monologic and dialogic communication. The obscurity of the ostensibly other-directed internal monologue is ultimately offset by the protagonist's interrogation of the status of her own discourse, a conscious shift in register denoting a problematization that reinscribes the deliberate marginalization of her position. But, given that this interrogation takes place in the same mode as the sequence it questions, the inherent instability of the discursive position is even further inscribed as a result of this interrogation. Such paradoxes clearly delineate the discursive and subjective interstices between desire, alterity, culture, and identity. The physical side of the relationship is inscribed as a sort of allegory, her virginal state representative of her lack of a cultural context as well as the embryonic condition of her relationship with Africa as it is allegorized through

Sory himself. Indeed, the admission that he is desirable "because he hasn't been branded" amounts to a recognition of her own "adulterated" cultural lineage. Yet, at the same time, the tentative and ambiguous aspect of this inscription is reflected in her problematization of the status of her own discourse, an act which reflects an awareness of the unsettled nature of both the discursive and the interpellative fields. For in wondering whether she is indeed speaking, a question posed through the inherently and deliberately circumscribed medium of her internal monologue, she redoubles and reinscribes the troubled status of the narrative discourse, displacing even further her own ambiguous interpellative position as it is represented through the conscious displacement implied by this discursive strategy.

This ambiguous otherness that situates the protagonist ultimately inscribes a textual poetics of place, the doubled ambiguity of the alienation it articulates re-presenting the ethnic and cultural creoleness whose polysemy is the mark of her discursive positionality. As the narrative moves its subject in a trajectory from absence to acceptance, Véronica's recognition that Sory's double, disjunctive inscription both as desired cultural symbol and as arbiter of physical desire has effectively masked the latent potential of her own Caribbeanness finally drives her toward a transformative resolution of her cultural pluralism.

While Veronica's awareness of the need for alterity is consciously undertaken and pursued, her simultaneous awareness of its limitations demonstrates a deeper knowledge of the true nature of her estrangement. Alienated from both the Caribbean and Africa, does she need, at bottom, "a certain idea" of them both to effect this reconciliation with herself and her past? "If he doesn't love me, if he doesn't let me love him, how can I return to my womb? How can I be born again? Free of shame and hidden contempt? . . . I'm convinced he can save me. Reconcile me with myself, in other words my race. . . . Do I love this man or *a certain idea* I have to have of Africa? What is this idea? That of an Africa, of a black world that Europe did not reduce to a caricature of itself" (66, 67, 77/100, 103–4, 119; emphasis mine). Here, she appears to recognize the reality that Sory is in fact mediating her ability to come to terms with herself as other, signified by this need for uterine return. Clearly, then, the reconciliation that she seeks is really in order to engender a new discursive space from the categories of past and present, allegory and reality, desire and ambiguity. This desire to be "born again" draws on an attempt to merge with her own projection of black linearity and legitimacy in order to achieve a new inscription within the field of the Other, to break new subjective ground by possessing the unadulterated, uncaricatured signifier of "Africa," an act which will determine the future by merging her with its idealized past.

Véronica's dilemma is thus a complex and multifaceted one, signified by an almost impossible mediation of a plethora of opposing signs within a single social whole. As Ajoké Mimiko-Bestman points out: "Véronica's dilemma is one of reconciling the dialectic of past and present . . . but don't the two temporal axes find their synthesis in Ibrahima Sory . . . ? She drifts between the two opposing groups in this African village, between Hérémakhonon and Saliou's household" (1987:166). The tensions between Sory and Saliou, her neighbor, simultaneously teacher-turned-activist, Sory's brother-in-law, and leader of the opposition forces, tend to sum up the similarities and contradictions of the alterity that Véronica must negotiate; these figures will parallel her growing recognition of the mythical oneness of the signifier of "Africa." The twin axes traced by these characters and their final, tragic encounter will assume a growing importance in her mediation of the dialectical relationship between Africa and the Caribbean which she both desires and denies.

Yet, for Véronica, love swiftly becomes equated to politics in the African context: "I'm wandering from one continent to another, looking for my identity, *dixit* Ibrahima Sory. . . . If I understand correctly, making love in this country comes down to making a political choice" (64, 69/100, 106). She becomes increasingly preoccupied with parallels between desire and identity, with whether she loves Sory, whether he loves her, and, most important, she begins to question the efficacy of the metonymic relationship she has established between him and the country he represents: "I begin to understand where I went wrong. If I want to come to terms with myself, i.e. with them, i.e. with us, I ought to return home" (71/110). The continued deliberate restriction of her discourse to an internal monologue only serves to problematize even further the role of the discursive process in the resolution of her relationships. Yet, at the same time, this recognition of the métissage signified by her cultural origin defines and particularizes the discourse of diversity that she embodies, for, as Françoise Lionnet suggests, "if . . . identity is a strategy, then *métissage* is the fertile ground of our heterogeneous and heteronomous identities as postcolonial subjects" (1989:8). It is by recognizing and valorizing this cultural and subjective status as a métis that Véronica will ultimately resolve the divided desires underlying her own ambiguity.

If love is assimilated to politics, then the pursuit of desire implies the taking of sides; her neutrality cannot be maintained forever. The mythification through which she had figured the Other dissolves; her primary narcissism enters a secondary stage, gives way to a dialectical exchange. The womb of the mother is that space to which one cannot return once having departed it; the goal at recognition must be to reframe that which she herself represents. Véronica must accept the separation from the Other in order to assume and valorize her own identity, to engender a discursive space for her diversity and ambiguity. Separation from the (m)other implies separation from its signifier, Ibrahima Sory, as well.

By deciding to abandon the Other, Véronica reverses the cultural codes through which she has operated; the burgeoning political crisis which Sory, as Minister of the Interior, must police, forces her finally to choose between Saliou and Sory, a symbolic recognition of the "Africas" they stand for. Suddenly Sory appears in a different light, one significantly illuminated by Saliou: "Well, Saliou was right. Ibrahima Sory is a feudal reactionary. . . . A cop. I realize I'm dealing with a cop. I'm looking for salvation in the arms of a cop. . . . Did I come to Africa for that? Will I find my identity in this role? To hell! Let's forget about my identity. Isn't all this searching in vain? *In vain*" (88, 91/ 130, 134; emphasis in the original). The significance of this new perception of Sory as politician rather than as cultural object of desire occurs in terms directly mediated by Saliou, his subjective counterpart within a framework of nationalism, and cannot be overstated. Her recognition that his inviolability is politically grounded is critical to her own understanding of the complexes inherent in her articulation of identity as a female Caribbean postcolonial subject. For in perceiving Sory as a cop, the protagonist is now finally aware not only of his impossible alterity but of her own as well. She also realizes that his role with regard to her has been to interdict her identity; inhibiting rather than mediating by virtue of the paternalism and authority bound up in his role as minister, he has in fact impeded her accomplishment of recognition while the elaboration of her own displaced desire must now confront its ineluctable foreclosure, the imposition of circumscription, repression, and restraint rather than reinscription and release. Indeed, she is also now able to infer that the social whole for which he is the signifier has carried out a similar function with regard to her interpellation; the myth of *la mère Afrique* was indeed just that, an empty sign whose reductive codification by the Other had inevitably determined her inability to withdraw from the misrecognition inherent in its discursive space. And so she is now in fact able to categorize her own activity as a *role*—a falsehood, a hollow construct antithetical to identity, a role doomed to dissolution and which must now be abandoned. For this postcolonial female subject, victim of a double subjugation that erases the very possibility of a place of enunciation, the discursive figure of the internal monologue now becomes a means of generating an alternative subject position from a framework of marginality and exile.

Meanwhile, the ongoing political tension marches toward its moment of crisis. Oddly, the continuing strikes, demonstrations, and arrests seem to have no perceptible effect on the trajectory of her relationship with Sory; she continues to either repress or ignore the likelihood of the latter's instigation of or involvement in political oppression. But when she discovers that Sory has apparently had her followed one evening, and that the safety of his own brother-in-law, Saliou, the opposition leader, is being openly threatened by forces operating under his aegis, things begin to take a different turn:

> This man is obnoxious. I am now fully aware of it. I'm the one who's fleeing the alienated of my native isle and I come to work on other alienations. That's it, isn't it? Yes it is. . . . I didn't find my ancestors. Three and a half centuries have separated me from them. They didn't recognize me any more than I recognized them. All I found was a man with ancestors who's guarding them jealously for himself and wouldn't dream of sharing them with me. . . . I'm an ambiguous animal, half fish, half bird, a new style of bat. A false sister. A false foreigner. It would have to start all over again from the beginning. I got off to a bad start in this country. I should have become interested. . . . Try to understand. (123, 133, 136–37/177, 189, 193–94)

Véronica's increasing recognition of the tenuousness of her African inscription forms the core of this extract, and, as we shall see, it effectively forms a turning point in the direction of her trajectory.

As her monologue becomes mediatory of subjective regeneration, her characterization of Sory as "obnoxious" marks the beginning of the end. She has finally achieved the realization that what separates them is difference rather than similarity, and that this difference must in fact become the (hall)mark of her own subjectivity in order for its full potential to be exploited. Interestingly enough, she characterizes herself as a traveler from Europe, rather than the

Caribbean, inscribing herself geopoliticlly as departmental subject and situating herself squarely at the middle point of the historic relationship of triangular exchange linking Africa, Europe, and the Caribbean, and re-marking the intermediate and overdetermined nature of her social and cultural space. Her position is now one of an exiled female departmental subject, a triple personification of the decentering effects of colonialism, class, and gender. This compounding of her situation is what is in fact engendered by "other identities . . . other alienations," as the multiplication and regeneration of her ambiguous perspective inexorably reframes not only the form of her discourse but her cultural location as well; she is now, literally, between worlds.

Sory's insistent efforts to "guard them jealously for himself" amount to repudiation of the subject by the (m)Other, an attempt to inscribe the separation of cultures and of discourses which should force the subject into acceptance of the laws of the symbolic Order. Véronica is able to reject Sory and Africa, but he has no understanding of her doubleness, thus limiting his utility as a cultural catalyst. For the paradox that ironically undergirds their relationship inscribes Africa as cultural (m)Other to the Caribbean subject, while, at the same time, colonial Europe inscribes itself as discursive (m)Other to the subjects of both Africa and the Caribbean. The repudiation carried out against the postcolonial African subject by the displaced departmental Caribbean Other seeking cultural and political contextualization is simultaneously recuperated and reproduced by this unwelcoming signifier for Africa against the European (m)Otherness that Véronica simultaneously embodies. She must now recognize this chiasmus and reappropriate the spaces of ambiguity and doubleness that will allow her to refine and embellish the creole culture by which she is ultimately framed.

It is within this frame of reference that Veronica can finally acknowledge the ambiguity of her position. This action does mark an important turning point: while Françoise Lionnet suggests that "Veronica reaches a new form of knowledge, if only a negative one, still based in a Nietzschean form of anarchic and negative *ressentiment*" (1989:175), I would like to contend that the negativity of her binary outlook has been successfully negotiated and replaced, allowing her to take the supplementary steps that will lead to her departure. For it is in these terms that her final deployment of a contestatory doubleness will take place.

In fact, this gesture toward accession and acceptance takes place simultaneously on two discursive levels. On the one hand, in defining herself in the previous extended excerpt as "an ambiguous animal . . . a false sister," Véronica uses this ambiguity in order to come to terms with the insufficiency provided by the African Other and her own lack of commitment. This sisterly role is also insufficient for the subject because of the paradox inherent within the relationship; whereas Véronica would appear physically and culturally able to exploit her ethnohistorical resemblance to her African counterparts, this relationship is simultaneously limited in that the Other has not acceded to her appropriation of alterity; her cultural sisterhood remains latent, unfulfilled, and false to the extent that the insubstantiality of the ground on which this role was based has now been exposed.

Similarly, the term "a false foreigner" assumes a parallel ambiguous stance, although the apparent tautology it contains also marks the adverse of its sisterly counterpart. She is a "false foreigner" through the paradoxes and contradictions of the Guadeloupean culture from which she derives, producing her alienation from this space through her departmental definition by both Africa and the metropole, a cultural sign of the colonizing Other. The paradoxes and pluralities within the terms "false sister" and "false foreigner" thus tend to cancel each other out, leaving the absence engendered by their mutual opposition as the ultimate marker of her subjective interpellation; the *place* of her belonging is still ultimately an open question. As an ambiguous subject, embodying a paradoxical, polysemic rootlessness, functioning through a specific discursive space that remains outside the linear strictures of metropolitan dialogism, Véronica Mercier can now synthesize her divided desire, working through her overdetermination to draw on, but yet remain separate from, the specific fields of African and French subjectivity to create a new, third sphere of identity beyond the boundaries of binary contestation. In mapping these contours, however, she must also come to terms with the subjective corollaries that are also specters of her intrinsic displacement, confronting her anxieties in the paternal authority of the Mandingo marabout, the mulatto charms of De Roseval, the metropolitan integrationism signaled by her white Parisian lover, the aura of authenticity symbolized by her "nigger with ancestors," Sory, and, finally, the critical threat posed by the looming confrontation with her historical counterpart, Marilisse.

Véronica: Desire and Creole Culture

The role of desire in generating the ambiguity of her identity is of paramount importance in explaining Véronica's relationship with the African Other.[4] She is painfully self-aware, and her words reflect an awareness at least of her subjective dilemma, although she may not yet have clearly grasped the means toward its resolution: "Saliou is an African, a man from Africa, but not my Africa and consequently does not crystallize the love I am seeking for myself through her" (146/207). It is precisely both the depth and definition of this absent self-love which she seeks *through Africa* that, once established, will point Véronica to the road back to self-affirmation. But the origins of her lack of rootedness are much farther back in her past, and it is this aspect of her identity structure that we must now explore further.

Véronica's depiction as a displaced mulatto bourgeois Guadeloupean woman, born into a social and familial structure desiring to erase its social inadequacy through assimilation to the white, upper-class stratum of island society, is central to the resolution of the complexities of her own divided desire. Within this doubly alienated world of the black bourgeoisie, then, Véronica Mercier is the embodiment of the basic condition defining Caribbean society; as the personification of a post/colonial hybridity, an icon of the region's ethnic and cultural overdetermination by the twin axes framing its ongoing encounter with colonialism, she is, in Homi Bhabha's classic phrase, literally less than one but double, shunned by both ends of the spectrum, unable to accomplish complete assimilation into or acceptance by either of the groups she simultaneously embodies. The resulting inscription in both the metropole and its Other is at the heart of her inability to locate or define a place for her dual subjectivity. In addition, her family's insistence on bourgeois class divisions tends to exacerbate her difference, imposing patterns of social and cultural exclusion that, paradoxically, seem to define her place in this neocolonial society. The function of these figures in the economy of the narrative are of key importance in articluating Véronica's alterity.

Véronica's predicament is in fact a cultural conundrum whose resolution demands the recognition of the critical intersection of opposing patterns of identity and difference. And indeed, the extent to which Véronica's dilemma renders her paradigmatic of the society at large compels us to consider the implicit link between individual and collective identity in the Caribbean women she re-presents. These issues are cogently summed up by Leah Hewitt in *Autobiographical Tightropes:* "But identity is that curious fiction that requires absolute difference . . . while situating its subject in a preexisting signifying chain of culture. . . . In Veronica's case, individual identity is intimately connected to the problematic of collective identity of the Antilles" (175). These issues of race, class, and gender converge to create a doubled subjective counterpart in the text (another who is me), a fictionalized, tropological representation of the subject to whom the latter refers constantly as Marilisse. This figure is a paradoxical one, the circumstances of her historicity embodying in turn the conflicting and contradictory desires of the subject to both subvert and submit to the cultural anxiety produced by colonial patterns of patriarchal authority. In her desire to both recognize and to disavow the ethnohistorical paradigm established by Marilisse, Véronica must face the cultural paradoxes that have overdetermined her subjectivity and that in fact endow her with a cultural hybridity whose potential she must now learn to exploit.

The unbidden series of associations that opens the novel is a point of convergence for her anxieties of authority, emphasizing the extent to which her lack of place is grounded in the surviving traces of her familial order: "The police officer really hits the nail on the head. . . . Surely from that part of the coast that produced my father's ancestors" (3/19–20). This metonymic slippage from one authority figure to another, from one iconic re-presentation of alienated cultural patriarchy to another mediated by the name of the father, encapsulates the axes of Véronica's alienation. But soon, by juxtaposing the two neighboring French Caribbean departments of Guadeloupe and Martinique, their women, who are in a sense a metonymic extension of herself, are soon also made the objects of a comparison in which the issue of métissage renders them symbolic of her own division and self-interrogation: "The French, and consequently everyone else, have always ignored Guadeloupe in favor of Martinique. The Martinique women are said to have a higher proportion of mixed blood. Hence, they are considered more beautiful. A whole lot of good that did them. Why am I here?" (4/20). By reversing the code and opening up the sign, Véronica's interrogation points inalterably to the primary role of métissage in perpetuating stereotypical myths of Caribbean culture. But it is the scope and substance of métissage that is really at issue here; she must work through the implications of this doubleness to be able to recognize the extent to which the complexity of her relationship with Africa is ineluctably bound up in and recuperated by the very métissage that grounds her familial relations. The importance of the tensions and dualities intrinsic to this background grows increasingly apparent as the text progresses.

It is the amorphous link between this complex, contradictory familial structure of her native Guadeloupe—torn between the middle-class conformities imposed by the metropole and the apparent ethnic linearities of its African axis—and the singular, legitimizing lineage that she has sought through them both, that marks the extent of Véronica's misreading of the unitary subjectivity that she seeks. Her attempt to appropriate Sory's ancestors for herself, thereby accomplishing a retroactive inscription in a racially recognizable civilization with which, however, she can establish only distant ties, is in fact an act of overt cultural possession whose innate illegitimacy is grounded in a desire not simply to know but to *become* the Other. The civilization of Africa is desirable both because her family rejects its symbolism and because it provides an appearance of continuity and ethnic legitimacy; given this patina of permanence, and with Sory as its iconic representation, he becomes desirable because of his enigmatic, unadulterated, "unbranded" difference. In seeking to own this history and to recast it in the image of her own desire, Véronica's cross-cultural encounter will ultimately reveal to her that the binary inscription of difference remains essentially a difference from, and is thus an inadequate means of subjective survival; only an abnegation of this economy of possession will prevent this subject from repeating the proprietary patterns of the colonial encounter. Ultimately, the double problematic of difference and the essential otherworldliness of both Africa and Europe must be resolved through the fugitive complicities of her Caribbean heritage.

The incessant discursive slippage that is integral to Condé's narrative strategy since it figures the ambivalence of Véronica's cultural inscription thus incorporates not only the primary communicative ambiguity that is perhaps the principal textual signature of both narrative and subject, but also a temporal elasticity that allows the narrator to accomplish necessary shifts of period, register, and perspective. The sudden proleptic or analeptic changes that this discursive elasticity permits result in moments of flashback or reverie that are critical to Véronica's eventual recognition of the ultimate futility of this search for ancestors. By using her imbrication with the African Other ultimately to confront the alienations of her Caribbean past, she is eventually able to perceive the formative subjective role of her bourgeois family origins, and to rec-

ognize, in the social complexities of a multiracial and multicultural francophone Caribbean background, the ghosts that must be laid to rest so that she
can finally move beyond them.

The exposure by degrees of the heterogeneities of her family history is thus
a necessary step in the fleshing out of a composite character who would ultimately have to "find herself" among the complexities represented by the counterpart. She will come to the key trope of patriarchal authority indirectly, acknowledging through the peregrinations of her Aunt Paula—from a distant,
almost unacknowledged branch of the family—the artificiality of the family's
all-important veneer of bourgeois respectability: "To make a long story short, a
down-and-out white, determined to finish his days under the Caribbean sun,
married her on his death bed. The priest had threatened to withdraw the last
rites. She was left the lovely French name of Delahaye and enough to build a
hotel-restaurant on the public square at Sainte Anne. They never mentioned
her name. Black-out" (10/28). The arbitrary combinations of chance summed
up in this little vignette encapsulate the inescapability of métissage in the complex patterns of Caribbean history. In the case of Véronica's family, their acqui-
sition of property, and of a respectable French name to go with it, submerges
the important corollary of means while inadvertently acting as a paradigm of
the random creation of creole cultures. The fact that no family member ever
spoke of the inadvertent, almost illegitimate nature of these origins, of the
intersection of black with *béké* that locates her family's real roots—given the
duality of the pun on ethnicity and erasure inherent in the term "black-out"—
confirmed the primacy of appearance over reality, driving an alienation whose
simultaneous recognition and denial of its metropolitan axis produced ethnic
and cultural patterns whose origins were as indefinable as their effects were
endemic.

At bottom, then, the duality of Véronica's position is figured by the paradoxes of her past. She has inculcated the stereotypes, inadequacies, and class
prejudices of bourgeois social climbers who, she claims, prayed thusly: "We
give thanks to our Lord for having made us different from the other niggers.
And equal to the white man, our former master" (45/86). Indeed, it is as a result
of this sense of class inadequacy conjoined with métissage that she seems paradoxically to claim the right to be a part of the Africa that she seeks to appropriate, in a bid to achieve legitimacy: "I could have vibrated to the word of the
griot. . . . Instead, I have in my family tree a white man's sperm gone astray in
some black woman's womb. It didn't seem to disgust the sailors on the slave

ships"(17/38). This alternation between the elusive affinities and differential temporalities of genealogy suggests a subject separated from Africa, an ethnic heritage inalterably marked by the notorious rape of African women during the Middle Passage; this brutal inscription into Caribbean social reality emphasizes the ineluctable imposition of sociocultural origins in which the notion of a unitary milieu is revealed as a chimera. Caught in the ambiguous interstices of a polysemic indeterminacy, Véronica continually crosses boundaries of time and space to confront a collection of counterparts and ancestors whose subjection to an overdetermined history may yet shape the ambitions of her future.

Thus the critical confrontation with the figure of Marilisse, representing the complex tensions, contradictions, and dilemmas attending the black woman's survival in a Caribbean context, will engender myriad subjective and textual implications for Véronica's constant temporal oscillations between landscapes and cultures in her quest for liberation. In a discursive conflation whose resonances are both analeptic and proleptic, the historical derivation of this haunting figure is inscribed through the dehumanizing scene of a slave auction, narrated in the first person: "They were all sitting around, hissing. 'Marilisse! You're making yourself Marilisse!' Due to his forthcoming departure, Sieur Cazeau, inhabitant of Cul-de-Sac, has put up for sale a young negro girl of pleasant features named Marilisse. Good laundress. Can be taken on a trial basis. . . . I was not doing a Marilisse. I was in love. That's all. A woman in love, isn't she always a Marilisse? Let the Feminists stone me if they want to!" (17–18/39). In its primary incarnation as counterpart, the figure of Marilisse at once fulfills a plurality of roles, among which the primary function, as we see here, is to serve as a cultural sounding board for a protagonist intrinsically unsure of her goals and motives. Through the tensions of temporal disjuncture, Véronica is dis-placed backward through time to *take the place* of a Marilisse who then voices her dis-location in the third person, in order to mirror the polyvalent paradoxes of Véronica in the present. But in fact, this complex contextualization of the figure of Marilisse provides but one of several terms and conditions by which its impact on the subjectivity of the protagonist is iterated.

On a primary level, then, through the social and cultural oppositions inscribed in this figural counterpart that is Marilisse—whose *métier* of laundress—or *blanchisseuse*, in French—is far from coincidental and, indeed, culturally and linguistically significant—the text opens up a modernist means of evaluating Véronica's strategy of self-liberation through the blandishments of an apparently uncomplicated desire, but one linked ineluctably to the field of the Other. For historically, the name refers to the conditions of a real relationship of concubinage between a slave woman and her white master, as Condé herself has indicated in a series of interviews with francophone cinema critic Françoise Pfaff: "I decided to use this historical character, Marilisse, a black slave woman who lived with a white man and had children with him" (1993: 65). Importantly, while the social resonances of this relationship within the black community would appear to border the fields of social betrayal and personal prostitution, there are several levels of signification to this complex relationship that might make it appear to be simply one of self-preservation or even liberation. As a result, Véronica's already ambivalent subjective trajectory is now rendered even more problematic. As Condé continues: "In this way I sought to stress both Veronica's desire for liberation and her sense of submission. The trap for her is that she seeks self-liberation through a man" (65). But in fact this simultaneity of liberation and submission frames a complex nexus of contradictory concerns, one complicated even further by the ever present figure of the colonized woman, and marked by the attempt to accomplish an illusory self-liberation doubly grounded in terms of racial difference and social hierarchy. In a supplementary intertextual and historical reference, she points out that she is no Mayotte Capécia and has no desire to lighten the race either symbolically or referentially.[5] But in these terms, Véronica's act of self-definition, framed as it is within the conundrum initiated by Marilisse, remains mired in a dilemma of Otherness whose metonymical, dependent relationship to both subjective and colonial patterns of patriarchy effectively nullifies the subject's goal well before it is even reached.

Further, by raising the troubled issue of power-based racial relations within a historical context of inequality, Condé is able to comment within the narrative frame itself on the ultimate end of Véronica's relationship with Sory, this self-reflexive turn giving first voice to the dilemma that Véronica faces by acceding to a desire grounded in the field of the Other. Through its implicit factors of ethnic and cultural difference, the inescapable imbalance implicit in these tensions of patriarchal power invalidates the solution proposed by Marilisse to the conundrum of cultural conflict. Thus Veronica's liaison with the son of the mulatto De Roseval family brings its own set of problems, their ineradicable pattern of colonial imitation articulating its own set of critical ambiguities: "The mansion was a fake, a mere copy of the Marins de St Sorlins mansion which had stood a few miles higher up only to be brought down in a slave uprising. The light-skinned De Rosevals claimed descendance from the Marins de St Sorlins. One of them had even attempted to prove it. All the whites rose up against him. Pretentious bastard" (6). With the mansion as a metonymic re-presentation of family legitimacy and respectability, grounded in the interstices of mimesis, it is significant that its original paradigm is brought down by a slave uprising, one of many events erased from a colonial history written by the colonizer. Further, however, this episode illuminates the intricacies of lineage wrought by the colonial encounter, and the inadequacy of claims of legitimacy to the maintenance of a neocolonial social hierarchy. Finally, the dual traces already at work in the narrative come together in the final exclamation, a literally double-voiced remark that is a conflation of Véronica's ongoing commentary through internal monologue, and her direct, quoted appropriation of the perspective of the rich colonial whites whose social superiority is threatened by an outsider, a pretender.

At the same time, however, she is perhaps not entirely disingenuous when she claims that for her, the attraction of Jean-Marie, "this light-skinned mulatto with green eyes and the complexion of a young Oriental prince" (7/24), goes beyond the superficialities of skin color. "Wasn't his color. I swear. That's what they all said because, naturally, they could not think of anything else. No, it was his freedom" (8/26). The social freedom to which she refers here stems from her metonymic relation to Jean-Marie's exclusion from traditional racial patterns and hierarchies, and her family's disapproval illuminates the pluralities and paradoxes of the French Caribbean's black bourgeoisie's constant struggle to achieve social inscription and metropolitan recognition. With Jean-Michel, the white French "architect with his long hair and rust-colored velvet suit" (14/34–5), she enters a relationship of sexual exchange of which she claims that "he was reassured. I was satisfied. Deuce" (23/46). Here, despite her professed longing for a sense of social and ethnic legitimacy, and the claims of reprobation that followed her earlier amorous encounter, she ultimately professes a critical blindness to race and its itinerant corollaries in her relationship with Jean-Michel, calling this relationship a "purely an individual adventure. With a man who for me was not a white man" (188/132). At this juncture, then, her subjective trajectory appears to lead from an intersection of race with class, to an attempted alignment with metropolitan legitimacy, while denying the importance of its gender and racial components. These intersections of gender, race, and desire are pursued and transformed with Sory's symbolic conjunctions of ethnicity and history within the African "heart of darkness"; the only firm constant, then, appears to be her paradoxical bent to achieve recognition through varying signifiers of socialized masculinity. So the bases of her relationships with the mulatto Jean-Marie De Roseval, and with the white Parisian architect, Jean-Michel, become increasingly significant, pointing as they do to a long-standing practice of subjective contestation through alignment with the masculinized, racialized other. Indeed, a disturbing parallel to the checkered sexual/subjective history of Aunt Paula (Delahaye) is already perceptible, one (re)traced by Véronica and which already serves as a primary foil for the initial turn to *africanité* of her rootless, composite character.

To sum up, then, since the act of submission ultimately implied by Marilisse's relationship with slavery-driven white patriarchy renders her in turn a false sister, apparently betraying principles of social and cultural resistance, this sign of bad faith impacts proleptically on Véronica, framing the tensions of her split subjectivity in exactly the same terms. For Véronica, as her cultural and historical heir presumptive, the relevant issues are now rendered even thornier by the creolized impositions of a much more complex world, one in which the barriers between self and Other, colonizer and colonized, are now blurred, multiform, displaying instability and permeability instead of binarism and linearity. As Veronica's journey toward a valorized hybridity continues, the uncertainties that these comparisons elicit are continually plumbed and extended by the probing elasticities and ambiguities of the narrative framework. In order to more fully exploit the potential implicit in this telling space of uncertainty, the narrative will reveal an even more critical subjective confrontation, as the protagonist is led to interrogate the tensions and parameters governing her bourgeois childhood existence with the family at Saint-Claude.

It is through this conscious and continuous self-questioning of her motives that Véronica effectively demonstrates how much is at risk for her in this venture. The pluralities of the past are unremittingly present, constantly (re)constructing the narrative and subjective ambiguities of the protagonist. For example, at her introduction to the president, Mwalimwana, when he greets her as one of the children that Africa lost, she interjects an interstitial commentary, a correction that immediately and irrevocably implicates both parties: "Sold, Mwalimwana, sold. Not lost. Tegbessou got 400 pounds sterling per boat load" (32/58). Such strategies decenter any fixed positions of guilt and innocence, and alienation assumes a pervasive character encompassing the zones of alterity traced by the creole conjunctions of Véronica's past and the dual desires of her present. The figure of Marilisse now assumes its complex affirmation of the significance of alterity in the configuration of the protagonist's subjectivity.

Véronica's recognition of the importance of her own childhood in the working out of her role in the growing political crisis speaks to the intractability of social strata, and this becomes increasingly apparent with her progressive revisitation of its boundaries. In describing these relationships to Ibrihama Sory, she is simultaneously avowing them to herself: "Let me go on. I wanted to escape from the family, the Mandingo marabout, my mother, the Black bourgeoisie that made me, with its talk of glorifying the Race and its terrified conviction of its inferiority. And then gradually I came around to thinking that this form of escape was not valid, that it was hiding something else" (52/86). This resolution to confront the origins of her alterity and what Sory derisorily terms her "identity problem" results in the inscription of a remarkable sequence into the textual economy. Successive fragmented articulations of a pervasive associative reaction finally give rise to a reincarnation of home, permitting her to confront her elusive counterpart through a re-presentation of the creolized past:

> What can Jean-Michel be doing at this moment? At home. The town seems so small, ridiculous! That's where I was born, however, and grew up. They show me the new district, the council flats that have replaced the huts made of soap cartons and corrugated iron; the motorways; the new hotels, and the wildlife park cut in two by an ice-cold river. I am sitting on a big grey rock, sucking my thumb. A dozen men and women are getting off the bus *Bienfaisante Providence*. They're beating the *gros-ka*. A couple undulates to the *bonda* and mimics the motions of making love. Mabo Julie is singing her head off. At the wheel, the Mandingo marabout sighs. (72/110–11)

The flashback that this sequence constitutes allows the narrator to view the social and infrastructural changes at work in her Caribbean departmental home from the perspective of an existence amid the norms of the metropole, such that the appearance of highways, hotels, and H.L.M.s that transform the traditional, once familiar landscape, the mirrored reflection of metropolitan patterns of development, does not immediately appear out of place. The heady mixture of old and new, of French and Antillean cultures, subtly changes the perception of the once-familiar landscape and puts into place that dichotomy between past and present, known and unknown, self and Other, that undergirds the creole parameters and hybridities of her difference. The return to origins becomes a necessary confrontation, a crucial encounter between what she once was and what she had now become that will mark and, ultimately, help resolve her future. Through the interpolations of the maid, Mabo Julie, a metonymic link to the paradoxical familial structure of her early childhood, and the paternal authority figure of the "mandingo marabout," whose ineluctable difference is relentlessly and metonymically re-presented to her through diverse authoritarian figures for Africa—first, through the immigration officer whose presence marks her arrival in Africa, and, most important, through the ongoing enigma of Sory himself—both the alienated past and the sense of alterity she desires of the African Other form forbidding patterns of authority that must be confronted and overcome. In this sense, the passage of time leads to a point of convergence for the subject's redefinition of her own alterity. As the alienated Parisian adult watches the bourgeois Guadeloupean child sitting on the rock, the imperative to negotiate between worlds of difference, the one grounded in patterns of colonial class structure and the other in the ambiguities of ethnic alterity, both of which are simultaneously engendered and imposed by the colonial (m)Other, becomes increasingly urgent. For it is only by recognizing and coming to terms with the transformative potential of her own dualities that Véronica will escape the concomitant corollaries of her desire for cultural appropriation and begin her repudiation of the conflation of sign and referent signified by Sory and the African Other.

The preceding episodes are interspersed across the first two parts of the novel, with Veronica drawing increasingly closer, as it were, to the final encounter between alternating spheres of subjectivity. Indeed, it is possible to construct a parallel between the increasing intensity of her subjective dilemma and the growing tension of the local political situation, reinforcing the novel's deliberate conflation of the patterns of passion and politics. With the latter approaching its culmination and climax in part 3, she attempts to escape by visiting a neighboring islet. But, through a process of metonymic displacement, the boat trip reawakens a reminiscence of a similar journey to Guadeloupe's neighboring isle of Marie-Galante, undertaken when she was a child. However, this parallel temporality quickly announces itself as a simple vehicle for a final engagement with the past, one which must ultimately be faced if Véronica is to be liberated from the throes of her binary patterns of desire and to find the means of claiming that tertiary subjective space which she still embodies. Reinscribing the temporal oscillation that has consistently marked the discursive boundaries of her self-definition, the subject signals the opening of this important flashback, finding it now increasingly difficult to distinguish between past and present: "Is it the present? Or is it the past?" (127/180). As the signifiers of her childhood slowly assume their position in the narrative sequence unfolding to her inner consciousness, and Mabo Julie, Dr. and Mme. Bageot, and the sights and smells of the five-hour trip become firmly contextualized, she is soon able to recognize and affirm, with a note of relief mingled, perhaps, with an apprehension that is signaled by verbal repetition, the return and reanimation of the past: "It's the past. The past" (127/181). As she makes her way among the onlookers for whom she now represents an object of desire, given her arrival from the "grande île of Guadeloupe," this episode appears to mark the earliest trace of her latent, pervasive desire for otherness, the primary instance of her unconscious revulsion toward her formative familial context.

The family, of whose name she says "I had nothing to be jealous" (8/26), usually spends this vacation at Saint-Claude, deftly and unforgettably described by the narrator as the "mulatto stronghold." But the usual effusive welcome, habitually extended to them by their counterparts in other parts of the island, does not occur here. Their exposure as the black bourgeoisie elicits vacuousness and rejection, their unbelonging recognized immediately by that true incarnation of creole mobility, the Bakra, or creole whites: "They were looking for an excuse to parade themselves at Saint-Claude, the mulatto stronghold where the Blacks used to walk on tiptoe, the Bakra having fled higher up. . . . And believe me, it was total anonymity. . . . *We were not intruders at Saint-Claude. We simply did not exist. . . . It was here that everything began*" (128–29/182–83; emphasis mine). The exposure of these hierarchical patterns of difference, made up of what Leah Hewitt calls "Veronica's chaotic recollections of a veiled racial inferiority in Guadeloupe" (1990:181), are of critical importance. For it is at this point that the ineluctable oppositions and convergences of Véronica's creole society emerge to engender that sense of absence and exclusion, that diffused displacement (the product of imposed anxieties constructed upon artificial hierarchies of colonial authority) which had brought Véronica to this symbolic juncture where both past and present are at play in a bid for the predetermination of her prepossessing presence.

The confrontation and disavowal that constitute the primary axes of this narrative sequence in fact take place simultaneously on two separate levels.

On the one hand, the appearance in Saint-Claude of her "mandingo mar-about" and his family constitutes a test, the ultimate proof of whether or not the racial and social ascendancy to which they have aspired and which they have practiced for so long is indeed real, its efficacy to be proven through their acceptance or rejection by the last bastion of the Bakra, or mulatto bourgeoisie, whose ultimate allegiance is to the ethnic exclusions of the metropole. For the Merciers, this desire for acceptance is the sign of a subjective alienation and cultural duality that, functioning as the corollary of departmentalization, pervades by extension the society at large. And in fact, on the face of it, their attempt at integration is an abysmal failure. By simply "not existing," Véronica's family cannot join in with the objects of their social desire but rather engender a prohibitive physical distance that emphasizes the difference that is the basis of their demeaning rejection.

Paradoxically, however, it is in the observation that "we were not intruders" that Véronica signifies the thoroughgoing nature of this deception. For her, it is the paradoxical capacity to be an intruder, to be perceived and recognized herself as a marginal subject—a false foreigner and an unwanted one—that signifies her distance from her family's values and ultimately imposes meaning upon her social interaction. The erasure of this paradoxical potential for difference—since, to all intents and purposes, her family is effectively effaced by the very group whose approbation they had sought—seems to mark a critical beginning of sorts: "It was here that everything began." Since her subjectivity is grounded in her desire to understand and come to terms with where her difference lies, this sojourn at Saint-Claude was a catalyst for her, the absence of a meaningful marginality proving to be as problematic as the familial difference by which she was already marked. For Véronica, the trauma of identity occurs precisely at the point at which she is *not* an intruder, for the pain of nonexistence that forces her confrontation with her own unresolved difference serves to increase the intensity of her sense of disjuncture. Eventually, as we shall see, it is the irresistible urgency of this innate sense of difference that will force Véronica, when she does leave Africa, to return not to Guadeloupe but to Paris.

As this panoramic re-presentation slowly clarifies the parameters of her present dilemma, she comes to realize that the critical connections of her creole culture still constituted the inauguratory gesture of her persistent and all-pervading alienation. And indeed, it is by confronting the dismissive derision of the Saint-Claude population that she will come to terms with these innate anxieties of cross-cultural desire and apply them diachronically to her present attempt to appropriate the cultural values of Africa. In other words, her original desire to be other, born of a lack drawn on the creole complexities of familial métissage and social difference by the colonial (m)Other, constituted in fact the origin of that desire to be other which had brought her to Africa, with its long ethnic history and aura of cultural legitimacy. She had not succeeded in abandoning the symbolic authorities spawned in childhood; they were still with her, still haunted her, and now must play their role in resolving the conflict that, symbolically, both draws Véronica and Sory together and simultaneously keeps them apart.

The key, now, is to apply the differential temporalities of both past and present in order to unlock a new vision of the future. This is a move that must be performed by the protagonist herself, as she moves beyond these disabling dualities into an alter/native position. As she waits at Hérémakhonon for Sory's return from the city, the last act of this interpellative drama begins: "The most illogical thing is that once I get to Hérémakhonon I don't know what to do with myself. . . . I wait in other words. For when I become Marilisse" (149/209). The importance of this self-deprecatory observation, equating her desire for Sory — and, by inference, for the symbolic African structures he so effectively embodies — to the moment when she becomes Marilisse, marks her final acknowledgment of the subjective alienation that has determined her peripatetic pattern from departmental to metropolitan domination to African politics, from class conciousness to a cultural alterity that must now be abandoned. The resolution of these latent, doubled forces of exile and liberation will prove to have interesting and far-reaching consequences for Véronica as creole subject.

Following the repression of the student-led uprising, the indeterminacy of the political situation forces everyone to reexamine their personal position regarding the climactic events. She is at last aware of her role as interloper and accepts its psychological implications of otherness: "I come here . . . to spoil other identities. I'm the one who's fleeing the alienated of my native isle and I come to work on other alienations" (133/189). Now she can acknowledge the need for a new beginning: "I'd need to be someone else to make this investigation. To start again from the very beginning. To emerge again from my mother's womb" (166/232). And it is in this context, just prior to the final catalyst of the announcement of Saliou's death, that Véronica's inscription of a differential alterity for herself takes place. In her newfound honesty, she refuses the proffered political explanation: "I don't believe it. Saliou wasn't a coward. Or else, and my intuition tells me that this must be the truth, they killed him and chose to camouflage his death by suicide" (170/304). Further, reason dictates a double responsibility for this personal and political tragedy, forcing a final rejection of Sory and recognition of the results of her blindness and inaction: "In a way nonetheless despicable and cruel, although bloodless, I've helped to kill him" (175/312). In this unsparing articulation of her bloody responsibility, facing and stating her complicity *en toutes lettres*, the subject signals her need for a critical change in positionality; no longer does she seek subjective rebirth by borrowing the structural symbolism of Africa, but rather embraces a recognition of the innate multivalences and complexities of a culture of métissage whose location has always, for her, been elsewhere. Abandoning the twin axes of desire which had bisected the field in which she sought to inscribe herself, this third issuance from "my mother's womb" marks the inauguration of a new site of symbolic otherness, an escape from the binary confines of a simple teleology of colonial difference.

In fact, the subject is in the process of abandoning the divided desires of her original alienation, adopting instead the principles of her own métis background as the most effective deployment of the self-assertion she has so long sought. She is in fact an interstitial subject whose intrinsic pluralities have become the distinguishing sign of a postcolonial *neither/nor*; outside the binary boundaries of the colonial self and Other, she can finally take advantage of her own creative instability. Symbolically, it is the principled stance she has witnessed in Oumou Hawa, Ibrahima Sory's sister and Saliou's wife, who calmly but persistently makes her way between opposing political and personal axes, that has made Véronica see herself as a false sister and spurs her recognition of courage. This initial but important moment of interstitiality will ultimately point the way to the resolution of her own positionality. Indeed, as the embodiment of an incipient hybridity, she repeatedly insists on the need for lucidity: "I want to leave with my head clear. Fully conscious of what I'm doing. It's nothing rash. It's not a spur-of-the-moment decision. I've understood. *Understood.* I must leave if I want to maintain a semblance of respect" (173/240–41). This desire for clearheadedness is an important correlative to her subjective restitution and symbolic rebirth, signaled by her reiterated and italicized voicing of "understood"; her deliberate objectivity and distance have finally been catalyzed.

Ultimately, the arc of African politics obliges her to make a personal decision; she is forced to confront her own desire and alterity, and, in so doing, to forsake the space of the Other: "My ancestors, my ancestors via Ibrahima Sory are playing a dirty trick on me. A very dirty trick. By imprisoning Saliou they are trying to force me to hate them" (160/224). Here, it is not simply that the African context would always remain other, but also that the insufficiency of the African Other was always already a reflection of her own, and that the impossible basis of her desire to *become* the Other was the issue that had finally to be addressed and resolved. Her imminent departure signifies the inaugural gesture of her renegotiation of this intrinsic, interstitial migrancy.

As she simultaneously approaches both the end of the narrative and a new subjective beginning, she is able to pass judgement on the episode just ended from the newfound perspective of a self-generated space: "And here I am. Face to face with myself. Trapped. . . . *One day I'll have to break the silence*. This mistake, this tragic mistake I couldn't help making, being what I am. My ancestors led me on. I looked for myself in the wrong place" (176/244; emphasis mine). Face-to-face with herself, ineluctably but creatively trapped, she can now construct a strategy of survival that will confront the difficulty she faces in integrating her pluralism into a positionality of her difference. Yet, significantly, her discourse continues to the end as internal monologue, and her acknowledgment of this configuration and of its continuation—"one day I'll have to break the silence"—suggests its role as an alternative framework for inscribing female creole subjectivity. By acknowledging the latent polysemy of her Caribbean otherness, whose pluralized displacement is made the overarching sign of a differential cultural idiom, she finally succeeds in appropriating her hybridity as a modernist site of creole subjectivity, and in allowing a transformative, gender-inflected economy of discursive difference to emerge within that Caribbean space. And it is in the coming political performativity inherent in the irruption of this postcolonial moment that the significance of Véronica's departure for Paris and resistance symbolically lies.

Prerogatives of Place

Finally, what we have witnessed, in effect, is the transformation of the interpellative trajectory of the subject of *En attendant le bonheur*: from a fragmented female subject from Guadeloupe's black bourgeoisie—a *négresse rouge* who is less than one but intrinsically, insistently double—in a fragmented postcolonial society marked by mimetism and métissage, whose African sojourn takes her through the singular veil of Glissantian Reversion, to a recognition and assumption of a valorized, contextualized pluralism that is the positional embodiment of a creole culture. Indeed, Véronica's predicament is largely paradigmatic of a sort of subjective dis-ease that afflicts the female protagonists of Caribbean literature, marked by an intrinsic inability to find a place in their societies, a predicament usually exacerbated by strong feelings of abnormality and patterns of aberration. These pervasive cultural and subjective disjunctures are partly the product of a postcolonial culture, and define what Marie-Denise Shelton calls "the contradictions and tensions characteristic of feminine existence in the Caribbean" (1990:352). By confronting and contesting the dilemma of displacement that, as Shelton sees it, accuses these women of "belonging nowhere, of being deprived of identity" (351), Véronica succeeds in supplanting the stereotype and engenders a differential discourse that effectively counters preceding paradigms of dysfunctional self-awareness.

This postcolonial narrative's visible, vigorous insistence upon retrieving or inventing lost homelands, as Elleke Boehmer argues, accomplishes the construction of creole identity through what she calls "the conversion of apparent deficiencies into definitions of self" (1995:117). In these terms, the subjective strategy outlined by Condé is articulated in tandem with the formal narrative structure, constructing a discursive dyad that specifically seeks to reflect a certain political and historical vision that would mark Véronica ineluctably as both product and symbol of a hybrid Caribbean culture. This "condition of placelessness," this "experience of cultural schizophrenia," in Boehmer's words, is ultimately translated into a "restorative dream" (117), allowing the subject to pursue the resolution of her alienation in a context that symbolizes the difference innate in her own sense of exile, while embodying her subtle difference from the practices commonly overdetermining the cultural background of her Caribbean counterparts.

It is important to note that her trajectory from alienation to self-awareness has itself been mapped through discourse—specifically, by an iconic re-presentation of her interstitial ethnocultural pluralism through the doubleness and foreclosure implied by internal monologue. It is this distance and separation from any recognition of a valid interpellative space from which to speak that creates the conditions of possibility through which the subject seeks to come to terms with the diversity that she embodies. Maryse Condé suggested such an interpretation in an interview with Ina Césaire: "All I saw in my people was an absolute imitation of the western life-style, an admiration of its values, in other words, a total assimilation. Since the Caribbean, during that period, rarely called into question the cultural images which had been im-

posed on it by its dependence, even when they claimed to be free of them.
. . . Véronica is nothing but a mirror who reflects the two sides. . . . One can see
in her a series of conflicts, of contradictions which many Caribbean women
certainly are familiar with, even if they do not always wish to acknowledge
them" (1979:125–6, 128). In these terms, the subject of the narrative may be
read as an interrogation of the disabling dualities that have historically figured
the construction of a feminine Caribbean identity structure. By making
Véronica the discursive mirror of the dichotomies of departmentalization, and
forcing her into a discursive contestation and avowal of the innate contradictions and pluralities marking the emerging postcolonial culture, Condé's view
of the disparate social and cultural patterns that ground this community is
recognized and recuperated. Further, as Susan Andrade argues, the characterization of Véronica operates on several levels to subvert a range of stereotypes
concerning the black woman: "Condé counters two of the symbols telescoped
into the negatively charged stereotype of 'the black woman': the white perception of her as sexually uncontrollable and the black male perception of her as
a sexual/racial betrayer" (1993:218). It is by inscribing Véronica as a multivalent
cultural and subjective sign, then, that this myriad of assumptions can be effectively confronted and transformed. The reinscription of these complex patterns of alienation as strategies of subjective possibility through the rigors of a
postcolonial discourse of difference is precisely the goal of this deliberately
polysemic narrative.

The novel's culmination with Véronica's departure from Africa for Paris,
rather than her native Caribbean, also marks a conscious strategy whose paradoxical import is intended to reinscribe her into the paradoxical space of exile
from which her sense of cultural displacement had originally sprung. Indeed,
the importance of this choice of the metropole in locating an alter/native discursive site for the hybrid differential subjectivity embodied by Véronica is not
to be overlooked; in the same interview, Condé insists upon it: "I think that
Véronica's flight is a very brave departure. She could have stayed in the arms of
her Minister, certainly with regrets, but going on in this way. She is brave
enough to break it off, to leave, to go somewhere where she can think about
her whole adventure, and eventually to draw a lesson from it. So I think that
there is a self-evaluation . . . and courage!" (128–29). Through this *prise de
conscience* implicit in the direction of her departure, Véronica announces the
strategization of the differential discourse that she has adopted as the sign of
her self-definition. Her departure for France does not constitute an embrace of

French culture as such, but rather the contestatory gesture of a subject forced to confront and come to terms with the original site of its alienation and displacement. The double vision produced by her position as both native and outsider works to consolidate her newfound hybrid Caribbean heredity. Indeed, following her attempt to resolve the dilemma of her cultural identity through a double displacement into the field of the Other, first to France and then to Africa, the persistence of the internal monologue suggests the appropriation of difference as a form of discursive and cultural positionality. Yet it is through this discourse that she is also able to crucially confront her idealized image of Africa, a task which, as Suzanne Crosta writes, "Condé feels is important . . . especially . . . in the light of personal and cultural definitions" (1999:172). Further, by writing in French while inscribing difference through the use of internal monologue, Véronica confronts and contests the historical tool of the colonizing Other, displacing linear colonial discourses to trace and relocate both center and peripheries in order to effect a transformation of perspective, a metamorphosis of method. Véronica's search for a valid self-image maps an interpellative triangle whose operative poles are Guadeloupe, France, and Africa, and this deliberate recuperation of the early triangular trade by which slaves were originally brought to the New World underlines the transformative reinscription of this historical path in the construction of a regional postcolonial perspective that adequately articulates the axes both of the subject and of its larger sociopolitical context.

By reworking the sense of cultural marginality that a hegemonic colonial discourse seeks to impose, Véronica's text effectively subverts its strategy, reframing the terms and teleologies within which difference is mapped and located. The terms of this alternative re-presentation re-place the cultural nightmare of perpetual unbelonging by underlining the possibility of engaging subjectivity through polysemic patterns of cultural and discursive articulation. This critique of the traditional roles imposed upon Caribbean femininity draws on alternative inscriptions of ethnic and cultural positionality to extend and transform the inherited boundaries of Caribbean identity. Both narrative and subject appropriate new terms for asserting female postcolonial agency without reinscribing the received hierarchies of a colonial perspective that alienates the articulative possibilities of the female "I"; ultimately, what is engendered is an autonomous discourse that, by transforming hierarchies of alienation and integration, positionality and place, self and Other, revises the terms of isolation, double displacement, and dis-ease that have beset the boundaries of Caribbean womanhood.

ℑ 3

L'Isolé Soleil/Soufrières
Textual Creolization and Cultural Identity

Eia pour ceux qui n'ont jamais rien inventé
pour ceux qui n'ont jamais rien exploré
pour ceux qui'n'ont jamais rien dompté
insoucieux de dompter, mais jouant le jeu du monde
Aimé Césaire, *Cahier d'un retour au pays natal*

Drawing the Double

As we have seen thus far, the discursive articulation of resistance in a departmental context tends to employ narrative strategies that exploit an ambivalence inherent in the process of departmentalization itself. These narrative forms expose and extend shifting temporalities and teleologies that effectively displace and subvert the neocolonial hierarchies imposed upon the departmental subject, translating them into a plural site that continually contests its inherited liminality and marginalization. For the French-speaking Caribbean, this discursive contestation forms the basis of a framework that, even as it elaborates a poetics of difference, also inscribes the regional resonances of the postcolonial. Daniel Maximin, a writer born in Guadeloupe in 1947, and whose background includes prose, poetry, and work in radio, and who for several years has been chargé of the *Direction régional des affaires culturelles de la Guadeloupe,* would successfully appropriate these ambiguities and omissions implicit in the colonial histories of the region. His work is in the vanguard of those attempts to articulate the multiple modernities of the postcolonial Caribbean through a supple narrative whose structural slippages and thematic complexity simultaneously embody and reflect the oppositional multiplicities of a creole culture. As we examine the discursive disjunctures and insistent patterns of pluralism that characterize his novels *L'Isolé Soleil* and *Soufrières,*[1] we shall see that even as he articulates the diverse cultural and historical patterns of his native Guadeloupe, his narrative discourse reflects a larger creole textuality of resistance that shapes and defines a postcolonial practice of migrant modernity, inscribing a counterdiscourse that successfully contests the historical obsession with origins and resolutions that marks the Caribbean region.

Language is critically important in the colonial relationship, since it is the primary means by which the oral and discursive domination of the colonized is put into practice, and its relocation in narrative would prove to be equally critical for defining postcolonial difference. We have seen, for example, that for Maximin's artistic prelector and predecessor Edouard Glissant, the dynamic discontinuities of poetic expression play a predominant role in creating new patterns of material representation. As Glissant writes in *L'Intention poétique*, "In the expression of being, language will no longer be pure obstacle and pure accomplishment; it will also include, in the most *contradictory* way, principles of possession and connection . . . as though it were already the language of a language" (46). These complex poetics of prose elaborated by Glissant prepare the fertile ground of the discursive heterogeneity that will be intrinsic to the articulation of an adequately differential postcolonial condition.

At the same time, however, the double disjunctures of colonial discourses, generating their own language of catachresis and ambiguity, can create complex patterns of domination and containment where the hierarchies of language and culture become the inescapable instruments of an inimical authoritarianism. As Frantz Fanon states in *Black Skin, White Masks*: "Every colonized people . . . every people in whose soul an inferiority complex has been created by the death and burial of its local cultural originality—finds itself face to face with the language of the civilizing nation; that is, with the culture of the mother country" (18). Language, in other words, in conjunction with the apparently monolithic discursive system of colonialism, erects a binary logic of domination that demands to be confronted and appropriated if it is to be successfully subverted and countered. These narratives of contestation, while tracing the trajectory of the Caribbean experience, simultaneously exploit the linguistic and discursive ambivalences of the colonial encounter to articulate the doubling of culture and subjectivity that must undergird the alternative temporality of the postcolonial condition. And it is precisely this question of language, coincident with an innovative interrogation of the authoritarian implications of linear narration, that sets Maximin's work apart from most nationalist narratives that have preceded it.

Maximin's narrative practice, by contrast, offers tacit acknowledgment of the fact that the discursive complexities of the colonial encounter are of cardinal importance in fashioning a framework for the articulation of issues of cultural identity in a postcolonial context. Responding to the oppositions embedded in the texts of colonialism on their own terms does nothing to dismantle these hierarchies of signification; as Benita Parry argues, "A reverse discourse replicating and therefore reinstalling the linguistic polarities devised by a dominant centre to exclude and act against the categorized, does not liberate the 'other' from a colonized condition. . . . the founding concepts of the problematic must be refused" (1987:28). Dislocating the focus of discursive articulation from assumptions of colonialist sovereignty to the deliberate dissymmetries of postcolonial discourse reveals the displacement and repression, the anxiety and apprehension that are the ground both of colonial authority and of its attendant narratives, and, as Homi Bhabha points out, generates a new hybridity from the instability and ambivalence of the colonial encounter which "enables a form of subversion . . . that turns the discursive conditions of dominance into the grounds of intervention" (1986:173). By acknowledging and appropriating the doubleness of the historical and cultural experience, writing the alternative temporalities of its difference in postcolonial terms turns colonialist domination into new categories of subaltern representation. The principles of creole performance are translated from the linguistic to the narrative level, generating a form of textuality whose multiple patterns and layers draw deliberate designs of doubleness in order to re-present the complexities of the postcolonial condition. Figures drawn on the ineluctably creole culture of the Caribbean colonial experience are ultimately exposed, translated, and exploded in Maximin's signifying network of postcolonial identity.

To achieve this novelistic representation of Caribbean culture, the primary patterns traced by these teleologies of difference appropriate a postcolonial praxis of resistance to enact the complexities of its contestation in primarily discursive terms, grounding its enunciation of alternative teleologies of culture on those patterns of division that disrupt the apparent authority of cultural representation. As Bhabha has suggested, "In signifying the present, something comes to be repeated, relocated, and translated in the name of a tradition. Such an intervention quite properly challenges our sense of the historical identity of culture as a homogenising, unifying force" (1989:128, 130). The translation of colonial ambivalence into conditions of postcolonial possibility entails subverting this artificial authority through complex, differential strategies of representation. If, as Ashis Nandy contends, "the liberation ultimately ha[s] to begin from the colonized and end with the colonizers . . . the oppressor too is caught in the culture of oppression" (1983:63), the latent cultural ambiguity of the colonial encounter instantiates a new register of postcolonial pluralism as an agential site of collective identification. Figures of dislocation and doubling at work within the narrative structure reflect the persistent pluralities and conjunctions of the colonial encounter, drawing patterns of creole production that signify a postcolonial problematization of the canonical confines of colonialism.

Any shift toward the initiation of a transformational temporality of difference must resite the original rupture, translating the traces of the original patterns of alienation and disjuncture. In a 1986 interview published in *Les Nouvelles du sud*, Maximin himself notes the inscription of this paradigm as an integral part of his discursive framework: "When one is dominated and one wishes to escape, one must take up the master's arms, and defend oneself with them" (41). Such a reappropriation of the discursive tools of colonial domination ultimately aims at creating a discontinuous creole subjectivity which draws on the uncanny doubleness of this differential discourse to develop alternative modes of authentication. By translating this experience from the subliminal realm to the performative, deliberately seeking to reflect the pluralities of history and culture, the discourse of authors like Maximin, argues Ronnie Scharfman, "defines the simultaneity of . . . a double form of resistance" (1995:126), averting the destructive divisions of a recuperative nationalism by locating the communal culture and the performance of its shifting polarities in a variety of sites.

The ambiguities and polarities of colonial authority must be exploded, exposed, turned inside out in order to resite these temporalities and teleologies as a hybrid heterogeneity. It is by relocating the diegetic traces of the colonial encounter in a new performative framework that the complex inscription of a creole discourse of doubleness will be accomplished.

L'Isolé Soleil: The Caribbean's Historical Hybridity

Overtly and even obsessively metafictional, a novel that constitutes the (hi)storied rewriting of a Caribbean discourse, Maximin's *L'Isolé Soleil* works principally through the re-presentation of key contemporary and historical events as it attempts to inscribe some of the dualities and paradoxes that ground the fragmentation and pluralism of the Guadeloupean postcolonial experience. While the book ostensibly traces the trajectory of its protagonist Marie-Gabriel's attempt to write the complex history of her family's existence in Guadeloupe, the author's interrogation and exploitation of the very notion of a writing project draws insistently on patterns of self-referentiality, inter-textuality, and repetition that permit the translation and relocation of various *topoi* of a differential postcolonialism, in which the epistolary dialogue be-tween Marie-Gabriel and her friend Adrien, and their respective writing projects, become the privileged signs of the contact, communication, and cre-ativity that must ground the discursive (re)definition of this diasporic creole culture. Through a remarkably decentered discourse whose hybrid inter-vocality comprises fictional narrative, letters, notebooks, proverbs, poems, and historical documents, Maximin succeeds in displacing Caribbean marginal-ity, rewriting stories of history and identity already written, and exploding the traditional vision of regional fragmentation and difference into a doubled performative site of cultural contestation and subjectivity. The deliberate self-reflexivity of this creole counterpoetics relocates the linear authorities of a Guadeloupean identity whose boundaries have been largely shaped and defined by the discourse of the metropole; Maximin's formal dialogue be-tween history and literature deliberately and repeatedly doubles figures of dis-course and character, voice and perspective in order to (re)invent both the past and the future of an interstitial, interactive community.

It is important to recognize that Maximin's contestation of prior narratives of colonial authority constitutes a major re-vision of binary boundaries of exclusion and erasure, articulating through its very form the complexities of its subject matter, and generating in the process a regional antipoetics of nonauthoritarian contestation. As John Erickson rightly argues, "Maximin's *L'Isolé soleil* . . . takes as its subject the rewriting of a history of his home islands; it seeks to wrest from the occupier the history of Guadeloupe" (1992:120). And Maximin himself, in his 1986 interview, addressed precisely this discursive privileging of the historical framework: "Our dominator was our historian . . . we did not control our history much less the telling of it" (38). Indeed, this is borne out by the primary role ascribed to representational rep-etition and structural displacement in the narrative, as the differences and affinities, the parallels and paradoxes intrinsic to the construction of a creole hybridity from the antinomies of colonial anxiety begin to take shape. His de-liberate discursive conflation generates what Clarisse Zimra has called "a diz-zying narrative space, the better to underline the collaborative, dialogical and tentative nature of all writing" (1999:191). Through this careful and consistent re-inscription of recurring characters, related events, and overlapping perspec-tives, the discontinuities and contradictions that have been the bane of French Caribbean colonial history emerge and are translated into innovative sites and signs of subjectivity, rendering this postcolonial society—one whose intrinsic ambiguity is figured by the doubleness of its departmental status—the product of the dualities of its colonial encounter. It is a place of community and of change where its indigenous heritage joined with the cultures of Africa and Asia and the metropolitan culture of the colonizer to be transformed into an uncommon site of innovative modernity.

It is Maximin's thesis that this plurality is the essence of the regional Carib-bean experience, and of the Guadeloupean experience in particular. For him, the Caribbeanness of the Guadeloupean identity is beyond dispute: "Thus one is Guadeloupean, and beyond that, West Indian. . . . I wanted to affirm this Guadeloupean, Caribbean identity as a fact, not to interrogate it" (1986:35–36). Maximin's thesis, then, is based on a revisionist rehistoricizing of key *lieux de mémoire* in the cultural trajectory of both Guadeloupe and the larger Carib-bean. The imaginative use of language is critical to this discursive refiguring, rendering the novel, in Maximin's words, "one which shows from beginning to end the memory of music and song" (1986:50). It is this insistence on discourse and the pluralized inscription of discursive form that has provoked a negative reaction to his work in some quarters, notably on the part of the well-known critic Bernadette Cailler. In her book-length study of Glissant, she describes Maximin's novel as one that diverges sharply from the Glissantian principle that conflates discourse and history: "What the author does not accomplish, and what needs to be for the novel to work, is precisely the interaction between poetry and history. . . . While this is the work of a gifted intellectual, it is not the work of a Caribbean poet" (1988:174–75). Yet I would argue that it is precisely this intersection between discursive form and historical fact that forms the core of Maximin's work. By insisting on a figural, rather than a linear or literal, approach to the task of (re)writing, Maximin reilluminates and reinvigorates events effaced in the continuum of colonial history by the discursive domina-tion of the colonizer.

One of the most striking aspects of Maximin's discourse is his insistence on the ineluctable presence of the Other; interestingly a primary sign of his appropriation of this site of alterity is his extensive use of the second-person singular. Indeed, following a brief opening prologue, *tu* is the first word in the abridged first section, titled "Désirades," and thus in the body of the novel proper, and as such constitutes a recuperation of the intertextuality and intervocality from which the novel derives the power and urgency of its perspective. By conflating the pluralized title, "Désirades"—the name of a small island of mainly Breton settlers off the coast of Guadeloupe—with *désir*, these initial textual traces of fragmentation, desire, and multiplicity come to play an early but key role in locating and shaping the direction taken by the discourse. The shifting presence of the novel's several narrators serves to accentuate this plurality, and as they address alternately both the reader and each other, the burgeoning network of signification generated by these discourses recuperates the polymorphous hybridity of Caribbean creolization. Maximin's attempt to inscribe a future for the region through recourse to its past is reflected in this ongoing construction of Marie-Gabriel's writing project, in which the collaborative constitution of her cultural identity is linked to this continual discursive dialogue between past and present, self and Other, grounded in a critical relational tension between text and form. The protean character of language, at both the narrative and subjective levels, in Maximin's textual creation of cultural identity is of paramount importance, entailing a (re)negotiation of key colonialist terrain. As Ronnie Scharfman writes, "Constituting an identity for oneself in language must not represent either a stagnant, repetitive, reverential regression, nor a substitutive, identifying, internalized parental superego" (1992:237). The novel manages to avoid these subjective excesses while producing meaning through complex processes of both reading and writing, engendering an identity for Marie-Gabriel and, by extension, for the creole culture she signifies, out of the turbulence of textual praxis.

The retelling of the 1962 plane disaster that opens the novel puts into place the intricate, extensive symbolic network that ties the historical experience of a liminally postcolonial Guadeloupe to the larger francophone world generated and governed by the metropole. The deaths of the anticolonial activists, among them Marie-Gabriel's father, that this event engenders foreground the struggle for autonomy and set in motion the poetics of place figured by the exchange of letters between Marie-Gabriel and her cousin, Adrien; the direct address by Marie-Gabriel both to her younger self and, by extension, to her reader-interlocutor voiced by the *tu* dis-places the burden of signification to areas of textual consumption as well as its production, and immediately creolizes the narrative site by emphasizing the political and cultural (dis)-continuities between colonial past and departmental present, self and Other, author and reader, center and periphery. For if, as Scharfman argues, literary creolization entails an "organizing, structuring principle" that "blur[s] the oppositions between writer, story-teller, reader public" (1995:133), then Max-imin's dissolution of colonial and narrative authority deliberately places post-colonial textuality within a context of cultural identity and subjective libera-tion.

Further, Marie-Gabriel's discovery of her eighteenth-century ancestor Angela's ring in the mango tree she is climbing on her seventeenth birthday provides a prefigurative glimpse of the important symbolic role to be played by historical objects in the novel: "Moonlight shimmers on beads of blood mixed with champagne set in the ring you discover in that hole where your rage came crashing down, a tiny ring placed in that hole two centuries ago, to be forgot-ten. You read the name ANGELA clearly engraved as if it conveyed property rights from the one who gave it to the one who wore it" (5/13). The determining role to be played by the past over both character and event in the present is clearly delineated here. The encounter symbolized by the ring found by Marie-Gabriel, as Erickson suggests, points to a "transformation of symbols effectuated in and through the Other's language, and directed towards the (re)inscription by Antillean writers of their own history" (1992:121); as it medi-ates discursive communication between her past and present selves, immedi-ately doubling the language of the postcolonial site, it prefigures the even larger symbolic role to be essayed by her ancestor Jonathan's notebook in the formulation of a new future.

The exposure of these unwritten histories of resistance and contestation helps to displace persistent myths of uniform subjection created by colonial univocality. Marie-Gabriel's undertaking of this writing project, of this novel within a novel that is the product of so many hands and voices, engenders a differential cultural temporality by subverting and displacing the very dis-courses that made the colonial project possible. It is this insistence on reflectivity and doubling that allows the text to inscribe an explosive, creolized Caribbean "I," multiply positioned and continuously self-generating. As Clarisse Zimra puts it: "A text arranged on the page even as it is projected in the imagination, since the novel to be written is the one which is being read. A volcanic 'I' erupts from the writing in *L'isolé soleil*" (1992:266). Ultimately, the novel's self-referential, creatively fragmented discursive framework will be constructed from an amalgam of writing notebooks.

Marie-Gabriel's initial task will be to (re)construct the lost notebook of her father, Louis-Gabriel; in this text, forever lost with his demise in the 1962 plane crash, was located the entire history of her Caribbean island(s) written through the (hi)story of his life. Marie-Gabriel's simulacrum of her father's journal, which will eventually become the novel *L'Isolé Soleil*, eventually encounters and intertextually incorporates the revolutionary notebook of her ancestor, Jonathan, the journal of her mother, Siméa, and the writing notebook used by her friend Adrien to take up with her issues of writing itself as they crop up during the invention of the novel. In this way, as Maximin's interviewer puts it, "we realize that the history of the island and the region are systematically displayed" (1986:37), but, even more important, the novel is inscribed as writing that takes writing as its subject in order to dis-place prevalent patterns of colonial discourse: "You will open the drawers of our confiscated history; drawers of heroism and cowardice, of hunger, fear and love. You will bring back to memory what was testified and what was told, making truth serve the imagination and not the opposite" (10/18).

In order to further emphasize the deleterious role of this colonial presence and the contemporary constructions of the creole this imbrication has produced, she then enjoins her younger self, at the end of this first section: "You will write to free yourself from paternalism, from the law of the return of the prodigal fathers and children, and from everything that tries to go back to itself" (11/19). These complex figures inscribe the necessity of a nonlogocentric, nonpatriarchal discourse to this novel project of communal self-definition, as well as the determining role of difference and pluralism and the integral part to be played by the textual uncovering of a history of resistance. At the same time, her warning coda—"However YOU will take care to never write I. When love is uprooted there's nothing but YOU and THEY to declare" (11/19)—ensures a discourse written in the name of the many rather than the one; by consistently doubling the formal constituents of the narrative discourse, Maximin's deliberately plural perspective negotiates the name of a collective, collaborative identification that succeeds in elaborating a strategy of selfhood for the emergent community whose history and future he is attempting to reinvent.

To help trace these trajectories from a historic as well as a symbolic perspective, Maximin then shifts the narrative register to one of omniscient narration and puts into place as his protagonists two twins, Georges and Jonathan; the offspring of an eighteenth-century mulatto woman, Miss Béa, they are the direct ancestors of Marie-Gabriel. Georges's impaired vision, and Jonathan's light skin and green eyes, function together with the métissage of their heritage to symbolically represent the ethnohistorical creolization of the colonial encounter through its cultural and discursive pluralism. Not only are they on occasion mistaken for mulattoes—Jonathan, for example, is taken for such by the vicar who ultimately baptises him (31/25)—in addition, Georges's expertise on the violin and Jonathan's ability to read inscribe them on the cusp of an artistic creativity that plays a critical role in engendering postcolonial subjectivity. An insistence on transgressing boundaries, particularly of the kind that marks Jonathan's identitarian struggle, amounts in effect to an overturning and reformulation of the status quo, recuperated in the discursive contestation traced by the novel itself.

For example, in section 2, titled "Jonathan's Notebook," writing, and its corollaries of fragmentation and displacement, are clearly primary in mediating the translation to the postcolonial. When we first encounter Jonathan, he is in the library at the Les Flamboyants plantation house, in the process of reading a long, italicized extract from the *Droit public des esclaves*, an extract that he tears from the text and later pastes into his secret notebook. This act of discursive appropriation and textual collage—an act of performative doubling that frames Jonathan as a progenitor of Guadeloupean and Antillean liberation—refracts and reframes proleptically the terms of both Maximin's and Marie-Gabriel's identitarian writing projects undertaken 150 years later; it functions in tandem with Jonathan's secretive discourse to engender an initiatory subversion, articulating alternative *topoi* of identity that bridge both past and present, and whose scriptive terms are effectively different from those imposed and disseminated by the master's discourse.

A short time later, Jonathan secretly shoots Elisa, the daughter of his mother's master, following the drunken attack on the plantation that occasions the rape and murder of his seven-year-old sister Angela by a group of colonial soldiers in search of two maroon slaves. More than a simple act of vengeance, this moment of sacrifice marks a parallel site of liberation on the ideological level, making possible a moment of *marronnage* that reinforces the notion of history as a protean force of translation and communication—punctuated by his symbolic planting of Angela's ring in the trunk of the mango tree, the ring retrieved by Marie-Gabriel centuries later at the beginning of the book—and leaves Jonathan free to initiate his own site of rebellion by himself joining a group of maroons, or runaway slaves.

The subsequent incorporation of the twins as autonomous subjects into the retelling of the epic episode of eighteenth-century Guadeloupean slave resistance to Napoleon's invading forces, led by the unheralded local hero Louis Delgrès—whose name finds an echo in Marie-Gabriel's prior naming of her father, "You'll call him Louis-Gabriel: Louis after Delgrès, incinerated in our memory, and Gabriel like your grandfather" (11/19)—valorizes Jonathan's seventeen years with the maroons as it simultaneously instantiates a performative site of discursive contestation, punctuated by a commentary made up of creole proverbs that generates a cultural counterpoint to Napoleonic efforts at the reinstallation of metropolitan domination and a discursive and ideological dispossession at the hands of the Other. From this perspective, Jonathan's linguistic ability and knowledge of the whites become a paradigm for a differential identitarian form of discursive contestation: "During seventeen years of freely chosen marooning, Jonathan was able to act as interpreter and coordinator, because he had learned several languages with his master, and was skilled at analyzing the whites' treatises and reports that fell into the maroons' possession" (49/53). The deliberate terms and conditions of Maximin's discourse allow it to compound the complexity of the notion of writing as a postcolonial praxis of resistance and recuperation.

Within the context of his own personal as well as the more general political background, the systematic program of pillage and revolt that Jonathan carries out against the slave society that subjugates him may also be read as resistance, the symbolic articulation of a figurative as well as a textual hybridity. As he seeks to inscribe his own trace upon the society through the institution of violence and terror, the métissage of his background effectively symbolizes both the need for a differential form of expression that goes beyond traditional boundaries and the culmination of the resistance carried out by Delgrès seen from a more creolized perspective, and this duality institutes the social and cultural ambivalence that his ethnic and political créolité represent.

As Georges and Jonathan meet their deaths through anticolonial struggle, the omniscient narrative that recounts this moment of Caribbean resistance is symbolically punctuated by a series of proverbs linking these acts to an indigenous network of cultural authenticity. While on the one hand these activities are meant to produce a valued sense of freedom, forged through struggle and self-affirmation, they simultaneously give rise to a critical doubleness of perspective whose practical paradoxes find perhaps their most forceful expression, in a further change of register, in the letter written to Jonathan by his brother Georges: "We reveal ourselves in the unnatural shades of our secret desires. . . . So thirsty to show that we know how to live and how to die, we go forward wearing a mask because the eyes of others have smashed the mirror of our brothers" (42–43, 37). Georges's articulation of the ambiguity and misapprehension permeating the structures of the social imaginary is effectively grounded in the space of the double displacement between the mask and the mirror, and acts as a harbinger of the binary oppositions bridging the roles of colonizer and colonized. This smashing of the image of the counterpart by the defining gaze of the Other has its roots in the desire and alienation of the colonial encounter, and the mask now marks an attempt, as Erickson suggests, "to counter this magisterial discourse that imposes upon the Antillean people the European Other's account and the Other's project for the future" (1992:126). Maximin's relocation and contestation of these canonical concepts of identity redefine the implications of a communal presence in the colonial project and, by deriving new paradigms and patterns of identity from acts of colonial resistance, establish a framework for the integration of hybrid sites of cultural and historical signification.

Perhaps the primary figure in this discursive and historical excavation is the reinscription of the 1802 Matouba massacre in Guadeloupe. In an episode that deliberately uncovers the untold history of resistance that figures a Guadeloupe discursively subjected to the interests of the colonizer, Maximin recreates the circumstances that had led up to Guadeloupe's submission to assimilation and Martinique's occupation by the British between 1794 and 1802—an act instigated by the Martinican planters to forestall the implementation of the abolition of slavery and the induction of the former slaves into French citizenship mandated by the Republic on 4 February 1794. When Napoleon dispatched his squadrons, led by Leclerc and Richepance, to reestablish the metropolitan rule of law, they were met by a nationalist group led by the mulatto governor, Magloire Pélage, commandant at Pointe-à-Pitre and of the entire region of Grande Terre, and the military officers Ignace and Delgrès. This group's insistence upon destroying themselves rather than submit to Napoleon's edict on the reimposition of slavery—and the armada he sent out to enforce it—is a key event of national resistance to colonial authority deliberately erased from colonial histories, and its symbolic significance as a site of identitarian independence cannot be overstated. Faced with an all but incluctable defeat, the Guadeloupean resistance forces, led by Louis Delgrès —a Martinican colonel who had settled in Guadeloupe—retreated to the Matouba heights on 8 May 1802, whence they threw themselves into the sea rather than surrender to the superior forces of the emperor.[2] While the importance of this act lies in its referential and symbolic resistance to imperial authority and to the inhumanity of slavery, its discursive recuperation renders it a strategic site of creolized identity construction both for the French islands and for the Caribbean at large. The participation of Georges and Jonathan in Maximin's re-citation of this occulted history is made an integral part of this act of discursive re-construction. Georges, who early on becomes secretary to Ignace, is blinded during the fray and dies with some fifty other survivors of a massacre on the Place de la Victoire when the ship on which they are eventually imprisoned is deliberately blown up in the harbor, and Jonathan meets his death fighting Richepance's troops alongside some five hundred other combatants, in an explosion caused by Delgrès's deliberate mining of the d'Anglemont plantation at Matouba. By re-citing these events as an integral part of the novel, Maximin endows them with an overwhelming cultural importance, inscribing through this discursive conflation of fiction and fact a framework for resistance and cultural identity that wrenches a symbolic victory from the jaws of defeat: "Guadeloupean resistance is certainly defeated, but a glorious, dignified defeat" (1986:37). This detailed integration of real and fictive characters with the unveiling of an indigenous history joins with the nonlinear, creatively fragmented discursive framework to interrogate the inherited bases, biases, and assumptions of Caribbean postcolonial history and subjectivity. Through this modernist decentering of narrative discourse and colonial history, Maximin clears the way for inscribing the conjunctions of a creolized Caribbean poetics, enacting new paradigms of postcolonial possibility. By exploding the principles of patriarchal linear narrative within a historicized context of Caribbean cultural performance, the novel connotes a metaphoric resiting of the discourse of the Other in order to inscribe new perspectives on the colonial encounter. Maximin's rewriting of historical events already written reveals the fragmentation and exclusion that have made this culture a reflection of the myriad influences underpinning its formation.

Thus the narrative also incorporates into the retold story of the revolt the characters of Miss Béa and Jonathan's mysterious younger sister, Ti-Carole, and implicates them, the "highly reputed old black woman who was always accompanied by a little girl with Yoruba braids" (59/63), in the death of Richepance, Napoleon's military commander; Miss Béa receives from him in return a letter detailing the cruelty of the whites toward the black slaves, which she secretly copies into Jonathan's notebook before passing it on to the Société des Amis des Noirs as a tool in the abolition struggle.

As Ti-Carole eventually learns to read and write from the same notebook (68/63), the role of discourse and fragmentation, repetition and doubling as talismanic icons of identitarian reconstruction is insistently and increasingly enhanced, emphasizing through the central, inescapable role given to writing and discursive appropriation the critical importance of Marie-Gabriel's writing project in the present for the (re)generation of identity from the traces of the past. Miss Béa perishes in the great Caribbean earthquake of 1843 that destroyed the entire city of Pointe-à-Pitre and decimated the neighboring islands of Antigua and St. Kitts, but the lineage of the family is tangentially traced through the repeated birth of twin sons and the symbolic repetition of the number seven as denotative sign of ages and time spans. In addition, Jonathan's notebook is continually passed on—Ti-Carole uses its secret texts in the lessons she gives in French dictation (68/63), and her granddaughter, Louise, will receive the notebook from her as a gift at age seven (77/72). Ti-Carole's sons are significantly given the names Ignace and Louis, and are born after a seven-month gestation in the same year that Basse-Terre is destroyed by fire. All three perish in the earthquake that leveled Pointe-à-Pitre on 25 March 1897—"the seventh fury of Shango since 1802" (79/75)—but Ti-Carole's granddaughter, Louise, survives by holding on to Jonathan's notebook, having sneaked outside early that morning to bury it at the foot of the silk-cotton tree. While the text reminds us that the eruption of Mt. Pelée in Martinique came almost exactly one hundred years to the day after the insurrection of May 1802, Louise, in turn, also gives birth to the twin sons Jean-Louis (named after her husband in an additional incidence of doubling) and Louis-Gabriel in 1917, thus perpetuating, as the text indicates, the initials of Georges and Jonathan as well as the historical memory of Louis Delgrès. Louis-Gabriel, having sneaked off to listen to a Haitian orchestra's rehearsal, will by pure chance be the sole survivor of a hurricane that will kill his parents and brother in 1928, and grows up to be the father of Marie-Gabriel, a jazz musician and, perhaps even more important, one "specializing in improvisation" (81/77).

Contrary to the Derridean position taken by Chris Bongie, whose claim that "for Maximin, the affirmation of an ancestral identity can only be a . . .

gesture that further distances us from it, and propels us ever deeper into a . . . culturalized present" (1994:629) appears blind to these (re)inscriptions of history, I argue that through the construction of the preceding genealogical chronology, fictive though it might be, and particularly through the diachronic inscription of repetition, coincidence, and difference, Maximin's discourse engenders a creole poetics of Caribbean difference that sets the parameters for future articulations of nonocculted identity. To this end, our *mise en valeur* of the importance of anagrammatic transposition in Maximin's discursive and cultural exegesis underlines the significance of symbols of doubling and repetition as they come to assume an archetypal force in the text, reiterating and re-presenting a new creole temporality of difference that bridges both past and future post/colonial discursive subjects.

It is, in fact, the very basis of the discursive context through which the Caribbean has historically been defined that Maximin effectively interrogates and relocates. He uncovers the unwritten history of the region by inserting into the narrative untold accounts of indigenous uprisings and the violence and brutality perpetrated against them, massacres which were the corollaries of colonial conquest and the revolts that were the hallmark of resistance. By locating and rewriting these postcolonial sites, Maximin's reinscription of these efforts at self-definition signifies the creation of a postcolonial counterdiscourse where resistance is grounded in the resonances of the creole, mapping a new space for identity which supplants the historical authority of the master's discourse. As Erickson points out, "Marie-Gabriel's/Maximin's rewriting of history involves not only a break from colonialist history . . . but from patriarchal history and the dominant male narrative as well" (127).

The deliberate disjunctures of this discourse thus accomplish the instantiation of a double time of difference. On the one hand, Maximin's institution of an alternative regional temporality demonstrates narratologically that since historical discourse itself is predicated on narrative structures, it is thus subject to the same undecidabilities as other forms of narration. As Hayden White argues, "This value attached to narrativity in the representation of real events arises out of a desire to have real events display the coherence, integrity, fullness, and closure of an image of life that is and can only be imaginary" (1981:23). The result of Maximin's deliberate conflation and subversion of history and fiction is thus to undermine the imaginary authoritarian linearities promulgated by the colonizer, to expose the misrepresentations inherent in the colonial monopoly of discourse, and to offer an alternative to this form of discursive hegemony. Second, by confronting the discursive assumptions of colonialism with the repressed figures of its Other, he succeeds in inscribing the pluralisms of a postcolonial alterity as a framework for cultural autonomy.

Maximin's incorporation of eleven Guadeloupean creole proverbs into the already complex discursive fragment called "Jonathan's Notebook" provides another striking aspect of narrative creolization. Inscribed as a subsection of the "Notebook" titled "Eleven Proverbs," enclosed in parentheses, written in capitals, and sequentially set off from the rest of the text, they symbolically punctuate and comment upon his extended account of nineteenth-century Guadeloupean resistance to French hegemony, which is itself enclosed within quotation marks. In short, both text and proverbs assume the function of an embedded narrative, a separate discourse commenting upon the structural and thematic assumptions underlying the encounter with metropolitan colonialism and culture. The strategic positioning of these proverbs in the text functions not only as a sign of *oraliture,* inscribing the oral trace of an indigenous collective memory, but also as a hybrid site of narrative transformation and difference. The syncopated structure of these alternative ideologies engenders a supplementary space, such that in the interval between their iteration there ultimately appears that alternate temporality of creole hybridity which is the mark of his postcolonial praxis. Through the discursive content of the proverbs themselves, "WHERE THERE ARE BONES, WHERE THERE ARE DOGS. . . . COAL IS NOT FLOUR, FLOUR IS NOT COAL" (40–41/45, 46, 52), the narrative articulates a symbolic level of creole cultural signification that opens up new sites and possibilities from the desiderata of the colonial encounter between Africa and Europe. Most important, however, the addition of a twelfth proverb as a specific counterpoint both to the subtitle and to Jonathan's interaction with the Guadeloupean national leader Delgrès embodies this supplementarity and functions both analeptically and proleptically as a thematic inscription of the role played by exile and resistance in the community of cultural identity: "Go to the village where you don't have a house, but take your roof with you" (56/52). The *bracelet à proverbes* that Jonathan passes to Delgrès, the last of twelve he has carved, while whispering to him the proverb whose meaning is hidden in the bracelet's form, just before the final battle (51/56), is eventually recuperated by this final phrase; its simultaneous fusion of the discursive and the creole herald the inscription of emergent paradigms of nation*ness* by tilling the new terrain of identity and culture. These analeptic and proleptic cultural references disturb the linearities of colonial diegesis; simultaneously, their inscription of resistance and contestation enhances the significance of historically marginalized discourses and subjects as creative sites of dislocation, difference, and identitarian definition.

Doubling the Frame

A short central section that mediates between both halves of the novel, itself also titled "L'Isolé Soleil," establishes a multiplicity of structural and thematic linkages between the twin writing projects of author and narrator. The section begins with a letter to Marie-Gabriel, "the chosen sister," from her friend Adrien, in Paris, who finds Marie-Gabriel "getting ready to rewrite the account of the epic of Louis Delgrès, so fascinating to our poets and historians" (81/85), the same epic, in fact, that we have just read. By thus deliberately breaking the narrative line, commenting on and taking stock of Marie-Gabriel's work-in-progress through the already read, the narrator's self-reflexive turn emphasizes the critical role of *writing* in this project, and her inclusion of Adrien's correspondence recuperates the repeated additions to Jonathan's notebook that we see at work in the narrative itself. At the end of this section, the metafictional structure of this novel that continually comments on its own ongoing construction has been clearly established, and Marie-Gabriel's response points out to Adrien that "the real pleasure of letters for me is when we can reread them together, with our eyes and voices in correspondence" (104/107), thus drawing on similar patterns of discursive linearity to refer proleptically to the novel itself as finished product. As the exchange of letters bracketing this section traces the novel's construction by conflating the absent epistolary object with the fragmentary extracts of these twin notebooks, the large central fragment comprising Adrien's "Writing Notebook," framed by these scripts, assumes increasing importance. Not coincidentally, it is narrated in the first person, and comprises thirteen numbered subfragments that echo, structurally and thematically, through the presence of a last, supplementary addition, the commentary included in the "Eleven Proverbs" (become twelve) of "Jonathan's Notebook." In their turn, these subfragments allow the narrator to speak, through the missives of Adrien, of desires and paradoxes underlying his cultural inscription in Guadeloupe since childhood. In these sequential subfragments, with titles like "Project, Africa, M.-G.," "Colonized Body," and "Project for a Novel," he chronicles a subjective trajectory of alienation: from romanticized schoolboy notions of an Africa that is "the absent mother of my childhood" (88/92), to racism at a Parisian lycée. This racism, intriguingly, is less disconcerting than the displacements of home, and not least because of the important role ultimately ascribed to his double: "Paris did less to alienate me than the Antilles of my childhood. Because the sun hid from me the shadow of my double, who grew up without disturbing my solitude, until the moment when I was uprooted" (93/96). The cultural and discursive binaries of this section make it a point of convergence for the tropes and figures of an articulative creoleness, and make writing the medium that enacts the double-voiced re-vision of the colonial encounter.

This passage, then, marks an important interrogation of the twin axes of colonialism and desire. As Adrien addresses the pervasive nature of alienation and doubling, repetition and pluralism in the colonial context, it is in this moment that the conjunction between colonialism and ambivalence is simultaneously appropriated and interrogated through the incorporation of the counterpart, an other of the complex, fragmented colonial ego: "My double has been settled inside me since I was a child. . . . . he protected me from alienation in a white world. . . . So what I did was to colonize my double. . . . I internalized the combat as a basic confrontation between my body and my conscience, my desires and my image; even when I am completely engaged in playing a role . . . according to my wishes or the wishes of others, I have always been able to keep silently sheltered behind the shield of my double that quality that remains essential for achieving real autonomy some day" (94–95, 97–98). Maximin's transposition of the ambivalence of colonial authority into alternating layers of autonomy and duality, through the multiple misprisions of the colonial relation, interrogates and relocates the entire colonial undertaking from the perspective of differential patterns of desire, recognition, and repression. For by colonizing his colonially engendered double—another who is me—to protect himself against white-engendered alienation, Adrien reverses and appropriates colonial patterns of power, inverting and translating this gesture into a hybrid metaphor of resistance, a resiting and reinvestiture of colonial paradigms of division that simultaneously animate the complex intersections of the colonial experience. Indeed, it is by intervening in the binary relation between recognition and alienation, through the dislocation of psychoanalytic structures that have traditionally been bound up with the patterns and corollaries of colonial authority, that Adrien subverts the ambivalence intrinsic to a colonial discourse in order to appropriate the paradoxical possibility of autonomy from the incluctable positional slippage between colonizer and colonized.

As a subversive attack upon the authority of colonial discourse, Adrien's gesture evokes the inversions that we see at work in Homi Bhabha's paradigm of colonial mimicry. This appropriation of the ambivalence that is inscribed within colonial hierarchies functions through key strategies of doubling and temporal disarticulation, in that the articulation of a simulacrum of colonial power allows difference as the not-quite-Other to become visible. As Bhabha writes, "Mimicry emerges as the representation of a difference that is itself a process of disavowal. Mimicry is thus the sign of a double articulation . . . which 'appropriates' the Other as it visualizes power" (1994:86). It is through the transformative tension implicit in the slippage of the sign that the repetition and recolonization of the double discloses the signature of ambivalence; within such a framework, as Bhabha continues, this discursive act of differential repetition "articulates those disturbances of cultural, racial and historical difference that menace the narcissistic demand of colonial authority" (88). The resulting alienation of colonial desire reinscribes the colonial subject as the product of a critical doubling, subverting the dominant discourse by revealing and resiting its structural modalities. The originary discourses of the colonial encounter are thus constantly revisited, resisted, and reversed through the inscription of an alternative set of hierarchies that explode these assumptions of colonial authority from within.

The ambivalence at work in this moment of translation also uses the uncertainties intrinsic to these doubled hierarchies of the colonial encounter to redraw certain constructs of the Lacanian model of the mirror stage. While in this context subjective definition by means of a fictional construct is at once definitive of alienation, it is in the distance and the ambiguity simultaneously linking and separating the subject and its reflection that subversion of this ambivalence is made possible. In the colonial context of confrontation between Adrien's desire and his image, between his desire—already the desire of the Other—and the reflection of alterity from which he expediently fashions a latent autonomy, the possibility of postcolonial subjectivity takes shape from the assimilation and appropriation of the Other. The specular space opened up between the fictional coherence of the image and the simultaneous disjuncture of its appropriation, generated by this recolonizing but transformative gesture whose constant axes are artifice and alterity, translates colonial polarities of self and Other into a hybrid sign of creolization whose selective shield recolonizes the double into a framework that remains similar yet is also critically different from its original site.

Maximin's goal, then, is to redraw the boundaries of the postcolonial condition by interrogating and contesting the traditional teleologies of colonial patterns and structures, instantiating a praxis that Clarisse Zimra aptly calls "the desire to rewrite Caribbean history from within" (1992:268). He achieves this by exposing colonialism's hierarchical patterns of duality and exclusion, subverting and displacing the dominant discourse of the colonizer's desire, and replacing the linear binarisms of the already written by appropriating and resiting the very boundaries of the colonizer's language in which he must write. Thus he rearticulates colonialism's anxious, ambivalent authority through a hybrid poetics of difference. In the penultimate twelfth section of Adrien's "Writing Notebook," titled "Genealogy," the structural and thematic preamble to the later section "Siméa's Journal" takes shape. Indeed, the text inscribes not only the named and symbolic counterparts of both Siméa and Adrien, but also, through the family's departure for France during the eruption of the Soufrière volcano in 1956, the sequel to *L'Isolé Soleil* that bears the volcano's name. Through the demise of her friend and namesake, and that of her only brother, Adrien, in French Guiana in 1943, Siméa is made the central figure in the complex network of doubled figures that grounds the remainder of the novel, allowing the narrative to trace a subjective and thematic genealogy that will culminate with the appearance of the author himself at the novel's end.

Thus the novel puts into place an alternative vision of the Caribbean cultural subject, contesting the terms of colonial history even as it constructs a framework for a creolized Caribbean subjectivity; as Zimra states, "Maximin locates this birth of Caribbean awareness in the present" (1992:275). Both Marie-Gabriel and her mother, we are told in the novel's opening pages, have read and reread Suzanne Césaire's poem that appeared in the last issue of *Tropiques*, published in the very month of Marie-Gabriel's birth; the marginal notes and annotations that are the mark of their own textual (re)construction of Caribbean subjectivity constitute an intertextual framework that again stages (re)writing as the core of the relational aesthetics that the novel seeks to inscribe.

The thirteenth and final section of this notebook, titled "Identity," inscribes the postcolonial imbrication of language and identity in anagrammatic form:

"I wanted to be SOLEIL / SUN / I played with words. I found ISOLE / LONE" (102/105). The principles of re-placement, re-citation, doubling, and transposition intrinsic to the figure of the anagram are of key importance in the wider web of signification woven by the text, and provide in fact a remarkable allegory of the novel's overall strategy of appropriation and reinvention. The protean intricacies of translation and recreation, of change and metamorphosis signified by this process recuperate, on a symbolic level, the goal of (re)constructing an occulted identity from the palimpsest of a dominant colonial discourse. As Erickson points out, "Its repetitive use within the novel transforms it into an allegory for the strategy of the novel itself (Maximin's), as well as the novel within a novel (Marie-Gabriel's) and the search by both author and character to recast past events into a new configuration, a new history of the Antilles" (1992:122–23). These hybrid patterns of change shift the locus of the (re)writing strategy from the colonial margin to the postcolonial center as they instigate a creolized process of discursive and subjective performance that (re)defines the Caribbean *logos*.

With the opening of part 4, the narrative undergoes a stunning structural and discursive reversal. To this point, as Marie-Gabriel concurrently addresses the reader as well as her younger self, using the death of her father, Louis-Gabriel, to contextualize discursive acts yet to come, the critical importance of writing has effectively bridged the autoreferential economy of the narrative's doubled temporality: "With natural colors close at hand you'll blacken all the pages whitened by his ashes" (10/18). Following the ruminations of this central, intermediary section, the alternative articulations of sections 4 and 5, "Siméa's Journal" and "Mother's Song," inscribe, so to speak, a discursive balancing act to the historical set pieces of sections 1 and 2. Set in early twentieth-century Paris, and working now from a perceptibly feminine perspective which simultaneously dismantles the authoritarian discursive and historical precepts that are the corollary of colonialism, these sections set up a narrative order whose persistent principles of discursive contestation and dislocation firmly establish the deliberate difference of postcolonial identity and culture. (Re)writing culture and subjectivity from the gendered perspective of the subjected allows the (re)creation of pluralized discursive sites; as Ronnie Scharfman suggests, "He [Maximin] thereby stages the writing issue as one of generation and engendering, but not one bound by the constraints of gender" (1992:236).

In "Siméa's Journal," then, in a major shift of voice and perspective, the first-person narrative constructs an (auto)biography of the generation of Parisian Antilleans of the 1930s and 1940s, taking negritude and the *Cahier* as its discursive *toile de fond*. By fragmenting the individual characters of Marie-Gabriel's mother's name, Siméa, and assimilating them to an assortment of artifacts drawn on an intertextual and intercultural framework, it generates a vision of synthesis and intersection that (re)defines francophone culture from a persistently extrahexagonal perspective. These discursive *lieux de mémoire* include Rimbaud's *Une Saison en enfer*, Breton's *Clair de terre*, Eluard's *Capitale de la douleur*, the negritude journal *Légitime Défense*, and Césaire's *Cahier d'un retour au pays natal*. While each letter of the name is simultaneously present in the title to which it corresponds, the intertextual crosstalk of these various discourses allows the first-person female Antillean narrator— and, by extension, the myriad counterparts in whose name she speaks—rebirth and self-definition by symbolizing the myriad influences, or métissage, of her cultural exposure, generating contestation and constitution as the ground of her own defining moment.

The pain of Siméa's pregnancy by a French architecture student and the subsequent forced abortion become the engendering events that make her cultural identity the product of the creole concatenations of the colonial relationship, constituting it through the figure of the aborted child she addresses in the second person, and through an affiliative discourse of loss and recreation. As Scharfman points out, "Siméa's journal is her attempt to deconstruct the hold these poetic voices have over her at the same time that she constructs her own text out of them. The verbal violence of this section is . . . an active response of revolt against the violence to which she has been subjected" (1992:239).

Indeed, on a more complex level of signification, the narrative uses Siméa's condition to engender identity out of subjection, addressing the aborted fetus through a combination of the second-person singular and the first-person plural and so inscribing herself and, metonymically, her Guadeloupean homeland as products of colonial miscegenation: "My whole land devastated, my vagina pummeled. Your corpse ripped out of my ruins; and now, isolation and darkness" (112/113). It is clear that this recuperated hybridization, this harmonization of voices, emphasizes the métissage and pluralism of creolization as the enabling gestures of a postcolonial identity firmly inscribed on the symbolic and the narrative levels. Through the address to her aborted offspring, Siméa effectively not only reconstructs the identity of this lost creole child but engenders an identity for all the victims of colonial and cultural oppression. The second-person address of Siméa also revalorizes the role of the feminine voice in Antillean history as it simultaneously enlarges on an earlier observation by Marie-Gabriel: "If we listen to our poets and revolutionaries, our novelists and their historians, the only function of black women is to give birth to our heroes" (105/108). Siméa's journal is thus a *prise de la parole* on behalf of those who cannot speak for themselves, a deliberate slippage from subjectivity to solidarity that reinvents identities even as it recuperates key discourses of the negritude movement in contemporary Paris: "I need the hand of a woman, sun-woman, black sun, good nigger black, good maroon nigger for my self defense, my legitimate defense" (115/117). As the names and discourses of Léro, Ménil, Damas, and Césaire repeat and circulate, their symbolic power seems to converge in a single remarkable moment of direct intertextual address: "Give me back my black poets, give me back my black doll, Damas. . . . And give back to me Césaire, of all the *Wills* offered in the *Notebook* that I've just learned by heart" (119/120). By appropriating and rewriting the terms of the French Caribbean discursive heritage, Maximin engages with and transforms the already written; such discourses also encounter the intertextual inscription of phrases that appear, remarkably, to echo themes and images from other writers working in the present. When Adrien, in his letter to Marie-Gabriel, points out that "to be born into real life we must by a second birth uproot ourselves from their paternal womb" (82/86), his words appear to echo those of Maryse Condé's protagonist Véronica, in *En Attendant le bonheur*, who voyages to Africa in order to fulfill her own wish to return to her "maternal womb." This network of textual references reinforces the impact of these works as icons of interstitial identity, analeptic and proleptic markers in a literary and cultural landscape of creole authenticity.

Section 5, "Mother's Song," functions as a re-presentation of the disjunctures and anomalies underscoring colonial alienation. Importantly, it opens with a critically differential reinscription of the twelfth proverb from "Jonathan's Notebook," but this time playing on the symbolism of *toit/toi* to reinscribe identity: "You traveled toward *yourself*, toward the village where you didn't have a house" (147/150; emphasis mine). By marking this site as one of textual and temporal transformation, this phrase re-cites and rephrases the symbolic resurgence of this critically important figure, successfully reorienting, particularly at this juncture in the narrative, the critical interaction between culture and resistance by doubling and modifying the discursive framework, and reminding us that, with their displacement to the metropole in 1956,

Siméa and Louis-Gabriel "didn't forget to take the island in their luggage, dreams, and daily meals" (101/104). Further, this phrase deliberately exploits an intrinsic phonic ambiguity in the text in order to emphasize the significance of the differential identity it inscribes, signaling Marie-Gabriel's (re)construction of the identity of both self and counterpart through writing.

Then, switching to the second person, a strategy which clearly reflects a fundamental displacement of identity, Marie-Gabriel recreates her mother's story, inscribing the second notebook she was found holding at the beginning of the novel, while inventing her identity through the second-person address. This interweaving of the analeptic and the proleptic joins with the ambiguity of alienation and intimacy inscribed in the second-person address to culminate in the account of Siméa's return from Paris, her death in labor in 1945 and the simultaneous (re)birth of Marie-Gabriel as a discursive figure, and, implicitly, her symbolic liberation from paternal paradigms of colonial authority and textuality. The deliberate instability of the narrative perspective works through the reinscription of a plethora of discursive figures already at work within the narrative, to show that writing as a project of self-constitution may ultimately be read as symbolic of the novel's entire narrative strategy. Marie-Gabriel is symbolically reinscribed here as the mother of her mother's text, the latter simultaneously her interlocutor and discursive progenitor of her daughter's textuality. In the symbolic circularity of these texts and subjects there lies a world of creolized displacement.

By extending the parameters of displacement, Marie-Gabriel's narrative re-reads and extends the doubling of the discursive frame signified by the twins to the discontinuities of France's wartime occupation of Guadeloupe and Martinique: "And yet the twins, Martinique and Guadeloupe, almost became the center of resistance of the Free French Movement" (148/151). The spirit of survival that is the corollary of this period is summed up by the eventual reappearance of Jonathan's notebook; along with such icons of cultural affirmation as Césaire's *Tropiques* and his *Cahier*, it eventually symbolizes the extent to which resistance to the discourse of the colonial encounter by appropriating and resiting its boundaries is ineluctably bound up with issues of transformation and hybridity. An extract from Siméa's letter to the Césaires makes this clear: "We will recreate the poetry of the Antilles, blues sculpted in stone, our cry of pebbles polished by the sea. Yes, let us make our insults into diamonds" (157/159). As the narrator proceeds to interweave figures from the African-American struggle of the late twentieth century with transformational metaphors drawn on the improvisational jazz played by her father, Louis-Gabriel, she again reinscribes the strategy of repetition and transposition that is at the basis of the project whose birth we are witnessing.

This fragment culminates in a critical encounter: Louis-Gabriel's reading of the well-known article by Suzanne Césaire, "Qu'est-ce que le Martiniquais?" in an issue of the periodical *Tropiques*, placed symbolically beside two textual icons of the negritude movement's contribution to Caribbean identity—Léon-Gontran Damas's *Pigments*, and Aimé Césaire's *Cahier* published in the periodical *Volontés*. Louis-Gabriel's perusal of the April 1942 article in *Tropiques* quickly becomes, more precisely, his reading of Siméa's marginal annotation of it, her first-person gloss of the dicta enunciated by Césaire: "It's up to us to invent a future, without expecting much from the African past and the European present. I think that *identification is the enemy of identity*. We shouldn't first look for someone to identify with before we act. . . . Don't all Antilleans belong to one civilization? . . . I am necessarily Antillean, and Guadeloupean only by accident!" (191/192–93; emphasis in the original). Critically, here, the value that attaches to this identitarian declaration occurs in Louis-Gabriel's reading of Siméa's gloss rather than in Césaire's text itself, drawing together the web of signification elaborated by improvisational jazz, principles of discursive translation and transformation, and his reading of this text that responds to Suzanne Césaire within the journal itself. Together, these patterns engender Marie-Gabriel's ongoing writing project to literally (re)invent identity, articulating new patterns of creole cultural authenticity. The future will be grounded and located not by the implied sameness and fixity of a single historical *identification*—echoing Glissant's description of the practice of Reversion from the *Discours antillais*, and contravening the openness of the multivocal writing project that refracts an *identity* in movement—or of the traditionally accepted cultural axes of this displaced and transplanted society—neither in the African past nor in the European present—but in a site of exchange and transition that is more than either or both, less than either one, but, significantly, symbolically double. The initiatory declaration of a pluralized, common regional Caribbean identity that is articulated here derives its importance from the place and context of its enunciation.

As Louis-Gabriel's ruminations continue, they are ultimately engendered from the ancestral traces of the letter addressed by Georges to Jonathan, "a letter he had learned by heart, sent in 1802, by a certain Georges to his brother, Jonathan. Louis-Gabriel offered himself the pleasure of believing that this

Georges was one of his ancestors, because he was a fine violinist and composer of merengues" (192/193). With the reinscription of the second of the creole proverbs punctuating the uprising of 1802, and taught to him and his twin brother, Jean-Louis, by their mother, Louise, the repetition and improvisation of creolization and jazz are now generative of this incipient, interstitial identity. Already a coda and commentary to the Delgrès uprising two hundred years before, this key phrase, "Coal is not flour, flour is not coal" (193/192), now serves to bracket the trajectory of the family history being traced from past to present by Marie-Gabriel, and to underscore once again the important role played by symbolic and iconic repetition in the text. For as the divisions marked by this proverb usher in an extract from a letter written by Georges to Jonathan and entered in the latter's notebook, a talisman passed down through the family from generation to generation and which Louis-Gabriel keeps always in his possession, the re-citation of this fragment, learned by heart by Louis-Gabriel although remaining dimly understood by him, describes and defines the dangerous dichotomies that strew the path toward identitarian authenticity: "Freedmen live in dread of being like trumpet-tree leaves, green on top and white underneath . . . a sort of supplement of humanity, which makes us endlessly give the whites proof of our merits, or their iniquity" (192/193–94). This symbolic resurgence of Georges's letter, which by being read across time by both Jonathan and Louis-Gabriel—and, presumably, by the family members in between—continuously redoubles its resonances by deferring its destination, engages the difficulties of self-definition and the risks of purely dialectical aproaches to cultural subjectivity. It is through these repeated moments of almost imperceptible difference that the cycle of repetition allows the opening up of a strategic discursive space, ultimately engendering new sites of difference and identity marked by the aggregate symbolic assemblage contained by Marie-Gabriel's writing project.

This continuous, insistent exchange and redoubling of letters and proverbs, fragments and meanings, symbols and subjective positions reassert the undeniable primacy of cultural translation and its corollary of diversity in a creolized context of difference: "Observe your identical portrait and see how it is so exactly false compared to the image . . . that image . . . that can only come to your eyes from the mirror of the eyes of the other" (258/258–59). It is the translation of that doubled displacement from the mirror into a differential discourse of contestation which ultimately formulates and locates postcolonial identity within the region; an identity which, as the narrator insists, must reflect the plurality of the regional subject as a site of identitarian inscription: "Of course, here in the Antilles, we're first of all blacks, but then we are blacks of America, and Europeanized blacks of America. Our authenticity must be based on respect for our triple origins" (224/225). By underscoring the ineluctability of these multiple subject positions that are the region's inheritance, the narrator's textual recuperation of the experience of fragmentation becomes the defining sign of the text's discourse of difference.

Ultimately, it is the ambiguity and pluralism that inescapably undergird the postcolonial process that Maximin seeks to underscore in this narrative. The continuous alternation between epistolary discourse and third-person narration in "Thus Exile Departs," the novel's sixth and final section, positions this postcolonial praxis under an overarching sign of protean possibilities. The section comprises a series of letters exchanged between Antoine, Adrien, and Marie-Gabriel; its headings count down, in reverse, from fourteen to one, the end of the novel in fact simultaneously constituting a beginning, as the text's final act takes us back to the threshold of the writing project we have just read. Not only do these fourteen subsections double the symbolic number seven that has recurred at several critical moments in the text, they revise and re-echo the thirteen subfragments of Adrien's "Writing Notebook" that Marie-Gabriel has already incorporated into part 3; the poetic, supplementary, interventionist coda, signed by Daniel, the author himself, sums up the differential space of the community in whose name this project has been accomplished.

Maximin's contestatory counterdiscourse re-marks this (non)ending by recuperating an economy of epistolary exchange for an ending that brings the text full circle, introducing characters and repeating proverbs and phrases already encountered to engender new metonymies of signification from the contiguity of old and new, past, present, and future. Letter number 12, signed by Eve, ends with an iconic reinscription of Jonathan's bracelet: "For tonight, lone sun slips on my wrist the bracelet of Jonathan" (262/261), while letter number 10, signed by Adrien, evokes Jonathan's notebook through its reference to the journal kept by his descendant, Louis-Gabriel—the very journal Marie-Gabriel awaits when the novel opens—and announces its inscription of an intersubjective, affiliative articulation of nation*ness* through its re-placement of a traditional salutation by the phrase "Beginning of my history" (264/263); the stories of Adrien, of Louis-Gabriel, and of us all are re-cited and relocated by our textual encounter with these ongoing moments of recreation and reiteration.

The ineluctable multivalency of cross-cultural identity for the postcolonial Caribbean subject is continuously reaffirmed in the narrative discourse through the continuous (re)invention and repetition of episodes and identities already read. In a letter to Adrien signed "Aime-Gabriel" (M-Gabriel), the narrator speaks of her intention to reformulate in her novel the scene of Elisa's death: "I'm going to change the episode in my novel where I describe the death of Master Alliot's daughter Elisa; I got the idea from one of the projects in your Writing Notebook (the death of the little Elisa before the eyes of Geneviève and Jenny, her two little slave companions)" (269/269), thus recalling both Adrien's version of this episode under the heading "Project for a Novel" (98–99/101–2), and its earlier appearance, in a slightly different guise, in "Jonathan's Notebook"; as metafiction is made to follow fictional history, "J . . . the young slave, will now be the one who shoots her" (37). And in a letter to Antoine, Adrien speaks of receiving from Marie-Gabriel Georges's letter to Jonathan from the latter's notebook: "Marie-Gabriel sent me her letter from Georges to Jonathan, the maroon of 1802; she wants to add it to her novel" (282/280). This is a remarkabe double citation of the original letter in this subsequent letter, which itself refers to a novelistic episode (not yet) already written, in the text whose coming creation we continue to witness.

Indeed, the associative, dialogic identitarian principle underlying the entire project is reiterated by Antoine: "First of all, the language: discoveries, turns of phrase, associations of words-ideas, but all so natural as if flowing from the source . . . the precision of historical documentation, a clear departure from common knowledge (major events) in order to show us the form of the chronicle. . . . *It's above all the exiled sun that I read between your lines, the search for a dialogue between writings, even more than the accomplishment of your writing alone*" (272–74/271–73; emphasis mine). It is by reading between the lines that this decentering of writing and history will achieve the inscription of a cultural identity that constitutes the communal experience through the discursive re-presentation of its intrinsic pluralism. Through these constant realignments and revisions of the narrative site, Maximin's principle of allegorical and anagrammatical dis-placement engenders the identitarian pluralism that both undergirds and is re-produced by these discursive intersections, thus ascribing to them a primordial value in his re-construction of cultural authenticity. For if, indeed, as Peter Brooks argues, "repetition always takes place in the realm of the symbolic—in the transference, in language— where the affects and figures of the past are confronted in symbolic form"

(1984:124), then it is in the nature of this discursive repetition and translation that textual strategies of representation are (re)defined and, in so doing, initiate new signs and acts of a collaborative cultural difference. The economy of exchange and transformation from which the novel takes its title enacts performatively its own authority while interrogating the discursive and cultural production that has preceded it.

As this insistent process of doubling and substitution ultimately joins the character of Angela to the American Black Power activist Angela Davis, based on a brief stopover she made in Guadeloupe in 1969, and Guadeloupe's Georges and Jonathan to California's Soledad Brothers, George and Jonathan Jackson, these temporal intersections of resistance and revolt continue to widen and redefine the context of regional identity through its pan-American points of reference and recall the narrator's concept of Caribbean identity as the product of an ongoing cultural interaction between the transplanted blacks of the Americas. Yet the commonality of their experience, the incessant repetitions of struggle against and subversion of a hierarchical discourse of history written by the Other, is what informs this re-vision of the borders of identity and desire: "We have to pirate history and writing, stick our hooks into their culture across the expanse of our three continents" (274/273). Having recounted the deaths of George and Jonathan in Letter 3, Marie-Gabriel makes a final discursive gesture to Angela in the re-citation of the original version of Jonathan's twelfth proverb; here, in its third iteration, it effectively joins *toi* and *toit*, past, present, and future, the Caribbean and the Americas, into a single identitarian sign of community and contestation: "Don't ever forget my bracelet: travel to the village where you don't have a house, but always take your roof with you" (280/279). End as beginning, the novel as days of future passed; above all, as Daniel points out in the first/last letter which he signs with his own name, finally adding his own voice to the chorus of epistolary communication: "No outcome, certainly no ending" (282/281); the deliberate displacement of the sutures and slippages of the narrative process render the end of this self-reflexive project also the beginning of a new era of writing and identity.

This text engages both the institution and the transformation of the postcolonial condition, generating agency from the resonances of a preterite colonial temporality; both discourse and characters "refuse the chronological linearity of ready-made narratives by the ancestors," as Zimra writes, preferring instead to generate a creative framework that "delights in multiple Caribbean intertextualities, openly as well as obliquely" (1999:193). Maximin re-presents Guadeloupe subject to colonial domination as a Guadeloupe become object of a profane desire, its struggle for affirmation that draws on the traces of its discontinuous history confronting the colonialist's desire for recognition, and generating in turn the multiplicity and intertextuality that form the crux of a discursive context of resistance.[3] His foregrounding of writing as a primary constituent of postcolonial praxis recognizes the important role of discourse in the contestation of colonial overdetermination, as the novel's conflation of fragmentation and pluralism instantiates temporalities that ultimately proceed of their own volition: "Desire will open our mouths to continue our story with the book closed" (282/280).

This work, then, articulates a counterdiscourse that effectively challenges the ineluctable continuity of the unitary colonial voice in working through the ambiguities of postcolonial identity: "From the debris of synthesis in fragments of a plural, isle and wing, *Ile* and *aile*, he and she, it is us, *désirades* outstretched close together in the agreement between names, music, and acts, an alliance of dreams and awakenings" (283/281). This counterdiscourse validates the complexities of Caribbean identity by grounding it in the attendant corollaries of a Caribbean history regained; in the larger symbolic order, its accomplishment, as Françoise Lionnet succinctly puts it, of "a means of cultural representation that can do justice to the heterogeneities of the present and to the absent categories of the past" (1995:40), serves to organize the complex re-location, identification, and refashioning of the borders of a regional culture in which its present dualities refract those of its past as well as its future intricacies.

Soufrières: Exploding the Encounter

Similar principles are also at work in Maximin's second novel, *Soufrières*. Ostensibly a narrative centered on the real, in that it takes as its point of departure the threatened eruption of Guadeloupe's Soufrière volcano in 1976, this work evokes the evacuations, departures, and spirit of endurance occasioned by the looming crisis. Maximin addresses similar themes of writing, vocality, and creativity in this work, in which the unstable temporalities and teleologies of a contemporary reality all but constitute a sequel to *L'Isolé Soleil*. Significantly, however, the trajectory of the action of *Soufrières* is completed before the manuscript of *L'Isolé Soleil* has been written. However, such an assertion should by no means be read as implying that the action of *Soufrières* is temporally located *within* the framework of its predecessor. Indeed, given the critical metafictional cast of *L'Isolé Soleil*, we should perhaps remind ouselves that its script was given over to the composition and consolidation of the *writing project* which would eventually become the published novel. Both novels may together be construed as a discursive and thematic whole, then, which explains their exegetical joining here; at the same time, enough parallels and differences emerge between both works that even given the reappearance of several of the main characters, *Soufrières* remains a narrative whose treatment of issues of culture and identity construction centers on a sense of survival, a context of contestation tempered by recurring resonances of modernism in the novel's discursive praxis.

Among those characters who make their reappearance, perhaps the most important are Marie-Gabriel and her friend Adrien. Having survived the complex devices and desires involved in generating cultural identity by rewriting both its past and its present, they find this existence threatened by the imminent eruption of the Soufrière volcano and the certainty of its disrupting even the limited cultural autonomy they have been able to put into discursive practice. By putting their physical and cultural courage to the test, the volcano forces them to come to terms with the fragility of their existence, the ineluctable resurgence of arbitrary patterns of authoritarian power, and to take stock of the resources that inform their resistance to its power of erasure.

As we have seen previously in *L'Isolé soleil*, a complex network of intertextual references grounds the modernist thrust of Maximin's narrative discourse. If, however, *L'Isolé Soleil* is to be seen as more than simply "a pointedly revisionist history of Guadeloupe," as Chris Bongie puts it (1998:355), and if Maximin's intertextual framework is indeed critical to the construction of a Caribbean framework for creolization, then we must see the primary context of its operation as instilling patterns of re-citation and transformation, rather than the deliberately subversive space-clearing gesture through which, as Simon Gikandi puts it, "the modern Caribbean writer seeks to rework European forms and genres to rename the experience of the 'other' American" (1992:20). Rather, Maximin's textual strategy is one that deliberately absorbs and reworks aesthetic and historical discourses to inscribe and valorize the nuances and multiplicities of Caribbean creolization.

This interplay between discursive form and cultural expression takes shape early in the novel, as Antoine, Marie-Gabriel's husband, stages rehearsals for a play. A quick series of important intertextual references, including Simone

Schwarz-Bart's *La Mulatresse Solitude*, Aimé Césaire's *Une Saison au Congo*, and Wole Soyinka's *The Dance of the Forest*, erects a network of thematic and contextual parallels that serves both to situate the novel in a context of cultural and discursive resistance, and, more precisely, to clarify the symbolic resonance of the impending volcanic eruption. Antoine's play, *La Danse de la femme-volcan*, which, we are told, takes its title from Soyinka's play, traces the teleology of the volcanic voice, eventually mediating its theme of rebirth through a remarkable representational event which, as in its precursor, is placed almost exactly at the novel's center. The articulation of both identity and resistance are thus predicated upon a set of discursive enunciations grounded in the complex contours of Caribbean and diasporic culture.

In fact, one might reasonably claim that a plethora of textual references and discursive appropriation permeates the novel. Early on, Antoine cites an exchange from a purportedly drunken conversation he had at four o'clock one morning in 1952 with the Guianese poet Léon Damas: "A poem is useful; it is as strong and as fragile as graffiti on a big, big wall. And I answered him, I agree with you; when the poem is good, one no longer sees the wall, one sees the graffiti" (20). A scant three pages later, he appropriates and transforms this metaphor in conversation with Marie-Gabriel to draw a survival metaphor based on lines of life and death: "Life against death is like graffiti against a wall. If life survives, you don't see the wall any more, you see the graffiti" (23). Through both content and form, this translation serves to reinforce the narrative link between writing and transformation, identity construction and cultural survival, and is in turn reinforced by the revelation that Marie-Gabriel is herself crucially engaged in the final stages of creating the novel that will become *L'Isolé Soleil*.

Indeed, the potentially eruptive Soufrière is itself also made evocative of writing, as shortly thereafter their friend Rosan re-cites the structural disjuncture and thematic tension both of Marie-Gabriel's novel-to-be and Antoine's play with the revelation of his own fragmented, disjointed response to the volcano's threat: he presents Gerty—already encountered, as we shall see, in *L'Isolé Soleil*—with a notebook titled "Volcano Trial: Defense Notes." The reproduction of this two-page extract within the body of the text, its differential text and type made up of notes, clippings, and comments on a series of dates tracing a variety of local, regional, and global seismic and political events, draws on the structure of the first novel and the state of tension (and, implicitly, of latent renewal) elaborated by the imminent eruption to construct the contours of a cultural defense whose strategy is a creative fragmentation and re-constitution of that which threatens it most. This continuous disjuncture, reflection, and recuperation of the construction of *Soufrières* itself ultimately constitutes a differential means of resistance to these potential sites of eruption and erasure.

Within the tensions and teleologies of *Soufrières* qua novel, the deliberate textual practice of fragmentation and dislocation, re-citation and transforma-tion is an integral part of Maximin's agenda of discursive renaissance. Contrary to the position taken by Bongie, who somehow seems to see the author's project as an innately regressive one, "stressing the ungroundedness of the modernist project in the wake of which he is writing, and fictiveness of the identities, past and future, he is (re)constructing" (1998:358), I argue that Maximin is firmly inscribed in articulating a concrete poetics of creolization, a performative tour de force that reframes and relocates the terms and param-eters both of Caribbean creole discourse and its corollary of cultural identity. For example, we soon become aware that there are multivalent layers of signification continually being generated by this complex representation of resistance. The primary inscription of characters and events takes place in section 1 under the symbolic rubric of a "Caribbean Parade," a resiting, through textual appropriation, re-placement, and exposition, of the plural resonances left behind by the colonial encounter. It is here that the narrative expands upon the eruptive possibilities of the Soufrière to shape a space for a creole Caribbean identity through the tensions evoked by volcanic destruction and the ongoing discursive constructions being undertaken by Adrien, Antoine, and Marie-Gabriel.

However, section 2, "The Jungle," opens with a letter to Marie-Gabriel from Adrien, now located in Paris. His missive and its postscript underline the sym-bolic importance of the work of the Cuban artist Wifredo Lam, whose con-temporary rehabilitation of Caribbean themes in the plastic arts was a strong source of artistic inspiration in the period. These two section titles echo paint-ing titles from his work and allow a deeper contextualization of the narrative to occur, such that it appears in fact to be "the intense secret dialogue between the signs of the painting and the pages on the table: his letter to Marie-Gabriel, and the poem he had just written. . . . For Lam, for her, for himself and others, renewed this night after so many months through the form and color of words" (73). It is not without significance that a number of Lam's artistic works create an intertextual framework for Maximin's discourse; not only do his paintings name the novel's first two sections, they also provide cover illustrations for the Seuil editions of both *L'Isolé Soleil* and *Soufrières*, since *La Marcheuse des Iles* and *La Rumeur de la terre* adorn the respective covers. Also, no doubt not coincidentally, what is probably the Cuban artist's most famous work, *The Jungle* (1942)—a painting that has been described as "a visual companion piece to Césaire's *Notebook*"[4]—found an uncanny titular and thematic echo in an essay by the same name, published by Pierre Mabille in the January 1945 issue of *Tropiques*, the journal edited by the Césaires and René Ménil that provides a counterpoint to the project of Césairean intertextuality in which Maximin is engaged. It is the symbolic substance of this influential artist's work that crafts new artistic concepts of Caribbeanness through this inter-textual network to coincide with the culturally critical and creative period of the 1940s and 1950s in the region, and accounts for Maximin's discursive ap-propriation and metafictional reinscription of his work. Indeed, the phrases that appear as possibilities for Adrien's poem's title—*la Rumeur de la terre*; *Les Frères*; *L'Oiseau du possible*; *Défilé antillais*; *Chant des osmoses*; *Apostrophe' apocalypse* (73)—are quickly recognizable as being in large part titles drawn from Lam's work to be given to the novel's various sections. If, then, this metafictional fragmentation and reintegration of the novelistic framework through the poetic intersections and artistic resonances of one of its intra-diegetic elements signify the author's inscription of the contours of a concrete creole pluralism, conflating art, history, and discourse to engender an alternate set of modalities for articulating Caribbeanness, the tension between erasure and resistance is ultimately elaborated in the differential discursive temporal-ity articulated by the Soufrière and the contestation that it both constitutes and commands. This sort of textual creolization or discursive doubleness creates a polyvocality that simultaneously decenters and determines the deliberately multivalent forms adopted by resistance in the text.

Indeed, the question of resistance is one that Maximin broaches both the-matically and textually in *Soufrières*. By virtue of the volcano's imminent erup-tion, the characters populating this figurative Guadeloupe are forced to come to terms with the possibility of their impending extinction, and to choose be-tween submission to erasure of their cultural identity, or through their resis-tance, a creolization of perspective and performance that seizes on the plural-ism and paradox of the cultural experience to write a new formula for the shifting boundaries of survival in the Caribbean postcolonial context. Again, such a reading is strikingly at odds with the position taken by Bongie, where the lack of agency he insistently perceives in Maximin's discourse is directly traced to what he terms the author's lack of engagement, his production of text as simply "a rhetorical *inventio*"; as Bongie writes, "The creolized subject finds her- or himself in a textual and geographical space that is at a definitive, and defining, remove from any and all cultural points of departure or ideological points of arrival: the origin and the telos can be present only as insubstantial yet eroticized traces, in the Derridean sense of the word" (1998:358). The remarkable lack of authorial rootedness in the Caribbean landscape that such a reading presupposes may indeed be suggested by Maximin's endless play of sign and countersign; but while it may be possible to read Maximin's incessant fragmentation, repetition, and doubling as paradigmatic of a purely Derridean deconstructive turn, I would like to suggest that an implied engendering of Caribbean agency is a critical component of Maximin's creolized discourse.

Drawing on the conflation of differential historical and aesthetic practices, this discourse opens new paths of discursive and subjective possibility from the intersections of postcolonial discourse and the concrete context of its praxis. His works, then, are discursive performances that appropriate and transform various resonances of Caribbeanness in order to redraw the boundaries framing a composite creole subject. The deliberate intervocality of Maximin's text reinforces the importance within this network of an infinite modification and renewal of the colonial trace. As his narrative glosses itself in continuous cycles of regeneration and re-citation, the strategies undertaken by both text and subject constitute continuous moments of rebirth and contestation such that for Maximin, writing new solutions ultimately keeps the historical threat of erasure at bay. This issue of choice, of a rebirth that preempts the volcanic eruption, is what undergirds the temporality of survival for Maximin; as Mireille Rosello writes of a key moment in *L'Isolé Soleil*, "It is perhaps in this distinction that the originality and the subersion of his work lies: the gift . . . is a symbolic gift, which reintroduces the idea of choice, and thus the existence of liberty at the heart of a terrifying universe (1992:58). Thus both character and text arrive at a sense of self-liberation that is simultaneously disruptive of an authoritarian discursive domination, constituting contestation from a discontinuous creole temporality whose uncanny differential doubleness of vision and voice generates paradigms of creative possibility even as it confronts the risk of its own dissolution.

Yet another aspect of the novel's persistent regeneration of signs of doubleness and hybridity retraces the patterns and principles of *écriture féminine* at work in parts 4 and 5 of *L'Isolé Soleil*; by separating the engendering of text from the double patriarchies of colonialism and discourse, Maximin avoids reinscribing their hierarchies of domination and alienation. Here, such deliberate dissymetries are accomplished by linking the volcano, and its critically symbolic role in the generation of a Guadeloupean identity, to images of female fecundity. Early on, in an extract from the play *La Danse de la femme-volcan*, the figure of the woman is yoked to that of the Soufrière: "But in the midst of the calm, a young woman emerges. . . . It is the young queen of the isle of Karukéra, the Soufrière, dressed in earth, air, and fire. The greenery applauds. The savannah's body shudders beneath her feet" (37–38). At this point, as the cycle of rebirth and continuity is re-presented through this dramatic text within a text—appropriating and re-citing the terms of Soyinka's original, written and performed to mark Nigeria's accession to independence in 1960—this performative doubling allows the discourse to reinscribe the critical duality of the Soufrière, poised between destruction and the corollaries of recovery and renewal. It is at this juncture that the pluralization of the novel's title becomes self-evident, as it recuperates the multivalent identitarian possibilities signified by the presence of the volcano and its imminent eruption. For if, as Siméa's rejoinder to Suzanne Césaire succinctly puts it in *L'Isolé Soleil*, "identification is the enemy of identity" (191/192), such an insistence on the possibilities of pluralism that are to be preferred over the chimera of unitary origin inscribes a double echo both of Glissant's injunction against Reversion (1981:30–32) and his valorization of rhizome over root in the articulation of identity's intrinsic multiplicity (1990:157–58). The principle of pluralism is thus multiply and intertextually inscribed, tracing a trajectory across texts and contexts to ground the several creole discourses of Caribbean identity.

But even this discursive gesture (re)naming the narrative's postcolonial praxis gives way to deeper resonances of cultural complexity as Angela's daughter Elisa falls ill. As Angela sings to this child, the descendant and namesake of an early victim of *L'Isolé Soleil*'s re-citing of the violent eruptions of the plantation era, the song becomes one which incorporates numerous linguistic and cultural characteristics, the whole more than the some of its parts, critically doubled, and "which was drawn from both a childlike romance and an old blues tune, neither creole nor French" (97). This creolization of both discourse—through the song—and character—through the symbiosis of singer and listener—is grounded in an ineluctably feminized economy, so that its openness and capacity for regeneration together trace metonymic patterns of creole postcolonialism. This economy of female fecundity ultimately contextualizes Maximin's polysemic textuality, his empowerment of the feminine axis allowing a transformative creativity of survival to emerge from the rupturing of the Soufrière.

But perhaps the most remarkable section of the novel is the one titled "Murmuring of the Earth" (Rumeur de la terre), significantly positioned almost exactly at its center. Here, recapitulating the structural strategy of its predecessor, the narrative shifts register to the first person, engendering through the mimetic self-reflexivity inscribed in this central fragment (we will recall both the thematic and the structural self-reflexivity of the central fragment of *L'Isolé Soleil*, and that Lam's *Rumeur de la terre* provides this text's cover illustration) a discursive site that mines the symbolism of title and theme even as it allows the Soufrière itself to be given voice: "I am a mouth of fiery flesh, but I have no language of disclosure. My dimensions are so spacious that I can speak through other bodies, and with a single gaze peer into all the recesses of my huge house. and my word is earth" (141). Simultaneously, through a series of polyphonic fragments that oscillate between third- and first-person narration, each of which begins with a temporal notation that, journal-like, marks the methodical, unhurried passing of the hours of the day, the island's crisis approaches its zenith. This complex strategy of mimetic re-presentation permits the inscription of a creole polyvocality that embodies much of the hybrid postcolonial culture of Guadeloupe, a culture caught in the very act of self-generation even as it contests the liminality imposed by the authoritarian ambiguities and hierarchies of a persistent, pervasive departmentalization.

Indeed, in its double role as salvation and threat, the volcano inscribes the imminent possibility of an explosive identity politics, tracing a translational, recuperative space for itself even as it articulates an ironic re-presentation of the people in whose name it elaborates this transformative perspective: "Death definitely holds no attraction for these people; they consistently seek survival in every evil, with neither remorse or atonement. They are not fleeing me, they are fleeing death" (150). When Rosan's pregnant wife, Gerty, confidante in Paris of Marie-Gabriel's mother, Siméa—herself engendered and encountered in an earlier text—gives birth to a daughter who shares the latter's name, in the midst of an eruption of rock and ash, surrounded by Marie-Gabriel and the familial elder, Man-Yaya, and metonymically inseparable from the former's fragmented manuscript, the event becomes "the double invention of a mother and child" (159), a dual fecundity of textuality and subjectivity that signifies the ineluctable imbrication of the postcolonial future with the colonial past: "A new and living Siméa, born from Gerty's desire to have a child one day from that *Siméa of Marie-Gabriel's 'Siméa's journal'* . . . placed in a cradle next to a bed of manuscript pages, themselves written with as much blood, flesh, love and ripping apart as had to be . . . searching word by word for the reason of her name" (160–61; emphasis mine). The symbolic relation between the birth of the child and that of the text position writing, birth, and eruption metonymically in a symbolic explosion of creolized feminine plurality. At the same time, the search for the name, for the sources of identity, makes this interconnectedness of history, discourse, and character indicate a voyage of cultural survival and self-discovery.

Far from framing a zone of Derridean unrepresentability, then, the intersectional space mapped by these two novels opens up new sites of discursive and subjective possibility, illuminating in their multiple points of convergence the temporalities and teleologies of a Caribbean creole discourse of difference whose analeptic and proleptic properties are yet to be fully articulated. Significantly, the novel's opening is marked by three points of suspension, followed by the reinscription of the very last line of *L'Isolé Soleil*, a letter signed, we will recall, by Daniel himself: ". . . and the leaf flies off at the risk of losing its green" (9). This issue of interconnectedness and intervocality itself is critical to the novel's inscription of self-generation; in fact, its phoenixlike re-citations of character, theme, and structure draw on its self-referential base to reiterate its formal standing as a historically-grounded discursive construct. To this end, there are two narratives simultaneously in progress in *Soufrières*, as well as the play *La Danse de la femme-volcan* and intermittent supplementary sites of intervocal commentary. For *Soufrières* is in fact a work in progress, an ongoing creation that Adrien refashions even as we continue to read it and watch its construction of cultural identity take shape. The repeated use of the second person that occurs in the text—and which, as in *L'Isolé Soleil*, opens it—is in fact Adrien addressing a series of realizations and conclusions to himself. These extracts from his notebook and letters gloss the primary site of writing, rendering its postcolonial praxis a signifying network of change, invention, and polyvocality. This sensation of an interlocking, infinitely discursive pluralism is buttressed by Marie-Gabriel's discovery of her mother Siméa's journal, a work that is at the center both of the creolized cultural polysemy of *Soufrières* and of the work that thematically and chronologically precedes it. The supposed referentiality of this fictional discursive construct compounds and

undergirds the interstitial complexity of such sites of resistance, where pluralism and paradox tend to render linearities of signification liminal at best.

These themes are encoded as a differential discourse near the end of the
novel, when Elisa, significantly driven to articulate her autonomy for the first
time, inscribes her hybrid subjectivity by evoking and resiting Aimé Césaire's
poetic elaboration of the inherent instability of the volcano itself: "There are
volcanos that die away. There are volcanos that survive" (249). This
reinscription of a Césairean discourse brings the wheel of doubling and
intertextuality full circle, as his phrase completes and anchors an arc of
signification in which the polysemic strata of the novels have continuously
reiterated and re-cited Césaire in order to ground the ineluctably composite,
fragmented, but contestatory world of the Caribbean experience. Thus the
novel's final section, "Flights of Possibility" (L'Oiseau du possible), functions
as a coda revalorizing the inventiveness of this discursive polyvocality; supposedly narrated in the first person by the vocal embodiment of Marie-Gabriel's
notebook, its protean possibilities of discursive transformation and metamorphosis are given pride of place: "For, between the past of exodus and the coming genesis, you chose to risk your own metamorphosis by synthesizing our
wanderings" (253). Addressing itself directly to Marie-Gabriel here, the text
highlights her own transformation through the creative, risk-taking act of writing, placing in tandem the twin axes articulated throughout the text by the
Soufrière. At the novel's end, Elisa, in a critical gesture—symbolically clutch-
ing under one arm a Wifredo Lam painting and the records made by Marie-
Gabriel's father as key icons of cultural creolization—glosses the final page of
Marie-Gabriel's text in front of the burning house by transforming the
Césairean poem "Oiseaux" taken from his volume *Ferrements*, whose beginning, "l'exil s'en va ainsi" (thus exile departs), consciously echoes the title of
the final section of *L'Isolé Soleil*. This final rewriting constitutes, in its deliberate circularity of endings and beginnings, both the re-citation of the entire
novelistic structure and the basis of an economy of protean performativity for
this creole postcolonial culture. In this novel, survival is a conscious act of will,
discursively constructed out of repeated resonances of refusal and remem-
brance.

Finally, as a conclusive, convulsive event, we are told at the novel's very end
of the destruction of Les Flamboyants plantation house by fire. The house has
long been a symbol of cultural and historical continuity, being also the location of young Elisa's death at the hands of Jonathan during the opening pages

of *L'Isolé Soleil*. What possible narrative or symbolic purpose could now be served, we may well ask, by its destruction at this final juncture? I would like to suggest that, far from being an inexplicable event, the climactic burning of Les Flamboyants serves a specific purpose: namely, to deliberately and brutally sever our ties with the symbolic icons of past and present generated by Maximin's narrative strategy. With the conclusion of *Soufrières*—which moment, in turn, marks the completion of *L'Isolé Soleil* by Marie-Gabriel—such icons are no longer necessary; indeed, it might be argued that they are now quite superfluous, given the proleptic perspective of Maximin's prose. With the task and the trace of writing now come full circle to mark the intersections of past and present, self and Other, discourse and subjectivity, a framework of future possibilities has been constructed on discursive ground, and with the threat of eruption and erasure rendered moot, the Soufrière volcano, interstitially double voiced, assumes its role as a modernist metaphor of creole aesthetics. In a Caribbean context of discursive performance, dominated, as Simon Gikandi argues, by "a certain anxiety about endings which is also an anxiety about new cultural beginnings" (1992:226), this symbolic and referential conflagration becomes a microcosm of the textual strategy, disrupting our assumptions of historical continuity even as it inaugurates new moments and metaphors of creolized subjectivity through discourse.

Maximin's narrative discourse, then, articulates complex, discourse-driven positionalities of creolized difference for the postcolonial Caribbean subject, primarily by inscribing identity through multiple narrative sites and strategies that simultaneously reflect and realize the pluralism undergirding regional experience; in the concluding words of Marie-Gabriel's narrating notebook, "I have always trusted in the suns of our history" (277). In the complexities of form, play, and *dédoublement* and the subtle pluralities of voice that re-present the relational aspect of this *domien* culture, Maximin constructs the discursive framework of a hybrid temporality, distilling from its doubleness the archetype of a differential identity that is demonstrably the product of the Caribbean's ethnic and cultural synthesis. Maximin successfully contests the authoritarian assumptions implicit in a traditionalist, colonially imposed narrative structure, recognizing that it is precisely at this juncture—that of discourse and subjectivity—that the critical choice between continuing historic patterns of imperial domination and articulating a cultural subject that is the embodiment of difference is to be made. As Edward Said indicates: "Conventional narrative is . . . central to imperialism's appropriative and dominative attributes. Narrative itself is the representation of power. . . . To tell a simple national story therefore is to repeat, extend, and also to engender new forms of imperialism. . . . A new system of mobile relationships must replace the hierarchies inherited from imperialism" (1993:273–74). By disarticulating these hierarchies of power, Maximin's narratives ultimately construct a new foundation for the articulation of identity in a postcolonial setting of interstitial pluralism and difference. His contestation of the discursive linearities of colonial authority enables the elaboration of a new order of resistance and recognition that rewrites the traditional teleologies of the margin into key strategies of identity and liberation. In this context of cultural hybridity, the polysemy of the post/colonial moment suggests a set of modernities that announce a resolute heterogeneity; as Françoise Lionnet suggests, "If *métissage* and *indeterminacy* are indeed synonymous metaphors for our postmodern condition . . . multiplicity flourishes when the shackles of homogeneity and rigidity are broken" (1989:17–18).

In sum, Maximin's principal achievement is perhaps the plural articulation of a communal voice, one which deliberately draws up a framework for the future through discourse: "I have never considered my island as a hell in which I must bury my memories and my imagination" (277). By repeatedly and insistently crossing discursive, spatial, and temporal boundaries, and by blurring the static categories of genre and gender, Maximin's fusion of re-citation and performance, of fiction and history, of subjectivity and community creates a composite cultural force of resistance and renewal. The deliberate disjunctures of these regional narratives interrogate the inherited discursive dynamic of colonial dispossession—through its functional dyad of history and textuality—while they simultaneously map the multiple metamorphoses of the creole Caribbean postcolonial subject, shaped by a context of contestation whose inventiveness is the necessary precursor to an alter/native identity that effectively escapes the intrinsic constraints of the written.

L'Autre qui danse
The Modalities and Multiplicities of Métissage

Ce sont deux hommes de chair et d'os; il y en a un qui lit et un autre qui danse;
je n'y vois pas autre chose.
Alfred de Musset, *On ne badine pas avec l'amour,* act 2, scene 5

Hybridity and Hierarchy

The pluralities that we shall be exploring in this chapter engage a form of
positionality that contests the basic essentialism grounding traditional perspectives on race and culture. The schismatic categorizations of self and Other that
provided the basis for schemes of colonial expansion found their justification
in the theories of scientific racism that pervaded the nineteenth century. By
constructing a pseudoscientific rationale for insisting upon racial difference,
the concept of the hybrid emerged at the bottom of this hierarchical framework, its dualities coming to be perceived as intrinsically degenerative. In
other words, the manipulation of categories of opposites had the effect of eliding any framework for intersection in order to preserve and protect the purity
of racial paradigms, their corollaries of hierarchical difference and colonial
expansion, and, last but not least, to avoid the possibility of racial extinction.
Instances of interracial mixing were eventually conjoined with the evils of
immigration to create a network of fears and phobias, a mountain of mon-
strosities whose ultimate expression of essentialism was the simultaneous apprehension and repression of the racialized Other.

In a postcolonial context, however, the resonances implicit in the term
"métissage" tend to open up and assume added significance. Indeed, the very
semantic instability of the root term "métis" points us toward the possibility of

new sites of cultural signification. A diachronic, cross-cultural glance at the varied uses of the term reveals variety rather than uniformity; in the French colonial context alone, as Françoise Lionnet has shown, the terminological resonances are continually transmuted as one travels from Canada, to Senegal, to the Indian Ocean, to the Caribbean. The fact that this constant metamorphosis remains contextually tied to a series of colonial sites allows Lionnet to conclude that "the very notion of métissage, then, is something culturally specific" (1989:13). The implications raised by this phenomenon of cultural specificities of difference are precisely the area we must explore in order to define the point where hybridity is transformed from biological monstrosity into an articulative discourse of alternative subjectivity.

In a specifically Caribbean context, this site of overlapping discourses marks a creative instability, a paradoxical indeterminacy that reflects and embodies the ambiguous geopolitical realities of the region. The complex structures of Caribbean society, encompassing as they do polyvalent issues of race, politics, history, and culture, point to the emergence of a community marked and striated by the traces of diverse indigenous and colonial practices, whose origins lie in Africa, Asia, Europe, and the New World.

More fundamentally, what is at issue here is the intrinsic ambiguity of the term "creole" itself, given its key role in the construction and maintenance of a formal contextualization of cultural métissage that will successfully contest the dominant hegemonies of the colonial encounter. As a form of decolonization, métissage functions on the discursive level to destabilize the "normalizing" mastery of authoritarian discourses, elaborating through the subtle ambiguities of its intervocalic structure an alternative to the strictures of the colonial double bind. By interrogating the fixed set of assumptions that have historically governed the conceptual singularities of ethnic and cultural "representability," these overlapping domains of difference ultimately renegotiate the intersubjective and collective nexus of values and constituencies that underlie our vision of self and Other, producing an affiliative engagement with the ambiguities of experience that help to define these polymorphous communities in the (post)modern world.

The creative ambivalence that locates this new world of creolized possibilities can serve as an apt figure for the métis subject herself, whose identitarian experience of multiple subject positions tropes and transforms the customary boundary between racial and cultural categories. This capacity to confound the strictures of an either/or division in fact engages a critical transformation of these categories to the contradictory negations of neither/nor, exposing colon- ialism's false opposition of cultural traits and its unsettling relocation of these anxieties of cultural difference, but at the same time opening up strategic new vistas of social and cultural production. Such a double gesture goes beyond initiatory concepts of cultural division and makes of the mulatta a polyvalent sign which, as Hortense Spillers points out, "has no personhood, but locates in the flesh a site of cultural and political maneuver" (1987:183). This strategic location of the categories of the creole in the interstices of signification is a signal, transformative contingency whose sundry implications must now be mapped and explored.

It is perhaps not only appropriate but critically important that the post- colonial subject produced by this plurality of cultural universes inscribes the trace of her or his difference in the space of this very "in-betweenness" from which its interstitial identity seeks to emerge. For if, at bottom, as Henry Louis Gates Jr. argues, "every black canonical text is . . . 'two-toned' or 'double- voiced'" (1984:3), these instances of intrinsic intervocality define the principal space within which alternative models of identity may be elaborated, models which themselves may also (re)trace internal patterns of oppositionality across the site of the collective.

Between the subjective and cultural divisions engendered by metropolitan domination of the DOM-TOM, and the discrepancies and disparities of exile within the domain of the metropole itself, the pluralisms of the imagined in- terstitial community are simultaneously contested and resited by the double displacements that mediate between Subject and (m)Other, between oppos- ing dualities of alterity and autonomy. The key question of identity formation within a context of cultural and communal pluralism opens up critical issues of discourse and modernity, given that, as Stuart Hall suggests in his Introduc- tion to *Questions of Cultural Identity*, "identities are never unified and, in late modern times, increasingly fragmented and fractured; never singular but mul- tiply constructed across different, often intersecting and antagonistic, dis- courses, practices and positions" (1996:4). It is this intrinsic complexity that undergirds issues of identity in global contexts of multiculturalism and post- colonialism that must, in turn, necessarily inform the narrative interrogation of a creolized cultural pluralism.

The attempt to create, and to define, new paradigms of social and national identity must confront these critical antinomies of difference. Creole identity patterns will draw on these polysemic patterns of positionality to generate new codes of cultural inscription, mapping a critical intersection between multiplicity and postcolonial articulations of alterity; as Hall continues, "Identities are constructed through, not outside, difference" (1996:4). In this way, issues of globalization and fragmentation are resited and reinscribed; by demystifying the ambiguities of the present, they expose the binary artificiality of borders and boundaries that impose the antithetical strictures of an either/or contrariety. As a way of contesting what Françoise Lionnet calls "this discord between a particular idealized racialized identity and the realities of the postcolonial world" (1995:96), novelists like Suzanne Dracius-Pinalie open up the fragmented and discontinuous world of the subaltern subject. By sketching through the pluralisms and ambiguities of its multivalent modernities new, discursive solutions to the alternating codas of dependency and dislocation, these extremes which have historically demarcated the conflictual, emblematic space of métissage now set as a strategic site of subjective renegotiation.

L'Autre qui danse: Exile and Identity

Suzanne Dracius-Pinalie, a professor of classics at the Martinique campus of the Université des Antilles et de la Guyane, published her novel *L'Autre qui danse* in 1989,[1] after growing up in both France and Martinique and returning to her homeland of Martinique after completing her studies in classics at the Sorbonne. Although the more "successful" of the two métis sisters whose subjective strategies are explored in her novel traces a similar formative path—Matildana is in fact a graduate student at the Sorbonne—Rehvana appears to reject such alliances in her search for cultural "authenticity," and it is precisely this question of the multivalency and malleability of boundaries and identities that the novel sets out to interrogate. Indeed, the novel itself articulates an important evaluation of the (im)possibilities of interstitial identity for the inhabitants of the DOM-TOMs as they appear through the symbolic prism of exile and métissage.

On a primary level, Rehvana—the sister whose ultimate death by way of a (re)turn to a self-imposed exile in Martinique to (re)integrate herself into an Antillean tradition and way of life provides the basic armature of the plot—is a woman whose lack of rootedness in the Parisian society where she has lived since early childhood drives her to behavioral and psychological extremes even before her turn to tradition. She traces a subjective trajectory whose complexities and contradictions incarnate, in Richard Burton's words, "that condition of doubleness and dichotomy to the utmost limits of its capacity to con-fuse, torment and fecundate" (1992:186).

Her peripatetic search for identity is inscribed in her nominal inscription in the root *rêve*; thus "Rêve-ana's" unsettled handle on *la vie quotidienne* com-bines with an overwhelming sense of fragmentation and dependence, visible as early as the uncanny plurality of narrative voices discernible in the novel's aptly named "Promonologue," to engender a desire for integration and au-thenticity that she seeks to fulfill through a number of convoluted and contra-dictory encounters. In this brief but critical opening section, the text initially locates her as being subject to an ongoing subjective and discursive fragmenta-tion; she speaks but has no interlocutor, receives no response and is quite evi-dently separated from any localizable milieu and from the Others who inhabit it. "She is perfectly willing to be his wife, she wants to be one of them, but not at this price! . . . 'I don't wish to be marked!' . . . But I am awake; their drug has no effect on me. . . . However, Rehvana is far from the horrifying discovery she has just made" (11–13). Through this series of short, staccatto, almost aggressive phrases, shifting imperceptibly from free indirect discourse, to direct speech, to internal monologue, to omniscient narration, Rehvana's fragmented positionality and interstitial, unlocalizable perspective are highlighted. Fur-ther, since this episode chronologically follows her escape from the the Fils d'Agar—an extremist cult of displaced Antilleans whose questionable attempts to erase the traces of their *francité* can be summed up by their abortive attempt to blow up the Centre Pompidou—and since the moment of her imprison-ment at their hands will be recounted later, this temporal displacement of the discourse serves only to deepen the sense of estrangement that reader and character must both now share.

In *Postcolonial Representations*, Françoise Lionnet suggests in a nuanced reading of *L'Autre qui danse* that strategic and subjective alternatives to the master narratives of Caribbean colonialism are what novelists like Dracius-Pinalie "offer through their implicit critique of the passivity of their heroines." At the same time, however, it should be noted that what the oppositional cast-ing of Rehvana and Matildana accomplishes, at least in part, is "a new way of denouncing the illusion through which the return to the past and physical suffering can play a mediating role in the search for authenticity" (1995:91). In this way, it can be seen that Rehvana's characteristics of passivity and malaise are symptomatic of her insistence upon an illusory absolute, alienating her in succession from her counterparts, beginning with the group of mainly

Martinican mulattoes who should constitute an initial site of metropolitan affiliation for her alterity. Yet her refusal of this identitarian refuge increases exponentially, articulated through insistent feelings and moments of displacement that are themselves formulated in the centripetal terms of free indirect discourse: "My God! How she would love to be elsewhere! She would like to scream at them that she was not in her place" (20). The centrality of this idea of place, with its corollaries of subjective location and definition, draws on the geographic and cultural difference between France and Martinique to construct a world within a world, a space of apparent belonging which itself maintains its separateness from the larger cultural spaces that surround it, a sense of difference that is ultimately the product of a double dis-location from the communal institutions of Paris and Fort-de-France.

The critical textual inscription of the increasingly ubiquitous *négropolitain*, the immigrant who remains marginalized from both the departmental and the metropolitan worlds, re-presents these inscriptions of exile and subjectivity. Those like Rehvana's boyfriend, Jérémie, have only tenuous connections to what is now only the land of their parents' birth and form a doubly disjoined category of their own; "born in the 14th arrondissement of Paris, of immigrant Guadeloupean parents, he [Jérémie] can only perceive the Antilles through the beat, Malavoi and Kassav, codfish fritters and punch, and Guadeloupe and Martinique meant nothing to him but a pleasant folklore, none of which he denied, but he displays his beautiful black skin with no complexes or bitterness through the streets of Paris and the corridors of the HEC" (30). Here, the somewhat ironic tone of distanciation that reduces cultural authenticity in exile to folkloric traces of food and music simultaneously subjects Jérémie and his counterparts to the transitive terrain of intersubjectivity, dispersing them into an identitarian void that becomes the dominant designation of their difference.

In these terms that evoke the critical paradoxes of cultural adaptation, the vacating of paradigms of collectivity and collaboration construct a forgetting of the terms of blackness, one that denies Jérémie even the stigmata of identity and removes him from the patent possibilities of recognition. "Jérémie had never known either fear or shame because of his deep black skin, *nor any personal disgust when looking into the mirror, nor any lowering of his curly black head before the world, nor rage, nor resentment, nor feelings of injustice,* by all appearances, nor an irrational camouflaging of the smells of the hold and exile which neither oceans nor centuries had washed out of his skin" (31; emphasis mine). This relationship to the mirror recalls Jacques Lacan's notion of alienation inscribed in the mirror stage; it marks the subject's intrinsic alienation from itself, deriving mastery and unification from an illusory external image: "The mirror stage is a drama . . . which manufactures for the subject . . . the succession of the phantasies that extends from a fragmented body-image . . . to the assumption of the armour of an alienating identity, which will mark with its rigid structure the subject's entire mental development" (1977:4). What is striking, however, is the absence of these alienating structures from Jérémie's overt psychic makeup; indeed, despite his overdetermination by patterns of cultural alterity, he appears to reflect nothing recognizable, whether positive or negative, into the mirror at all. Literally caught in the interstices of opposing cultural systems, Jérémie represents the unnameable impossibility of cultural location, that point of intersection between the dominant and the marginalized where subjectivity is effectively erased; he is a victim of the fictions and realities of a doubled social inscription that renders him fully neither self nor Other. Instead of the initial category of ineluctable duality produced by the subject's identification with the (m)Other—a paradigm of metropolitan misrecognition, in the postcolonial context, that produces a subjective fragmentation which may, as we shall see, be much more applicable to Rehvana—his innocuous sense of self seems to have neither other nor counterpart through which to accomplish his self-definition. Jérémie's critical lack of a self-image, of a stable subject position that is the product of a functioning cultural constituency, ultimately revokes his cultural potential, rendering him an unavailing subjective site that is in excess of the sum of the "parts" of difference. This prevents Rehvana, in her turn, from participating through or with him in a meaningful, foundational sociocultural framework that will endow her with subjective and agential significance, and that she can feasibly call her own.

The problem of double cultural displacement that Jérémie "successfully" confronts is one that must be faced by all *négropolitains*: the binary oppositions that stem from continuing to integrate oneself into and functioning within a dominant metropolitan French culture, while maintaining an identitarian inscription in the differential, communal culture represented by the polysemic space of the DOM-TOM. Born and raised in Paris, the son of émigré mulatto parents from Guadeloupe, Jérémie has known only the metropolitan culture of the city; the reality of his parents' homeland remains a distant, inaccessible dream, made present only on the discursive level, through verbalized reminiscences and iconic traces of a displaced cultural production. Neither totally French nor completely Antillean, Jérémie is a curiously vacuous hybrid; theoretically, perhaps, one might expect him either to partake in the great French phantasm of assimilation, becoming a subject who consciously articulates the mantra "nos ancêtres, les Gaulois," or to acknowledge and act upon the disjunctures of his difference. But paradoxically, both the place and situation of his birth—although of Antillean extraction, he is also literally a Parisian born to French nationals—appear to interact disjunctively with the inherited double displacements of an émigré belonger now internally exiled from the periphery to the center.

Jérémie appears to re-present rather the absurdities and absences of the neither/nor; his tenuous links to an unknown culture to which he can yet lay claim, combined with his seemingly untroubled assimilation into French metropolitan culture, represent something less than the sum of these unequal parts, a space of in-betweenness whose transparency is ultimately, at bottom, more conflictual than commensurable. Interestingly, it is Rehvana who sees most clearly through the veneer: "In any case, Jérémie, you just can't understand this kind of thing; the only thing that interests you is to conduct your pathetic little assimilated life, and be swallowed and digested; so you can't even see that you are nothing but a whitewashed blackman, socialized and shameful" (27). It is this paradoxical lack of conflict by which Jérémie is figured, the critical absence of slippage between his self-projection and the image he perceives in the mirror, that renders him almost but not quite Other, an inadequate approximation of the authoritarian anxieties of the metropolitan culture in which he participates.

Thus, then, her affiliation with the Fils d'Agar; the displaced, deceptive family structure that the closed composition of the group re-presents is meant to (re)construct for Rehvana the sense of authenticity, affiliation, and acceptance to which she somehow still remains a stranger. Yet her choice of this alternative space of subjective inscription turns out to be a singularly unimaginative one. Marginalized itself, the group employs a conflictual strategy that effectively places its members on the borderlines even of the multiple identitarian modalities of the metropole; an association with the members of the Fils d'Agar can do no more than exacerbate Rehvana's already acute sense of alienation.

The impossibility of the Ebonis-Vrais-Fils-d'Agar serving as an adequate sheltering space for Rehvana's fragmented subjectivity has more to do with the double displacement of the group within the metropolitan social structure than with her own sociocultural dualities and insufficiencies. For example, the primary symbolic paradox that emerges from the group's inception is the insistent slippage between who its members are and what they seek to represent. Despite their claims to radicalism and cultural purity, ostensibly authentic representatives of African identity, the Ebonis are in fact displaced Antilleans; "Diop, Abdoulaye, Babacar and the others—whose Christian names were Jean-Loup, Marc and Thierry" (30)—progressively proceed to alienate both metropolitan whites and those Africans in whose name they articulate terrorist strategies of cultural contestation.

Interestingly, within the nominal framework of the Ebonis is a complex construct that locates both the referential blackness that ebony traditionally inhabits, as well as phonetic traces of groups of runaway slaves, in particular the "Boni," or Aluku maroons, who successfully contested the tyrannies of slavery in British, French, and Dutch Guiana (now, respectively, Guyana, "la Guyane française," and Suriname). Given that both Rehvana and the Ebonis are of Antillean origin, the primary element that separates them is the same mark of difference that separates her from Jérémie; while she was born in Martinique and now lives a metropolitan existence in a form of self-imposed exile, the tenuous connection between the group and the Antilles—albeit one that they effectively renounce and deny—is the fact that they are in reality second-generation *négropolitains,* who have never set foot in their parents' homeland and who speak an artificial, imperfect creole. "They suddenly hid themselves behind their clumsy, difficult Creole, a banana Creole learned more or less on the sidewalks of Barbès—for they had never set foot in the Antilles, not a single one" (23). The question of the linguistic role of creole in the construction of an effective subjective identity is an important one, and is an issue to which we shall return. For the present, however, let us pursue the devolution of the double displacements of the Ebonis onto the recalcitrant subjective structures of Rehvana.

Unlike their counterpart, Jérémie, whose identitarian reflection in the mirror is apparently absent, the Ebonis, through the prism of their desire, see in the mirror the trace of the African Other, locus of an ideal ethnic and cultural purity that simultaneously reinscribes the bipolar axes of the colonial self/ Other conundrum. Ironically, however, they are rejected by the very cultural body in whose name they speak, framing themselves within a conflictual strategy of self-definition. They manage somehow to simultaneously alienate both the white and black axes of France's increasingly diverse metropolitan culture; "there had been increasing conflicts with the purebred Africans, the non-mixed ones who carried authentic passports from compromised Africa, of whom the least aggressive allowed himself to ignore with a majestic disdain these enlightened Ebonis" (57). Ironically, in this reversal the issue of (non)métissage becomes the final arbiter of the specter of authenticity, placing the paradigm of an *africanité* of "pure souche" at odds with the modernities of the metropole, while eliding the incommensurable multiplicities of a burgeoning creole culture. Doubly disengaged as they are from both the Other and the counterpart, disenfranchised by canonical extremes of both ideological camps, the Fils d'Agar frame through the depth of their isolation the impossibility of a collective experience of refuge or sanctuary that will allow Rehvana to reappropriate a composite identitarian experience grounded in stability and self-recognition.

At the same time, however, Rehvana herself articulates through this series of alienated actions a pressing condition of deficit and dependency that, as we shall see, plays a cardinal role in the unfolding of her race-based dualism.

It is precisely Rehvana's background as a métisse, as "a historic mulatress with slight aristocratic ties" (18), that lies at the heart of the diverse disjunctures and divisions that she attempts, unsuccessfully, to confront and correct throughout the course of the novel. These sociocultural tensions and teleologies of the intrinsically ambivalent aftermath of the DOM-TOM, and whose complex implications we have explored on the thematic and discursive levels in previous novels, are here translated to the psychological level of a split subjectivity whose disturbing divisions are grounded in a racial and a geopolitical duality. Here, the constant challenge will be to articulate a generative sense of creolization out of an ethnocultural experience of métissage. What sets Rehvana apart from the compulsive contradictions of her fellow Caribbean exiles, like Jérémie and the Fils d'Agar group, is the fact that she, like her sister Matildana, was born in the Antilles; both were formed by that paradoxical difference-within-sameness that is the ambivalent corollary of departmentalization, and both are still inhabited by an ethnocultural interstitiality that sees "her native but still foreign Fort-de-France" (18) as a doubled identitarian space of inscription, with which a cardinal cultural contact must be re-established at all costs. The sisters' (re)negotiation of the binary boundaries that separate metropole from department, and their respective attempts to turn these discursive and subjective ambiguities into transformative patterns of pluralism, emphasize the problematic of the interstitial impasse that is symbolically recuperated by Rehvana's doomed but insistent search for a redemptive racial authenticity, and her sister's transformative, enthusiastic embrace of her own multiple modernities—divergent paths whose opposition between métissage and creolization is mediated through the connective counterpoint of the creole culture of their native Martinique.

Exile and Métissage

The double nature of Rehvana's sociocultural situation is a rather specific one, and it both reflects and refracts the complex shades of signification that beset the extremes of exile that confront so many Antilleans both at home and abroad. Indeed, from one perspective, community identity has been fostered and expanded in both locations through the postdepartmentalization wave of migration that took thousands of French Caribbean subjects to the metropole after 1946; the postwar phenomenon of anglophone Caribbean migration to Britain and North America in the 1950s and 1960s traced a similar parabola of physical and cultural displacement. These transplanted subjects transferred with them to the former colonial capitals their indigenous patterns of cultural practice, giving rise to a form of transnational identitarian affiliation that increasingly influences both the shape and performance of popular culture— particularly in the areas of music, film, television, drama, dance, and fashion—in those metropolitan centers that now serve as axes of association. Yet such phenomena of recolonization, in which the imperial metropole is in its turn made subject to the paradoxes and pluralities of the Other, come at a price; the realities of their exile are relative but permanent. The sense of displacement that Rehvana experiences is indicative of the persistent historical, geopolitical, and cultural distance that separates France from its Others, and that insists upon the recognition and inscription of an inescapable alterity that, as Frantz Fanon has pointed out in *Black Skin, White Masks*, finds its origins in long-standing perceptions of difference grounded in notions of race and place: "But in my case everything takes on a new guise. I am given no chance. I am overdetermined from without. I am the slave not of the 'idea' that others have of me but of my own appearance" (116). This ineluctability of the racial marker, or, more precisely, the place of its splitting, re-cites the hierarchies of the colonial encounter; its misapprehension will act in conjunction with her exile to become the generative ground of Rehvana's double displacement and subsequent (re)turn to tradition.

The double perspective that guides or drives these protagonists is simultaneously recuperated by their double inscription in the interstices of race and gender; the ineluctable identitarian impositions that are the product of racial overdetermination marginalize the creole siblings of this novel through the indeterminacy of their métissage as well as through the otherness of their inescapably biracialized femininity. The resulting double bind tends to exacerbate the already split and splintered uncertainties of racial and cultural identity, with the apparent impossibility of the successful synthesis of these categories for the subject leading to the temporary valorization of one category over the other as a possible solution. As Paul Gilroy has cogently suggested in *Small Acts*, when "racial identity appears suddenly impossible to know reliably or maintain with ease, the naturalness of gender can supply the modality in which race is lived and symbolized" (7). Can this formulation account for the subjective trajectory traced by Rehvana? Does she in fact attempt to come to terms with herself as a female creole subject by suffering the traditional subjections of the regional modalities of gender? In the incessant redoubling and splitting of the ties between sister and sibling, home and exile, DOM-TOM and metropole, biraciality and biculturality, the oppositional paths traced by Dracius-Pinalie's creole protagonists ultimately will engender alter/native perspectives on the pitfalls and possibilities intrinsic to an effective elaboration of Caribbean female subjectivity.

Misrecognition and Unbelonging

The complex subjective dilemma that Dracius-Pinalie presents for our perusal is, in a certain sense, the culmination of previously inscribed patterns of feminine disjuncture, those archetypal attributes of an experiential alienation that abound so readily in Caribbean literature of feminine expression. The paradigm of double colonization to which the women of the region historically have been subjected produces what Marie-Denise Shelton has called "a different 'knowledge' of being Haitian, Martiniquan, or Guadeloupean. . . . feminine writing tends to expose conflicts and mutilations that characterize the being-in-the-world of women in the Caribbean" (1990:346–47). The result of this conflictual relationship to a masculinized world of simultaneous domination and disjuncture produces patterns of dispossession and degradation that tend toward thematic re-presentations of the disintegration of the feminine self. Primary among the symptoms of affective disorder are patterns of madness and withdrawal, of silence, solitude, and suicide that trace the paradox of spiritual deterioration and physical survival that follows the deprivation of identity and the dissolution of subjective coherence. These narratives of the Caribbean's pervasive *mal féminin* have been produced by such authors as Michèle Lacrosil and Myriam Warner-Vieyra, and it receives perhaps its most notorious treatment in Mayotte Capécia's *Je suis martiniquaise* (1948).[2]

Of interest here, however, is a narrative and psychosocial phenomenon that Shelton identifies and terms autophobia. Drawing on psychologist Erik Erikson's work in the area of shame, Shelton explores how the ultimate effects of this self-hatred and desire for invisibility clearly become gender-marked in the appropriation of these tensions to a context of Caribbean female subjectivity.[3] Her contextualization of autophobia draws on an extract from Michèle Lacrosil's novel *Cajou* (1961), where the female protagonist is consumed by anguish, self-doubt, and a desire for invisibility. But it is the explanation of her dilemma advanced by Cajou herself that so interestingly illuminates the argument advanced by Erikson: "When a little girl discovers, in the dim light of her experience, that all the ugliness of the world has gathered in the *mirror* she consults, instead of viewing herself as a monster, she at first directs her anger at the *mirror*" (30; emphasis mine). The implications of this interaction of fiction with the psychoanalytic phenomenon of autophobia for the Caribbean female subject together frame the argument that I now want to address.

At first glance, it would appear that the subject's ineluctable involvement with the images generated by her interaction with the mirror must result in a self-directed anger. Such an internally driven form of resentment does create the appearance of avoiding the aura of an unnameable monstrosity by redirecting the terms of the displacement into a schema of self-blame. But upon closer inspection it becomes increasingly clear that the target of this specular redirection must in fact be the image of the (m)Other, the displaced double of this already alienated subject. For, as Lacan reminds us in the *Ecrits*, the symbolic matrix of the specular image tends to "situate the agency of the ego, before its social determination, in a fictional direction" (2). In other words, it is this very misrecognition that ultimately (re)locates this subjectivity as a fictional construct; the resulting crisis of ambivalence and alienation is engendered by the mirror image, since, as Kaja Silverman's gloss on Lacan shows us, "to know

oneself through an external image is to be defined through self-alienation. . . .
It loves the coherent identity which the mirror provides. However, because the
image remains external to it, it also hates that image" (1983:158). Seen in these
terms, then, the displacement from self to re-presented Other (re)traces the arc
from department to metropole, building a bridge that inscribes these protagonists within the terms of a sort of "dualized subjectivity," a doubling of the
subjective matrix that draws its polysemic, oppositional patterns from the
subject's intrinsic fragmentation. But it is within this differential dualism, this
world of seemingly infinite dislocation and disjuncture, that a generic "double
colonization" also engenders a perpetual distance between the subject and the
object of its desire, producing a multipartite alienation that is seemingly the
ineluctable domain of the female Caribbean postcolonial subject.

Given the inescapable context of cultural multiplicity and geopolitical
doubleness that constitutes the functional framework of the French Caribbean experience, an alienated femininity that assumes an identitarian
identification with opposed subject positions renders this female postcolonial
subject an iconic re-presentation of the very paradoxes that structure and stri-
ate the social space she inhabits and of which she is a product. For if the inscription of Caribbean femininity inherited from colonial discourse—in
whose terms the economy of colonized woman was first circulated and circumscribed—turns upon furthering stereotyped figures of enclosure, of
subordinacy, of inadequacy and alienation, in short, upon being not even that
which the colonized male is not, then a discourse of feminine postcolonial
identity for the Caribbean must begin by reframing and transforming these
regional resonances of feminine fragmentation. The turning of these dualities
to the deconstruction of monolithic models of womanhood must address the
"double unbelonging" of women who inhabit a Caribbean creole context.
And it is here that the critical difference signified by the multiplicities of the
métisse finally comes into its own.

In *Woman Version*, an analysis of West Indian fiction by women, Evelyn
O'Callaghan remarks upon the pervasive nature of the "alienating, neo-colonial middle-class world" of the Caribbean woman (70), a world riven by
conflicts of class, culture, gender, and language. The paradoxes and dualities
of the relation to the metropole allow us to postulate a number of penetrating
parallels that impact the female subject caught in the neocolonial departmentalization strategy operated by France, reflecting the attendant dualities of the
British imperial colonialism that O'Callaghan so trenchantly analyzes. The

presence of these multiple models of class, color, and political allegiance that result in the articulation of an artificial economy of choice tends to impose a telling polarization upon the perspective of these female postcolonial subjects, generating a pattern of mimesis that O'Callaghan sums up as "conflicting gender roles from which she must choose"; the subject's subsequent acquiescence to the linear disjunctions of this model results in patterns of "doubleness, self-estrangement, [and] a loss of sense of self" (70). Yet, at the same time, it is important to note that these externally driven impositions of division, exclusion, and subjection, from a cultural and subjective point of view, mark precisely the sorts of oppositional ambiguities that are recuperated in the figure of the métisse. However, by creatively recuperating, expanding, and re-citing the influence of such bipolar sites of alienation, these complex subjects can inscribe difference by interrogating the diverse, conflicting paths that an interstitial neocolonialism imposes upon this latent postcolonial femininity. And so it is by bringing this complex set of moves full circle that we are able to return to the network of cultural, geopolitical, and subjective complexities signified in Dracius-Pinalie's text through the paths taken by the siblings Rehvana and Matildana.

Together, these sisters signify a complex web of contradiction and recognition that contests and relocates the series of assumptions attaching to the issues of exile, biculturality, bilingualism, and femininity in the French Caribbean. The parameters of this conflicted relationship that is the bane of departmental francophone culture are marked by the very questions of assimilation and acculturation, of the absence of a stable sociocultural position and the paradox of exiled presence in the heart of the metropole that define these Martinican sisters. The constant sense of displacement and lack of belonging that enervates Rehvana's metropolitan existence eventually engenders her return to Martinique, setting in motion a tragic trajectory that ultimately ends in a vicious cycle of pregnancy, poverty, disgrace, and death. Yet, on the other hand, her sister Matildana's relative success at the process of sociocultural integration, first as a student at the Sorbonne, then, following her own return to her homeland, as an engaged teacher and journalist, raises critical questions concerning the divergent paths and possibilities produced by the dynamics of cultural authenticity. As French Caribbean female subjects, inscribed as oppositional signifying systems that renegotiate the relative failure and success of cultural coherence and cultural pluralism, this conjoining through the polyvalent social structures that link these intrinsically multiple subjective sites is recuperated and refigured through the shifting, interstitial space of the métis.

This inherent multiplicity allows the figure of the métis to encompass the far-flung diversities of a postcolonial subjectivity for the francophone Caribbean, serving as a metaphor for the sweeping range of ethnic, cultural, and political possibilities that frame the paradoxical realities of the Caribbean diaspora, and of the *domiens* as borderless imagined community. In this regard, it is interesting to note that a latent ambiguity concerning the role and positionality of women has historically informed Caribbean literature, creating a thematic and discursive complexity that increasingly compounds the nexus of national identity. As Simon Gikandi points out in *Writing in Limbo*, "To consider the question of gender and subjectivity in modernist discourse is also to confront the ambiguous role women play in the construction of national identity. . . . the end of colonialism does not rescue women from their historical confinement—they still remain modernism's 'other,' excluded or marginalized from the signifying systems of the new nation" (197–98). By exploiting the latent displacements and dualities that simultaneously separate the symbolic schema sketched by each of these sisters, and yet paradoxically also join them into an intricate figure of fragmented feminine difference, we may come to a fuller understanding of the composite and transformative web of signification woven by these contradictions of exile and integration, ethnicity and positionality, in Dracius-Pinalie's relocation of the boundaries of francophone feminine subjectivity.

Return, Revival, Resistance

The presence that most effectively mediates the transition in the novel from the "Chant premier" to the "Chant second"—marking the moment of Reh vana's memorable return to Martinique—is the figure of Eric, an irresistible young man she meets at a party and with whom she pursues a relationship and suddenly and inexplicably decides to return home. Confronted with this dominating and debilitating presence, she finds herself "defenseless and without will" (80), trapped by an overwhelming masculinity and a complete loss of self-control: "Rehvana has no idea where to go. . . . She has never felt such pain, such shame and such confusion. She is ashamed to be there, blushing and frozen in place" (76). Transfixed, she can do nothing, say nothing, but continue to suffer his domination in silence: "She hates him as he continues to dominate her with his height, his haughty look, and his self-assurance" (76). Indeed, she finds herself unable even to dance. By contrast, her sister, Matildana, in a symbolic precursor of their twin trajectories of displacement, seems to be dancing herself into oblivion at the precise moment of Rehvana's deepest confusion: "Matildana, dizzied, carried away, dances . . . in the exaltation of her being" (74). By the party's end, Rehvana's life has taken a new and unforeseeable turn: "Inexplicably, a single glance, a single second had been enough for Rehvana to make Eric the man of her life" (83). The oppositional axes of their reactions to the musical expression of their cultural heritage—inscribing them both between constraint and autonomy—set in motion the repeating patterns of dualism and disjunction that define their divergent reactions to the larger issues of departmental dependency and cultural authenticity at work in the novel.

This singular new path that Rehvana decides to follow with Eric is meant to counter the pervading sense of exile and unbelonging that we have observed in her behavior to this point. She will return to Martinique and reintegrate herself seamlessly into the society; indeed, it will be as though she never left. If, however, as Gilroy has suggested, the modality of gender through which she attempts to come to terms with herself as métisse is signified through her subjection to and subsequent terrorization by Eric, then this choice certainly constitutes an overt interrogation of the hierarchical pattern of gender relations and the destructive role played by a dominant masculinity in the (de)construction of a valid, independent feminine identity in the Caribbean context.

Rehvana's approach to accomplishing her double goal of subjectivity and authenticity involves little questioning either of herself or of the categories she has in view; rather, it is to adopt a strategy that, in a certain sense, is perception based, and it is in the interstices of these gradations of appearance and reality that her search ultimately loses its way. Her alienation has always been in search of a mythic, overarching authenticity; from the beginning, "she wished to be authentic, more authentic than those who had never been to the Other Shore, and displayed her pretty little feet, the feet of a historic mulatress with slight links to aristocracy, on the uncaring macadam of a Fort-de-France which was both her birthplace and foreign to her" (18). Already, Rehvana's unfamiliarity with the metropole is leading to the authenticity she seeks, while ignoring the potential doubleness of the *mulâtresse historique* that she embodies. As a result, the Martinican capital of Fort-de-France remains an impenetrable paradox for her, simultaneously *natale* and yet *étrangère*, its enigmatic identity capable only of reflecting her own displacement.

It is both striking and paradoxical that the contours of the native country-side to which Rehvana wished so strongly to return appear so strange, if not downright foreign, to her upon her arrival. Sights, smells, and sounds all seem distant and unknown to this prodigal daughter: "The smell of ylang-ylang, the caresses of frangipani, the violence of the red balisier, the dizzying sound of Creole, the universal trembling at the scent of sweet sweet, Rehvana gathered from all these gifts, piously, her inheritance, what was expected" (88). The day-to-day aspects of island life are increasingly striking—"At Sainte-Thérèse, at the entrance to the city, the traffic jam is monstrous, the heat infernal" (93)—and even the architecture appears decidedly "unmetropolitan"—"All the huts are in some way or another 'colonial'—but in such a modest way, in style rather than in substance" (95). This supposed distinction between style and substance, however, may well be a subconscious desire for a subliminal authenticity engendered by Rehvana herself. For indeed, an inscription in this particular desire becomes the motor of Rehvana's lifestyle once she settles in, apparently driven to recuperate an almost mythical, idealist authenticity displaced by her time in the metropole: "Rehvana left the hut hurriedly to take in the washing she had spread out on the grass, faithful to the traditions of old-time Antillean washerwomen. . . . A whole congregation of former beliefs, all badly understood, badly overcome, has found a place through voluntary fervor in the young Foyalaise of Paris, and controls her movements, gives rhythm to her life, and inhabits her tormented nights" (99). The text leaves us in no doubt here as to the implausibility of Rehvana's vision of "authenticity"; her desire to return to the past, to the One, is, as we have already seen, doomed to encounter only failure; this search for Glissant's moment of "Reversion" visualizes an originary site of agency that will be forever ephemeral.

In these terms, Rehvana's desire is effectively the desire of the Other, as she is alienated and overdetermined by subjective structures that she imagines to be those of the society in which she hopes to find herself. As a result she manages only to reformulate the basis of her own alienation, since the codes and practices she sees in her mind's eye no longer ground the society she left behind.

Her decision to forgo the luxury of modern conveniences, and to concentrate instead on eschewing technological progress and rediscovering national dishes and condiments, marks in fact a fundamental misrecognition of the forces that give rise to the regional realities of exile and departmentalization. For the (re)discovery of a true Caribbeanness does not lie in such trivial articulations of consumption or self-sacrifice; by attempting to recreate the superficial structures, sites, and sounds of a vanished colonial era, Rehvana responds ultimately to the covert, sedulous demands of the Other when she should in fact be seeking alternatives to them, exacerbating rather than apppropriating the unspoken doubleness of the departmental dilemma.

What takes place, instead, is that the complex, anomalous terms of the Martinican relationship to the metropole remain completely unaddressed by her; the cornerstone of this intrinsic cultural and political doubleness, of which Rehvana's métissage is perhaps the ultimate symbol, remains aligned along its metropolitan rather than its Antillean axis, the binaries of the subjective hybridity produced by the colonial encounter simply relocated rather than resolved. Indeed, the very fact that "Rehvana had deliberately cultivated this blind faith and this forced credulity . . . *determined to be Antillean, to make herself totally Antillean*" (100–101; emphasis mine), renders this deliberateness of her gestures a sign of the alienation and displacement she is attempting so desperately to contest. Through her inability to come to terms with—and to profit from—the pluralities of her own perspective and experience, Rehvana effectively discounts the very multiplicity, born of the dilemma of her own double inscription, that holds the greatest potential for transforming her Martinican métissage. In this regard, then, the origins and peculiarities of the drive for nativism that appears to occasion Rehvana's return to Martinique are of critical importance; the terms, conditions, and contingencies of this return instigate the disjunctions that separate Rehvana's ongoing métissage from Matildana's assumption of the modernities of creolization.

Commensurability and Authenticity

The differences that separate these two sisters are of such cardinal importance that they transcend the merely significant to approach the realm of the socioculturally symbolic. For the fact is that together Rehvana and Matildana represent the complex network of pluralisms and ambiguities that construct the character of the Caribbean basin. The essence of their creoleness goes beyond the interstitial individualism of skin color; at the critical ancillary conjunctions of language, culture, class, and the ineluctable dualities of *dom-tomisme*, they

inhabit the articulative ambivalences and polysemic possibilities that are symbolically summed up by the intrinsic dissonances of their metropolitan exile.
On a primary level, then, the divergent symbolic directions of these siblings
suggest opposing conceptions of the greater imagined community that encompasses both the Caribbean and its diaspora; a subtle yet complex framework for
indigenous identity, a discursive inscription of a multivalent Caribbeanness
that simultaneously binds the French Caribbean to its metropolitan center
while still separating it from the vaunted unicity of the center's sense of
francité. But on another, more abstract level, it is the depth and persistence of
Rehvana's drive to redefine herself, her assumption of the linearities of misrecognition by essentially renaming and reinscribing herself as an authentic
Martinican native, that open up new perspectives on feminine subjectivity and
creolization in an ambivalent postcolonial context, interrogating our fixed assumptions of the function of class and ethnicity within the cultural framework
of the DOM-TOM.

 If Rehvana's ultimate goal is the rediscovery, or rearticulation, of her cultural essence, then, on the face of it, her plunge into the Martinican peasantry
should theoretically provide the enabling conditions for the accomplishment
of this goal. Rehvana therefore appears to seek the literal exchange of one
identity for another, simultaneously surpassing the interstices that bind the
DOM-TOM to the metropole while bridging the binaries that define and divide
the bipolar categories of colonizer and colonized. But even beyond the hollow
politics of Reversion, how effective a counterfoil to the departmental politics
of division is this exchange of the modalities of class for those of race?

 Ultimately, Rehvana's error here is one of vision, the inability to fully comprehend the array of antinomies that undergirds the network of departmental
ambiguities within which she is inscribed. Her goal is to change the terms of
her social inscription by dis-placing its terrain; to move from rootless departmental reject in exile at the margins of the metropole, to the comprehensive
certainty of a nativist position that excludes and negates the interstice by virtue
of its assumed authenticity. But it is precisely at this juncture that the ineluctability of her error is to be located; since the ambivalence of the departmental
experience is itself founded upon an expedient extension of the colonial encounter, a rehearsal of old hierarchies of dominance, exclusion, and dependence disguised as egalitarianism and inclusion, a simple shift in positionality
within the boundaries of a metropolitan domination of the DOM-TOM does

nothing to contest effectively the strictures of this determinedly bipolar relationship. Further, the assumptions that undergird such searches tend to be grounded in the fabric of metropolitan patterns of alienation. As Robert Young reminds us, "There can be no such nativist alternative history. . . . it is worth pausing to consider . . . to what extent an 'alternative' simply represents the narcissistic desire to find an other that will reflect Western assumptions of selfhood" (1990:165). In the end, Rehvana is simply extending her inscription in colonial binaries; neither her situation nor its proposed solution is effectively problematized, so that the terms "authenticity," "métissage," and "peasantry" continue to structure a framework grounded in and bounded by an ineluctable duality constructed and dominated by the metropole.

This is what ultimately constitutes Rehvana's blindness; by engaging in a posture that ultimately produces only a distinction without a difference, she transforms neither the terms of her dependence nor the dualities of her subjectivity. In any event, even a politics of identitarian exchange based on considerations of class, as Rehvana visualizes it, would be equally ineffective at formulating strategies of freedom able to articulate the complexities of a creole culture. From the plantation to the H.L.M. (Habitations de Loyer Modéré), from the béké (Caribbean creole white planter class) to the bourgeois, differences of class within the DOM-TOM have always been a function of the implicit presence of colonial hierarchies; the principles of relative privilege and social exclusion that have shaped these societies have inevitably extended the hegemony of the colonial principle of divide and rule.

And so even the empyrean promises held out by the attempt to elude the class struggle cannot bring the authenticities of antillanité or créolité into being for this Antillean subject. Indeed, since such class concerns must function within the neocolonialism of the departmental moment, the intersection of class with the contingencies of colonialism engages only, as Ato Sekyi-Otu points out, "a modulation of the exclusionary politics of the 'colonial context,' the degree to which the dream of the colonized to 'take the place' of the colonizer is partially consummated or hopelessly doomed to frustration" (1996: 159). Simply "going native," then—whatever that means—cannot produce a functional identitarian framework for Rehvana; the essence of creoleness lies outside the binary boundaries of race and class, a cultural composite continuously reconstructed by recognizing the liminal, polysemic postcoloniality of the DOM-TOM. The idea of nativism itself, on which her search for identity appears to depend, poses an alternative set of difficulties, raising issues of cultural specificity whose implications are at the heart of creolization's modernity.

Given its recent insurgency within the polysemic patterns of postcolonial identity, the principle of creolization has increasingly characterized the subjects and objects of contemporary cultural studies. Modernity, in turn, draws upon a concatenation of political and cultural phenomena to inscribe an all but intangible sense of ongoing newness, a drive for the disparate and the disjunctive that has been succinctly defined by Paul de Man: "Modernity exists in the form of a desire to wipe out whatever came earlier, in the hope of reaching at last a point that could be called a true present, a point of origin that marks a new departure" (1983:148). In these terms, what is most compelling about the quest for modernity in a postcolonial context is its ineluctably dual relation to both past and future; since its points of departure simultaneously (re)inscribe the past upon which they draw, as Rey Chow writes, "Modernity is ambivalent in its very origin . . . It must incessantly deal with its connection with what *precedes* it . . . in the form of a destruction" (41; emphasis in the original). Modernity, then, effectively (re)stages the confrontation between the first and the third worlds that lies at the heart of contemporary postcolonial theory and its corollary of cultural identity politics. And so these are the terms within which the quest for authenticity practiced by Rehvana in this novel rehearses the intrinsic ambivalences not only of the modernity of postcolonial discourse but also of the attendant positionalities it is meant to inscribe.

Both Rehvana and Matildana are, in a sense, two halves of a matching pair, a dystopian duo marked most trenchantly, perhaps, by the stark contrasts that define and demarcate their lives and that appear, on the surface, to restrain them within the binary ambit of neocolonialism and métissage. These differences and contrarieties are all the more striking given that both siblings share an ethnic and cultural background, an ineluctable métissage of ethnicity and location that is augmented by their dual exile within the alienating confines of the metropole. But where Rehvana encounters rejection, Matildana encounters acceptance; where the former suffers isolation, the latter finds inclusion: and where Rehvana's world seems one that dooms her to failure, her rival sibling progresses from success to success. It is this deliberate dichotomy between subject and counterpart, between these polar opposites who are yet so much the same, that compels us to interrogate both the basis of Rehvana's dissolution and the progressive path traced by her more successful sister. How, then, does the latter's deeper inscription in the culture and society of the metropole, and the tacit acceptance and transformation of its implicit divisions that increasingly inscribe her in creoleness, play in the elaboration and evolution of her success?

Assimilation and Alienation

The context through which Rehvana's sister Matildana is figured appears on the surface to be one of assimilation to the values, practices, and traditions of the metropole. However, we shall see that her métis subjectivity is equally predicated on her acceptance of her ties to Martinique as well. On the one hand, not only does Matildana achieve ascendancy by virtue of a thoroughgoing attachment to metropolitan culture—as a graduate student in classics at the Sorbonne, she epitomizes the very paradigm of traditional socioacademic conservatism—the patterns through which this assimilation is practiced do not, on the face of it, diverge from the historical norm of colonial/departmental migratory movements. Matildana's resolute absorption into metropolitan life reverses the traditional hierarchy pitting department against metropole by having her symbolize one of the more than 400,000 people of French West Indian descent or origin currently resident on the French mainland, with more that three-quarters of this figure resident in Paris and its environs. And if, as one study has shown, this population stood at over 320,000 as early as 1982— a figure more or less equal to the individual population of Guadeloupe or Martinique, and nearly three times that of French Guiana—then Alain Anselin's conclusion that "a third island is situated in the heart of Europe . . . one West Indian in three lives in France" (1990:110) is by no means an overstatement of contemporary realities. The sociocultural complexities generated by the population of this "third island," circulating as it does between department and metropole, enlarge the concept of a regional diaspora and are of just as much concern, perhaps, as the dislocation and dispossession that are the more obvious signs of departmentalization's imagined community.

These hybrid communities maintain a level of ties with and travel to their homelands that effectively problematizes perceived notions of belonging, of the difference between "home" and "away." As a result, there is also a doubling of these sites of affiliation that blurs fixed notions of identity and erases the distinction between positionality and place. As Richard Burton points out in his introduction to *French and West Indian*, "Almost all French West Indian families have members living in France. . . . The constant crossing of the

Atlantic tends to undermine the distinction between 'France' and the West Indies" (12). Such social patterns ultimately have the effect of repositioning and globalizing identity as a product of the departmental encounter itself; as Anselin points out in his full-length study *L'Emigration antillaise*, "French West Indians no longer migrate, they circulate" (266), their ceaseless, circular movement creating a modernist nomadism where migrating metaphors of difference disturb the hierarchic assumptions of both center and periphery.

The psychocultural chasm, then, that separates these siblings has its roots in a migratory movement of Antillean peoples from margin to center, encouraged and developed through active bureaucratic efforts by France to increase its own labor pool; the primal role played here by the state agency BUMIDOM strongly marks the postdepartmental period but perhaps reached its zenith in the decade of the 1960s.[4] As paradigmatic products of this migratory phenomenon, Rehvana's and Matildana's resemblance to and difference from each other epitomize that "double consciousness" that tends to be manifested within the colonial trace. But to see more clearly the extent to which these captious coalitions of metropolitan exile intersect with the complex patterns of cultural and subjective alienation drawn by this sibling rivalry, and to clarify the way in which they inform and impact the structure of the narrative, we must examine more closely the terms in which Matildana herself confronts the multilayered terrain of the metropole and the compromises, if any, she is made to accept.

If the parabola of failure traced by Rehvana in the novel marks a simultaneous pattern of success for her sister Matildana, it is significant that these differences are apparent from the opening moments of the narrative. Where our first view of Rehvana underlines the fragmentation, pluralism, and alienation that are the generative ground of her shifting subjectivity, when we first encounter Matildana these patterns of progressive dissolution are notably absent; indeed, she appears to be firmly ensconced in the precepts of affirmation and acceptance that lie at the opposite end of the subjective spectrum. The contrast between them is a deliberately multivalent one, operating on a variety of levels. As Françoise Lionnet argues, "In contrasting the character of Rehvana to that of her more reasonable and well-adjusted sister, *L'Autre* sketches out a solution to the problems of identity. . . . Matildana represents the self-possessed Caribbean woman, comfortable with her body and able to negotiate the contradictions of her past and of her cultural and racial present" (1995:99). Further, and perhaps most important, Matildana is marked not by the fragmented voices and visions, nor by the dis-ease or the need for recognition that beset her sibling, but by the golden glories of her Afro-Caribbean métissage.

Symbolically, when we first encounter her, she has gone to the hospital along with Jérémie to help Rehvana after she has been locked in a trunk and has refused to have her face tattooed, followed almost immediately by her beating in the metro, all at the hands of Abdoulaye of the Ebonis: "Jérémie had found an ally for himself in this endeavor: Rehvana's older sister, a big, healthy girl with heightened Caribbean cheekbones . . . comfortable with her own strangely polychrome self . . . ebony-colored along her long, unending hands, covered with rings up to the curving nails, smoothly cinnamon-colored on her arms, and light sapodilla, satiny apricot on her face" (39). There can be no question here of the active articulation of Matildana's *antillanité*: from her "heightened cheekbones" which, significantly, are wholly "Caribbean," to the multicolor of her polychromatic skin, inscribed and signified through the symbolism of cinnamon and Caribbean sapodilla, she is totally at home in her Caribbeanness and rejoices in the apparent polysemy of her ethnicity. She has no need to search for a space to provide her with an identity, for she already inhabits and embodies several spaces, and whether she is located in Paris or in Fort-de-France, she incarnates its symbolism through her very being.

It is important, indeed telling, that the narrative positions Matildana at the virtual center of a maelstrom of multiplicity, providing her with an ethnic and cultural identity that not only is beyond question, but which also allows her to act as a protective and regenerative shield for her sibling; the creoleness that she has adopted comes to the rescue, in a sense, when Rehvana's fails. For Matildana, identity is grounded in the secret strata of a history whose polymorphous precepts stretch back through the mists of colonial time, and whose lineage leaves Jérémie speechless: "At first he hardly knew what to say to this girl, this moving wave, this vine, this incredible new beauty *who brought together so many centuries*, this magnificent contrasting harmony of all races joined together" (39; emphasis mine). As the amalgamation and assimilation of the cultural complexities and temporal discontinuities that make up the Caribbean diaspora, Matildana is the fruition, the culminating point of a Caribbean creoleness re-presented as a symbolic "harmony of contrasts."

Yet above all, Matildana is at ease, comfortable and unconstrained in the unbridled acceptance of the sociocultural plurality that this identitarian space necessarily constructs. Indeed, not only does she symbolize the multiple modalities of Caribbean history, she personifies them: "In herself she set in opposition her striking profile from the Ganges shores . . . with her callipygian stature of a Yoruba princess. A marvelous aberration of history, she blended it without comment, her mixed blood. *It was as if each race, each people had added to her flesh everything within it which was most beautiful.* There she was, untouchable, a freed Pandora, solid in the confusion of her blood" (40; emphasis mine). As the text deliberately emphasizes the continental differences that, paradoxically, come together to create Matildana's identity, it simultaneously stresses the pluralities of race and ethnicity whose confusion locates and liberates her transcendent self-sufficiency. The product and progeny of colonial practice, Matildana now re-presents that network of signification that colonialism sought to foreclose but to which, paradoxically, it ultimately gave rise: a polysemic subject whose deliberate disjunctures act as a corrective to the presumed univocality of colonial discourse.

From the outset, then, Matildana as a character is put into place as one who inhabits and personifies the multiple materialities of Caribbean culture. But of critical importance here is the fact that the basis of the polysemic creole subjectivity that she so successfully embodies appears to be drawn on the symbols and figures of racial difference. Indeed, the discourse is at pains to point out that the multiple ethnicities of Matildana's background, those that provide the subjective framework through which she is figured and by which she achieves self-representation, are subsumed and summarized by the intrinsic complexities of her skin color. This conflation of blood and melanin that acts as a signifier for the plural encounters of the Caribbean historical and cultural experience is explicitly framed as the visible locus of Matildana's identity, the site and symbol of her subjective strategy.

It is therefore at this juncture that these patterns of textual signification encounter the established myth of race as a verifiable biological category. The argument is not a new one, and the notion that the external physical characteristics upon which we depend for our superficial system of racial and ethnic classification—a notion that reached its zenith in nineteenth-century French metropolitan discourse with the publication between 1853 and 1855 of Count Arthur de Gobineau's *Essai sur l'inégalité des races humaines*—has been repeatedly and effectively debunked and disproven by such critics and theorists as Nancy Stepan, Claude Lévi-Strauss, K. Anthony Appiah, and W. E. B. Du Bois.[5] Appiah, in this regard, in a well-known essay on the subject of Du Bois and race, puts the argument well: "Given only a person's race, it is hard to say what his or her biological characteristics will be, except in respect of the 'grosser' features of color, hair, and bone" (1986:31). To grasp the obvious conclusion to be drawn here, one need not look much farther, "The truth is that there are no races: there is nothing in the world that can do all we ask 'race' to do for us" (1986:35). And yet, if we accept as a primary premise the logic of this racial argument, which is, in sum, that the concept of race cannot contain the ethnic distinctions and coalescences of humankind, then it immediately appears to undermine the racialized basis for this textual re-presentation of Matildana's creole identity.

But perhaps the issue we really need to interrogate is the role to be played by the discursive re-presentation of nuances of pigmentation and skin tone in such a context of creolized identitarianism. Further, and perhaps even more important, is the fact that this issue is linked to the terms in which race itself is inscribed in the text as a means of embodying both character and representation. For these twin terms to articulate the material totality of Caribbean history and culture that are located within Matildana's subjective space, both siblings must be recognized as textual signs, as signifying vessels capable of carrying a multitude of creole contexts. These sisters are more than simple formulations of character; they embody and respond to the myriad patterns and possibilities that together have shaped the multirelational essence of the Caribbean creole experience. Seen in this way, Matildana's polychromatic skin, the racial sign that identifies her as a métisse, functions as a signifier of cultural pluralism, a coded re-presentation of the many historical encounters that have produced this polysemic creole society. The very unlocalizability of her racial heritage, functioning as a signifier of difference, is made to stand in for the oppositions and possibilities of cultural change. As Appiah puts it, "Where race works . . . it works as an attempt at a metonym for culture; and it does so only at the price of biologizing what *is* culture, or ideology" (1986:36; emphasis in the original). In inscribing biology as metonym, then, this textual re-presentation of creole polysemy through the racial complexities of ethnicity and culture is effectively probed and problematized; Matildana is made to inhabit the spaces of both self and Other while transforming them into a network of commonality that is less than either of its primary axes yet effectively more than both. This biologization of the creole experience, functioning primarily as a signifying structure, works to present the identitarian complexities of the region by preserving the conflictual traces of the historical encounters between civilizations that inaugurate the affiliative strategies marking the regional present.

This problematization of the historical and the cultural, which locates and actualizes the warp and the woof of common experience that binds the region together beneath the shifting sands of colonial history, both joins and separates Matildana and Rehvana while articulating the themes of continuity and authenticity that escape the latter. In fact, Matildana's double difference, from Rehvana and from the binaries of the (neo)colonial Other, allows us to posit, in a certain sense, her identitarian incarnation of Caribbean creoleness as a practical example of identity production as it has been visualized by Stuart Hall: "Perhaps instead of thinking of identity as an already accomplished fact, which the new cultural practices then represent, we should think, instead, of identity as a 'production' which is never complete, always in process, and always constituted within, not outside, representation" (1994:392). Hall's vision of identity formation in postcolonial societies paints an interlocking pattern of divergence and commonality that is the core of a Caribbean framework of signification: "This 'oneness,' underlying all the other, more superficial differences, is the truth, the essence, of 'Caribbeanness,' of the black experience. It is this identity which a Caribbean or black diaspora must discover, excavate, bring to light and express" (1994:393). Here, the presence of scare quotes denotes the conscious problematization of both oneness and its categorical opposite of Caribbeanness, and this paradoxical pluralism thus becomes the basis of a new grammar of nationness, in which the practical positioning of the subject within a discourse of difference can frame the simultaneities of subjection and rupture through which the Caribbean has been figured as "Other."

It is by appropriating and transforming this Otherness into a site of affiliative transcendence that Matildana ultimately re-presents the core of the Caribbean character; her inclusive positionality now initiates new strategies of creole recognition. As Hall sums up this process, "The rift of separation, the 'loss of identity,' which has been integral to the Caribbean experience only begins to be healed when these forgotten connections are once more set in place" (1994:394). Through this play of difference within identity, the essential doubleness of the Caribbean diaspora is repositioned and re-presented in terms of Matildana's acceptance of her racial and cultural complexity, engendering a multivalent subjective site which is itself further underscored by Rehvana's misrecognition of its innate possibilities.

This critical contrast that the text establishes between the siblings' differing perspectives on the patterns of ethnicity and duality within which they are both initially inscribed is thus in play from the outset, simultaneously marking the identity of both sisters and determining the opposing paths upon which they each embark. Importantly, the rootedness that is Rehvana's ultimate goal is assumed, transformatively, by her sister and is already an integral part of her social and psychological framework.

This dissimilarity of perspective is quite apparent when the sisters attend a dance party hosted by a young professional academic Afro-Caribbean couple. Matildana has insisted that Rehvana go to the party, although she knows no one there. One of the most significant aspects of the proceedings, excluding, of course, Rehvana's encounter with Eric, and from a strictly sociological point of view, is the ethnic and cultural diversity of the invitees; not only are the host husband and wife from Cameroon and Martinique, respectively, we are told that "it's true, there are all kinds of people, from France, from Spain, and from everywhere—*le gai Paris*—Africans, people from the DOM-TOM, mixed couples, a Pakistani woman who does't wear her sari and her French-German husband, the woman from Abymes in Guadeloupe living with an upper class guy, pale, dignified, and who listens, amused, and complicit" (71). Ill at ease in this métis group of yuppies who delight in the diversity that provides them with just the sort of identitarian affirmation that she so sorely lacks, Rehvana feels abandoned and afraid. (Ironically, it is here that later, despite her sense of isolation, Rehvana meets and bonds with Eric.) It is quite striking that while Rehvana wanders the room in a state of deadly boredom, Matildana not only feels completely at home but is immediately entranced and enraptured by the insistent polyrhythms of the music.

However she interprets the call of these Afro-Caribbean cadences, Matildana is drawn to respond; it is the sense of oneness that simultaneously joins her to the music and to this métis, multicultural group of exiles that inscribes her through involvement rather than isolation, and signals participation rather than withdrawal. This associative framework is signified in the text through both movement and voice, "through African heat flowing through the body, a heat that undoes, that leaps and drags her arms up as she cries out the same OUÉÉÉ, as she submits, lawlessly, to the same chords" (72). What Matildana responds to in fact is, in a sense, the call of hi/stories, the transmutation of the slave rhythms whose call-and-response signaled community and resistance into the transnational, cross-cultural cadences of zouk and calypso, whose polyvocality is the hallmark of Caribbean expression. Even here, her capacity to distance herself from the intrinsic, isolating paradoxes of her own academic pursuits does not go unremarked. "I'm talking about the night festival. This is the same one which shook the chains, in the evening, on the plantations; it can't be learned academically, and Matildana knows it. . . . tall, shameless, in the glory of her being, here she is, taken over to the depths of her self" (73–74). It is this bridging of the binaries that separate the world of the DOM-TOM from the world of the metropole, an act that simultaneously diffuses the disjunctures of race and place, history and culture, that ultimately separates Matildana's world from the summary stalemate that is Rehvana's.

For both sisters, then, the primary factor that grounds their respective subjective fields is the play of difference. For Rehvana, this difference is intrinsically negative, oppositional, generating a condition of fragmentation which is re-presented through the tensions of a narrative of displacement. For Matildana, on the other hand, this very condition is ordinary, unsurprising; it locates her psyche and positionality within a framework of liberatory pluralism. While it is true, as Stuart Hall has suggested, that all identities are essentially fictions, the construction of these symbolic selves is produced by the intersection of difference and diaspora, of discursive performance and the identity politics of the affiliative postcolonial community. But it is the insistent, re-iterative doubleness of this question of difference—of one sibling from the other, of métissage from creoleness, as well as of both from the metropole— that lies at the heart of this cultural and subjective negotiation. As Hall points out, "It is an immensely important gain when one recognizes that all identity is constructed across difference and begins to live with the politics of difference" (1987:45). It is the complexities of working through this politics of difference that explains the arc of antipathy eventually traced between Rehvana and Matildana.

For Rehvana, her descent to the depths of degradation and despair takes place fairly quickly. Initially, she plunges into her rediscovery of the "authentic" Martinique with an enthusiasm that borders on fanaticism. Without respite, she cooks, cleans, and reconstructs, but inscribed within it all is an ironical subtext of ineluctable failure and misplaced perspective: "She pruned the hedges, cared for all the plants, fertilized all the flowers. More royalist than the king, aggressive, carried away with militant Caribbeanness, Rehvana took arms against all those who, according to her, did not possess incontestable authenticity. She started raising chickens. She has nothing to do with household appliances or other examples of modern laziness: anyway, what would she do with them in this house without any electricity?" (115, 119, 121). Indeed, in short order, this deliberate plunge into a traditional, mythicized past—one upon which Antilleans themselves had turned their backs, in their ongoing journey into modernity—becomes unalterably entwined with her tacit subjugation in terms of gender, an ongoing process to which she appears inexplicably blind. "Everything would be wonderful if only Eric appreciated her efforts for what they were worth, if he only gave her some word of encouragement, if only that beloved man didn't come home so late at night—if he came in!—to shove his feet under the table, only to wolf down his food without speaking a word, fast, swallowing his fish soup which she had delicately simmered, after having, she herself, scaled and gutted the fish with her own delicate city girl hands" (119).

It is this double, misplaced subjugation to both gender and culture—and its attendant, implied blindness—that leads Rehvana inexorably to the point of subjective dissolution. The simultaneous narrative critique, always surreptitiously present in tone, sums up the double bind of her misprision in a single, succinct phrase: "She does all this for Eric, and because it's the Caribbean way" (122). The depth of the irony by which Rehvana is figured here recuperates the extent to which the complexities of authenticity and exile, of "home" and "away" remain as patterns of protean elusiveness for the female Caribbean subject. This constant sense of displacement and lack of belonging that enervates Rehvana's existence signals the presumptions, practices, and positionalities that historically have informed the actions of generations of Antillean women, and which are finally taken to task and effectively dismissed.

This blindness is in fact continually represented as a deliberate refusal to see, and the text leaves us in no doubt as to Rehvana's responsibility in the matter. "Since her return to Martinique, Rehvana had deliberately cultivated this blind faith and this forced credulity, for in that she perceived the dark essence of the Antillean soul . . . determined to be Antillean, to make herself Antillean, totally. . . . Rehvana buried herself, in a hallucinatory, haggard way, in the nightmare of the intense nightwatch she had inflicted upon herself" (100–101). In this insistent process of self-transformation, her mind remains firmly closed to whatever does not fit neatly into her preconceived notions of Antillean reality, but her own responsibility in creating a real-life nightmare for herself somehow escapes her.

By adopting the positionality of the victim, she rejects the subjection that should be her salvation, and this stance is rendered even more painful when it comes to Eric's thinly disguised adultery: "Gradually, all around Rehvana, floats the penetrating female vapor the man carries back with him from outside, and which is emitted by his entire body, leaning over her" (103). By giving in to Eric's desire, she tacitly accepts his adultery, although it becomes increasingly impossible to disguise "the scent of the unknown woman" (103). Through the metonymic presence of this unseen but felt rival, the narrative sums up both the depths of Rehvana's despair and her refusal to countenance its implications, a position which is tantamount to psychic self-immolation on the altar of an unalterably elusive authenticity.

From here, it is but a short step to the depths of physical abuse. Most often, Eric beats her with his belt, and perhaps the most brutal of these beatings occurs after she becomes pregnant. Since, crucially, the father is Jérémie, the batterer displays the usual technique of blaming the victim: "All she sees is the heavily buckled leather, he's speaking too loudly for her to understand, he has no idea how her ears are buzzing, he laughs when she vomits, he is furious that she got up, complains of her bad manners" (131). In vain does Matildana encourage her to file a police complaint; her friend and mentor Cidalise, on the other hand, at first, surprisingly, counsels resignation — "After all, if this man is pleased with you. . . . Even if the child you are making is not for him" (185) — but, in a striking reversal, redeems herself by insisting on an end to Rehvana's victimage when the child is threatened. While, on the one hand, much of this woman's experience has long been familiar lore in the Caribbean, the intensity of these episodes draws in large part on their chronology, an implied chain of cause and effect instantiated by an insistence on the efficacy of Reversion and a repudiation of proferred alternatives. By conflating these twin teleologies that Françoise Lionnet calls "a sometimes poorly repressed tradition and the lure of a passively lived femininity" (1995:99), Rehvana, perhaps, dooms herself to an increasingly inexorable downfall.

Together, the contrasting experiences of these sisters map a new, alternative strategy for the construction of postcolonial identity, one whose signal liminality draws on the ambiguities of the DOM-TOM and its diaspora and is reflected in the creole complexities that they both resolve and reproduce. The persistent discourse of doubleness that we have seen at all levels of the narrative is of key importance in the construction of the open, affiliative identity that Hall envisages: "It is possible to think about the nature of new political identities, which isn't founded on the notion of some absolute, integral self and which clearly can't arise from some fully closed narrative of the self" (1987:45). Pursuing the trail of disjunctures integral to this strategizing of discursive subjectivity leads us to examine those contexts of communication that they share, articulated antinomies that simultaneously unite our siblings while separating them one from the other. Let us take a closer look at the tensions of their relationship during Rehvana's sojourn in Martinique, a site of communication which, significantly, takes place largely through a remarkable trio of letters directed from Matildana to Rehvana.

Epistolary Economies

Matildana's first letter to her sister Rehvana appears several pages into part 2 of *L'Autre qui danse*. This long middle section, titled "Chant second," covers the period of Rehvana's return to Martinique and traces her decline from idealistic participant to despondent outcast. Appearing unannounced as an untitled subsection of a chapter titled simply "La Martinique," the entire letter is italicized, drawing attention to its peculiar, particular status as a text within a text. Before we consider the narrative content of Matildana's missive, and what it says and suggests about the relation between both writer and her interlocutor, we need to examine the question of the letter's discursive form, particularly as it relates to the status and function of epistolary conventions as they are inscribed within the larger framework of a discourse of postcolonial identitarianism.

The issue that first engages us here is the overall nature and function of epistolary discourse. The use of the epistolary form in fiction puts into play a number of interesting and important possibilities that impact the key areas of gender, reflexivity, and representation, areas that hold particular implications for the analysis of a liminal, polysemic, feminized postcolonial subjectivity. The broad lines of the epistolary code suggest that the appearance of the letter implies, at bottom, a distinctive doubling of the narrative discourse, what Linda Kauffman, in her key study *Discourses of Desire,* calls "the letter as literature, literature as a letter" (17). The problematics of presence that lie at the heart of epistolary communication insist on this act of discursive doubling, since what is implicit in any fictional letter-form is an address to an invisible other, an attempt to transform absence into a proxy of interlocutory presence through a reply to another implicitly absent text. Integral to this performative moment is the duality of the writer's desire: as Kauffman puts it, "The heroine ... dedicates herself to nurturing her illusions. ... Yet her strategy is simultaneously subversive, for she contests. ... Her epistle is ... a revolt staged in writing" (17–18). These are among the formal qualities that characterize fictive letter writing, producing a discourse that simultaneously undergirds and undermines stereotypes of gender and authorship, authority and subjectivity.

In tracing the trajectory of creole subjectivity for the DOM-TOM, we have sought to stress the openness and the polyvalence of the complex situation faced by those doubly disenfranchised métis women of the francophone world who must negotiate the anxieties intrinsic to their simultaneous complacency and dis-ease within the confines of both the metropolitan and the departmental contexts. The insertion of an epistolary discourse takes the politicization of these complexities one step farther, since what is resited at this intersection of writing and ideology, gender and desire is the very notion of positionality, as epistolary writing ultimately comes to mark, in Linda Kauffman's words, "the process and strategies by which ... writing women transform themselves into artists, taking control of the production of writing to challenge ... the fundamental tenets of representation itself" (22). For if epistolary discourses effectively stage the fundamental dramatization of the inscription of desire, their teleologies of transgression can also undermine traditional concepts of desire, gender, and subjectivity. And it is precisely here that the polyvalent rhetoric of desire that grounds Matildana's unanswered letters encounters the alienated axes of Rehvana's narrative of duality and displacement. In this interrogation of the interstices of métissage, revolt is inscribed within each iteration of its axes; in the heart of the contrarieties that separate both sisters, in the paradoxically affiliative antinomies that bind them while banishing them from each other.

If the goal of Matildana as writing subject is to wrest control of the terms of sibling representation, her first letter begins by berating Rehvana—albeit in a lovingly reproving tone—for the silence of separation that the family has had to endure since her departure for her homeland and her attempted re-cognition of "authenticity." Through the extensive use of the second person singular, she registers her worry, dismay, and disapproval of her sister's actions while encouraging her to resume communication with the family: "Believe me, you're making a mistake, deciding to stay cut off from everything, cut off from us, even from me!" (105). Here, the exclusion to which Rehvana has felt subjected for so long has been effectively turned against her erstwhile protectors, in an inversion of subjective hierarchies that signals her intent to forgo previous protocols of safety and now leaves her family unit feeling alone and abandoned. At the same time, Matildana is able to communicate Rehvana's overwhelming importance to her—her salutation is "Rehvana de ma vie"—while signaling, through an important interplay between subject pronouns and disjunctive and indirect object pronouns, her own singularity of vision and of purpose: "For *I* have things to tell *you*, yes I do. Even if *you* don't want to talk to *me* anymore, *my* far-away beauty" (105; emphasis mine). In this way, Matildana sets up a revolving register of opposition between Rehvana and herself that reinforces the recurring cycle of love and anger, presence and absence, itself metonymically signified and deepened by Rehvana's appellation of "belle lointaine."

Matildana's criticisms of Rehvana's choices in this first missive are articulated primarily through the latter's multiple relations with the three arbiters of masculinity in her life: their father, Jérémie, and Eric—although the last is named only in disparaging terms. As a result, the efforts at revolt and re-vision by both sisters are inscribed through their analysis of an ideology of masculinity to which they take opposing views. The divergent attitudes shown toward these figures of masculinity trace the tensions of both internal and external difference; Rehvana displays singular attitudes toward each of them—although these can only be inferred—while Matildana's overall perspective devolves specifically into a difference from each aspect of her sibling's. By articulating her disapproval through this critique, effected through an epistolary discourse and aimed at freeing Rehvana from the social stereotypes written into traditional gender roles, Matildana implicitly inscribes the terms and conditions of her subjective revolt.

For their part, the sisters' parents have cut off all communication with Rehvana since her decision to return to Martinique to live with Eric. While she evenhandedly writes no letters to anyone, they would still like to hear from her, although her father in particular appears to have disowned her altogether: "The parents would really like it if you wrote to them from time to time, real letters, even if Papa has pretended to deny you. . . . he never speaks of you, out of pride, but I can tell that this hardness is just pretense" (106). At the same time, the monthly allowance that Rehvana receives has also been stopped, accompanied by a series of parental—or paternal—injunctions to be followed for the cash flow to be reinstated: "Here's the bad side of things. . . . Papa apparently won't go back on his decision to 'cut you off' until you get back on 'the right track,' until you've gone back to being a 'good girl,' until you've come back to the behavior of a 'girl from a good family' until you've stopped 'sowing your wild oats,' until you've left your 'gang of niggers,' and 'gone back to your studies'" (106–7). It seems that Rehvana indeed has done the unthinkable and, through her actions, offended her parents' delicate middle-class sensibilities and set about the ruin of their good bourgeois name. She needs to get back on track, to make up for her thoughtless flings with both Eric and the Ebonis, and to resume her studies. It is to be noted that these concerns are communicated to Rehvana indirectly, her absence mediated by her sister's discourse, such that the discursive aspects of the paternal edict are deliberately presented in scare quotes.

However, even as she conveys the content of the parental mind, Matildana is able to register her double disapproval of both parent and sibling several sentences later through the form of her expression: "In the meantime, I'll keep sending you half of whatever he gives me; don't thank me, this is just normal, since you still have the right to half of the studio where I'm living alone now since you've run off, you bad girl!" (107). Matildana's re-presentation of their father's wishes becomes a discursive doubling of his decisions, coupled with her own decision to share her allowance while remonstrating with Rehvana for her departure and her ongoing silence; this allows her to appear to be pleading while in fact she registers her strong sense of separation from the actions she reports.

Jérémie seems to occupy the literal and the figurative middle ground here; as Eric's predecessor, and Rehvana's nominal rescuer from the Fils d'Agar, he appears to symbolize the possibility of a return to stability and security. Indeed, a projected reunion with him seems to meet with Matildana's approval: "I was able to console myself for your absence when you left me by going to live with Jérémie, and if you come back to him, you already know that it would be with my blessings" (107). But this may be only for form's sake, since she knows that Rehvana attaches little importance to news of Jérémie's well-being: "I'm sending you news of Jérémie on purpose, even though I know perfectly well that he means nothing to you" (107). This acknowledgment serves to undermine whatever note of regret or remonstration may have lurked in her references to Jérémie, and in fact both reader and interlocutor are quickly confronted by the specter of Eric, cast in such snide and sarcastic terms that the extent of the hierarchy that separates them soon becomes evident: "In fact, there's one thing that I don't understand: since Jérémie is ten times more handsome, a hundred times nicer, a thousand times more intelligent than that idiot from la Pelée, and at least as much 'son of Africa' as he is, why in hell did you chose the worse of the two?" (108). The complex and effective use of metonymy in this fragment is quite remarkable and deserves a closer look.

The criticisms leveled here by Matildana against Rehvana's choices are all the more penetrating given the fact that the object of her criticism is never identified by name. Using Jérémie as a *point de repère*, she is able to implicitly critique his competitor without according him the status of discursive subjectivity. The phrase "the idiot from la Pelée" uses a combination of geography and historical event to locate Eric through his Martinican origins while both disparaging his intelligence and simultaneously differentiating him from Jérémie, the second-generation Antillean who paradoxically recognizes Paris as home. The geometric progression of the resulting comparison, from "ten times" through "a hundred times" to "a thousand times," places Eric on the losing end of a sliding scale of values; but then by turning to "sons of Africa," and particularly by enclosing it in quotes, she is able to undermine the central criterion of Rehvana's search for identity, one that she has carried out successively through Abdoulaye and Jérémie, vainly seeking to locate an elusive authenticity of which Eric is only the most recent arbiter. Such a strategy simultaneously allows her to collectively critique these masculine figures in whom her sister has invested the possibility of her own identity, making liberal use of irony and sarcasm to cast doubt upon the validity of what is in reality her continuing subjugation through gender, at least in the terms in which Rehvana has sought to locate it.

Interestingly, the subtle terms in which this critique is couched follow a more overt attack, one which involves the capacity for judgement of both Rehvana and her chosen paramour. Here, Matildana opens by ostensibly allowing her sibling a measure of accommodation, but this impression is quickly stifled by what follows: "I know very well that you are not a pure spirit, I have a hard time visualizing how you can cling for so long to that illiterate who can't even hold a conversation. Still! I suppose that Mister Muscles must have all kinds of hidden charms" (107). This turn to the sardonic again does not identify Eric by name but rather relies on drawing an implicit distinction between the lovers based on the levels of education and class that separate them. This implicit reference to the upbringing that they share is Matildana's verdict on her sister's chosen path, its penetrating allusion to his lack of letters and her lack of prudence swiftly followed by a mocking, acerbic sexual aside that deprecates Rehvana's discretion and disparages both sibling and her lover. This broadside gives way to a final cutting remark, issued in the same vein: "So, fine! Go on and cuddle with your caveman, but don't forget, still, that I can barely forgive you for the way you're making me suffer, for the hurt you're giving Jérémie, and especially for how you're destroying your life" (109). Here again, Matildana delivers her commentary in terms that are deliberately double voiced; Eric is again described with irony, but only indirectly, as "your caveman," while what can only be categorized as the cutting satire contained in the verb "cuddle" is completed by the triple "gâchis" that she has made of three lives. Rehvana takes Jérémie's side, we may conclude, as a proxy for the implied ruination of both Matildana and herself. But it is Matildana's refusal to accept Rehvana's choice that is of the greatest overall interest here; the difficulty in forgiveness is in fact a warning, a foreclosure of continuing pardons and a signal of her need for independence, and her intention to eventually abandon her sibling to the persistent ineluctability of her own devices and desires.

Matildana's second letter to Rehvana comes nearly eighty pages after the first and takes a decidedly different tone from its predecessor. It takes up barely two pages of text, as opposed to the five-page length of the first, and this new-found brevity is matched from the outset by the impersonal character of its salutation. Addressed this time simply to "l'étrangère," it soon paradoxically displays her awareness of changes in Rehvana's material condition even as its opening sentence signals the growing distance and estrangement between the siblings by Matildana's inaugural use of the unfamiliar *vous*, since, as she states, "I have no idea how to address You from now on, Dear" (188). After this lapse, however, she quickly reverts to the familiar *tu*, inquiring after Rehvana's health during this period of pregnancy and announcing her intention to be present for the birth. But the damage has already been done, and in spite of her ongoing concern for her sister's welfare, Matildana will not hesitate to signal her discursive separation from Rehvana's isolationist posture.

Again, Matildana remonstrates with her sister, but significantly, she does so this time in tones that border more on the prosaic than the reproachful: "You still haven't called, you don't even send a little letter" (289). By recapitulating the status quo in declarative terms, without problematizing her sister's absence or protesting her continued, insistent refusal of communication, Matildana tacitly signals her acceptance of it, and this act functions to reregister her own insistent, pluralist difference, one that is thus inescapably creole. She cements this impression when she conveys the news of her own social and cultural stability through the discursive appropriation of a phrase from her chosen intellectual field, the classics: "As for me, I don't have anything especially new to tell you; *nihil novi sub sole,* nothing is new under the sun; I'm studying for my midterms, the Sorbonne is the same as it always is, but the statue is in a different place" (189). In this apparently laconic reference lies what is perhaps the key to Matildana's secure subjectivity; she is able to accept her interest in other worlds and other cultures as valid precisely because she sees them as interconnected extensions of her own complex historical experience, and she rejects notions of oneness and univocality as anathema to the polyvocalic perspective she embodies. Her affirmation of this sense of pluralism through the key reference to the Sorbonne and the use of the Latin phrase is the subtle sign of a vibrantly polymorphous subject. All this contradicts the turbulent state of affairs symbolized for her through the suggested displacement of the institution's hallmark statue.

Matildana ends her missive by equalizing the situations of both siblings in terms of a discursive confrontation: "I'm going to stop here; it's impossible for me to tell you about my life when I know nothing, or so little, of yours" (189). She insists on a fair exchange of information, registering her protest by withholding her own narrative, uneventful though it might be. But significantly, this second letter is followed immediately by a discursive commentary, communicating the reasons for Rehvana's inveterate lack of response. These letters have all "gone unanswered" (190), for symbolically, and in contrast to her sister, writing is not Rehvana's medium of choice. In fact, the communicative preferences of each sister have been apparent since childhood: where Matildana has always favored the infinite play of discourse, Rehvana prefers not to display her "uncontrolled, capricious spelling" before the "Miss Perfection-first-prize-in-dictation" (190) of her sister. This ease of inscription and intrinsic preference for polysemy that Matildana exhibits are directly at odds with the insistence on origins and their corollary of unicity heralded by Rehvana's search for a cultural authenticity she is already convinced exists. Thus her wish to keep to herself the "stony crucifixion of vain efforts and sterile outbursts"(190) of her self-styled grand return is symbolic of this differential attitude toward the discursive that reinforces the twin registers of creole subjectivity signified by these siblings and reinscribed by their isolation across the divide of the epistolary.

It is thus perhaps not surprising that Matildana's third and shortest letter should be reduced to a series of disjointed fragments barely four lines long, miming ironically the condition of its interlocutor as it finds Rehvana in a subjective state of siege, disoriented, afraid, cowering from Eric's wrath while vainly seeking to maintain her self-respect. Despite the joy associated with her daughter's birth, and the visit made to them both by Matildana, the salutation bottoms out here in the unmistakable tones of "abominable little sister" (280). There then follow only hints of the immoderate succession of issues that have intervened between the siblings: "Pardon me . . . police . . . lying to Maman . . . it doesn't matter" (280).

In the form and the function of these letters, then, Rehvana is both physically and symbolically absent, caught in an insistent silence that verges on the autistic. Her increasing fragmentation is underlined by the presence of ellipsis dots, particularly in the brief last letter which she cannot even manage to render coherent. Compared to Matildana, in fact, Rehvana speaks relatively little in the novel, with a turning inward that is symbolic of her inscription in Reversion. The subtle staging of these discursive strategies through the epistolary mode permits Matildana to separate herself from the succession of disjunctures and misapprehensions that characterize Rehvana's search for an authentic identitarian inscription, while inscribing both her own spirit of revolt and independence and her insistent recognition of the importance of cultural diversity and difference. By dis-placing the traditional subject of an epistolary discourse, she is able to engage an alternative site of enunciation, refracting the creative fragmentation and possibility of the DOM-TOM through the deliberate presence and absence of her letters' dissymmetry. But ironically, it is as early as the first of these epistolary inscriptions of independence that we can also remark a material sign of Matildana's capacity to distinguish and demarcate the imprint of cultural difference, a marker of recognition uttered but unidentified by Rehvana, yet grounded in the complex articulations of creole expression.

Language and Authenticity

What Matildana recognizes and linguistically valorizes in her sister Rehvana can be coded as a verbal signifier of indigenous Caribbean cultural specificity, an appreciative inscription of the Africa-derived act of "sucking one's teeth."

This capacity to produce an expressive, onomatopoeic *cheups* (Fr. *tchips*) of disgust or disapprobation is one of the cross-cultural hallmarks of the Caribbean vernacular, conveying wordlessly but effectively the mind-set of the speaker with regard to the subject at hand.[6] At the same time, it remains almost unknown (and practically inexpressible) outside the Caribbean region and the ethnic African lexicon from which it was originally adapted. Given the specificity of these parameters, it is thus all the more significant that when Matildana raises the cultural flag by referring to Rehvana's "tchips," she does so not only in an epistolary context but by simultaneously enclosing the reference in parentheses: "(I even miss our arguments, and I even go so far as to miss your inimitable 'cheups,' you remember, the lovely resounding cheups that only you could do . . .)" (105). On a primary level of signification, the use of parentheses would appear to impose a symbolic line of demarcation, restricting the reference to the valorization of verbal exchanges between the siblings while enacting a further refraction of the textual framework. The term is thus clearly valorized by being positioned in a text-within-a-text-within-a-text. At the same time, however, there can be no doubt of the importance that Matildana attaches to this catchall Caribbean neologism. Indeed, she insists upon exploiting and extending the image, rendering an absent Rehvana metonymically present through sound, yet within the parentheses: "Yes, I can hear it, that remarkable dry little sound that you just made with your lips, the air whistling through your teeth, I'm coming to drag one out of you, oh, how lovely it is" (105–6). It thus becomes increasingly clear that Matildana's discourse here turns on a particular practice of cultural expression.

Between the parenthetical and the epistolary, then, lies a critical area of creole expression that is enhanced and enlivened through Matildana's recognition of the cultural value articulated by the Caribbean vernacular; at a symbolic level, it is not by coincidence that it is she, rather than her sister, who engages and valorizes this aspect of their culture. By bracketing her own discursive re-presentation of this typically Caribbean ejaculation, and conflating it with the apostrophic address of the letter, she is able to reflect the complex intersection of ethnic and linguistic experience symbolically embodied in this creole utterance, while using it to challenge the traditional tenets of regional re-presentation displaced by the expression itself. The world of historical and cultural specificity contained in Rehvana's titillating cheups signifies a microcosm of performative Caribbeanness, a vocalized vision that distills the essence of the Caribbean character. This irruption of creole expression in the text marks an initial site of cultural identitarianism, a singular event that ultimately leads to the extensive distribution of creole across the discursive spectrum. Matildana's identification of this signal space remains in stark contrast to Rehvana's refusal to acknowledge it, and simultaneously signifies Matildana's integral inscription in the creative creole culture of the region, whose pluralized openness she effectively inhabits. But it is the symbolic significance of vernacular communication in this context of Caribbean pluralism that leads us to consider the role of the creole language itself in the signifying structure of the text.

While it is not my intention to provide, at this stage, an extended analysis of the social role played by Creole languages in the Caribbean context, an effective reading of the incorporation of this form into the novelistic discourse requires some historical background. It is critical to recognize initially that, as Peter Roberts points out, creoles are not dialects but are full-fledged languages in themselves: "A creole represents a stage in a developmental process which started as an unstable, structurally restricted, non-native form of communication between peoples of different cultures. This communication has become stable, and more expanded in roles, functions and structures and represents the native language of the descendants of those originally involved in the contact situation" (1988:13). In other words, such creole languages have become the communicative vehicle for those societies identified under the same rubric; rather than a simple process of homogenization, this linguistic creolization typically marks a society constructed out of the tensions and teleologies of the colonial encounter, both its population and its language the product of this cultural intersection. This cultural contact between colonizer and colonized, both of whom, in the Caribbean case, were transplanted subjects from a variety of African and European ethnic groups with no common language, functions as the dominant marker of a creole Caribbean society. As Mervyn C. Alleyne observes, "It was contact among immigrant groups of diverse origins . . . that became the most significant factor for the emergence of West Indian societies, because nowhere else in the hemisphere was the destruction of the indigenous peoples and their civilization more complete" (1985:158). It is this important link between linguistic transplantation and (re)construction, on the one hand, and cultural re-presentation, on the other, that we must now explore in Dracius-Pinalie's text.

The critical conjunction that exists in the region between historical experience and linguistic development becomes the basis in the novel for the metaphorical articulation of collective identity. Indeed, language and linguistic form are intrinsically associated with the growth of the Caribbean creole continuum. As Alleyne continues, "The language situations existing in the Caribbean are mirrors through which the complex cultural history of the region may be observed" (1985:158). As a means of contesting the colonial phenomenon of mimetism that institutionalizes the colonizer's model among the colonized, the view of creole as a valid form of cultural expression has long been subject to opposing opinions concerning its relative value as a language, a patois, or dialect, or even a pidgin, signifying nothing more than a typically imperfect assimilation of colonial culture. As Alleyne suggests, "The general feeling is that creole languages and dialects are defective—that they may be suitable for the expression of 'folklore' . . . but that they are quite inadequate for the expression of complex and abstract thought" (1985:160). When such attitudes are joined to historical patterns of prejudice that encourage colonial subjects to master colonial speech and vocabulary patterns in order to better ensure social and educational advancement and recognition, it is no wonder that creoles continue to sustain an ineradicable social stigma. It is this crucial field of contestation that Dracius-Pinalie's discursive use of creole seeks to address.

Much of the creole dialogue in *L'Autre qui danse* is located in a long, untitled, largely monologic section of part 2. In this scene, Rehvana is made to listen to an extended mini-narrative recounted by Man Cidalise, an older peasant woman and storyteller of traditional values who befriends her; as an icon of cultural complexity "whose syncretism combines Christianity and obeah, sweets and fasting" (221), Cidalise's embodiment of strong matrifocal values sustains Rehvana during her progressive falling-out with and escape from Eric. The bulk of this episode thus constitutes an embedded narrative, a tale-within-a-tale whose structural characteristics and self-reflexive thematic relation to the main text produce what Tzvetan Todorov terms "causal explanation" or "thematic juxtaposition, as with arguments or examples or stories that form a contrast with the preceding one" (1981:53). This extended articulation of creolized language in the text is a comment on the more linear narrative and communicative patterns that surround it, and through its difference exhibits several key characteristics: first, reprising the principle that form follows function—and theme—it comprises an oral mini-narrative told by a member of the lower classes to one whose social identity grows increasingly indeterminate. Further, in syntactical terms, the passage does not quite conform to the oralities of the creole commonly spoken in the French Caribbean; doubling its difference in its diversion even from traditional creole forms, it appears to retain a number of trace elements that are closer to what we might term a colloquialized Caribbean French, and certain phrases are provided with footnote translations.

Given the symbiotic relation that we have noted between the articulation of Caribbean culture and the idiosyncracies of its language, it seems fair to postulate that such an inscription of creolized language in *L'Autre qui danse* functions as a discursive re-presentation of the cultural complexities framing the Caribbean diaspora that the text seeks to open up. Upon closer reading, then, it becomes quickly apparent that this sequence displays a crucial dichotomy between speaker and interlocutor; although the series of mini-tales told by Man Cidalise takes creole as its basic reference, Rehvana maintains a stony silence in response. Reinforcing the symbolic significance of Rehvana's refusal of speech, here her distance paradoxically valorizes the linguistic difference she refuses. Indeed, the extended monologue that this quickly becomes bears an uncanny yet significant resemblance, on the symbolic level, to the silence Rehvana maintains with regard to the letters Matildana writes, suggesting a further withdrawal of this subject from the creolized patterns of difference set into motion by both her lingual and her literary interlocutors. It remains one of the novel's supreme ironies that Rehvana's search for cultural authenticity, one of the primary axes of the plot, leaves her unable or unwilling to acknowledge the articulation of such indigenous patterns when they are inscribed in the character, actions, or words of her others. The persistent disjuncture between these audibly and visibly creole sites and strategies that proffer a transformative pluralism, and Rehvana's inability to recognize the various modes by which it functions, stigmatize both her as subject and the search in which she is engaged, making her insistence on homogeneity the very sign of her positional stalemate.

The importance that can be ascribed to these deliberate (dis)articulations of authenticity leads us to consider how—and why—creole establishes its difference of form and function in the text, in its dual role both as discourse and as polysemic cultural sign. As was suggested earlier, we are confronted not with a phonetically accurate, morphologically distinct re-presentation of creole, but with a creolized (re)construction of a culturally drawn colloquial French, a distinction which at once begs particular questions of the formalized textual structure of narrative, language, and communication in the novel. Specifically, this sequence uses current creole expressions, along with words and phrases from a standardized French lexicon, but modified and metamorphosed into an effective but intelligible approximation of a vernacular creole. Thus we see the construction of linguistic simulacra, such as "couri-vini" (140) and "toutes bagailles" (143), along with such creolisms as "sa ki rivé'w" (141), "sa sa yé sa" (142–3), "passe que" and "missié" (144), "kouté sa," "ka pasé," "manzèl," and "ay fè zafè'w" (165), and with the whole periodically punctuated by typical creole onomatopoeic expressions such as "wacha," "plim," and "wabap" (145). Further, within the overall framework of the sequence, the narrative commentary that resurfaces between monologues maintains its linear inscription in standard French, creating a polyvocalic discourse whose several levels of linguistic expression reflect the overwhelming complexities of communication in a culturally creolized environment. The resulting conundrum locates creole language structures in a plurality of sites that restructure, through the parabola of plural presence engendered by the intersection of ethnicity, language, and gender, our very understanding of what a larger vision of creolization might entail.

Over against the complex creole patterns of language and culture, the vision of métissage in which Rehvana remains inscribed is contrasted with an unmistakable polysemy drawn on regional realities forged from the tensions of the colonial encounter, a re-presentational grammar that encompasses the split racial, cultural, and linguistic levels of articulation that frame the functioning of the Caribbean diaspora. These forces interact despite Rehvana's intransigence, locating and valorizing a pattern of creole pluralism that avoids Rehvana's positional extremes while revealing the ubiquity of the very identitarian strategies she seeks. Matildana functions, then, as the signifier of a differential creole subjectivity, tracing the contrarieties of perspective that separate her from the demand for an overarching procedural unicity that will ultimately prove to be Rehvana's downfall; the patterns of race, ethnicity, culture, and language in whose interstices both siblings are intertwined offer strikingly differing paths toward the open-ended challenge of creative possibility that creolization offers.

This constant valorization of Matildana's position, constituting an implicit inscription in the interstices of the creole, reaches periodic crescendoes in the text, in which the siblings' oppositionality of perspective is rendered even more penetrating by the persistent discongruity by which they are figured. One of these episodes occurs more or less at the narrative center of the text, and the other is placed much nearer its end. Let us take a closer look at the first of these episodes, the one in which these patterns of creolization are subjectively verbalized.

Receiving no response to her succession of letters, Matildana decides to fly to Martinique herself to locate her errant sibling. Their meeting occurs in an untitled chapter of part 2, the reunion of the sisters remaining unrecorded until we confront them deep in conversation on the veranda of Rehvana's house. Significantly, the opening words of the episode convey Rehvana's inability to withstand the intense Caribbean sun, its heat the overarching signifier of the very tropical ambience which, ironically, her vaunted return had led her to rediscover: "This sun is making me crazy! I hate this direct light!" (191). But this is followed by an even more significant exchange, one dominated by Matildana's scathing dissection of her sister's insistence on locating a palpable, material authenticity.

In thundering tones of ironic objection and dissent, Matildana rails against the core of her sister's position; that there is a discernible and definable essence that compartmentalizes humanity into ethnic and cultural categories whose poles are destined never to meet. The logical implications of this position are too much for Matildana to contemplate: "I am unnegrified! . . . Yes, I forgot dear Abdoulaye's catechism, that holy man! Article One, identity: since I didn't start out completely white, if I don't negrify myself, I am nothing. I have neither race nor color, nor identity nor culture, I am nothing. I am a nothing, a nothing at all. A less than nothing. And it is so important, so primordial, to be truly something. Even if, in order to cultivate authenticity, one must force it a bit and use tricks" (196).

The extent to which Matildana's use of irony in this passage is able to undermine the basic premises and assumptions that govern the perspective of the purblind Abdoulaye and the Fils d'Agar and, by extension, her sister Rehvana, is really quite extraordinary. In fact, a close reading of the passage indicates that each metaphor used to prop them both up is introduced only to be immediately subverted and undone. Thus any merit to be attached to the "catechism" of Abdoulaye, the "holy man," is at once called into question since it has been forgotten; the legalistic resonances of "Article One" bestow upon him the profile of a political leader, but this suggestion of command and authority is erased by her ironic insistence that ultimately "I am denegrified." But critically, this process turns upon a perception of individual racial inscription: Matildana, who speaks, by proxy, for Rehvana as well as Abdoulaye, is categorized not as black, or métisse, but as "not completely white," displaying an almost criminal pattern of ethnic betrayal that by implication renders her un-knowable and indefinable, requiring her immediately to "negrify herself" in order to avoid being reduced to "nothing." This, by extension, has proved to be the path of least resistance down which Rehvana has been led. But by now, the structure of the argument is visibly faulty, and the center cannot hold; Abdoulaye's principle of authenticity, whose intrinsic unicity Rehvana adopts, refuses to countenance the symbolic function of a cultural crossroads for fear that it will undermine the fragile essentialism of his binary, and thus implicitly still colonial, world, which ultimately rings hollow before Matildana's mul-tiple modernities of the creole.

Ultimately, then, Dracius-Pinalie's discourse seeks to valorize a vision of the Caribbean heritage as a composite, cosmopolitan, polysemic presence, a creoleness that David Lowenthal calls "an expression of condition rather than of nationality" (1972:32). Even beyond the oppositional trajectories traced by Rehvana and Matildana, the textual strategy of *L'Autre qui danse* envisions an inscription of a creole society in terms that underscore the fact that it derives its value and its raison d'être from the intersection and interplay of the multiple cultures and ethnicities that together signify beyond the subjective strategies of métissage. This creole culture of the Caribbean embodies difference through the confluent character of its collective identity, creating, in the words of Anto-nio Benítez-Rojo, "a supersyncretic culture characterized by its complexity . . . and its instability . . . whose seeds had come scattered from the richest stores of three continents" (1992:46). It is this inscription of instability that Matildana as textual subject seeks to transform into performative possibilities of presence.

If, as Benítez-Rojo argues, the mission of the Caribbean text is to go "in search of routes that might lead . . . to an extratextual . . . psychic reconstitution of the Self" (1992:28), it is perhaps the nonconflictual ease of Matildana's cul-tural performance that allows us finally to posit this reconstitution in discursive terms. Equally at home in Paris or Fort-de-France, a subject who "loves Terence as much as Senghor" (325), she exemplifies the basic polysemy of a métis subjectivity that turns heterogeneity into an elemental principle of epistemic cultural praxis. In contrast to her ironic outburst to Rehvana—that, from the latter's point of view, "outside of race, no salvation" (197)—her own chosen path is one that personifies her commitment to pluralism. Moving back to Fort-de-France after completing her studies, Matildana immediately locates the linguistic and cultural principles at which the complexities of the creole intersect: "She studies linguistics and Creole, and works as a collaborator, in her free time, for a new Caribbean weekly which is trying to take into account . . . the cultural, political and social issues of the Antillean world" (323). By conflating creole's metaphoric polyvocality and transcultural linguistic structures with the dynamics of political action signified by the deliberately pan-Caribbean perspective of the new journal, Matildana inscribes herself in her own culture as an icon of its profuse possibilities, actively inhabiting and embodying the infinite many-sidedness of her Caribbean world.

The rhythms and resonances of the creole language are inscribed as a singular metaphor for this network of cultural possibility: "She learned Creole . . . like a language whose mechanisms and richness she is trying to plumb. . . . the durability of Creole strikes her as a necessity, she is on fire for Creole, she dives into it, mines it, and Creole inhabits her, overwhelms her" (323–24). Matildana's immersion in the creative disjunctures of creole's figurative feasibilities thus brings to fruition the spectrum of linguistic pluralism that serves as the founding framework for this vision of Caribbeanness, and effectively inscribes what Benîtez-Rojo calls the "local truths, displaced truths, provisional and peremptory truths . . . that barely make up a fugitive archipelago of regular rhythms" for the postmodern Caribbean (1992:151). For as the symbolic inheritor of a cultural cornucopia, Matildana now not only inhabits but manufactures and extends the many spaces of difference through which she is defined; importantly, her conflation of the language and politics of the creole inscribes her at the center of a geopolitical axis that is intrinsically and overwhelmingly Caribbean, generating a sense of community and identity that transcends the boundaries of the local from her immersion in these twin defining signs of an indigenous regionalism.

In a didactic riff that tacitly recognizes the growing empirical centrality of the creole, the text maps the terrain of a cultural self-constitution now almost global in its reach: "Nothing human, no matter what its color, whether white, black, yellow, or tricolored, *nothing human is foreign to her.* In opposition to her younger sister, Matildana is not one of those who punishes herself with impossible blacknesses" (325; emphasis in the original). In this subtle yet overt contrast in subjective strategies, the italicization of the text underlines the global reach of her cultural pluralism. Matildana has successfully avoided the binary colonialist essentialism of racial typing; the singular factors undergirding Rehvana's attempt at authenticity are contested and overturned by her sister's personification of a differential, collective Caribbean identity, grounded in what Richard Burton calls the "continuum of cultures that have coexisted and competed in the Caribbean ever since slavery" (1997a:2). This suggestion of affiliation and evolution constructs a composite from the multiplicities of the margin, teasing out from the tensions of the colonial encounter a coherent framework for the challenge of everyday existence.

In this way, the intrinsic pluralisms of both language and ethnicity in a Caribbean context are metamorphosed into cultural signs, re-presenting the complex, multilayered network of associations that has wrought the characteristics of this creole society. Matildana's effortless skill at symbolizing the successes of this identitarian strategy is firmly and unalterably grounded in her Caribbeanness: "She knows very well, in any case, that she has never stopped being Antillean, that these innumerable years of exile haven't changed very much in terms of the depths of her nature" (324). This embodiment of a pluralist cultural praxis ultimately locates the misplaced unicities of her sister Rehvana in a revealing light, enacting a striking positional contrast that emphasizes the creative capacities of creolization and the protean possibilities of métissage while illuminating the shortcomings of an elusive, illusory authenticity based on the binary assumptions of racial division. For importantly, not only does Matildana personify the substantive originality and self-invention of the métis, she is also an integral part and product of a commonwealth of cultures that cultivates a novel modernity out of the ruptures and disjunctions of the past. As Nigel Bolland puts it, "The image of creole culture and a creole society emphasizes social unity: the new nation as creole *community*" (1992:51; emphasis in the original). By inscribing the diaspora as imagined community, then, these textual designations reframe creoleness and are crucial to any understanding of Matildana's true achievement.

This emphasis on the constitutive and transformative role of language revises and reforms our notions of both identity and community. Indeed, it is the very instability and polymorphism of creolized language forms that enables the transition to cultural and identitarian pluralization. As Françoise Lionnet cogently explains: "Language reinforces a phenomenon of creative instability in which no 'pure' or unitary origin can ever be posited. A linguistic and rhetorical approach to the complex question of *métissage* thus points to the ideological and fictional nature of our racial categories while underlining the relationship between language and culture" (1989:16). In these terms, the multiple modernities implicit within métissage supplant the chimera of unitary origin that is Rehvana's goal, exposing the stony ground at its source and erecting in its place an affiliative network of creole creativity generated from the kinetic polyvocality of Caribbean culture and language. So that while Rehvana's fundamental error consists, even from her formative years, in finding herself "already just a bit too black, always just a bit too black" (341), Matildana, on the contrary, "feels herself a whole person, she doesn't conceive of herself as anything other than Antillean, but still refuses to be put into bottles of artificial scent" (325); she thus crucially distances herself from Rehvana's misplaced vision of overarching oneness and sets up the appearance of the final textual arbiter of these siblings' critical difference.

Death and Survival

The novel concludes with a "Chant Ultime," a final coda to the divergent destinies of these two sisters in métissage. Matildana's comfortable creoleness is inscribed and encoded in a chapter titled, symbolically, "L'Autre Martinique," articulating an otherness that is at once entirely Martinican and yet distinct from the "authentic" Martinique whose discovery Rehvana desired. The text takes up the downward spiral of Rehvana's final days in the subsequent chapter, appropriately titled "Quelque part entre L'Une Et L'Autre." This in-betweenness, originally the sign by which, ironically, both Matildana and Rehvana are figured, now marks the boundaries of the latter's destructive displacement, the space of incessant slippage that separates both sisters.

The seriousness of this slippage is formally inscribed in the text by Rehvana's almost total absence from it, a symbolic and progressive erasure of Rehvana as subject that, beginning with her inhibited speech patterns, increasingly reveals her unsettled condition by proxy, through her disappearance from Martinique and in Matildana and Jérémie's discussions of her whereabouts. In this roundabout way, Man Cidalise suggests that Rehvana has probably left for Paris, thus accomplishing a mysterious and elided disappearance whose disturbingly enigmatic silence is filled by the counterpoint of Jérémie's impending marriage and Matildana's decision not to disclose the fact of his paternity to him. But these corollaries soon give way to a detailed re-presentation of Rehvana's approaching agony.

Even before this final section gets under way, Rehvana's inexorable decline becomes increasingly poignant; the text makes it clear that "Rehvana has become the shadow of herself" (252). To make ends meet, she takes a job as a secondary school teacher—"without receiving either instructions or teacher training" (240)—in the ghetto-like town of Remorville, where "the sub-basements . . . harbor a rat-like people, crawling with excrement and filth" (238). Yet, even here, she insists on dressing "in boubou and African sandals" (239) as a sign of her difference and authenticity. Subsequently, she is finally abandoned by Eric, while an increasingly worried Man Cidalise turns her daughter Aganila over to a relative for safekeeping. Meanwhile, profoundly apathetic, Rehvana falls ill and, significantly, begins to bleed mysteriously and incessantly in a symbolic portent of the suffering and death to come; indeed, she has "the feeling that she has never stopped bleeding. . . . Rehvana bathes in her own blood" (297, 299). Returning somehow to Paris, she succumbs to poverty and the death that it eventually brings.

The cramps and hallucinations that she is made to undergo are now the final arbiters of a constant subjection to alienation and dis-location, translating her childhood rivalries and complexes into a pattern of subordination whose concluding chapter is about to be written. "Rehvana thinks that reality exists only because she is aware of it, that she perceives it, and that all she has to do is to close her eyes in order to make things stop being visible" (350). But accepting these divergent images and positionalities as a simple product of sibling rivalry would be much too reductive a reading here. While it is clear that the young Rehvana "is not quite with it," and that Matildana "possesses . . . the capacity to feel comfortable with herself" (342), it is the latter's striking capacity for substitution and transmutation that is the symbolic key to the creole pluralism that she re-presents. The early importance of this polysemic perspective is underlined by its inscription through the multivalent signature of writing, reaffirming the critical role of discursive form in the the novelistic articulation of Matildana's relational vision: "Matildana writes two Latin compositions, her own and Rehvana's . . . and sprinkles into Rehvana's work the strings of frightened little demons that are Rehvana's adorable spelling mistakes" (341). It is this early capacity for discursive doubling and identitarian transformation that functions as the overarching figure for the cultural polyvocality that Matildana will untimately embody; as she reproduces on the page the identifying traces of Rehvana's presence as well as her own, she embodies the strategic tensions that secure and separate self and Other, subject and object, sameness and difference. And it is these opposing patterns of affiliation and indivisibility, pitting the confines of ethnic homogeneity against the possibilities of cultural heterogeneity, that ultimately dictate the novel's twin teleologies of death and survival.

Rehvana's death, when it finally does occur, is, in a sense, reported rather than re-presented. It appears, in the chapter "Nulle Part," as an innocuous newspaper item read by Matildana's seatmate on a flight from Fort-de-France to Paris. This anonymous leavetaking is all the more ironic given Matildana's simultaneous distance from her sibling's death and proximity to its discursive reproduction; the old woman she has just helped heave her bag into the overhead compartment, and who then reads "that a young Antillean woman had been found starved to death with her child in a housing project in the Parisian suburbs" (358) can have no inkling, despite the tears of sympathy that she sheds, that the article's unfortunate subject is her neighbor's hapless, long-lost sister.

Metaphorically, Matildana's imminent arrival echoes her sister's definitive departure. In a final, symbolic gesture of transformation, the original metropolitan site of binary division and colonial transgression is rewritten as an infinitely malleable cultural and subjective space, one that metes out both the ineluctability of erasure and the infinite promise of creolized climates of change and survival through the plethora of discourses and desires it re-presents as part of the transformative terrain of present-day postcolonial culture. In the complex context that undergirds the disjunctures of French overseas departmentalism, working through such pluralized patterns of creoleness and métissage can illuminate the dilemma posed by a sense of exile and the search for oneness, even as new fields of discursive and subjective possibility for Caribbean women are opened up. As Françoise Lionnet points out, "Rehvana and Matildana are certainly two sides of the same character: the one who feels exiled and the one who feels anchored, the one who searches for origins and the one who comfortably assumes global citizenship" (1995:99). In the incessant, dialectical oscillation between the incommensurable opposites of tradition and modernity, adulteration and authenticity, these sisters' twin trajectories instantiate the double Caribbean problematic inscribed between the lines of ethnicity and identity: Rehvana, ironically, becomes "that unknown young woman who allowed herself, at la Corneuve, at Quatre-Mille, a death worthy of the African desert since she was incapable of living as an African" (358), as she refigures that imaginary insistence on intangible modes and models of an absolute authenticity that ultimately proved her undoing. Matildana, the "other" for whom dance proved an early metaphor for her openness, spontaneity, and active acceptance of and participation in a creole network of cultural signification, reframes the Parisian discursive space as one of both exile and return, articulating a critical metamorphosis that, in Stuart Hall's words, gives rise to "a new conception of ethnicity as a kind of counter to the old discourses of nationalism or national identity" (1987:460). In this way, an identitarian strategy inscribed through and across difference defines a new space for the *dom-tomienne*, finally subordinating traditional metropolitan claims of mastery to the differential, discursive claims of a heterogeneous creolization.

The complex concatenation of dilemmas that confronts the métis female Caribbean departmental subject is complicated even further here by the issues of exile, integration, and positionality that frame the construction of cultural identity in the region. But within these multilayered modalities we can locate two specific but divergent subjective strategies vying for a strategic space of survival that can empower a disenfranchised Antillean femininity struggling against the exacerbating forces of racial and cultural displacement. Dracius-Pinalie's discourse of liberation has deliberately articulated a wider vision of creoleness for the contemporary *dom-tomienne*, avoiding the inviting but ultimately reductive scenario in which, as Gayatri Spivak has suggested, "contemporary neocolonialism is seen only from the undoubtedly complex and important but restrictive perspective or explanatory context of metropolitan, internal colonization of the post-colonial migrant or neo-colonial immigrant" (1992: 98). Thus the construction of an effective subjective strategy that will reflect the paradoxes of an interstitial composite of identity, ethnicity, and place for the Antillean woman remains a vital discursive challenge. For the French Caribbean female writer, then, the overriding concern must lie in this critical conflation of discourse and identity, working, as Françoise Lionnet states, "to elaborate discursive patterns that will . . . displace the traditional distinctions of rigidly defined literary genres" (1988:261). The pressing problematic of strategizing alternate terms and conditions for Caribbean female authorship and the corollaries of subjectivity it constructs are effectively yoked together in Dracius-Pinalie's striking subversion of the traditional images of Caribbean womanhood. The search for self-definition whose boundaries are charted by this text install new, affiliative categories for female socialization in the region.

In his seminal study of the origin and development of cultural métissage in the Caribbean, René Depestre insists upon the relational dynamism integral to the double phenomenon of marooning and admixture that is the region's primary social and cultural heritage. The re-vision resulting from this se-

quence of marooning and identitarian mutation eventuated an interculturality which is the basis for a specific subjectivity founded on reconstitutive
practices of pluralism and difference. According to Depestre: "Interculturality
is the characteristic, the common denominator of the Caribbean people on all
levels of their psychology and their behavior in society. They have created new
values and in as much as these were lived values, they carried within them the
universal" (1984:7). These intercultural values help to expand and redefine the
boundaries of a departmental culture marked by its difference from the European and the African axes while mapping a discursive space for itself that is
more than both. Transforming these terms, Dracius-Pinalie's discourse maps a
modernist space for the métis female voice, delineating and interrogating a
cosmopolitan politics and poetics of place that helps to redefine Caribbean
womanhood.

It is not coincidental that the title of this novel is itself also an exercise in
intertextual doubling: in a kind of discursive synechdoche, it is drawn in part
from Baudelaire's poem "Le Serpent qui danse" in *Les Fleurs du mal*, from the
intrinsic opposition between freedom and restraint inscribed in the line "One
might say that it was a serpent dancing at the end of a rod" (57). Here, the baton
serves to maintain the dance through the implied threat of force, but ultimately it cannot control the snake's dangerous, innate liberty. More important, perhaps, the author also draws on a critical scene in Alfred de Musset's
On ne badine pas avec l'amour, in which Perdican and Camille are at odds
over the impending marriage planned for them by the Baron.[7] In act 2, scene
5, Camille explains at length to Perdican her reasons for returning to the con-
vent instead of remaining in society. In order to demonstrate her argument,
she then describes to him a painting in the château in which there is a monk
sitting in his cell, bent over his missal; visible through the bars, there is also an
Italian-style inn, in front of which a goatherd is dancing. Asked which of the
two he prefers, Perdican replies, "Neither one nor the other and both of them
. . . one of them reads and the other dances" (64). But there is more to this pair
than just a simple binary opposition. Linked by their similarity as much as their
difference, these figures seem to inhabit discursive spaces that tend to oppose
as well as to merge with each other; activity is set against passivity, intellectual-
ism versus participation, but both subjects, in the end, are engaged at some
level with existence.

What does this dichotomy—one for whose axes Perdican indicates no preference—symbolize for the discursive worlds of Matildana and Rehvana? Per-

haps, in the double gesture of métissage, these figures are not as opposed to each other as they at first appear; by choosing "both" over "one" or "the other," that is, through his preference for the advantages of admixture, the full cultural and historical measure of the subject can finally be explored to its fullest extent. It is the judicious conflation of the historical hierarchies of métissage that frames both Rehvana and Matildana, that transmutes the colonial trace through the cultural interaction that highlights both their differences and their similarities as symbiotic sites of creole possibility.

Given the constructed constraints and commonalities of the modernities that frame both the "third island" of the metropole and the DOM-TOM, identity must, in the end, be ineluctably plural. But as Evelyn O'Callaghan reminds us, "There is no *one* authentic West Indian identity, much less a definitive female one" (1993:13; emphasis in the original). The survivalist strategies inscribed here reflect the multiplicities of an interrelational model of difference that disturbs prevalent notions of origin and return even as it relocates and transforms the heterogeneities of a collective consciousness. It is the richness and variety, as well as the expansiveness and unpredictability, of this cultural interplay, its re-formation of the old into a new order of values and practices, that Jamaican critic Rex Nettleford sums up as "an organic whole inextricably bound up and expressive of a new and rich phenomenon which is neither Africa nor Europe, yet embodying the two in unprecedented and creative modes of relationship" (1970:173). Métissage is grounded in the interstices of this paradoxical neither/nor relationship, dis-placing and re-placing the binary-driven boundaries of a dominant departmental neocolonialism through the creative expression of the multiple modalities of creoleness that are the heritage of the colonial encounter. Its effects reshape and redefine the boundaries of regional identity by dis-placing the double colonization that has historically insisted on positioning the feminine Caribbean subject.

5

Solibo Magnifique
Carnival, Opposition, and the Narration of the Caribbean Maroon

Chaque livre est un homme. Chaque
  mot tremble du fourmillement des siècles d'écriture.
Patrick Chamoiseau and Raphaël Confiant, Lettres créoles

Marooning the Text

Comparatively speaking, the rise of the Martinican novelist Patrick Chamoiseau to the pinnacle of contemporary francophone fiction writing might
appear to certain eyes to be somewhat precipitate. Born in 1953, Chamoiseau
grew up the son of working-class parents in the island that remains his home.
He studied sociology and law in Paris, moved back to Martinique and became
a social worker, and indeed still works as a probation officer. Yet, prior to 1992,
when he received France's most prestigious literary prize, the Goncourt, for
his third full-length novel, *Texaco*, an allegorized retelling of Martinican life
through the inhabitants of one of Fort-de-France's principal shantytowns,
Chamoiseau was known primarily as the author of several collections of short
stories and a couple of original, even inventive novels, and also recognized as
the coauthor, along with the linguist Jean Bernabé and the novelist Raphaël
Confiant, of a duo of theoretical works that sought to ground the French
Caribbean experience in the principles of *créolité*, a cultural and discursive
framework originated by these authors that valorized the pluralisms and
discontinuities of language, history, and ethnicity that had eventuated the
commonalities of the Caribbean diaspora. The fact that Chamoiseau was cata-
pulted to the heady heights of international fame through the inescapable
paradox of metropolitan recognition of the cultural production of the

postcolonial periphery that it still maintained in neocolonial thrall was not lost among the many plaudits and commendations that followed. While metropolitan recognition of his literary prowess went a long way toward finally moving French Caribbean literature as a whole closer to the center of a long notoriously narcissistic canon, at the same time, the process of centering brought about by this act of approbation raised the inevitable question of the literary and cultural assimilation of a field whose origins and very raison d'être resided precisely in its historical determination to assert its difference from the metropole.

However, somewhat contrary to the direction of this contemporary canonization, I focus in this chapter on one of Chamoiseau's earlier works, *Solibo Magnifique*,[1] in which, as I hope to show, his self-reflexive inscription of traditional Caribbean tropes based on a carnivalesque sense of parody and play and a whirlwind of verbal manipulation succeeds in re-presenting the complex, interwoven structures of a society tracing a fiercely independent path between cultures, between worlds, between the disappearing patterns of an evanescant, plantation-centered age and the plural possibilities of a developing, heterogeneous creolization.

This is not the moment to interrogate the intricacies of créolité, or, for that matter, to outline the historical framework that undergirds Chamoiseau's vision of contemporary Caribbean creole culture. Indeed, much of this subject has already been rehearsed in the introduction. But any reading of *Solibo Magnifique* must come to terms with the slave-based phenomenon of *marronnage*, or marooning, and with the figural role of the maroon, or runaway slave, as an identitarian icon of rebellion and liberation for the Caribbean diaspora. It is this figure that both informs and determines not only the paradigmatic persona of Solibo but the patterns of parody, pastiche, and self-reflexivity that structure the discourse of the novel.

The roots of the maroon figure lie in the veiled colonial mists of slave rebellion, and the reality of the runaway slave has been recognized as being of pivotal importance, a fundamental element in the construction of an indigenous opposition movement for the Caribbean people. Indeed, even apart from acts of individual or group rebellion, of which the plantocracy lived in constant fear, the ubiquity of runaways was inescapable. As Michael Craton points out: "Wherever there were slave plantations, there were runaways; wherever runaways banded together and sustained themselves in the wilds, they can properly be called maroons. True maroons were found at one time or another in virtually every plantation colony, however small" (1982:61). Overall, then, the plantation hierarchy suffered a number of large and violent slave revolts, but it was certainly also faced with a sliding scale of acts of marronnage, since these were by no means limited to the larger islands. There can be no denying the fact that slaves generally resisted their treatment as chattel and came to revere the successful practitioners of both the individual acts of petit marronnage and the installation of larger, self-sustaining maroon communities that, in the most successful cases, evolved a level of military effectiveness that forced the colonial administration into signing peace treaties with them. The importance of these maroon rebellions as models of autonomy and independence cannot be overstated. As Craton writes: "Maroon communities were deeply inimical to the slave plantation nexus because they offered a rival version of creolization. . . . Maroon communities and their life-style were bound to provide an admired ideal for those still enslaved" (1982:64). It was the twin tensions inscribed between an idealized self-determination and the inauguration of an indigenous creole consciousness that would provide the impetus for the construction of modernist metaphors of cultural opposition based on models of maroon courage and defiance.[2]

The important parallel to be established at this juncture is the gradual transformation of the model of the *marronneur* into the *paroleur,* or the *conteur,* a metaphorical transposition of acts of opposition from the sociopolitical to the discursive plane. In the search for a subaltern subject capable of serving as an idealized paradigm of heroic opposition, one capable of encompassing the entirety of the physical contestation and verbal dissimulation that grounds the temporal trace of the Caribbean experience, the maroon figure became the embodiment of a native creole independence of wit and will that traversed the period from the arrival of the earliest slaves to the gradual disappearance of the plantation era. These pulsating patterns of cultural contestation help to explain Chamoiseau's choice of the *menu peuple* to shoulder the oppositional role that seeks to keep both the *békés* and the metropole at bay; as Richard Burton explains, "The day worker is the perfect maroon, except that the town becomes the site of his tasks and that it is within the system itself that he carries out his complex opposionality" (1997b:167). For if the history of the Caribbean region was, in large part, a history written by the colonizer, one which tended to stress the colonizer's view that the slave subject was marked by his or her natural docility and acceptance of subjection, then the very ubiquity of slave opposition across the length and breadth of the region would provide

the discursive and metaphorical framework for the construction of an autonomous, emancipatory model of creole consciousness that the social phenomena of carnival and departmentalization might transform but not transcend.
Chamoiseau's work, like that of the créolistes, is a discursive act inscribed as a
response to colonial elaborations of authority and forced subordination, and
must ultimately be read within such a framework. As Burton continues, "As an
oppositional culture of the dominated, *Créolité* can only be understood
through the structures of power which it opposes, and only through them, and
their implied connection of power and writing, can any critical discussion of
Chamoiseau's work take place" (1997b:158). It is this interplay between discourse and power, between orality, tradition, and the problematics of re-presentation, that informs in its turn our reading of Chamoiseau's *Solibo*.[3]

For the French Caribbean, just as for the rest of the region, the history of
rebellion against colonial imposition was long and persistent. The first slave
rebellion broke out in Guadeloupe in 1656, barely twenty years after the
island's colonization in 1635 by Cardinal Richelieu's Compagnie des Iles
d'Amérique. In the eighteenth century, revolts broke out again in Guadeloupe
in 1737 and in Martinique in 1752, and the revolt in 1802 in Guadeloupe provided, as we have seen, much of the discursive background to Daniel
Maximin's *L'Isolé Soleil*. With the entire region galvanized by the great slave
rebellion of Saint-Domingue in 1791, Martinique found itself forced to quash
a series of rebellions in 1822, 1824, and 1831. Thus this was a period that, in Eric
Williams's words, "afforded the slaves . . . examples of the success of the policy
of revolt," and bore witness to "the passion for freedom among the slaves and
the will to fight for it" (1970:198, 199). The task now would be to transpose this
tradition of refusal and revolt into a tropological framework of opposition and
enfranchisement for the protagonists of regional fiction. For an account of
Chamoiseau's vision of the marronneur's role in this discursive process, we
must turn now to a reading of his *Lettres créoles*.

A Creole Caribbean History

Patrick Chamoiseau and Raphaël Confiant published *Lettres créoles* in 1991,
two years after their publication, in conjunction with the Guadeloupean linguist Jean Bernabé, of *Eloge de la créolité*, their manifesto articulating the
terms of a creoleness to be pursued in art and letters. The subtitle of the *Lettres*,
Tracées antillaises et continentales de la littérature, 1635–1975, summed up its

authors' intent: to trace the contours of literary development in the French Caribbean overseas departments, and to explore the wider relation between history, politics, language, races, cultures, and literary genres, as they have all been eventuated in the fertile basin of the Caribbean Sea. The growth and development of this pluri-ethnic culture, and the integral role played in it by the descendants of black African slaves as the primary social group, is well documented. As Josette Fallope explains: "The Caribbean region is of overwhelming importance in realizing this creole culture. . . . The appropriation of this space was both transformative and adaptive. Since slavery, Blacks have explored the Caribbean in all its myriad possibilities" (1994:45). The task of exploring and re-presenting the myriad of plural possibilities inscribed in this geopolitical space would demand an intrinsically polyvocalic perspective, since it both assumed and sought to animate the network of affiliations and alliances engendered and transformed in combination with and promoted in the wake of the colonial encounter. The complexities of this cultural configuration bring us in turn to the metaphorical evolution of the historical figure of the maroon.

In the *Lettres*, then, Chamoiseau and Confiant were at some pains to trace the path taken by and the symbolic importance of the figure of the maroon in the exigencies of historical and cultural experience in the region to link him to the emancipatory, tricksterlike figure of the conteur. For a variety of cultures, the figure of the storyteller has long fulfilled a key symbolic and transformational role, both as transmitter of identitarian traditions and as the signifying center of the constituent community; it is a double challenge whose contours have been succintly mapped by Walter Benjamin in his essay "The Storyteller": "Experience which is passed on from mouth to mouth is the source from which all storytellers have drawn. And among those who have written down the tales, it is the great ones whose written version differs least from the speech of the many nameless storytellers" (1968:84). By conflating the inscription of community identity with a form of discourse that most resembles speech, Benjamin effectively valorizes that very category of oral cultural production framed by Chamoiseau and Confiant in the *Lettres* as oraliture, and whose importance to the recognition and continuity of the social whole Chamoiseau seeks to re-present in *Solibo Magnifique*.

However, in the context of a francophone Caribbean literary history of resistance upon which this generation of writers could draw, the act of marronnage from which the figure of the conteur derives was perhaps first discursively valorized by none other than Aimé Césaire in "Le Verbe marronner," his circa 1950 poem to his Haitian friend and colleague René Depestre.

Here, the ambitious ambiguities of negritude provide a self-assertive historical context; maroon liberation is clearly conflated with the scriptive project that envisions a regional cultural identity: "Shall we turn maroon? Depestre, shall we turn maroon? / . . . Bah! Depestre the poem is not a mill for / grinding sugar cane absolutely not / . . . it is undoubtably a very serious problem / the relation between poetry and Revolution/the content determines the form" (1983:368–71). By placing poetry and the concept of revolutionary change in the Caribbean into close proximity, Césaire succeeds in appropriating discursive invention to transformatively engender a framework for the articulation of the regional experience. As Gregson Davis points out, "In inventing a verb, 'to maroon' (*marronner*), based on the noun denoting slaves who escaped from the New World plantation to live in autonomous communities, the speaker hoists aloft the banner of artistic freedom and resistance to cultural totalitarianism" (1997:17). By joining the idea of resistance to the reality of marronnage through discourse, then, Césaire's gesture serves as an effective paradigm for the later development of the maroon model as an effective formula for constructing new narrative possibilities from the material historicity of the French Caribbean.

In the orality-driven communities of the Caribbean, the subtle strategies of tradition and change were also embedded in the complexities of the creole language and its critical mediation of social resistance; as Edouard Glissant succinctly states in *Caribbean Discourse*, "Camouflage. The creole language was constituted around such a stategy of trickery" (21/33). Thus the seeds of this transformative tension that bind the conteur to the maroon take hold almost from the inaugural moment of the slavery/plantation regime itself and, indeed, recur consistently in Glissant's creative and theoretical work. As he suggests in *Poetics of Relation*, "In the silent universe of the Plantation, oral expression, the only form possible for the slaves, was discontinuously organized . . . the same discontinuity the Maroons created through that other detour called *marronnage*" (68/82). The key parallel of discontinuity that Glissant draws between the verbal act of expression and the physical act of marronnage demonstrates the simultaneous importance of rupture and of the transmission and transformation of tradition that came into being in the plurality of voices and beliefs forced to coexist in the hold of the slave ship, in the cry of protest and bewilderment that Chamoiseau and Confiant see as issuing from this cradle of colonialism's depravity: "In the ship's hold, there are several African languages, several gods, several ways of perceiving the world. Where does the cry come from? From which cultural basis, from which language? Will its poetics reveal itself as a whole which will save all? We must imagine this, for this outcry contradicted the colonial purpose" (1991:33). It is this inaugural, emancipatory cry that will ultimately give rise to the verbalized acts of contestation and identity inscribed in the discontinuous discourse of the conteur. In this silence that marks "the first rupture" (33), there are already the traces of an insistent difference. For if, as Chamoiseau himself insists in *Ecrire en pays dominé*, "the hold of a slave ship is not a point of departure, but a fulcrum leading towards incredible possibilities" (1997:203), it is the signification intrinsic to these newfound fields of possibility, resited and restructured in the wake of the colonial encounter, that opens up the relational, foundational forces of social survival that engenders, in turn, the conflictual synthesis of this cultural mosaic.[4]

Almost immediately, then, the historical link between the *nègre marron* and the conteur is established and inscribed, a link that draws its figural power of contestation from the strategic doubling of dissimulation and difference. "The inheritor of the cry," write Chamoiseau and Confiant, "will be the maroon (the one who escaped from the household to hide his resistance in the hills), but the artist of the cry, the recipient of its poetics, the progenitor of the literary trace who stays on the plantation will be the Speaker, our creole storyteller. It is he who, in the midst of the fields and the sugar factories, will take up in his turn the resistance to the colonial order, using his own art as a didactic mask" (1991:35). By stressing the difference between the "inheritor" and the "artist" of the "cry," the text accentuates the strategic importance of this symbolic discontinuity that is doubled and reenacted through discourse. With the *conteur créole* now inscribed as a primary figure of opposition, and the creative power of this *paroleur* made even more intrinsic to the elaboration of identity, it is critical to note that combatting the colonial will through the articulation of deception and disjuncture is in fact the role of the conteur, but that he is a figure, as Chamoiseau and Confiant point out, "who . . . does not exactly resemble the maroon" (1991:59). Indeed, far from overtly embodying the characteristic spirit of revolt symbolized by the marron, the conteur as artist and symbol seeks to give voice to that vast majority of slaves who did not succeed in making good their escape from the plantation but yet embodied a spirit and praxis of resistance in the carrying out of their day-to-day existences. In this way, the conteur can in fact appear to create almost exactly the opposite impression; Chamoiseau and Confiant call him "a peaceful fellow, *almost* an Uncle Tom, that the Bakra does not fear and in fact trusts, to the point of letting him speak" (1991:59; emphasis mine). But it is in the tension between his *apparently* peaceable character and this very authorization to speak that the subversive potential of discursive displacement lurks.

What draws these figures together is their shared capacity for contestation, albeit on different discursive planes. But where the marron carried out a military and political program of subversion and revolt, the conteur set himself apart by disturbing, and ultimately reversing, the tranquil superficiality of the plantation's set hierarchy of domination and dependence. "Tolerated by the colonial slave system, the *conteur* is the vocal representative of a shackled people, living in fear and attempting to survive," write Chamoiseau and Confiant (1991:59). Voice of the voiceless, adopting and adapting a variety of discursive postures aimed at taking advantage of his systemic invisibility, the praxis of the conteur is ultimately of the same order as that of the marron: the subversion and overturning of metropolitan domination. Expertly intertwining voice, content, and delivery, it is the artistry of both sign and act that gives significance to this nascent poetics of the people, marking out a discursive space whose identitarian opposition is the product of the disjunctive metaphors of creole artistry.

This mode of artistic production hinges on language and is grounded in the historical construction of creole languages; such structures, as we have seen, facilitated the various levels of communication that contested colonial dominance and hegemony while articulating a new, collective identity for the inheritors of the displaced African diaspora. It is here, then, at this point of colonial mimesis and conjunction that transforms African and European patterns into Caribbean cultures, that the beginnings of a creole consciousness are instantiated; the historic polarities that separate colonizer from colonized are transmuted into the patterns of cultural appropriation instilled by displacing the linearities of colonial domination. Already, then, through this vision, the foundation for the conteur's role as contestatory vox populi has been firmly laid; the ineluctable disparateness and difference of his Caribbean heritage translated into a multiform discourse of opposition and identity that seeks to transmute the conteur's verbal acts of resistance into a fully constituted affiliative discourse that embodies the past and present community spirit.

With the exigencies of the Caribbean plantation system therefore mediating what Chamoiseau and Confiant call "the birth of the creole storyteller within the framework of nocturnal liberty" (1991:56), it is possible to see the production of discursive strategies of dissimulation as part and parcel of an overall pattern of revolt and self-definition that functions through the interstices of language and culture. It is this conflation of culture and orality in a polysemic context of protest that transforms orality itself into a culturally specific form of performance, ultimately producing the conjoined creole conundrum of oraliture. "Creole *oraliture*, write Chamoiseau and Confiant, "was born in the plantation system, both within and against slavery, in a questioning dynamic which both accepts and refuses. It confronts the 'values' of the colonial system, and subversively inscribes its counter-values, a counter-culture" (1991:57). Here the ambiguities of Caribbean identity are not only acknowledged but appropriated and re-placed within a continuum of colonial contestation whose simultaneities of revolt and acceptance ultimately produce the modernist multiplicities of a creole counterculture. And in this primal framework that inscribes the critical plurality of the word is drawn the framework for a consolidated discourse of cultural opposition.

Chamoiseau's discourse, then, is articulated through a subtle strategy of doubling, drawing on the twin axes of culture and history to arrive at a complex elaboration of the temporalities and teleologies of the common Caribbean experiences of exile, displacement, and creolization. Further, the centrality of language and its role on the plantation are here both acknowledged and transformed. As Jane Brooks suggests: "The folktale . . . is dominated by three major themes . . . ruse, hunger and revolt. Traditionally, the tales are told outside at night . . . and . . . have four functions: to give the community a medium of self-expression, to store memories, to entertain and to voice resistance" (1999:131–32). In his social role, then, the storyteller adds a critical dimension of self-assertion to a community already displaced to the margins.

It is thus the tension at work within these linguistic and subjective conjunctures of the creole that is of cardinal importance in fashioning a diachronic framework for the textual elaboration of an oppositional strategy of discursive identitarianism. It should by now be clear that the creole constructs that were articulated over time in the Caribbean were not the product of a simple process of blending and homogenization of subtly variant elements, but rather the heterogeneous outcome of the constant conflict and contention that accompanied the colonial encounter. The resulting ambiguities and contradictions signal the inscription of critical patterns of doubling and dissimulation that help to strategize a framework for an identity drawn in oppositional terms, tracing the transmutation of the historical site through the radical transformation of its key tenets and tensions. As such, this process draws on Michel de Certeau's critical operational distinction between resistance and opposition; by stressing the positional difference between an *internally* derived strategy of *opposition*, re-writing and re-placing the tools and customs of the system itself, and an *externally* derived strategy of *resistance*, in which change is wrought by bringing to bear concepts and policies from outside the system, de Certeau articulates the basis of a discursive praxis that allows the incorporation of those key metastasizing metaphors that have shaped the oppositional contours of a creole poetics.[5]

Language assumes pride of place, then, because it becomes the primary weapon in this identitarian arsenal; in this context, it allows the conteur to vitalize a collective voice of protest and parody that speaks to metropolitan domination in the name of the people. In this sense, the communal spirit of revolt that is at the core of marronnage is rearticulated as a vital collective memory; as Elias Khoury points out, "Language is the repository of the collective memory. It is the basic national value which must be preserved" (1982: 245). Language mediates the composite field that links the marron to the conteur, signifying in its disjunctures the complex struggle continually being waged by the linguistic and cultural axes of the creole. As such, it is in the vanguard of the array of strategic approaches to cultural difference and cultural identity, acting as both vehicle and arbiter of this composite network of opposition and contestation. Its importance in a sociopolitical context of struggle cannot be overstated; as Barbara Harlow indicates, "Culture, then, and language are critical as an arena of struggle, no less than as a part of that struggle, as one of the weapons. . . . The use of language is crucial, both as challenge to the antagonist and in redefining the identity of the protagonist" (1987:55). The persistent proliferation of these overlapping axes of doubling grounds these articulations of identity and allows this process of discursive marooning to take shape.

Such a framework would appear to be appropriate to the task at hand, taking adequate account of Caribbean specificities of history, culture, and social structure to construct a theoretical basis for the discursive disposition of revolt and dissimulation in the region. But it is precisely this framework, and its supposed capacity for propagating gender-based disjunctures of homophobic and phallogocentric domination, that have come under fire from the critic A. James Arnold. Firing the opening salvo in the 1995 collection of essays titled *Penser la créolité*—one whose original title, interestingly enough, was to have been *Repenser la créolité*—Arnold assails Chamoiseau and Confiant in particular for deliberately excluding women from the creole tradition and, further, for a discursive overinvestment of the figure of the maroon, and indeed challenges the very validity of the maroon paradigm: "We should note, however, that in the French West Indies these are imaginary, rather than historical, heroes. Moreover, within this model of a nascent creole culture, the maroons could not . . . be the effective vehicle for transmission of the syncretic new culture that would come down to the present day" (1995:29). Arnold's attack, launched as the keynote address of a francophone Caribbean colloquium in October 1993, titled "Expanding the Definition of *Créolité*" and held at the University of Maryland at College Park, remained until the original publication, in a 1997 number of the journal *Cultural Anthropology*, of Richard and Sally Price's piece "Shadowboxing in the Mangrove," perhaps the most thoroughgoing interrogation yet published of the tenets and principles that undergird the créolité movement. Both articles seek to call into question the basic criteria within which the movement exists as an effective vehicle for Caribbean cultural contestation.

The charges laid by these authors are critical enough to warrant a reading before proceeding from an outline of the maroon model to an assessment of its discursive praxis. What do we make, first of all, of Arnold's excoriation of the French Caribbean maroon, and of Chamoiseau and Confiant's attempt to turn him into an iconic champion of a downtrodden people? We do not need to recite the details of each maroon uprising and settlement in the Caribbean between the inauguration of colonization and the arrival of emancipation in order to recognize the overwhelming symbolic importance to a people held in bondage of even the smallest act of rebellion and autonomy. As we have seen, the great maroon uprisings documented in Jamaica, Dominica, Grenada, and St. Vincent eventually combined with the smaller slave revolts that consistently occurred on most of the islands—including, as we have seen, both Guadeloupe and Martinique—to function as idealized paradigms of the possibility of subaltern identity. This folklore of revolt produced larger-than-life figures like Cudjoe, Tacky, and the female Jamaican rebel leader Nanny, whose strategies of subversion inscribed events that told their enslaved counterparts of heroism, resistance, and the innate possibilities of a flight to freedom. Indeed, no less an authority than Edouard Glissant has in *Caribbean Discourse* defined the terms within which the marron functions as a heroic figure for the regional population: "It is nonetheless the case, and we can never emphasize this enough, that the maroon is the only popular Antillean hero, and the incredible sufferings which marked his capture show the measure of his courage and determination" (104). Given the entire region's subjection to an unvarying regime of slavery, racism, and colonialism, then, these events did not need to have occurred on the neighboring plantation for them to take fire in the imagination either of the slave subject or of his or her descendants. On a larger scale, history has shown that a people denied the birthright of its own identity will ultimately salvage their own myths and heroes from the detritus of their indigenous traditions, whether or not, in this particular context, large-scale maroon movements took root and flourished in each and every Caribbean colony, since the success or failure of such movements does not intrinsically deny the symbolic value of even the smallest act of resistance or opposition.

It is not simply the content but also the form of the discursive articulation undertaken by the figure of the conteur that arouses Arnold's ire. Indeed, he is at particular pains to point out that the *béké*'s trust and lack of apprehension of the conteur conveyed in the phrase "presque de la qualité de l'Oncle Tom" (59) from the *Lettres créoles* is tantamount to "the total rehabilitation of the Uncle Tom. . . . the only position remaining to those who would declare themselves the heirs to the *oraliturain* is that of castrated storyteller whose language remains obscure, muffled or screamed (read: hysterical), at all events turned away from the direct production of meaning" (Arnold 1995:31–32). Here, the extent to which Arnold's reading is based on the misrepresentation or distortion of specific historic patterns and traditions of Caribbean discursive resistance from past to present must nevertheless be unpacked. For the patterns and principles of quiet anarchy that reside here in the tension between the word *presque* and the implicit acquiescence of the Uncle Tom figure mark the world of difference that separates the subversion enacted by the one from the subjugation of the other, in a framework where language as ruse and camouflage takes pride of place. It was precisely through this slippage between appearance and reality that this conteur was able to carry out his double duty of subversion and cultural continuity and transformation, his tales and songs eliciting countervailing patterns of subversion and ridicule ranged against symbols of colonial authority. The interaction resulting from such cycles of domination and resistance between colonizer and colonized, both dislocated *creole* subjects (from an etymological perspective) from the African and European continents with no shared language, becomes the primary marker of a creoleness made increasingly and insistently Caribbean.

From a more contemporary point of view, the historical transformation of these discursive patterns into strategic articulations of subjectivity is in fact a particularly Caribbean site of cultural expression. Any modicum of familiarity with Caribbean life would clearly tend to suggest that the evolution over time of the musical art form of the calypso, and the tradition of topical commentary, satire, and social protest embodied in its primary exponent, the *kaisonien extraordinaire*, has its roots in the practice of parody and dissent that emerged among the displaced African slaves on the plantation; the ability to ridicule the blissfully unaware plantation owner to his face in song is one that continues to play a defining role in this society whose most distinctive feature is perhaps its pervasive and multivalent orality. Indeed, not only in the French-speaking but in the English-speaking Caribbean, where this art form has arguably attained a pinnacle of perfection, the calypsonian's choice of parodic, even impossible stage names, such as Lord Kitchener or the Mighty Destroyer, belongs to a resistive tradition of social protest in which the core social values and figures of the colonizing power are ridiculed and undermined, even as the physical prowess and verbal stylings of the calypsonian himself are elevated, praised, and even overvalued. Further, since the construction of creole society in the Caribbean was the end product of the transformational tensions inscribed in the colonial encounter, it stands to reason that, as Keith Warner suggests in his history of the calypso as art form, "of the many traditions that combine to make up the contemporary calypso, the West African *griot* also plays his part as distant forerunner or influence" (1982:38). This combination of storytelling, praise singing, and the exaggerations of comic burlesque is at the core of the deliberate indirection and polysemic patterns of double entendre upon which so much of the calypso tradition is based, and allows the present-day calypsonian, the inheritor of the tradition begun by the conteur and the griot, to regularly and effectively articulate the people's protest and outrage, an overtly oral gesture of critique aimed at confronting, in coded terms of social dissent, the powers-that-be in the name of a people who cannot speak, or sing, for themselves.

From the beginning, then, the conteur's double role as conscience and mouthpiece of his fellows has been at the core of his discursive appropriation as a figure of revolt. Indeed, Chamoiseau and Confiant point out that "the storyteller is first *he who gives a voice to the group* . . . the delegate of a collective imagination who adds his own art" (1991:62; emphasis in original). In an uncanny parallel that demonstrates the long heritage of oraliture, the role of the contemporary calypsonian renders him the community's social conscience as well, a rebel interpreter and transmitter of the myriad complexities of the contemporary condition. As Warner points out, "The calypsonian constantly monitors what is happening around him and uses the platform of the calypso to expose to his listeners a point of view that is not only his personal one, but more often than not is indicative of what the man in the street is thinking about a particular situation" (1982:59). While this tellingly trenchant social and political commentary mediates unspoken but popular attitudes toward any number of regional issues, scandals, or events, of even greater importance is this praxis of commentary, parody, and protest that goes back to the earliest days of the plantation and the confrontational figure of the *béké* master. Quoting the seventeenth-century West Indian historian Bryan Edwards, Warner establishes the roots of this penchant for targeting the powers-that-be through a barrage of verbal ridicule and indecorous innuendo often disguised as simple satiric censure: "There is, however, evidence that calypsoes—or at least the forerunners of these songs—contained social commentary long before 1898. Historian Bryan Edwards described the ability of slaves brought to the West Indies to give full scope to a talent for ridicule 'which is exercised not only against each other but also, not unfrequently, at the expense of their owner or employer'" (1982:60). Thus, the conteur or *paroleur* who derides and disparages his colonial master while giving the appearance of articulating another subject entirely can locate plantation oral practices as the mediator of an Africa-based tradition of oral resistance and the immediate harbinger of the contemporary *kaisonien*. This verbal skill combined deception and derision, and, as Bill Ashcroft and his coauthors point out in *The Empire Writes Back*, was born of the need for plantation resistance: "Transplanted Africans found that psychic survival depended on their facility for a kind of *double entendre*. They were forced to develop the skill of being able to say one thing in front of 'massa' and have it interpreted differently by their fellow slaves" (146). Far from being an Uncle Tom figure, then, the practitioner of this brand of discursive subversion was in reality only flattering to deceive, his primary aim being the accomplishment of his subversive agenda; as Burton argues in *Afro-Creole*, "By voluntarily becoming the smiling, fawning dullard that Massa or Busha believed him to be, the slave could adroitly turn the stereotype against them, preserving an inner free-dom beneath the mask of compliance" (49).

Historically, then, if the discursive resistance framed in contemporary French Caribbean musical styles such as the traditional, Africa-derived *gros-ka* and the polyrhythms of present-day *zouk* are the direct descendants of a covert, clandestine plantation communication system shrouded in secrecy and arcana and based on drumming and patterns of dissimulation, tracking this historical trace makes it evident that far from embodying subservience and docility, the conteur was in fact a rebel and revolutionary of the first water, carrying out a radical program of discursive and political insurgency under the very noses of those in authority, who saw in his innocuous inoffensiveness nothing but an amusing apostate to be exploited and inveigled into betrayal. Instead, such authoritarian icons were themselves made the unwitting victims of an ongoing revolutionary practice of mockery and contempt meant to desta-bilize the corrupt colonial edifice from within.

Notwithstanding these complex actualities of the Caribbean postcolonial experience, Arnold goes on to claim that the authors of the *Lettres créoles* have simply summarized the position articulated by Edouard Glissant in *Le Dis-cours antillais* on the advent and evolution of "Le Détour." In fact, not content with simply characterizing French Caribbean Creole as an "elliptical, hyp-notic, obscure means of expression," he goes on to extricate from the text the hypothesization of "a transpersonal motivation" to the development of creole, located in the "collective unconscious" of the slave population (1995:31). But a close reading of Glissant's vision of "Le Détour" in *Caribbean Discourse* re-veals a construct whose very heterogeneity functions in direct contrast to the reductive hegemonic unicity of what he terms "Reversion . . . the obsession with a single origin . . . to negate contact" (16/30). This drive toward a mythical oneness tends to disappear, however, when confronted with the complexities of forced exile and the face of the unknown. In these terms, he continues, this drive "will decline, therefore, as the memory of the ancestral country fades. . . . it will recede little by little with the need to come to terms with the new land" (18/31). The dissimulations necessary to the slave population, then, render cre-ole a *transformative practice*; "the slave takes as his own the language which his master imposed on him, a simplified language, appropriate to the demands of work (a black pidgin) and which pushes simplification to the limit. The end result of creole discourse does not produce an indulgent smile but rather a participatory laugh; it draws attention to itself, bringing together a common practice of storytellers the world over, poetic competitors, griots, etc." (20/32–33). As an indigenous, oppositional linguistic code of communication, then, and the daily lingua franca of hundreds of thousands of subjects in a multiplicity of Caribbean islands from Haiti to St. Vincent, creole is elliptical and obscure only to those unable, or unwilling, to decipher the lexical and cultural particulars of its standards and practices. At the same time, however, it would be foolhardy to deny the potential identitarian and oppositional value to be ascribed to possessing and manipulating a language whose content and form remained completely impenetrable to the uninitiated outsider, or the contestatory value to be derived from concealing either vital information or, perversely, even the most insignificant detail from the colonial masters. It is in this demonstrable degree of defiance that we may locate the capacity of creole to "effect opposition to slavery, to colonial ideology, to inhumanity," as Chamoiseau and Confiant put it (1991:61); together, the vicissitudes of language and the varieties of its articulation enact alternative temporalities of parody and opposition that inscribe identity through linguistic acts of cultural contestation.

In other words, the choice of the conteur as the primary symbolic figure of Caribbean cultural resistance is an inclusionary, rather than an exclusionary, gesture; it acts as an affirmation of the ongoing orality of the Africa-based traditions undergirding the social whole, and grounds the specificity of its social structure in a historical continuum of cultural transformation and opposition that by its very nature is both plural and continually present. It is perhaps even more important to point out that the figure of the conteur functions discursively as a sign of communal opposition to the hierarchies of slavery and colonialism grounded in a violence both verbal and political; indeed, it is in this moment of differential transformation that the basis of Chamoiseau's discursive praxis may be located.

In Richard and Sally Price's recent piece "Shadowboxing in the Mangrove," however, the insistence on prejudicial misreading that undergirds such analyses is taken to a new level of discursive effect. Here, despite the inferences that will likely be drawn from their opening statement that for the last decade they have chosen to spend half of each year in Martinique, the Prices consistently betray their formative vision as non-Antillean academics. Such attitudes are put into place early on with their beginning characterization of Martinique as "tiny" (126), the same pejorative appellation that the majority of Americans tend to use when referring to any country that happens to be smaller than, say,

Texas, California, or even Delaware. From here, despite the caveat that "we are not studying people out 'there' from a home-base back 'here'" (124), they go on to analyze the historical and epistemological foundations of the créolité movement in terms that seem determined to posit only instability and absence of historical rigor as the ground on which the movement is apparently founded. But I would like to suggest that a closer look at the terms of such a reading betrays a positionality whose claimed "Caribbeanness" must ultimately be questioned.

Such claims of the absence of a binary approach notwithstanding, the critical terms of this piece appear to pit créolité (creoleness) against *francité* (Frenchness), suggesting either an overinvestment in the metropole, on the one hand, or an overvaluation of the French Caribbean—to the detriment of the historiography of the rest of the archipelago—on the other. They open their argument by describing Césaire's seminal *Cahier* as being "written in what was at once extraordinarily powerful, masterful, and subversive French" (126), thereby at once establishing the implicit superiority of hexagonal French usage over the créoliste praxis they claim to be objectively assessing. From a larger perspective, the whole sets out to expose the supposedly flimsy philosophical foundations of créolité yet does so from a decidedly referential perspective on history and culture that quotes selectively and atemporally from both creative and critical works in order to illustrate the innate weaknesses of the movement's discourses. For example, their critique of the créolistes' "exclusively Francophone" vision of the creole experience (128) cites cultural historians who themselves engage the creole through the specificities of their anglophone and hispanophone antecedents. To illustrate their conclusion that the créolistes "rewrite central aspects of the Caribbean past" to "depict maroons as somewhat uncultured isolationists" (129–30), fragments of phrases and collections of references are thrown together across several pages from, inter alia, Chamoiseau, and Confiant's *Lettres créoles*, Chamoiseau's novel *Texaco*, Bernabé, Chamoiseau and Confiant's *Eloge de la créolité*, Confiant's *Contes créoles des Amériques* and *Les maîtres de la parole créole*, and Chamoiseau's *Au temps de l'antan* and *Solibo Magnifique*. But even more important, even if we were to accept the historically referential context that claims that "the central creolization process in those maroon societies was inter-African syncretism" (130), the implicit interculturality of artistic expression that the créolité of the *Eloge* has always reserved for itself—"*full knowledge of Creoleness will be reserved for Art*, for Art absolutely" (90; emphasis in the original)—and that renders it a *symbolic, metaphoric* framework, remains completely unacknowledged here. Such a reading, for example, is implicit in Simon Gikandi's vision of the deliberate displacements and pluralisms that comprise Caribbean modernist discourse when, in his introduction to *Writing in Limbo* he posits the Caribbean maroon as "the most visible *symbol* of this gesture of cultural *dédoublement*" (20; emphasis mine); it is the implicit existence of this symbolic framework and its intrinsic enabling of resistance that allows the créolistes' figural shift from the maroon to the conteur to take place, and that conversely links the Prices' positionality to that of Arnold.

Most telling of all, perhaps, is their description of the praxis undergirding the *marqueur de paroles* as "the agent of a ruse-based subversiveness comparable to that of the slave-era *conteur*," the whole stemming from Martinique's "deep imbrication in France and Europe" (131). Here, the inductive reasoning that forces their insistence on Martinican *francité* leads to a complete and total misapprehension of the discursive, self-reflexive role of the marqueur. As the figural representation of the impossibility of re-presenting the immediacy of play and pluralism intrinsic to creole speech and social structure, the marqueur has the goal of realism as well as resistance, a displaced re-citing of sociocultural norms that preserves a sense of social immediacy rather than exposing it to the codifications that are the corollaries of fiction. Such an avowal of the limitations of their diegesis is an unconscious one and places the coherence of the entire analysis at risk.

The Prices go on from here to question Martinican claims to ethnic and cultural diversity. After they define the Caribbean early on as "quintessentially Western," this unproblematized cultural appellation is soon extended into the area of ethnicity: "From a broader Caribbeanist perspective, however, the society of Martinique looks anything but diverse" (132). This conclusion appears to remain at the superficial level of "racial" attributes instead of taking into consideration the complex possibilities of ethnic and cultural admixture and exchange. Here, however, in a vague generalization, Martinique is classified as not "especially differentiated internally," a claim that ignores the real traces of the British, French, Spanish, Dutch, Portuguese, African, East Asian, Lebanese, and Chinese postcolonial presence over time in the region, and the concomitant patterns of difference inscribed, inter alia, in language, music, religious practice, and popular culture. At the same time, such a claim implicitly inscribes a hierarchical sliding scale of ethnic and cultural creolization in the Caribbean in which each island and, presumably, each group would have its rightful and unalterable place. But even this conclusion leads to a further binary comparison, conflating "Caribbean settings" with their concomitant "diasporic spaces like New York or Toronto, Miami, Paris or London" to then inscribe Martinique as *"relatively* homogeneous" (133; emphasis in the original), an act of discursive sleight-of-hand that insists on a metropolitan hierarchy of pluralism while effectively masking patterns of subversion of the (neo)colonial site through the process of postcolonial métissage and transformation enacted by the migratory movements of its formerly subjugated populations.

In a similar vein, a single choice quote from Derek Walcott's *Arkansas Testament* is used to generalize more globally about his take on the seeming Frenchness of Martinican culture and its "nauseous sense of heritage and order" (75), an act of omission that somehow manages to ignore, or exclude, his panegyric missive to Chamoiseau that followed the poet's reading of the former's *Texaco.*[6] His judgement that this "great book" (48) was a text that he would have liked "to press . . . into the hands of every West Indian as if it were a lost heirloom" (45), and that this re-presentation of "what [they] both grew up with" (45) was signified by the fact that when they met, they spoke in Creole, certainly would not have fit into this discursive and critical schema.

These examples might suffice to demonstrate the selective claims that ground this attempted deconstruction of the philosophical bases of créolité, and to illustrate, as I argue, the extent to which recent readings of these authors and their texts cannot shake off a grounding in the very metropolitan binarisms and prejudices that they accuse the créolistes of themselves. The critique of Martinican modernization undertaken by the Prices, while rightly characterized as "imposed from the metropole," is not altogether accurate in its claim that the former is "profoundly assimilationist in spirit." Indeed, their critique of metropolitan television programming, "electronic front gates, home security systems, travel agents, and canned dog food" (136) could just as easily be applied to the neocolonial influences to which the anglophone, hispanophone, and Dutch Caribbean are subject, and appears through its generalization to implicitly negate the very possibility of modernity for the peoples of the region. Yet it can be claimed that the very problematic of departmentalization finds its origins in such calls for modernization, as Aimé Césaire points out in his *Discourse on Colonialism:* "It is the African who is asking for ports and roads, and colonialist Europe which is niggardly on this score. . . . it is the colonized man who wants to move forward, and the colonizer who holds things back" (25).

The Prices attempt to resolve such a discursive dilemma by demonstrating a desire to reinscribe Martinique into an impossibly mythical colonial or precolonial past of ethnocultural purity, a position which goes against the grain of the very process of creolization that these authors are supposedly attempting to defend. Indeed, the modernization to which they refer is a global phenomenon that in the final analysis differs little from the (neo)colonial domination of the independent anglophone Caribbean, for example, first by Britain and now by America; whether it be by cultural and media infiltration meant to change the tastes and priorities of independent countries of the region, or through the ongoing fiction of the "Commonwealth" that joins Puerto Rico and the Virgin Islands to the United States. And we should recognize that it was colonization, and not just French television, that originally made "the French language an omnipresent part of everyone's daily life" (136); French has historically been the language of business and of instruction, and French and creole have coexisted—as they continue to do—in the region for centuries, whether or not the intrusions of modern-day television and radio have extended the reach of the French language. A similar parallel of linguistic doubling may easily be traced in the "English"-speaking Caribbean, one whose multiple trajectories and precipitations—and their critical role in social and discourse formation—have been most effectively described, perhaps, by Derek Walcott. Finally, if the créolistes' "masculinist position," critiqued by the Prices from a rather Arnoldian perspective, indeed stems from "the routine sexism of Martiniquan daily life," in which apparently most Martiniquan women are "complicitous" (140) (whether or not we agree that such a scenario, like it or not, has long been a pan-Caribbean gender phenomenon, inscribed in word, in song, and in deed, and from which no regional society is exempt), do not the very terms of such a claim simultaneously beg the question of French sexism? Of American sexism? Are we meant to recognize a culturally relative sliding scale of greater and lesser sexist guilt? Or are metropolitan societies themselves exempt from this social scourge, allowing their subjects to pass judgement on others?

To sum up, what has been missing in this sequence of argumentation is that very sense of intersectional pluralism that is at the core of the creolization process. The problem with such critical approaches is that they end up rehearsing and reinscribing the very positions that they set out to critique, grounding their arguments in discursive patterns and prejudices that maintain the neocolonial binaries of self and Other. It is in the strategies that make up the work of Chamoiseau himself that countervailing creolized structures are encountered, embodied, and most effectively articulated.

I would like to suggest, then, that in the final analysis, Chamoiseau's discursive gesture should be read from an inclusive and overtly plural perspective. In this regard, the author's recent discursive reflections, in *Ecrire en pays dominé*, on the cardinal role writing plays in fashioning alternative multivalent strategies for articulating cultural identity make the point well: "I saw myself deconstructed to the depths in order to be reborn, flexible, with multiple origins. Writing should know the exact point of this dizziness" (123–24). From this visionary genesis, grounded in a confident, pervasive pluralism, the important social roles that have been and continue to be played in the French Caribbean by women, by the métis, the *coulies*, and others are not ignored but can be seen to be distributed across the discursive field such that the intrinsically plural structures and possibilities of ethnic admixture and the continued transmission of creolized practices that together comprise this complex society are functionally instantiated and inscribed in the narrative through the intrinsic interplay of character and voice in its discursive and subjective structures.

Ultimately, the value to be ascribed to the phenomenon of marronnage lies precisely in its affirmation, despite all odds, of a communal spirit of creole affirmation and identity in a historical context of domination and opposition that continues to hold symbolic value for the community into the present, and Chamoiseau and Confiant put this well in *Lettres créoles:* "Even though it is repressed, marooning has remained the only spot where the colonized creole manages to express its defiance or its refusal of a destiny of which it has no part" (115). With Solibo himself as textual sign of what the narrative calls "our maroon way of life" (47), it is to the intersection of such indigenous patterns of opposition with the particular polyvalence of the Caribbean identitarian affirmation of carnival, and its role in appropriating multiple patterns and sites of expression to elaborate effective patterns of cultural affirmations, that our exegesis of *Solibo Magnifique* takes us next.

Interrogating "Vaval"

The complex network of figures and discourses that undergirds the texture of *Solibo Magnifique* is impressive, at first glance, but a more in-depth interrogation of its textual tropes reveals a reciprocal system of interactive signs that functions simultaneously on several different levels to destabilize narrative norms and to re-place select particulars of a creolized cultural tradition in the forefront of the critical imagination. The details of these interlocking patterns of discourse and culture emerge from a reading of the deceptively simple plot, which can briefly be summarized here: Sometime between the evening of Dimanche Gras and the morning of Ash Wednesday—that is, the two days that mark the boundaries of the climax of carnival—the conteur Solibo dies before an audience, having choked on what is termed an "égorgette de la parole," or fragment of the word, and having just uttered the pivotal phrase "Patat' sa!" (8/25). Since the powers-that-be cannot allow such a mysterious and unprecedented form of death to go unexplained, a criminal investigation is launched by the "Sûreté urbaine de Fort-de-France," led by chief inspector Evariste Pilon. With poison the leading suggested cause of death, a number of key witnesses are interrogated and released, and two further deaths ensue in somewhat short order. While the testimony of these witnesses serves to illuminate the character and lifestyle of the deceased, in the end Solibo's death remains "mysterious from a medical point of view" (151/216); ultimately, the primary question with which we are left is one of identity: "Who, but who was this Solibo, and why 'Magnificent'?" (154/219).

There is a triple-layered narrative code driving the organization of this poetics of performativity, and the way that these layers reflect and refract reciprocities of discursive signification also becomes the primary motor driving the vehicle of the plot. In this case, by carefully timing the moment of Solibo's demise, and engaging the disjunctures of analepsis and metacommentary to re-present the community around its dead storytelling subject, Chamoiseau has combined the opposition, parody, and play of the Caribbean carnival tradition both with the identitarian subversion embodied in the discourse of the conteur and with the interrogation of the particular narrative structuration of the detective novel. At the same time, the pressing fact of Solibo's inexplicable yet carnivalesque death subjects the whole to a self-reflexive, metafictional form of play that ultimately places narrator, storyteller, and tale under the sign of a parodic mimetism that continually collapses upon its ephemeral attempts to construct signifying contexts of social or investigative logic. The result is a whirlpool of wordplay, a ludic interrogation of clues and content, character and form that regressively refracts into an improbable, indiscernible infinity. But in this narrative schema of reflection and reversal, all is ultimately subject to the bacchanalian bravado of the Caribbean's creolization of carnival celebrations.

Traditions of the carnivalesque have been in existence, primarily in Europe, ever since the dawn of the modern age. It is therefore unsurprising that fragments and remnants of these traditions should have surfaced in the European-held Caribbean colonies of the eighteenth and nineteenth centuries, transported to the region along with the horde of expatriate planters out to join the ever-growing classes of the nouveau riche. Even today, carnival celebrations are an integral part of the pre-Lenten festivities of such European cities as Venice, Frankfurt, and Zurich, but, as I hope to show, the process of creolization that spawned the transformative tradition of performance that grounds Caribbean carnival effectively separates the latter from the essentially Catholic European model from which it sprang. As a result, any understanding or analysis of the social role played by the cultural pluralisms driving the carnivalesque in the Caribbean must be fundamentally at odds with the premodern patterns produced initially by Renaissance Europe.

Carnival festivities, then, are seen mainly from the oppositional perspective of the ribald, parodic, and grotesque subversion of established social norms and religious rituals outlined by Mikhail Bakhtin. In *Rabelais and His World*, Bakhtin analyzes carnival as a social practice of release, a communal extravaganza of liberation and renewal: "During carnival time life is subject only to its laws . . . the laws of its own freedom" (7). This sense of social freedom produces its own framework for self-expression; in their gloss on Bakhtin, Katerina Clark and Michael Holquist support his contention that carnival celebrates the recognition and reversal of society's seamy underside: "Carnival is a minimally ritualized antiritual, a festive celebration of the other, the gaps and holes in all the mappings of the world laid out in systematic theologies, legal codes, normative poetics, and class hierarchies" (1984:300). It is this transgressional dialectic between the sacred and the profane that creates a space of sedition within which, as Richard Burton puts it, "the foundational oppositions of 'high' and 'low,' 'inside' and 'outside,' 'male' and 'female,' and the like are joyously and extravagantly subverted to give birth to a utopian universe of play, appetite, and unbridled sexuality and pleasure" (1997a:156). However, relocation of this essentially European subversion of the social order to a colonial Caribbean context of the creole engenders the renegotiation and repositioning of the ideological and performative parameters of carnival as it is (re)made into a vehicle for identitarian and cultural contestation.

The society eventuated in the Caribbean by the complex circumstances of slavery, emancipation, ethnic admixture, and colonial subjugation ultimately effected a complete transformation of carnivalesque principles and practices, appropriating and refashioning its potential for subversion and liberation into the polysemic contemporary round of revelry that is the basis for Chamoiseau's text. From its beginnings during slavery as the monopoly of the white planter and creole classes, carnival was slowly infused by the growth of the slave population and the arrival after emancipation of indentured laborers from Africa, China, India, and Europe, all of whom brought with them their own indigenous religious practices and social and cultural rituals. As Judith Bettelheim, John Nunley, and Barbara Bridges point out in *Caribbean Festival Arts*, the upper classes slowly withdrew from carnival, following which it increasingly took on the trappings of masquerade competition, neighborhood rivalry, and a religious, cultural, and aesthetic diversity embodying and reflecting the particularly Caribbean eclecticism of its celebrants: "The Caribbean's ethnic complexion, as well as its dynamic economic and political history, are the ingredients of its festival arts. . . . Caribbean festival arts are evidence of the transformation worked by a creole aesthetic" (34–35). In other words, the ethnic and cultural pluralism that had become the defining sign of the region was itself now reflected and refracted in the multiple manifestations and metamorphoses of kinship and belief systems that carnival came increasingly to convey.

Addressing similar issues in the same collection, Rex Nettleford makes this point well: "They adapted and adjusted, creating in the end expressions appropriate to their new circumstances. . . . But the sustaining lifeblood of these events was the creation by the participants of masks to disguise, of music to affirm, of dances to celebrate, as well as the germination of ideas beyond the reach of those who brutishly supervised them for the rest of the year" (184). Structuring and participating in the creole content of Caribbean carnival, then, is an activity of a different order from briefly reversing the oppositional dichotomies of "discipline" and "license," or "good" and "evil." It is inherently a postcolonial celebration of resistance, of identity, multiplicity, and ethnic and historical survival, in which parody and performance play equally critical roles in defining and disseminating a national sense of self; it is a moment of inordinate intensity, in Richard Burton's words, "in which the forces that govern 'ordinary' life are expressed with a particular salience, clarity, and eloquence" (1997a:157). Not so much a celebratory flouting and reversal of society's accepted rules and norms as an engine of cultural empowerment, it is a mirror held up to the intrinsic radicalism, flamboyance, and composite creativity of that society.

How, then, does this carnivalesque ludism impact upon the content and discursive form of *Solibo Magnifique*? Or, to put this question another way, if, as John Nunley suggests, Caribbean carnival praxis reflects "a national history in which cultural clash, rebellion, liberation, and African heritage were most important" (1988:116), in what sense do these forces undergird the outwardly parodic polysemy of Chamoiseau's conflation of the drama of the conteur with the narrative rulebook of the *roman policier*? I would like to suggest that this novel functions primarily as a mirror of reversal held up to the dissonant, composite temporalities and teleologies of the eternally evolving Caribbean diaspora. To examine this aspect of the narration more closely, we must look particularly at the way in which carnival reflects precisely the performativeness and slippage that render its polysemic essence theoretically inadmissible to the linear rigors of logic represented by the *roman policier*.

If Chamoiseau appropriates new discursive terrain by deliberately intertwining the disjunctures of the carnivalesque with the themes and tensions of the *roman policier*, then, let us examine the ground upon which these twin typologies prove emblematic of the marooning that reflects the difference of the Caribbean condition. While carnival celebrations in the French departments of Guadeloupe and Martinique are indeed marked by a conflation of the cultural heterogeneity, costumed tradition, and performative panache similar to the bacchanalian generalities noted above, conforming as well to a pre-Lenten temporality—unlike some non-Catholic islands, where carnival is explicitly linked to celebrating emancipation—they do incorporate certain transformations and specificities that are particularly reflective of their island experience. Chief among these is the eventual appearance of the god of carnival, Vaval, and the implicit importance of his likeness, or effigy, to the success of the festivities. In a text written to accompany a photographic guide to her native Guadeloupe, Maryse Condé discusses the centrality of Vaval to the climax of carnival: "Carnival winds down on Ash Wednesday with the traditional black and white figure. . . . in the waning light we praise Vaval, that dislocated puppet Bwa-Bwa, and then we burn him. It's over" (1994:48). This construction and destruction of the god of carnival by the people themselves may be read as symbolic of a resurgent control over this moment of pagan intoxication, when the full panorama of religious beliefs, ethnic admixture, and cultural traditions that subtend this society are briefly given full rein.

Chamoiseau's own text on Martinique in the same series reads the phenomenon of carnival in similar fashion: "And to end, Wednesday. . . . On this day diablesses covered in the black and white rags of a joyous mourning. . . . We danced around the effigy of Vaval, this pagan god of joy, and drowned him in the bay while screaming our hearts out amid the flames" (1994:40). The fearsome triad represented by Vaval, the "diablesse," or legendary Caribbean she-devil linked to the syncretic traditions of *vodou* and *obeah*, and the implacable approach of Ash Wednesday and the season of Lent illuminates the composite character of Caribbean life, the creolized, cross-cultural, atemporal whole now driven to fever pitch by the combination of license and licentiousness that carnival brings. By positing carnival as an articulative *lieu de rencontre* for the symbolic binarisms that have historically functioned to structure this society— black versus white, African versus Indian, slavery versus freedom, birth versus death, joy versus sorrow, Christianity versus paganism/voodoo—the intrinsic oppositionality of these dualities is shattered, substituting instead an open, flexible framework that functions through the pluralisms and possibilities of the public sphere to mirror the inherent multiplicity that remains the region's paradoxically pervasive identifying sign. As Maryse Condé argues: "Because of the composite, even disparate character of its population, Guadeloupe was seen as a 'patchwork,' a mosaic of elements from different ethnic groups living together as well as they could. . . . the entire Caribbean should be seen as a single entity, in spite of variations in colonizing languages" (1994:78). It is the discursive unrepresentability of this characteristically Caribbean performative presence, heralded by a constantly metamorphosing mosaic of peoples and cultures, languages and religions, that leads Chamoiseau, as we shall see, to mine the serpentine, subversive, self-reflexive terrain of metafiction.

What renders this regional patchwork quilt essentially unrepresentable is precisely its uncanny site in the interstices, its location outside the linear on-tologies of the historical and social sciences that were the product of nine-teenth-century European thought. Indeed, one of the primary paradoxes of colonialism is the way in which its ultimate dislocation of its own driving con-cepts such as nation and identity is the end result of the very imposition of hierarchies of inferiority and imitation that drove the colonial process from the beginning. As Patricia Waugh points out in her book *Metafiction*, the tradi-tional linear narratives of European colonizing nations sought to reflect the subject's inscription in the large-scale social and political processes through which the nation was constructed, but the vagaries of an insistent modernism would undo the fixity of these categories: "In eighteenth- and nineteenth-cen-tury fiction, the individual is always finally integrated into the social structure.

. . . In modernist fiction the struggle for personal autonomy can be continued only through *opposition* to existing social institutions and conventions" (10; emphasis in the original). Here, the issues of autonomy and authenticity that are so critical to any characterization of Caribbean life are transmuted into discursive structures that articulate their oppositionality through their very resistance to categorization, their simultaneous, ongoing re-siting of the many and the one. It is this unity in diversity, this ineffable creole essence that explicitly subverts the risk of Glissantian Reversion, that Chamoiseau himself emphasizes in his description of his island's capital city: "Fort-deFrance was able to transform itself from a colonial into a creole city. . . . The city is strange, beautiful and melancholy, youthful through composite antiquities resembling the mosaic that governs our identity" (1994:8). Again, the concurrent complexities of this Caribbean culture insist upon their innate capacity for modulation and metastasis; in the intricacies of the mosaic lies the very stimulus of its insistent slipppage.

Chamoiseau's appropriation of the intrinsic self-reflexivity of metafiction, then, becomes a meditation on the character of the Caribbean condition — an ongoing interrogation and exposition of the cultural contestation and pervasive polysemy that are both filtered and framed by the figure of the conteur. Thus the text opens *in medias res*, confronting the reader with a dead Solibo found amid continuing carnival celebrations; by subversively fragmenting and imploding the reverse narration of the *roman policier*, the narrative adopts the search for the cause or agent of his death as the pre-text for locating the core of an evanescent, shifting Caribbean identity. Here the salient facts are shielded from view and principles of observation and deduction, while of overwhelming importance, may yet prove insufficient.

His choice of detective fiction for the novel's discursive framework is thus not simply fortuitous or incidental, for it plays a cardinal role in the contemporaneous processes of discovery and displacement that allow the author to attempt to represent the unrepresentable. At the heart of detective fiction is an intricate progression of inference and perception, cause and effect, tied together by the linear logic of narrative, and that, by retracing events in reverse order, lead to the revelation of the killer's identity at the end of the novel. As Glenn Most and William Stowe point out in the introduction to their collection *The Poetics of Murder*, the genre "emphasizes the relation of detective fiction to the art of storytelling, to 'narrativity' as it is called, the structure of stories and the nature of narration" (xii). In the same collection, Roger Callois neatly summarizes the genre's subtle interweaving of plot and character that leads the way to resolution: "This progression sketches out the usual structure of the detective story: a series of hypotheses is first laboriously constructed and then summarily rejected until one last theory is found to fit all the facts which have forced previous theories to be abandoned and demonstrated the innocence of previous suspects" (2–3). Further, along with the presence of the overarching hypothesis, we should note that the mysterious circumstances surrounding the death also usually demand an explanation. As Callois continues: "Rarely has the crime been committed in banal circumstances. It must be enigmatic, and seem to mock natural law, verisimilitude, and good sense" (3). These, then, are among the key strategies and practices that Chamouseau must absorb, appropriate, and transform as he seeks to explore the uncharted territory of carnivalesque creoleness embodied in the Caribbean conteur; the mysterious demise signaled by the discovery of Solibo's body parallels the dislocation of the narrative discourse that the delineation of this cultural conundrum makes necessary.

This reverse chain of cause and effect should logically lead to that key moment of identification which is the high point of the narrative; all other things being equal, we should expect similar sorts of overarching revelations in the cultural sphere which should logically indicate the key political and historical patterns that subtend the social role played by a Solibo. But these are precisely the traces that, as we shall see, must remain unnarrated and unrevealed; the implications of linear fixity that would follow from such resolution would reinscribe French Caribbean culture into the very metropolitan hierarchies it has so long been trying to escape. It is this eventuality, perhaps, that marks the text's passage into metafiction. Helmut Heissenbüttel, in his article "Rules of the Game of the Crime Novel," singles out the critical role of narrative in the plotting of detective fiction; using Ernst Bloch's phrase, he points to the "reconstruction of the unnarrated" as the primary function of the discourse of detective fiction (83) and goes on to posit the symbiotic relationship between the corpse and the suspects: "The first characteristic shared by this group of suspects is that they each had some relation to the corpse. . . . The ties of the characters to the corpse reveal themselves furthermore to be the same ones that make the characters recognizable among themselves as a group" (88).

But the progressively orderly pattern that typically throws light on victim, suspects, and motive will incessantly be frustrated in Solibo Magnifique, and the ties that bind the suspects to each other and to the victim will be undermined and undone by the ebb and flow of linguistic, cultural, class, and racial differences, all of which themselves provide the foundation for the unnarratable, polysemic, social whole whose discursive re-presentation insistently and incessantly announces itself to us as a construct. Its affirmation of its own difference reflects the composite character of its object while meditating upon the impossibility of the task before it, a dual duty which is precisely the key property of metafiction. As Patricia Waugh suggests, "Metafiction re-examine[s] the conventions of realism in order to discover—through its own self-reflection—a fictional form *that is culturally relevant* and comprehensible to contemporary readers" (1984:18; emphasis mine). Ultimately, with metafiction as a discursive tool of formal revision that simultaneously signifies and re-presents a plethora of pluralisms, it is this very insistence on unrepresentability, on the impossibility of resolution and the persistence of a pervasive incommensurability, that becomes the hallmark of Chamoiseau's text.

If this novel continually calls attention to its status as a novel, as a literary artifact or cultural object, whose rules it deliberately flouts in order to expose the artificiality and embedded power patterns that govern those rules, it does so with one overriding aim in mind: to suggest the possibility of an alternate temporality, a different material inscription of the complex, differential tensions and teleologies that have eventuated the Caribbean diaspora. As the rules of the game are simultaneously observed and exposed, both convention and difference—the twin tenets of the creole—are discursively resited and reinforced. By constructing *Solibo* as an ongoing paradigm of discursive doubling and displacement, in which fragments of language, plot, and character work to destabilize metropolitan norms, this strategy, as we shall see, also allows Chamoiseau to posit the multivalent patterns of the lived experience of the French Caribbean within a framework of both immediacy and impossibility, acknowledging the infeasibility of his discourse even as it is progressively inscribed.

Narrating Solibo

Perhaps the primary discursive paradigm against which Chamoiseau writes here is the concept of the modern nation and its concomitant master narratives. Recent re-visions of the constitution of the national space reveal hierarchies of difference rather than harmony, demonstrating, as Homi Bhabha puts it, that "the ambivalent figure of the nation is a problem of its transitional history, its conceptual indeterminacy, its wavering between vocabularies" (1990:2). Chamoiseau's narrative feat is precisely this simultaneous, insistent inscription and definition of difference, in which the impossibility of discursively re-presenting the oral essence of the conteur's art is repeatedly expressed to the author-narrator—and paradoxically reinscribed within the framework of this narrative-that-is-not-one—by Solibo himself. But before turning to the narrative implications raised by this double conundrum, let us look first at the terms within which the narration itself is ultimately framed.

The novel's insistent interweaving of several key patterns of dislocation continually alerts us to its ongoing status as a novel about writing a novel about a subject so present and immediate that its secondary re-presentation is intrinsically impossible. But by far the most striking structural phenomenon is the framing of the narrative proper not by one, but by *two different*, discourses: the novel opens the body of the text with the section "Before the Word"; this is followed immediately by a five-page "Incident Report," a formal facsimile of the police report of the events surrounding the death of Solibo, signed by the investigating officer Evariste Pilon, which in its turn is followed by the main text. In this sense, the entire novel proper is simply prologue; the narrative closes with a fragment titled "After the Word," made up of the alliterative "Sequence of Sucette's Solo" from the protagonist's final moments, and the collection "When Solibo Spoke," constructed utterances whose status is repeatedly interrogated in the main text. By including these end pieces Chamoiseau constructs *Solibo* as a frame narrative; indeed, the subtitle to the section "Before the Word," "Document of the Calamity," underlines the discursive aspect of the frame while opposing it to the shifting substitutions of *Solibo*'s verbal performance, with the main text functioning as the primary embedded fragment of the discursive schema. The result bolsters a reading of *Solibo* as an archi-narrative of the francophone Caribbean tradition. Tzvetan Todorov explains the practice: "Embedding is an articulation of the most essential property of all narrative. For the embedding narrative is the *narrative of a narrative*. By telling the story of another narrative, the first narrative achieves its fundamental theme and at the same time is reflected in this image of itself" (1977:72; emphasis in the original). In this way, the doubling and development that insistently occurs between the "Incident Report" and the main text tells the story of the oral community, mirroring the disjuncture between what the punningly named chief Bouaffesse will term in the novel "un français mathémathique," reflecting the linear, universalist hierarchies that ground the metropolitan imagination, and the artistic blend of humor and history, community and commentary, that Solibo's interlocutors call his capacity for a "discours sans virgule."

The parodic discursive framework that the "Incident Report" provides also allows the self-reflexive inclusion of the author as one of the novel's key characters. The authoritative, first-person narrative voice that opens the novel proper breaks off less than five pages into its tale to produce a bracketed list of witnesses to Solibo's demise, a purportedly even more authoritative though problematic subtext headed, in italics, ". . . extracted from the general report of the preliminary investigation submitted by the Chief Inspector of the precinct" (11/29) This reincursion of the legalistic discursive frame into the novel proper, differentiated as it is by the double sign of parentheses and italics, has a twofold purpose: while it is meant to give credence to the admittedly suspect account of Solibo's death by choking on an "égorgette de la parole," it also allows the inscription of one "Patrick *Chamoiseau*, nicknamed Chamzibie, Ti-Cham, or Oiseau de Cham, claims to be 'word scratcher,' in reality has no occupation, lives at 90 rue François-Arago" (11–12/30), both as one of the witnesses/suspects and as the discursive double of the author himself. This creative conflation of author, narrator, and character produces not simply an additional layer of subjective refraction but a veritable Gordian knot of self-reflexivity, a Chamoiseau-character who figures in an ostensibly authentic police report that is part of a novel by a Chamoiseau-author about the impossibility of writing that novel. This ongoing revision of the formal structures of metafiction, of the whodunit, and of the creolized narratives of the conteur accounts, as we shall see, for the important professional appellation of the character as a "word-scratcher"; the impossibility of the novel suggests, implicitly, the impossibility of the novelist, and of the questions of presence and absence upon which the impossible narration of Solibo ultimately rests.

In a sense, then, the deconstructive dichotomy between presence and absence and, more important, speech and writing is what ultimately grounds the novel's strategic subversion of the traditional typologies of plot and narration associated with the *roman policier*. While, in this formulaic approach, the carrying out of the crime itself must remain shrouded in mystery, in this case it is clear to all but the police that there has been no crime; refusing to countenance the death-dealing capacities of an "égorgette de parole," they decide to launch their own investigation. But it is this aura of the clandestine that itself engenders the second, but paradoxically primary, act of narration, a technique that Henry Louis Gates Jr. outlines in his important reading of the revisionary black thriller: "The story of the crime is a story of an absence, in that the crime of the whodunit has occurred before the narrative begins; the second story . . . the plot, generally depends upon temporal inversions and subjective, shifting points of view" (262). These shifts in time and perspective will play a critical role in the narrative *enquête* into the persona of Solibo, as the re-presentation of the police inquiry attempts to discover, retrospectively and testimonially, the true nature of the victim's life and times. But this inquiry itself becomes subject to the paradoxical re-visions of writing and speech that are at the core of deconstruction.

Given the critical interplay between writing and orality—and the impossibility of the former to re-present the latter—that provides the novel with its narrative motor, a review of their paradoxical symbiosis is perhaps in order here. The oppositional hierarchy separating speech and writing has traditionally relegated the latter to a secondary position, constructing a framework, as Jonathan Culler succinctly puts it in *On Deconstruction*, "in which speech is seen as natural, direct communication and writing as an artificial and oblique representation of a representation." The immediacy and presence that are part and parcel of speech, in this view, cannot possibly be recuperated by writing; as Culler notes in the same work: "Speech is seen as in direct contact with meaning: words issue from the speaker as the spontaneous and nearly transparent signs of his present thought. . . . Writing thus seems to be not merely a technical device for representing speech but a distortion of speech" (1982:100). Such a schema inscribes the spontaneity of speech as indicative of its incontrovertible presence, with writing as the supplement that "functions in the absence of a speaker," and conforms to Solibo's position on Chamzibié's efforts at transcription or narrative re-presentation: "Solibo Magnificent used to tell me: 'Oiseau de Cham, you write. Very nice. I, Solibo, I speak. You see the distance? . . . you want to capture the word in your writing. . . .Me, I say: One writes but words, not the word, you should have spoken. To write is to take the conch out of the sea to shout: here's the conch! The word replies: where's the sea?'" (28/52–53). Here, then, is the crux of the matter, the spontaneity and orality of the conteur that insists upon the irrecuperability of its gestural presence through a displaced discursive re-presentation whose presence, in turn, is predicated upon the absence of the very speaker whose words and actions it re-presents.

However, the relational identity that governs the inscription of linguistic units demonstrates that the arbitrary inessentiality separating these units from each other leads to the inescapable conclusion that speech is indeed a form of writing, implying not only a reversal of the hierarchy speech/writing but an inversion of the binary pair presence/absence. An inscription within the framework of this now foregrounded space of absence hierarchizes writing by placing both orality and transcription on an equal footing; as Culler puts it, "This gives us a new concept of writing: a generalized writing that would have as subspecies a vocal writing and a graphic writing" (1982:101). With both these subspecies sharing the qualities of absence and misunderstanding, the laws of supplementarity and resemblance emerge to govern the metafictional entirety of Chamoiseau's literary undertaking; both the plot that seeks to re-cover the trace of the absent, since deceased Solibo and the discursive re-presentation of this paradoxically secondary story-in-reverse are ultimately governed by a logic of absence and lack that figures the cycle of displacement and deferral that encapsulates the unrepresentability of a creolized Caribbean difference. Ultimately, in terms of content as well as form, *Solibo Magnifique* is determined by an incessant slippage between its mode of re-presentation and its intended object, engendering a discursive simulacrum, grounded in what Jacques Derrida terms "the supplementary mediations that produce the sense of the very thing that they defer: the impression of the thing itself, of immediate presence. . . . Immediacy is derived" (1974:157). This impressionistic palette, with its incessant sense of doubling and ineluctable derivation, is the product of a discursive and narrative conflation, in which, as we shall see, the use of footnotes, of references to earlier novels by Chamoiseau, of the insertion of the author as character, of the victim's inexplicable death from an "égorgette de la parole" and the mysterious changes that afflict the body after death, along with the inclusion of the "Incident Report" and the "After the Word" fragments as discursive endnotes, all conspire to construct constant reminders of artificiality and improbability that undermine any surviving impressions of an immediate realism.

What we are left with is the impression of a text, one that itself seeks to re-present the unrepresentable presence of the storyteller's art. Chambizié himself explains this to the Inspector during the interrogation: "The storyteller's art encompasses the sound of his voice, but it's also his sweat, the rolling of his eyes, his belly, his hand gestures, his smell, that of the crowd, the sound of the ka drum and, of course, all the silences. Then there's the surrounding night, the rain if it's raining, and the silent vibration of the world" (99/147–48). Such a cultural cornucopia is certainly a textual impossibility; thus it engenders impressions of the deceased victim, the witnesses, the episodic recreation of incidents and interlocutors that stem from the inquiry that follows his death and which, as readers, we hold in our hands. The resulting verbal and discursive play precipitates a strategy of parody, erasure, cross-referencing, and substitution that, as Derrida notes, creates a carnival of signification and opposition even as it simultaneously undermines it: "Also the destruction of discourse is not simply an erasing neutralization. It multiplies words, precipitates them one against the other, engulfs them too, in an endless and baseless substitution whose only rule is the sovereign affirmation of the play outside meaning" (1978:274). With this resurgent reconfirmation of the pluralistic paradigm of play that we have already noted as the preeminent trope of Caribbean creolization, the full import of Chamoiseau's accomplishment is now increasingly apparent; given his social role as conteur, Solibo's death at carnival's climactic moment requires that the re-presentation of this death, with all its discursive corollaries, be read through the infinite prismatic refraction of the Caribbean carnivalesque. As a result, both *Solibo* as discourse and Solibo as narrative subject reflect the paradoxes of play, presence, and pluralism that evoke and encapsulate the Caribbean creole, the impression of shifting ambiguity at its core the insistent insignia of its incommensurable difference.

Writing, then, is simultaneously and paradoxically the death of the word, as Solibo makes clear to Oiseau de Cham: "Stop writing, scratch scratch, and understand: to grow stiff, to break the rhythm, is to summon death. . . . Ti Zibié, your pen will make you die stupid" (45/76). If the narration of Solibo, then, is dependent upon a summoning up of the social and cultural inscription of the carnivalesque, the importance of this ambient atmosphere is immediately set by the narrator: "And so, fatal evening—after the parades, the crowd breaks up into the smaller parties (*gragé jounou, touffé-yinyin, zouks . . .*) that Carnival sows in its wake, from Balata field to the hutches of Texaco" (10/28). Between the double gesture of "fatal" (end of carnival, end of Solibo) and the critical personification of carnival itself through the absence of the article, the myriad performative possibilities of this moment of cultural multiplicity are made apparent; to locate the role of the *bals, zoucs,* and *grajésjounous* in the lives of the inhabitants, we would do well to turn first to the agents of that carnival culture inscribed within the boundaries of the narrative. The witnesses to Solibo's enigmatic demise are, or were, his principal interlocutors, the conteur's primary listening audience and social counterparts who make up, as Richard Burton puts it, "that underworld of men and women of African or Indian origin who barely manage to get through life" (1997b:157); these familiar figures now are of key importance in the official investigation into his death. The intrinsic discrepancy between the perplexing verbal re-presentation of the "scene of the crime" and the need for an "official," judicious explanation provides the raison d'être for the police interrogation that takes up most of part 1. It is this drive for narrative testimony and its implied corollary of order that leads us from the bare fact of "the corpse of a man under a tamarind tree in a place known as the Savanna"(3/17) to the intriguing parentheses that insistently and significantly surround the "liste des témoins" of part 1 (29) in which, as we have seen, the author-narrator himself is interpellated and implicated as a principal witness in his own narrative investigation.

This list of fourteen witnesses appears, as it must, in alphabetical order, since it has purportedly been extracted from an official document and inserted into the narrative: it is a fragment "extraite du rapport d'ensemble" and thus constitutes an additional—since exterior—level of discursive complexity. As a result, the first glimpse we have of such key characters as Doudou-Ménar, Bête-Longue, and Congo is through the prism of a constructed police dossier, complete with categories covering aliases, address, and profession. But it is critical to note how many of these principal witnesses are listed as "sans profession" or "sans domicile fixe" (S.D.F.),rendering them, in the eyes of the police at least, marginal and somewhat suspicious members of an already isolated social group. And indeed, this is the principal paradox that undergirds and inscribes this motley group of protagonists; as the invisible, borderline inhabitants of the DOM-TOM, they represent a vanishing era, that class of artisans and djobeurs that symbolizes the disappearing traditional world of peasantry, small farming, and craftsmanship whose remarkable orality reflected the Africa-based traces of their sociocultural origins on the slave plantation.

By choosing to focus on this little-noticed segment of the Martinican population, Chamoiseau endows the *menu peuple* with that capacity for oppositionality and transformation that is their heritage from this contestatory era. Richard Burton explains their social significance in Martinique's post–World War II temporality: "However, at their zenith, immediately before and after the 'Robert period,' the jobbers were resourcefulness itself, the collective incarnation of a world and a culture of oppositionality . . . whose origins were to be found in the survival tactics of the underclass" (1997b:158). Here, with the name of the naval officer running the Occupation providing a convenient nomenclature for the entire period, it is this incipient social slippage, marker of a contestatory community in crisis, that accounts for the predominance of S.D.F.'s among the primary characters; as Marie-Agnès Sourieau suggests, "The witnesses of the Solibo case display the deep splits in the society of Martinique, and the ambiguities and uncertainties of its linguistic and cultural situation that little by little obliterated oral discourse" (1992:135). By inscribing both discourse and characters on the cusp of cultural and social change, then, Chamoiseau is able to draw the reader into the search for lost tradition that the inquiry into Solibo's disappearance signifies; the fact that "these beings symbolize an outdated economy, a bygone era to which they try desperately to cling" (135), as Sourieau puts it, allows him to recuperate the rhythms and movements, the immediacy and spontaneity of this evanescent community—one about to be erased by the approaching modernities of departmentalism—while re-citing the unrepresentable storyteller's voice of Solibo himself.

Through his re-creation of the conteur's final storytelling moment, the narrator is able to inscribe the multiple patterns and rituals that adorn the world of Caribbean orality, the interplay between the storyteller and his audience and the whirlwind of sociolinguistic signification that is the Caribbean's creole. Symbolically, it is the re-citation of the list of witnesses that breaks the signifying chain linking the *announcement* of Solibo's impending arrival with the eventual *actuality* of his presence. And appropriately, the announcement itself is inscribed in cultural terms, with the harbinger of this almost Messiah-like figure of cultural contestation and authenticity being played by the drummer, Sucette; beating on the *gros-ka*, a traditional French Caribbean drum of African origin, Sucette calls the company to order by simultaneously inscribing indigenous rhythms and suggesting the conteur's increasingly rare appearances; we are told that the crowd is "avid already for the appearance of Solibo Magnificent, all the words of the old storyteller, rare these days, were good to hear" (10–11/29). Here, the cultural significance of the reciprocal relationship between storyteller and audience is immediately and clearly established.

Solibo's arrival is striking in two primary respects: on the one hand, little detail is furnished with regard to his physical appearance. This is somewhat odd given that he is the long-awaited protagonist from whom the novel draws the totality of its title. We are provided just the following description: "Bushy mustache, straw-broom goatee at the tip of his chin, he had the tafia expert's red-yellow eyes. . . . ah, Solibo had really earned his name's other half!" A few additional details of dress then give way to the overwhelming virtuosity and intensity of his opening "sentence": "Ladies and gentlemen if I say good evening it's because it isn't day and if I don't say good night it's the cause of which the night will be white tonight like a scrawny pig on his bad day at the market and even whiter than a sunless béké under his take-a-stroll umbrella in the middle of a canefield *é krii?* . . . *É* kraa! The company had replied" (13/33). Here is perhaps the classic example of the protagonist's famed *discours sans virgule,* the absolute lack of punctuation and the enigmatic cultural allusions and references to local plantation life—incomplete, of course, without the usual disparagement of its chief symbol of colonial hierarchy, the *béké*—framing an ocean of shared understanding between teller and listener, with the whole culminating in the traditional question and answer, the coded "cric-crac" call-and-response to which the waiting audience joyfully provides the answering chorus.

Similarly, while the core of Solibo's tale-telling that final evening is elided in the narrative, it is the moment of his demise that draws the most attention, not least because it is this event that permits the entire narrative to proceed. As Solibo's narrative draws paradoxically to a close with the approach of the impending dawn, there is an inexplicable break in his verbal rhythm: "And when at last the sky paled and a foggy wind announced the dawn, that's when Solibo Magnificent hiccuped on a turn-of-phrase" (14/34). Here, the storyteller's words are personified, taking on the textures and teleologies of misdirection and ending; it is Solibo as subject of the discourse whose unprecedented hiccup signifies an intensifying lack of control. Further, the ubiquitous narrative commentary resurfaces, breaking the rhythm of reported events with parentheses this time, to underline the enigmatic importance of his final phrase: "Patat' sa!" The explanation, which itself serves only to deepen the mystery of the event, is rooted in the codes and rituals of creole storytelling: "However, patat' sa does not exist in krickrack. The storyteller says *E krii,* asks *Misticrii,* probes to find out *Can someone tell me if all's abed here?* . . . demands his tafia, a drumbeat measured to his speech, but never calls *Patat' sa!*" (14/34; emphasis in the original). And so with Solibo's departure from established discursive norms, reinforced by the narrator's conflation of commentary and dialogue, thereby himself subverting the narrative through discursive codes that have traditionally governed the daily rhythm and resistance of French Caribbean peasant life, the reader accompanies French police authorities as they set out to uncover the Martinican mystery of Solibo Magnificent.

The first witness to testify will be Lolita Boidevan, aka Doudou-Ménar, described in the police report as "a street vendor of candied sweets" (11/30).

While she is the classic embodiment of the Caribbean sweet seller, her curiosity and outspokenness make her stand out somewhat from the group, a characteristic not without its own importance, as we shall soon learn. Physically, her chief attribute is certainly her imposing size: "Her big breasts jumped up and down, but the fat woman ignored them (never burdensome for a chest, these things cannot fall, no)" (24/47). While, on the one hand, her size may to a certain extent render her a stereotypical figure, her name aptly recalling the subservient assimilationism of the creole *doudou*, on the other, Chamoiseau again makes use of parentheses to interpose a telling paraphrase drawn on Caribbean creole intertextuality: he inscribes an almost exact rendition of the grandmother Toussine's verbal admonition to Télumée, taken from Simone Schwarz-Bart's classic Caribbean text of feminine empowerment, *Pluie et vent sur Télumée Miracle*: "No matter how heavy a woman's breasts, her chest is always strong enough to bear them" (24/5). This feat of discursive cross-referencing allows the narrator to tacitly inscribe Doudou-Ménar as an icon of female cultural resistance, an intertextually drawn, larger-than-life figure whose capacity for suffering and sacrifice will soon be put to the ultimate test.

It is Doudou, then, who, racing off to seek medical attention for the victim, encounters the "guardian of the peace" Justin Philibon; it is he that she urges to find a doctor for Solibo, although, in an amusing turn of phrase, she refers to them both metonymically, by their respective professions: "Law! Call Medicine, there's Solibo fighting an evil spell in the Savanna. . . . you hear me, Law?" (25/49). This encounter inaugurates the series of interrogations and introduces us to Philémon Bouaffesse, "brigadier-chef," or chief sergeant, who will serve as chief interrogator of the unfortunate band of witnesses. Both Bouaffesse and his boss, Chief Inspector Pilon, as black Martinican police officers, are implicit enforcers of colonial law, signifying, in the duality of their fragmented allegiance, the subjective splitting that increasingly pervades this society on the brink of change. Both characters "represent the broken unity of the Caribbean people," as Marie-Agnès Sourieau puts it (1992:135), and embody, as we shall see, the double disjunctures of an imposed sociopolitical alienation that is diametrically opposed to the cultural contestation that the figure of Solibo represents, a social role that can be summed up as "the Magnificent's words . . . the shelter of his voice" (25/48). But for now, it is the hint of a history between Doudou-Ménar and Bouaffesse that allows us to take a closer look at the latter.

As the primary agents enforcing colonial law in the community, Bouafesse and Pilon both embody a fundamental conflict that illuminates the pervasive social and subjective divisions generated by colonial domination. The ensuing struggle of the two (born and raised in Martinique among the very djobeurs they must now interrogate) strikes a resounding note of discord, announcing and inscribing the novel's insistent dissension between the oral and the written, between the immediate, unconstrained, performative spontaneity of creole and the metropolitan, mathematical linearities of "official" French.

As Bouaffesse assumes the full discursive authority of his role as chief sergeant, it illuminates the multilayered complexity of contemporary Martinican cultural identity at work in the text. For identity in Chamoiseau's narrative is a discursive construct, grounded in the antagonisms and anachronisms of class and culture, ethnicity and language. The text is thus an interactive and transactional space, in which subjectivity becomes a dialogic process that is the product of social hierarchies and tensions generated by the colonial encounter and its legacy of conflict and contestation. As a result, even before we encounter Bouaffesse's acrimonious exchange with Doudou-Ménar, we are presented with the complex social background of the former; a descendant of the type of common-law relationship common in the Antilles, he is the product of one paternal line but bears the patronymic of another (29/54). This initial social ambivalence, a microcosmic re-presentation of the fragmented Martinican authority he comes to symbolize, is further exacerbated by the fact of the brutal reputation for massacring helpless civilians gained by his regiment in the Algerian War of independence and his subsequent marriage to a woman of East Indian extraction, "a coolie, they say" (29/55). Bouaffesse is thus increasingly inscribed as the ambivalent icon of metropolitan domination in Martinique: he is a paradoxically parodic authority figure, whose rotundity has been blessed with the soubriquet "Ti-Coca," yet he is also importantly assimilated to that ambiguous plantation official drawn from the ranks of the very slaves under his charge, the *commandeur*. Indeed, he is "short, massive, almost round like a bottle. In fact, you'd really think he was a good guy if he didn't have those shaggy eyebrows which add an extra visor to his cap" (31/57), and it is in this metonymical inscription symbolizing his subjective double vision that the crux of his identity is located.

This interstitial inscription of Bouaffesse is not without importance. In fact, it announces a ribald, riotously funny satire of the macho West Indian "sweet man" that occurs as a flashback at the moment that Bouaffesse and Doudou-Ménar both realize that they were once quite well acquainted during the heyday of their youth: "A-ah! Philémon, I didn't recognize you standing there like that, no! So you're a policeman, a shit-guard, huh? . . . You don't recognize me, Philémon?" (32–33/59). Here Bouaffesse, revealed as a former *kalieur*, is compelled to recognize the aging Lolita, and in so doing, to be textually re-viewed through the lens of "a studied stride which constituted the ritual of the kalior, the ladies' man: to see and be seen" (33/60).

This performative moment is of overwhelming discursive and cultural importance, and this on two fronts: first, Chamoiseau's detailed reconstitution of the *rituel du kalieur*, of the step-by-step seduction driven by the rhythm of the dance, evokes a well-known masculinist Caribbean tradition, in which the seductive performance is aimed equally at the seductee as at the audience ("to see and be seen"). As cultral praxis, it is a key aesthetic trope in the construction of Caribbean folklore. Roger Abrahams notes, "As the expressive and aesthetic dimension of the culture of tradition-oriented groups, folklore is made up of items and performances that are self-consciously and artistically constructed" (1983:1). As a form of homosocial bonding, the carrying out of this contest across the body of the female is geared primarily at enhancing the social—and more particularly the prurient—reputation of the seductor: "Men may be judged in terms of reputation, [and] reputation is established by the dramatic performance of what are considered rude acts from the perspective of the yard" (146). A pattern is established for the performer, one that must be adhered to in every detail, from dress—including choice of jewelry and cologne—to walk to brand of cigarettes to the manner of consuming drinks at the bar and surveying the room for prey; the visible conquest of the female serves to prove knowledge of social codes, to elevate one's social stature, and to enhance male social bonding, since, as Abrahams continues, "one major feature of designation is how effectively a man handles male-female relationships" (124). Bouaffesse, then, having proven himself a *kalieur* par excellence through his earlier seduction of Doudou-Ménar, will now be torn between the sexual and social links—and their concomitant contestation of class—forged during his youth, and the overbearing icon of colonial authority he has since become, raising the key question of the tone of the passage itself.

For in fact, it is the insistent irony subverting Bouaffesse's performance that is most at issue here. By consistently undercutting the detailed, ritualistic re-presentation of the *kalieur*'s precise performance with a creole subtext made up of commentary, asides, parentheses, and understated explanation, Chamoiseau detracts from his character's performance in such sweeping fashion as to thoroughly discredit any possibility of approval or acclaim. Here, each detail of hair, jewelry, and clothing is carefully to be assessed: "Show off the tucked-in Pierre Cardin shirt open on a fleecy chest, the tiny Martinique charm at the end of a gold chain, and (oh yes!) the little cross cradled under the collarbone on a shorter chain" (33/60). And ultimately, as the rules and ruses are scrupulously followed, from "winning her over . . . in the course of which Bouaffesse executed the latest steps, bending his knees, chain bracelet jangling, cologne trailing" (34/61), to their conclusion "en D.S. climatisée" [in an air-conditioned Citroën], both Bouaffesse and the not incidentally named Lolita are similarly and simultaneously implicated in this performative ritual: "The decisive stage: you reappear, fresh, smiling, and invite from afar (always get her to walk toward you, son). Either she accepts or refuses. . . . Ladies and gentlemen, Lolita Boidevan accepted" (35/62). This deliberately dual-voiced narration draws a divided Bouaffesse ever deeper into a labyrinth of contested signification in which his commuted colonial authority will be pitted against the maroon tradition of opposition symbolized by Solibo and his peasant cohort. And in this discursive schema, a contentious metropolitan mastery will ultimately take full measure of its victims.

The interrogations undertaken by Bouaffesse and Pilon are justifiably at the core of the narrative; all else, including the *liste des témoins*, the self-reflexive insertion of the *marqueur de paroles*, and the frenetic flashback that links Bouaffesse and Doudou-Ménar, is really prologue. It is here that the variations of speech and language that act as signifiers of race, culture, and class are recoded and rewritten into oppositional ordinances of difference and disorder. These divisions in linguistic production illuminate the binaries that separate the oral from the written, emphasizing the gulf of incomprehensibility that separates an "official" French and a creole vernacular that recuperates the resistance and authenticity that provide the novel's founding principle in the openness of oraliture.

If the primary function of an interrogation witness is to report what he or she has seen, thereby corroborating or refuting the official record of events, then the search for the trace of Solibo will independently and repeatedly encounter the "égorgette de la parole" that unaccountably felled him. Bouaffesse's initial response to Doudou-Ménar's disconcerting presence is dissimulation, explaining that "the lady in question was his cousin by his uncle's left hand" (36/64) and seeking reasonable explanations of the incident in medical coincidences; meanwhile, the whole paradoxical sequence is inscribed in free indirect discourse with Bouaffesse's direct address to Doudou-Ménar enclosed in parentheses (36/64). At the same time, in a critical development, as "Lolita took shape in front of him despite the apocalyptic evidence of the breasts" (37/ 65), the social division and subjective fragmentation that the interrogation engenders occur separately but simultaneously in contrasting locations. On the one hand, there is Bouaffesse's assistant Justin Philibon, whose reaction to the affirmation of authority symbolized in the locked door before him inscribes him as "sitting behind the béké's counter like a cartoon character!" (38/ 66), while Doudou-Ménar herself, under police escort back to the scene of the "crime," "has broken into legitimate existence, suddenly realizing that she had been living like all of us, on the margins, on those paths which trace a country other than that of the colonial roads" (39/67). These unannounced irruptions of colonial power are harbingers of its insistent hierarchies of difference and point, in the indistinct trace of an alternative topography, to the persistent pervasiveness of a creolized opposition in the cultural landscape. It is this ongoing sense of opposition to the lived materiality of colonial domination, and the cultural affirmation that emerges out of the symbolic confrontation between the police and the people, that the verbal testimony of Solibo's cohort finally accomplishes.

It is significant, therefore, that the textual re-presentation of this cultural resistance by which the core of the Martinican social whole is defined again takes dual form. On the one hand, as the testimony of the witnesses begins, their discursive delineation of Solibo takes place almost exclusively in creole. At the same time, the process of metonymic re-presentation that allows Solibo's social counterparts to recount and reanimate the key moments of his storyteller's art—albeit in fragmented form—enacts a crucial gesture of repetition that mediates the continuum of presence and absence marking both the text and its subjects. This critical double gesture forms the discursive core of *Solibo Magnifique*, subverting the supposed coherence of these testimonies through the apparently anomalous footnotes that subvert the narrative line through their very presence. These glosses translate creole phrases, explain cultural practices, supply extracts from the "official" autopsy report, and refer to previously published efforts from the *marqueur de paroles* to re-present the elusive immediacies of a cultural identity grounded in orality, (re)constructing an unrepresentable creoleness from the disparate divisions of colonial hegemony.

Thus it is that the testimonies of Sidonise, Didon, and Charlot, each in turn, are articulated in a creole whose tornadic turns of phrase immediately inscribe its difference from the binary linearities of the *français mathématique* that signals the pervasive presence of the colonial power structure. It is a creole whose syntactic structures till the fertile terrain of cultural complexity, bridging the binaries that link Africa to the Caribbean while expanding and erasing them, compounding the constituents of ethnic and cultural admixture and the maroon tradition of slave resistance into a hybrid metaphor of discursive self-definition. As Solibo's cohort effectively appropriates his storyteller's place in the narrative, the warp and woof of the testimonies that they weave tell his story as well as their own, actively inscribing them into the continuum of protest, dissent, and difference in which they had tacitly, or even passively, participated through the reciprocal relationship that binds storyteller to audience. For all practical purposes, then, these testimonies re-place Solibo's narrative discourse of performance: the text thus confronts the entirety of the French Caribbean colonial experience, the trajectory from Didon's *créole de Guadeloupe* to Charlot's *créole de ville* tracing an inscription of authenticity and oppositionality that makes Solibo's demise a foil for the articulation of the affiliative resonances of the post/colonial site in the Caribbean. And ultimately, as we shall see, it is the moment at which these linguistic modalities meet that comes to define one of the key polarities separating the metropole from its Others.

It is this Caribbean coalescence of linguistic and cultural opposition that *Solibo* as text so effectively articulates, mining the plethora of popular pluralisms that re-presents the region, in Michael Dash's words, through "its history of repopulated space, the shaping force of the plantation and the resulting experience of *marronnage*, multi-lingualism and creolisation" (1995:149). And since the symbiosis that joins storyteller and audience is both spawned and shaped by a particular experience of opposition that its ongoing orality makes manifest, it is this very orality that must be probed and plumbed in order to locate the core of a transformative terrain of representation for the Caribbean people. These, then, are the modalities that converge in the pair of mini-narratives through which the witnesses re-present the stunning subjectivity of Solibo in this section: Didon's "histoire de la bête-longue" (43–44/74–75) and

Charlot's "histoire du cochon" (47–48/80–82). By re-citing rather than re-presenting the events of these narratives, the paradox of absence and presence that produces the multivalences of oraliture is preserved, generating a logic of textuality governed by displacement and doubling that is simultaneously linked to the absence of the figure of the narrator, and the crucial appropriation of his position by that of the marqueur. Thus the textual traces of the figure of Solibo uncovered in the narrative must be framed and instituted by the trajectory of these oral testimonies; they become the discursive sign of the combative role that a tradition of orality and protest assumes in this polyglot society.

What links and undergirds both these mini-narratives, then, is a combination of confrontation and transformation that converges in that moment of crisis upon the figure of Solibo. Both the *bête-longue* that attacks Man Goul in the marketplace and the *cochon fou* that confronts Man Gnam signify a community without constraints, a social covenant gone so awry as to be unable to curb those forces normally held in control. But of even greater importance here is the way in which the forces signified in Solibo's dispersal of an imminent crisis are marshaled to defuse the threat and restore the balance between society and situation. In Charlot's account, despite his expertise, he admits his helplessness when faced with such a predicament: "Even I, who had come as the bleeder, despite my experience, I was shocked and helpless" (48/80). Similarly, in the case of the *bête-longue*, we encounter a group almost frozen with fear; none of the bystanders moves a muscle, and Man Goul herself is unable even to scream. No one, that is, except Solibo: "Man Goul was glued before the hissing death. . . . And the same went for us. That's when Solibo Magnificent came forward" (44/75). And through the fullness signified by the double appellation, we can finally grasp the complex significance of a Solibo within the social whole.

Solibo's strategy is seen to be an overtly transformative one, and it is here that we may locate the core of his insistent orality. The key lies, perhaps, in Man Gnam's reminder that "Mister Solibo isn't some other bleeder, but a wordsman" (48/81); it is not simply that his words become weapons, but that the manipulation of the word in the name of the people has the salutary effect of warding off the forces that menace the social whole while mediating the elimination of the threat by confronting it with its own other. Thus Didon's incredulous insistence upon having seen two snakes: "There was no hunter and no prey, but—forgive me everyone, I want to say it the way I saw it—but two hunters! In the market, at high noon, near Ma Goul resurrected, there were *two snakes!*" (44/75; emphasis in original). Solibo's oral strategy establishes a signifying chain that links him transformatively to his discursive object through the communal force of his discourse, becoming the image of the counterpart to adulterate its power to harm; similarly, Charlot's account of Solibo's feat inscribes his accomplishment as a purely discursive performance: "I don't remember what he said to the pig, but even without words or stories, Solibo was a Voice before the animal" (48/81). Solibo's feat, then, through the personification conveyed by the *majuscule*, is to respond to this sign of social pandemonium on its own terms and on its own ground; with colonialism and departmentalization recuperated as essentially discursive acts, both Solibo and the community in whose name he speaks are able to articulate the principles of their difference, confronting and contesting metropolitan domination through a transformative poetics of cultural identitarianism grounded firmly in the plural. The history and politics of maroon opposition thus come full circle to take up the relay, maintaining the coherence of cultural tradition for the community through a defensive gesture that shapes the differential contours of discursive contention.

This, then, is the legacy and the lesson of the man-of-words in the West Indies; through his performative speech-acts of social protest, he inscribes a double discourse of difference and dissent that protects his community even as he speaks for it, registering its own response to the complexities of colonial imposition. Solibo's accomplishment here instantiates this double praxis, quelling anxiety through the telling transformation of everyday norms. Yet as we are about to learn, this symbolic capacity for doubling and dissimulation has always been inscribed in the very paradoxical pluralisms of his name, a multilayered double entendre that also gives a title to our text.

The revelation that the twin terms by which Solibo is inscribed trace the opposing axes of an oxymoron is not without textual significance; indeed, this construct is at the core of the problematization of creole tradition articulated by this protagonist. Already elaborated as the symbolic center of the community's conscious apprehension of its cultural identity, Solibo is ultimately transformed into a nucleus of relationality by the double crossings drawn across the body of the character by his social and cultural inscription. For name and function are conjoined in Solibo; the multiple reciprocities and points of contact engendered by his social role make possible the linguistic and cultural pluralisms that his nomenclature signifies through its trenchant double discourse.

The terms of this crucial, creative paradox are carefully inscribed by the marqueur: "Around here, we say *solibo* to designate the fall. Every blackman, and the blackwomen more often than their due, have had their solibo" (45/76–77). During the period following the unfortunate, ironic ends of his parents, Amédé and Florise, the complex character we would come to know as Solibo disappears, Christ-like, into the countryside to reemerge several years later, the direct product of a creolized form of contemporary marronnage that symbolically links him to the peregrinations of both past and present that his orality constantly reinscribes: "It's our maroon way of life, those hours when the blackman from around here beholds in his conscience only that echo of himself . . . that has helped him become what he was" (46/78). Through Solibo, then, the text sums up an essential constituent of the Caribbean experience in both sign and act; in the alienation and disjuncture traced by the colonial encounter we may find the transformative teleologies that are the echo of the self. Indeed, in *Le Roman marron*, Richard Burton indicates that the linguistic and cultural associations that supplement the term *solibo* in creole are almost infinitely regressive: "'Fè an solibo' (faire un solibo) veut dire bien 'se cassez le nez,' mais, en langage de laghia, 'pwan an solibo' (prendre un solibo) se dit de la phase initiale du combat, alors que 'bay un solibo' (donner un solibo) en désigne la séquence finale" (1997b:172). Solibo as protagonist is thus increasingly inscribed in unnameable creole figures of orality, protest, and resistance to submission; later, the latent sign of storytelling subject that completes the paradox is added to his nomenclature by none other than another conteur: "Furthermore, he mysteriously distilled the tales in such a way that he seemed to have derived their innermost meanings from himself. It was an old storyteller, a serious talker, who upon hearing him at the market one Saturday morning pronounced him Magnificent" (46–47/79). Resultantly, as Richard Burton puts it, it is "thanks to his mastery of this miraculous weapon which is the word" (1997b:172), along with the centrality of the experiences he has interiorized, that now allows the discursive re-presentation through which Solibo inscribes both himself and his others to take place; the oppositionality of the oxymoron he inhabits erodes the boundaries that contest the community even as it expands the resonances of the relational. But of even greater importance in this saga of naming and becoming is the crucial role performed by the women of the community.

In marked contradistinction to a number of recent *idées reçues* that posit the supposedly reduced role ascribed to women in the world of the créolistes, it is striking to note that the female elders of the community are figured here as socially and discursively indispensable to the extent that, in essence, they make Solibo what he is. Indeed, the marqueur is at pains to point out that not only have these women provided him with the tales and legends through which he re-articulates the substitutive strategies that form the core of the society's trans-formative traditions, it is they, in a ritual of renaming, who have reengendered the person born Prosper Bajole as Solibo. At his reappearance after his period of marronnage, it is the women, keepers of historical tradition and guardians of the communal memory that Derek Walcott has termed "the source, fountain-head, and oracle of all Caribbean legend" (1997:45), who define his condition: "A few old women at the market where he parked his distress named him Solibo, Creole for *blackman fallen to his last peg—and no ladder to climb back up*" (46/78; emphasis in the original). Thus, to be defined as the material result of a *solibo magnifique* is to be inscribed in impossibility, to be framed by that gloriously Caribbean enigma that recreates triumph from tragedy, and whose most remarkable trait is that it cannot seem to cancel itself out.

But even the presence of the discursive paradox of the name here precedes the essence of Solibo as sign, such that the *rebirth* of Solibo the storyteller becomes an act of matrilineal mediation: it marks a critical moment of simul-taneity, a symbolic conflation of the feminine and the masculine axes of the tradition of oral protest and social opposition that was first articulated in the appearance of creole on the slave plantation and now resonates, as we have noted, in the conteur and the *kaisonien*, in the tornadic teleologies of the man-of-words: "As is done in such situations, the old women on lunch breaks of-fered him tales, oh words of survival, stories of street smarts where the charcoal of despair watched small flames triumph over it, tales of resistance, all the ones that the slaves had forged on hot evenings so the sky wouldn't fall" (46/78). It would not be in the realm of exaggeration to suggest that the implications of this passage are literally legion: ultimately, it is clear that the women of this community have acted over time as the guardians and inheritors of those criti-cal practices of protest and orality that have descended from slavery and through which the community itself constructs its larger subjective claims; in sharing the symbolic structures of this inheritance with Solibo, they recognized in him not only the signs of a level of distress, subjugation, and social dislocation to match their own, but also the possibility of cultural reanimation and renewal through recourse to a discourse of difference whose double disjunctures would ultimately reinscribe the group in whose name he would act. On a larger scale, it is also clear that by incarnating this protagonist as a purveyor of doubleness whose simultaneity articulates such multivalences of culture and difference, the text transforms Solibo into an avatar of the multitude of sites and temporalities marking Martinique's encounter with the metropole, distilling the disjunctures of colonialism and departmentalization into a cultural signifier of polyvocalic performance.

Solibo as protagonist thus occupies a multiplicity of positions; conteur, marronneur, and djobeur, he is a polysemic cultural sign whose pluralism recuperates both the multifaceted modalities of the society whose resistance he symbolizes and the many fissures and fragments brought about by the colonial encounter. He speaks both to and for those upon whom the metropole imposes its departmental disjunctures, traversing the dislocations of both past and present to give voice to the patterns of tradition and the tensions of protest. "He would captivate the company with the rhythm of his gestures, no longer spinning the word in the vanishing scene of a traditional wake, but back in the mountain refuge of the blackmen of yesteryear, the new maroons, the lost blackmen, the abandoned ones, the bad apples on the brink of outlawry" (42–43/20). Yet, paradoxically, this is the character that the text will reveal as not having existed, in any official, administratively demonstrable way, thus illuminating the disjuncture between the patterns of perception that separate metropole from colony. The occasion purports to be a note to Pilon from the chief of records, a fragment again set off from the text that we read literally over Pilon's shoulder: "Name of the victim (with some reservations): Prosper *Bajole*. Born approximately 192? in Sainte-Marie. . . . Note: no official document confirms his civil status—something not unusual around here. *Solibo*: was that his only nickname? Such information would help me get further details" (113/166; emphasis in the original). Shrouded in mystery and with even his date of birth doubly displaced into nothingness, Solibo may be as much figment to the authorities as he is fact to the world he re-presents.

But Solibo's particular gift is the recognition and recuperation of the gamut of the Martinican social experience; in short, he is an overwhelmingly interstitial figure, one who exists between classes, between discourses, adopting and adapting roles and modes of speech in order to elaborate and articulate creole patterns of tradition, resistance, and transformation. At the same time, it is this uncanny "in-betweenness" that provides the critical link between the djobeur and the marqueur; since, in fact, he is neither narrator nor, despite his scriptive presence, an active participant in the narrative, the latter occupies a limited discursive position that deliberately distances him from the characters and events he seeks to inscribe. If the goal of the marqueur is to record rather than to re-present, his desire at the same time is to preserve the particularity and immediacy of an oral discourse by refusing the secondary reengagement that is the corollary of narrative re-presentation. The result is a textural and textual *impression* of immediacy, in which the marqueur's simultaneous absence from and presence in the text generate a signifying simulacrum of authorial omniscience, generating a mimetic re-presentation of social reality precisely because he is neither quite narrator nor character but more than both at the same time. And although our marqueur does, to a certain extent, explain and present, he is at particular pains not to adulterate the discourse of Solibo; while he cannot solve the mystery of his death, he can help to map out the traces of the protagonist and thus provides us with differential discursive extracts which, significantly, are always set off from the rest of the text and presented in the first person.

These fragmented, oral impressions of the protagonist serve to fill in the space once occupied by Solibo while retaining both the aura of authorial omniscience and the unmediated exposition of the marqueur. The fertile ground of this insistent duality is perhaps most clearly exposed during the interrogation, when the self-reflexive narrator again adopts a dual-voiced discourse to expand upon the nonmediating role of the marqueur and the simultaneous resemblance and difference this dualism engenders between him and his subject, Solibo: "The writer with the curious bird name was the first suspect to be interrogated. . . . No, not writer: *word scratcher*, it makes a huge difference, Inspekder, the writer is from another world, he ruminates, elaborates, or canvasses, the word scratcher refuses the agony of oraliture, he collects and transmits. . . . he never really got interested in me. . . . He wasn't interested either in my plans to write about his life: writing for him caught nothing of the essence of things" (115–16/169–70). In a key moment, shifting suddenly from a third-person self-reference to first-person direct speech, the marqueur must take on the role of cultural translator; by explaining in linguistic terms the impossible intricacies of Solibo's discourse, he instantiates a recognition of the protagonist's interactive, socially driven interstitiality that is a reflection of his own social role as cultural chronicler: "Solibo Magnificent used the four facets of our diglossia: the Creole basilect and acrolect, the French basilect and acrolect, quivering, vibrating, rooted in an interlectal space that I thought to be our most exact socio-linguistic reality" (22/45).

This awareness of the "expansive syntax" of creole, driven both by its historical grounding in the dual experience of contestation and communication, and a delight in an immediacy of wordplay that makes it, as Walcott explains, "a language audibly aware of its melody, its pauses and flourishes, its direction toward laughter even in tragedy" (1997:47), clarifies in turn the striking self-referentiality of an earlier passage, in which the text not only refers, in footnote form, to a previous novel by the author but also describes the routine and technique of the work of the *soi-disant* cultural ethnographer among the djobeurs: "I had known him during my visits to the market when I had a work on the life of the jobbers in mind.* With patience, I got them to accept my notebooks, my pencils, my little tape recorder with batteries that never worked, my unhealthy appetite for tales, all tales, even the most trivial ones" (20–21/43; asterisk in original, with accompanying footnote: "*See *Chronique des sept misères*–ed. Gallimard"). Thus it is precisely through their mutual recognition and difference within this interlectal space, where the notebooks, pencils, footnote reference, and nonfunctional tape recorder of the marqueur function as simultaneous signs of his inscription in and distance from the very social patterns that he seeks to transcribe, that the double, mediating role of the marqueur comes to resemble that of the djobeur, since, in a sense, they both function within this world without actively participating in it or subscribing to its values. As a result, the key parallels of symbolism and functionality undergirding both roles come to be increasingly important; as Glissant states, "The storyteller is a handyman, the *djobbeur* of the collective soul" (1997:69/83). Similarly, as Richard Burton explains, together they provide a disinterested framework that allows cultural continuity to take place, through a critical process of positioning that places them neither fully inside nor outside: "Straddling these two worlds, distanced from them both and yet mediating them, there is the writer, or rather the word-scratcher, whose interstitial position recalls that of the jobbers and other marginal beings" (1997b:157). Yet on a larger scale, this textual mapping of the space once inhabited by Solibo simultaneously resites and rewrites those liminal figures with whom he interacts, and it is to the shape and substance of their social positions that we must now turn.

Solibo's Others

The voices that people *Solibo Magnifique* are collective rather than individual; indeed, the stature of Chamoiseau's Caribbean subjects deliberately reflects the complex resonances of their history. As Derek Walcott explains: "The agonies it describes are not individual but those of the entire race, not unique but those of the whole chorus of the settlement. The tribe discovers its voice in defiance and by survival" (1997:47). And here, in these twin terms that inscribe and frame the tensions and teleologies of the francophone Caribbean, can be located the conflicts and contradictions that illuminate its Caribbean characters. As the tensions of the police interrogation come increasingly to resemble the strictures of the ongoing encounter between colonizer and colonized on the Caribbean terrain of Martinique, they simultaneously assume the disturbing, dualistic shape of the conflict between self and Other, of an oppositional paradigm of recognition and misapprehension inflected by hierarchies of colonial alienation and domination. This history of intersubjectivity links Bouaffesse and Pilon to Doudou-Ménar and Congo, the two symbolic victims of the interrogations, and is at the heart of the complex tensions that link metropole to DOM and produce these patterns of Caribbean creolization. As Chamoiseau himself explains in *Ecrire en pays dominé*, his treatise on the complex intersections marking writing and neocolonial domination: "Each was present in the mind of the Other; each affected the Other without really changing it. Everyone experienced the Other according to brutal laws which had no consciousness of the whole. A prize for European colonists" (113). As the interrogation proceeds apace, the succession of social and cultural conflicts that are exposed by the encounter between the police and the witnesses is reframed as a microcosm of the complex, multilayered dynamics of contemporary departmentalization.

We have already noted the importance of language and linguistic forms to the processes of identity formation and self-recognition in this strategic site of créolité. We should therefore not be surprised to learn that the creole which is central to Solibo's articulation of tradition and community is of similar importance in the disarticulation of self and Other, in the critical disjuncture between creole subjectivity and the imposition of metropolitan alterity. Indeed, his death is perceived as a climactic, epoch-changing event that leaves the community voiceless, lost, and abandoned: "In dying, Solibo plunged us where words become worthless and things are senseless" (104/155). The insistent temporality of the interrogation, then, inscribes this creoleness as a diachronic process, in which the resulting elaboration of creole identity as a product of conflict and confrontation both acknowledges the necessary imbrication of history and articulates identity as an interstitial inscription of duality and pluralism. As R. Radhakrishnan cogently explains: "Patterns of identity and difference, selfhood and alterity are always historically produced in a world where different histories respond to and acknowledge the reality of one another. And any acknowledgment of another's reality necessarily involves the acknowledgment of 'the self in the other' and 'the other in the self.' Neither identity nor difference, neither self nor other is an immutable state of being: the two are necessarily inmixed" (1996:84). The climactic events that will shortly befall both Doudou-Ménar and Congo are framed within precisely these parameters, symbolically reiterating and reinscribing the paradoxical patterns and tensions that link all of the players in this colonial drama. But this time, even the investigating avatars of authority are drawn into this venomous vortex of identity and difference.

While we have already seen the way in which Bouaffesse's anxious articulations of authority are inscribed in a complex, striated local background that comprises, *entre autres*, military service for the metropole, a common-law life with a "coulie concubine," and the praxis of the *kalieur*, it is important to note that his superior, "Chief Inspector Evariste Pilon," is similarly defined by social patterns of paradox and compromise. As black males born and raised in Martinique, they are the primary symbols of metropolitan authority in the narrative; indeed, through the free indirect discourse that suggests to us Bouaffesse's alienation and subjective splitting, we learn that Pilon "was from here, a learned blackman who had combed the universities before landing in the police force in France, then in the Criminal Brigade of this country" (66/ 104). Pilon himself is so riven by conflict and contradiction that he becomes a figural archetype of colonial mimicry and the complexes of insufficiency that are the corollary of the encounter:

> At the time of the Solibo affair, he is living with a freckled chabine, petitions for Creole in the schools but jumps when his children use it to speak to him, crowns Césaire a great poet without ever having read him, venerates the Antilleanity of the July cultural festival with its outdoor theater but dreams of Jean Gosselin's variety shows, commemorates the self-liberation of the slaves and frets at the Schoelcherian masses of the liberating God ... votes Progressive on the municipal ballot, abstains from the legislative

one and screams *Vive de Gaulle!* at the presidential polling places, cultivates a sob for Autonomy and the rest for Martinique being made a
département. That is to say, he lives like all of us, at two speeds, not knowing whether he should put on the brakes when going uphill or accelerate
going down. (76/118–19)

The range of tensions embodied in this extract shows clearly the extent of the
division and duality that have penetrated the psyche of Evariste Pilon. Running the gamut from language to politics and from history to culture, Pilon is
perhaps Solibo's symbolic Other; that is, nothing but a mass of creole conflicts
whose duty and defensive armor are afforded by the authority of the metropole. From the personal to the political, Pilon is paradigmatic of his post/
colonial counterparts; his domestic relationship — with a "chabine," or woman
of mixed race — is common-law rather than legal, and he simultaneously accepts and rejects the cultural authenticity of creole; he fights off the sun while
keeping his feet warm with wool socks, reveres Césaire while leaving his books
unread, and is riven between sign and act when it comes to the intricacies of
local politics. The fact that this existence "at two speeds" is significative of "all
of us" ultimately refigures Pilon into an Everyman, paying lip service to notions of independence and autonomy while living the contradictions of departmentalization that are recognizable to all but himself.

These are the contradictions that ultimately collide head-on with the brutality of Bouaffesse when the interrogations begin. And significantly, it is on
the shifting, problematic terrain of language that this conflict takes place; as
Bouaffesse remains silent, and, indeed, almost threatening, Pilon informs the
witnesses that they should consider themselves "in custody for the purposes of
a preliminary inquiry." The latter are immediately and overtly "frightened by
Ti-Coca's presence" (94/141), although this nervousness is somewhat nullified
by the subversive use of his youthful nickname. Both begin to question Bête-
Longue, who evinces increasing difficulty with the linear authoritarianism of
the *français mathémathique* of the metropole, unable even to supply his
official, baptismal name to his interrogators. Bouaffesse's attempt at translation
is met with an indication from Pilon that he understands creole perfectly well,
a disclosure that gives rise to the following exchange:

—Just trying to be helpful! You're an inspector, you shouldn't delve into
the patois of these bums.
—It's a language, Chief Sergeant.

—Where did you read that?

— . . .

—Well then, if it's a language, how come your tongue is always rolling off such a polished French? And why don't you write your report in it? (95/ 143)

Interestingly, the re-presentation of this age-old debate as to the linguistic properties and status of creole has Pilon, the senior officer, defending it before Bouaffesse's disparaging sarcasm. And sure enough, in order to bridge this impasse of incomprehension, Bouaffesse is soon required again to translate these linguistic linearities of the metropole into a series of comprehensible colloquialisms, inscribed in a localized language of events significant only to the circumscribed community:

—Mr. Longue-Bête, what is your age, profession, and permanent address?
—Huh?
—The Inspector asks you what hurricane you were born after, what you do for the béké, and what side of town you sleep at night? Bouafesse specifies.
—I was born right after Admiral Robert, I fish with Kokomerlo on Rive-Droite, and I stay at Texaco, by the fountain. (95–96/143)

This remarkable moment of discursive exchange is not simply indicative of a temporary breakdown in the prevailing line of authority. Of equal importance is the disagreement between these two symbols of metropolitan superiority as to the true status of creole, given the capacity for communication and translation held by Bouaffesse (which Pilon, despite his spirited defense of creole, does not share). While Pilon's position can perhaps be read as one of enlightened condescension, the paradoxical pluralism that the material realities of Martinican life have made of their joint alienation turn the infelicities of verbal practice into a test of authenticity and cultural allegiance. It is a question that goes beyond a simple matter of expertise. By implying that the orality of these creole conventions cannot be transformed into an iterable, transmissible, metropolitan discourse because the necessary phonetic and lexical codes do not yet exist, Bouaffesse is able to infer a host of cultural insufficiencies through his translation of Bête-Longue's speech, drawing on the supposed inadequacies of this "language"—which defines him as well as his counterparts—to engender a world of inferiority, an entire cross-section of critical and cultural disjunctures that, from a historical and political point of view, separate metropole from colony through a differential pattern of critical temporal and linguistic difference. It is precisely this difference that, in Marie-Agnès Sourieau's words, "exemplifies the process of self-mutilation inflicted by colonial domination: to express oneself in creole goes beyond depreciation; it is not to speak" (1992:136). The re-presentation of these patterns of silence implying cultural dependency and subordination paints a picture of that insistent disjunction between metropole and DOM that is crystallized and contested by the soliloquies of Solibo, and that continually subverts the ongoing myth of metropolitan mastery.

This cultural conflict that is waged on the terrain of language is also used as a weapon of deception and guile by the police as metropolitan proxy against an unsuspecting and unprepared public. The form and function of the interrogation procedure lend themselves to this armature of plot with particular effect; as it turns out, the critical and hierarchical disjuncture between creole and metropolitan French is maintained and even exacerbated, as Bouaffesse turns his divisive and derogatory attentions from his juridical to his social peers, from Pilon to the unfortunate Congo. Here, Bouaffesse deliberately sets out to entrap Congo through the use of language, seeking to capitalize upon the limitations of his orality and his complete ignorance of the niceties and nuances of metropolitan French. The text leaves us in no doubt as to either his ultimate aim or his insistent alterity, signaled again by the use of free indirect discourse: "The best way to corner this vicious old blackman was to track him down in French. The French language makes their heads swim, grips their guts, and then they skid like drunks down the pavement. The Chief Sergeant's sixteen years of career policework had roundly shown this technique to be as efficient as blows with a dictionary to the head" (66/105). Thus the alienation that has built within Bouaffesse is of long standing, grounded in the metropolitan source of his authority and predicated upon the control of language or, more precisely, upon the fact that Bouaffesse applies his dual facility with the discursive domains of both the metropole and its colonial outpost to dupe and delude those of his counterparts who practice only an oral, creolized discourse. The effect of the discourse of the metropole upon these disadvantaged unfortunates is like a blow to the head, a physical confrontation with the forces of law and order which they are sure to lose.

As Congo feels increasingly menaced by metropolitan authority, the contrast between discourses is couched in unmistakably binary terms, as

Bouaffesse knowingly asks the impossible: "Good. Now, Papa, you are going to speak in French for me. I've got to write what you're going to tell me, this is a criminal inquiry now, so no black Negro gibberish, just mathematical French" (67/105). This authoritarian conflation of linguistic and racial categories becomes a cultural sign of social subjection, a metropolitan discourse defining Congo's alterity and difference from itself through discursive insufficiency and racial dissimilarity. Congo's subjectivity is effectively erased by the poverty of his performance, as Bouaffesse's translations of this oral "gibberish" into the metropolitan machinations of a "mathematical French" turn into demands for identity couched in legal terms: "I am asking you for your City Hall Social Security name" (67/105). This position of legal and linguistic authority allows him repeatedly to posit Congo's inability to respond in kind as proof of his cultural ignorance and social incompetence: "You don't speak French? You never went to school? So you don't even know if Henry IV ordered 'chicken-pot-pie' or 'pork-redbeans-and-rice'?" (67/105). Ultimately, it is the imbrication of history and politics undergirding this confluence of identity and difference that drives the doubled alterity of Bouaffesse, divided between metropole and colony, between a colonized, subjugated self that must face one other denied and a second that demands absolute allegiance, separated in turn both from Pilon and from Solibo's others, and unintentionally but inevitably highlighting the indissoluble hierarchies that rend this creole society.

The pattern of colonial brutality that these metropolitan divisions inscribe in terms of the linguistic economy articulated by Bouaffesse functions as a harbinger of the violence soon to be unleashed by the investigative process itself. The text leaves us in no doubt as to either his character or his proclivities; in fact, we are warned that he is a figure "whose implacable cruelty seemed to pour into the dark red of his gaze" (55/90–91). These violent tendencies, through which the insistent intricacies of colonial dominion maintained their stranglehold on this subjugated society while suborning key elements of the colonized, are also metonymically displaced onto Bouaffesse's henchmen; these "guardians" are like the harmoniously designated figure of Figaro Paul, who acquires a sobriquet that sums up his fearful character: "The name of the first was Figaro Paul, legendary for his long-lasting grudges and underhand vengeance and thus nicknamed Diab-Anba-Feuilles" (53/87). This is the framework for the forthcoming encounter between Doudou-Ménar and the forces of colonial authority, one that will clearly illuminate the pervasive dichotomy that colonialism's double vision maintains between the suborned and the subordinated.

What Doudou-Ménar, "still believing herself legitimitized" (55/91), remains critically unaware of is that the Bouaffesse she manages to unearth is no longer the carefree *kalieur* she once knew. He is now a crucially split colonial subject imbued with the representative authority of the metropole, and it is this divisive dislocation that will metonymically determine the merciless assault meted out at the hands of Diab-Anba-Feuilles and the subsequent subjective transformation of Doudou-Ménar into colonial victim. Here, we should also note that Doudou-Ménar herself is now no longer what she was; time and circumstance have made her a pillar of the community, an icon of respect, solidity, power, and tradition whose fleeting importance to the investigation engenders an ephemeral sense of social legitimacy. Now, with tough supermale ritualistically facing off against tough superfemale, even Bouaffesse hesitates, and the community holds its collective breath: "Even Bouaffesse steps back . . . the rising thirst to see the fight . . . dissipates the witnesses' fright" (56/92). This knot of tension and misrecognition seems resolvable in only one way, but even before that point is reached, there is an even more arresting act of self-immolation that precedes it; in what appears as an extraordinarily contingent act, Diab-Anba-Feuilles bites his own finger, draws blood, and taunts Doudou-Ménar with the resulting gore.

This apparently inexplicable moment is itself framed by several telling references. For essentially, Diab's verbal tirade preceding his physical assault conflates a metonymy of colonial authoritarianism with a perceived fear of gender reversal, resulting in a drama of debasement and denial: "Just because I'm wearing the police blues of the Law you think: Oh yeah he's probably an auntie! . . . Well, I'm no auntie, I'm no auntie, just you see if I'm an auntie" (57/93). Here, it is the blue of the official police uniform that confers authority on Diab, so that it is the Law itself that is being ignored by Doudou-Ménar. The eternal masculinity of colonialism's paternal precepts is then immediately laid over against the arrogance of an implied absence at its core, one which threatens to transform the authoritarian Diab-Anba-Feuilles into a *ma-commère/makoumè*, or passive homosexual, arguably the most execrable of masculinist Caribbean insults.

While acknowledging that the very use of this term has the capacity to open up a veritable can of discursive worms, what is immediately and pellucidly clear is that the inscription of the figure of the *makoumè* is contextualized against a female, rather than a male, counterpart. The rather contentious debate that frames perceptions of sexuality and gender roles, as well as associated rituals of naming and verbal performance in the region, is not really an integral part of this study, although the term and its corollaries have been addressed somewhat at length in a critical framework. In any event, this articulation of one of the region's key social tropes insistently frames a critical moment in the investigation.[7] It is the social significance of being termed a *makoumè*, or "auntie-man," then, that most concerns us here. Essentially a figure of derision, defined in the *Dictionary of Caribbean English Usage* as "a general term of abuse for any male considered to be lacking in the masculine qualities" (48), the auntie-man, or *mako*, in the Creole-speaking territories, is above all a powerless, derisory figure, a disenfranchised male who cannot even be a true female, deprived of any discursive capacity or social worth. This, then, is the fate that ultimately threatens to dismantle Diab-Anba-Feuilles's aura of colonial authority, erasing his masculinity and the social identity that is its corollary. Seeing himself about to be defaced by Doudou-Ménar, bested, brutalized, and ultimately forced to admit to a lesser femininity, Diab's first thought is to head off this double disenfranchisement, this public defrocking, so to speak, by any means possible.

The act of biting his own finger and drawing blood, therefore, is meant to preempt public embarrassment and humiliation at Doudou's hands, and indeed, the animalistic act of self-mutilation he undertakes effectively redefines the colonial framework: "Lips open on a set of bloody teeth, he holds his wound out before his prey" (57/93). On a larger scale, it is apparent that this inexplicably self-destructive act simply allows a larger bloodletting to take place, drawing blood to beget blood, and functioning as an extreme rationalization of the colonial violence to follow. For Bouaffesse, true authority does not require such antics—"He's no longer enjoying this. Diab-Anba-Feuille's freak show slightly lacks official dignity"—while for Diab, in fact, it falls under the rubric of a paramount, exclamatory self-sacrifice: "FOR YOU I HAVE BLED! . . . Chief, don't get mixed up in this, squeals the mad policeman, I have bled for her now" (67/93). And it is at this juncture that the true face of colonial domination explodes, unexpectedly and unreservedly, proceeding, as was the colonial wont, from vindication to violence, as the narrator enters the discursive frame to describe both act and reaction: "And with his club he hits Doudou-Ménar, who doesn't see it coming, the meanest bash in police history—I still weep over it" (57/93). The Otherness inaugurated by the politics of the colonial encounter achieves its first, climactic moment of revealing truth.

As this encounter continues, the problematics of cultural identity are once again played out on the fertile terrain of language. Notably, Diab's verbal and physical onslaughts are followed immediately by an outburst in creole: "I'm an auntie? So I'm an auntie? Me, I'm going to pound you into the ground, yep!" (58/94). This defiant repetition of the figured threat is certainly meant to force Doudou-Ménar into abject submission and an implicit acknowledgment of the hollowness lurking at the threat's core, but even more important, given the prominent role that language and orality, and creole in particular, have been shown to play in this text, its appearance here is important for two reasons. First, Diab's reversion to creole seems almost to occur in spite of himself; his outburst is described as being "in a Creole he could no longer hold back" (58/94), and signals the resurgence of the more familiar, mundane character who is an integral part of this subaltern community. Given his social role as colonial peacekeeper, his facility in both French and creole, with his critical shift from the former to the latter mediated as it is by his attack on Doudou-Ménar, this metastasis in the communication code signals a psychic and social alienation inaugurated by his colonial role and played out within a framework that conflates physical and linguistic violence. His turn to the subaltern code is in fact a return of the repressed, a double displacement of colonialism's desire for conformity that resurfaces as an alterity inscribed in violence and repetition where creole joins with a fear of feminization to become the verbal figure that de-scribes the de-masculinization implicit in colonial subjection.

Second, despite the periodic irruption into the text of other footnotes, serving other explanatory purposes, this moment of identitarian contestation remains the only instance when creole dialogue has been *translated* at length and rendered in footnote form. While the implications of the tonal shift compulsorily enacted by the inclusion of explanatory footnotes in a purportedly literary text have already been explored, showing that they necessarily draw attention to and emphasize the self-reflexive, factitious, fabricated nature of the literary artifact, the question raised by the difference between this translated creole passage and the presence of other, untranslated ones is ultimately one of accessibility to the authorial gesture, a problematic register that mediates here between author and reader. We have also seen this problematic in the work of Suzanne Dracius, who resolves it by providing a creole glossary at the end of the text. If, as seems clear, Chamoiseau has deliberately chosen this passage for self-referential footnoting and secondary re-presentation in order to highlight the problematic politics of language and creole identity as they intersect with and implicitly transform both colonial authority and textual re-presentation itself, then this episode of confrontation and contestation of social, political, and literary boundaries takes on added shades of resonance and discursive subtlety.

Doudou-Ménar is but the first victim of this pattern of displaced colonial violence; an even more excruciating experience awaits poor Congo. His torment is parenthetically prefigured on the title page to section 4 ("Weep? For Congo") (111/163), just as Doudou-Ménar's fate was at the beginning of section 3 ("Weep over whom? Doudou-Ménar") (74/115), and, retrospectively, Solibo's as well, at the beginning of section 1 (Tears for whom? For Solibo) (7/23). By now the representatives of metropolitan power are convinced of the existence of a premeditated plot to poison Solibo with one of Doudou-Ménar's sugary *chadecs*—a confection made primarily of grapefruit whose origin is explained in another footnote purporting this time to be an extract from the Coroner's report—a plot with Congo as primary perpetrator, but one in which the entire community has conspired and in whose cover-up they continue to participate. Pilon's alienation here is clearly signaled once again through the use of free indirect discourse, whose ambiguities penetrate even this fog of inductive reasoning: "It was abnormal that the listeners to the one named Solibo manifested no surprise when, having collapsed after a cry of pain, he interrupted his statements in such an illogical way. This permits the hypothesis that the listeners *knew* that the man was going to die and that *they came to observe the spectacle*" (102/152; emphasis in the original). Able to perceive the mote of illogic in his counterpart's eye without taking cognizance of the plank in his own, Pilon, whose distance from his own sun-drenched tradition is so marked that he "stood in full sunlight like a tourist" (103/153), is determined to get to the bottom of the affair.

Yet the unplumbed complexity of the affair itself is aptly summed up in the person of the peasant known as la Fièvre, in the bus on the way to the police station, not so much by what he says but by who he is, or, more correctly, is not: "He's a featureless man, at the intersection of some fourteen ethnicities whose traits he's carefully avoided. We know him without knowing him, he's from Fort-de-France but he's not from here, and even his Creole has creoles from elsewhere in it" (105/155). This oracle of opacity inhabits a masterful metaphor of contradictions; a métis of undiscernible traits, simultaneously congenial and elusive, his racial and cultural indistinctness, coupled with a social and linguistic inscription drawn on the unknowable, combine to make him perhaps the ultimate icon of creole unrepresentability. It is thus more than appropriate that it is his plaintive query—"*What's happening to us, Lord? What's happening?*" (104/155; italics in the original)—that summarizes the communal condition upon the death of Solibo. But this turn to the Almighty is a rhetorical question that finds its material response in the interrogation, beating, and humiliation of the not incidentally named Congo.

Although the latter's creole has been described as incomprehensible to all but a very few, "more unfathomable than a Lorraine cliff" (68/107), the interrogation is enthusiastically undertaken once again by the guardians of metropolitan authority: "Jambette and Diab-Anba-Feuilles twist his arms behind his back, slam him onto a chair, face under a desk lamp's incandescence. . . . Mr. Bateau Français, inform us of the nature of the poison you supplied for Solibo Magnificent's murder" (139–140/200–201). And again, Congo, caught in the interstices of competence and performance, responds as before not in French but in a creole that requires a translator, a task, as we now know, of mathematical precision, undertaken this time, immediately and unmediated by any observation of the rules of re-presentation, by the intrepid Diab-Anba-Feuilles: "Hot ahan an hahê houazon, dit Congo, hantan-an hé an hojèt pahol la hi hépann Holibo.". . . "In front of the faces his superiors were making, Diab-Anba-Feuilles translated without waiting: He says that you are looking for poison though it's a strangulation that has culled Solibo" (140/202). Diab's recodification of Congo's "incomprehensible" non sequitur reveals the many nuances of division that pervade this maelstrom of colonizer and colonized, linking these various layers of colonial alienation through an incessant re-vision of the boundaries and disjunctures of colonialism's composite language forms.

Congo's ultimate fate requires a two-step process. In the first, his interlocutors revisit the fate of Doudou-Ménar with only slight changes in the cast of the drama. Meanwhile it is Bouaffesse's turn to marshal the misrecognition of the colonial counterpart, as he effortlessly perpetrates a supplementary colonial violence: "Papa, listen to me, we respect your white hair, but for us, murderers like you don't have any hair. . . . The Chief Sergeant seized a huge register he had set aside and brought it down on the old blackman's skull like a plague [the bad kind]" (141/202–3). This discourse emphasizes colonialism's symbolic erasure of identity, a fragmentation and dispersal of subjective boundaries exacerbated by interrogation procedures that expose the cultural void left to the voiceless by the demise of Solibo Magnificent. Given this colonial erasure of the collective memory and its voice that Solibo's disappearance represents, even the very Africanness of Congo's origins is held against him, negating his ethnic homogeneity and valorizing by default the marker of heterogeneous admixture: "His clients called him 'Congo,' his father having been one of those men transported to the country well after slavery. Their African purity had seemed a defect in the middle of our mixed population, and one said 'Congo' with as much disdain as 'Negro'" (142/204). This nomenclature stands in contrast to his "nom de sécurité sociale," Bateau Français, generating a supreme sense of irony through this figure who inhabits the triple terms of the colonial triangle; for if the search for Solibo's identity is meant to be the key link in the chain ultimately establishing the true cause of his death, the construction of Congo as primary suspect is also shown to be the catalyst that exposes the French-framed sea of divisions and social prejudices that are engendered in the wake of colonialism's construction of metropolitan authority.

The nadir of this colonial encounter finally is reached as Congo is systematically tortured. But interestingly, his victimization at the hands of Pilon, Bouaffesse, Jamette, and Diab-Anba-Feuilles marks an evolutionary stage in his instantiation as colonial martyr, in a gesture whose accomplishment ultimately comes, as it must, through an independent, contestatory act. In the meantime, this brutal process of "chosification" continues: "They hammered his skull and ears with thick phonebooks, they kicked him, and made him crawl under office chairs, they knocked him in the liver, the balls, the nape, they crushed his fingers and blinded him with their thumbs. . . . there was nothing human around there" (143–44/206). But it is in the moments following their respite—taken only to visit their colonial violence upon Sucette—that Congo manages to seize the initiative. Already inscribed as a symbol of social and historical resistance, he symbolizes the sufferings of slavery and the people's survival, "for those who saw him they saw four hundred years of our past" (143/204). From this perspective, in an act of supreme self-sacrifice that stands in stark contrast to Diab's act of self-mortification, he hurls himself through the window in a suicidal gesture that promises group reprieve as well as individual surcease: "Diagram in one hand, a glass of coffee in the other, the Chief Inspector was getting his questions in gear, when in a single leap the old man flew right through the window. There was a brief silence before they heard him crash two floors below" (145/208).

Crucially, it is the form, rather than the simple fact, of Congo's death that renders it an act of opposition to the continuation of colonial control; by intervening in the cycle of metropolitan violence, taking his own life and therefore the moment and manner of his death into his own hands, Congo takes his place beside Solibo as an icon of cultural independence, a symbol of opposition whose disappearance is fundamentally linked to an impending change in regional outlook and perspective. For if, as Marie-Agnès Sourieau suggests, "*Solibo Magnifique* establishes that the cultural dependence of the Martinican people brought on the escheat of a tradition that is fundamental to their identity" (1992:136), then Congo's sacrificial suicide must also take its rightful place as a survivalist act performed for and in the name of the people, a supplementary cultural and geopolitical inscription of an identity whose dual protagonists signify it as African and West Indian, indomitable and independent in its continuing struggle against metropolitan mastery. If the presence of the storyteller is critical to the continuity of the communal identity, then the Congos of the Caribbean are the final arbiter of colonialism's Others, modern-day maroons, if you will, who prefer the obstinacy of opposition and the dignity of death to a life of suffering, slavery, and subordination. Through Congo, Solibo's others attain that sense of survival as a community that was threatened by the latter's demise, acting out the identitarian tradition of creole enfranchisement and self-sufficiency made latent by Solibo's stories and confronting the violence that was ultimately unleashed by the insistence on locating the fundamental signification underlying his death. The methodology of the official inquiry, combined with the terrorist tactics of police procedure, produces a series of communal acts that results in the resurgence and reinscription of the very maroon identity that was thought to have disappeared with Solibo, valorizing the tradition of oraliture which he obviously not only personified but was able to vivify in his creole counterparts. As these symbols of metropolitan authority are slowly stripped of their colonial mystique, it is the polysemic, polyvalent character of the people, of the popular, communal voice so long thought to be oppressed and repressed, that finally comes into its own as a discursive articulation of oppositional identity.

Impressions of (Im)possibility

As the murder investigation inexorably approaches its end, the key issues of identity, means, and motive paradoxically become less rather than more clear.

Indeed, if the expectation of the investigators was that clearing up the "who" of Solibo would lead logically to the "why" of the crime, they are to be deeply and painfully disappointed. After taking pains to ensure that the written record reflects that "Congo's window suicide became an escape attempt" (147/211), thereby hopefully engendering the continued security and superiority of the metropolitan discourse through which their supplementary superiority is ensured, Pilon, with Bouaffesse in tow, returns to Doctor Lélonette for the results of the autopsy. But in point of fact, since the good doctor cannot provide an adequate response to the question of how Solibo died, he is thus equally unable to clarify the "who" aspect of the mystery, leaving the "how" that subtends Solibo's life and death still an open question for the metropolitan authorities: "The man was in perfect health, of exceptional vitality. . . . The problem for me is that he presents all the symptoms of death by strangulation. . . . however, on the neck's exterior, yes, yes, look, the neck shows no hematoma, not a trace, it's perfectly normal: this Mr. Solibo would then had to have been strangled from the *inside* (Whaat? Bleat Pilon and Bouaffesse) which literally makes no sense, you'll agree"(150/215). Both Solibo's death and Solibo as subject thus seem destined to remain shrouded in mystery, as the metropolitan authorities are forced to confront a logical and physical impossibility that now parallels the discursive impossibility within which this subject is framed.

If Solibo's beginnings are fundamentally untold, his end is no less enigmatic, as the doctor makes clear: "This death is mysterious from a medical point of view. . . . I can already say that there hasn't been a crime" (151/216). Caught in this maze of cultural signification, where the solution to the enigma of identity appears constantly elusive, Bouaffesse and Pilon proceed in a manner that becomes ever more surprising; by turning to a quimboiseur, or obeahman, known to Bouaffesse, they effectively abandon the logical straits of metropolitan linearity for the syncretic strategies of the creole. This tacit recognition of the colony's pervasive polyvalence is borne out not only by the enigmatic explanation proffered by this visionary of *vodun* — whose socioreligious role awards him a position of power within the community that rivals, and perhaps surpasses, that of these icons of imperialism — but through the significant fact that he makes his response "in his ageless creole," conflating form and function, history and opposition in a culminating moment of continuing orality. Last in a line of creole inscriptions that frame critical moments in the narrative, the quimboiseur's linguistic, identitarian gesture is an echo of the ageless, slave-engendered code that cleaves Solibo to his community, and joins language, history, and tradition in a final affirmation of pluralist mysticism: "In the body, Inspekder . . . there's water and breath, speech is breath, breath is strength, strength is the body's idea of life, of its life" (153/219). By equating speech with the ineffable life force, the quimboiseur succeeds not only in restating the value of the complex social role traditionally inhabited by the conteur—with its corollary of cultural affirmation for the community as a whole—but also in inscribing that elusive immediacy that has both characterized Solibo and defied discursive transcription.

It is here, then, in the spiritual core of the community, that the true import of Solibo's identity may finally be located; through the mediation of the marqueur, we come face-to-face with these impressions of (im)possibility, with the deliberate discontinuity between sign and act that ultimately transforms the text into a self-reflexive simulacrum of discursive representability. It is through this re-creational network that the marqueur seeks to convey his realization that "to write down the word was nothing but betrayal, you lost the intonations, the parody, the storyteller's gestures" (158/225), and that what was lost with Solibo's demise was in fact a way of life, a world within a world. If, as epilogue, the marqueur presents us with Pipi's performative reconstruction of the verbal exchanges of Solibo's final moments, a displaced, othered, re-presentative translation of what Solibo was, "a reduced, organized *written* version, a kind of ersatz of what the Master had been that night" (159/226; italics in the original), then the endgame essayed by this translation, while insisting on its constructedness, functions simultaneously to signal a coda for a society systematically—although perhaps unknowingly—destroying its traditions and practices from within. For with all that Solibo was, in the end "this man . . . was the suffering pulse of a world coming to an end" (159/227); as these festivities of bacchanalian intensity wind down, as "Vaval, in flames, reddened the whole harbor" (154/220), the social whole seems to slowly slide into an unrecognizable, impressionistic imitation of its complex, creole cultural heritage. It is this history, this discourse, these sites of violence, tragedy, and survival, that above all must not be forgotten.

If, in the end, Pilon has no answer to the question upon which his investigation has been predicated—"Who, but who was this Solibo, and why 'Magnificent'?"(154/219)—this need not be the case for us. Solibo's importance as subject of this text lies both in his social role and in the arresting absence caused by his death. As the society's storyteller, inheritor of that fierce desire for autonomy and self-assertion symbolized from earliest slavery by the figure of the maroon, Solibo functioned as the primary repository of a communal memory whose orality was the defining sign of an entire era. The Caribbean conteur was an intrinsically oppositional figure, one whose oraliture spoke in the name of the people to inscribe and reassert the tensions and traditions that had eventuated the community itself. In understanding the importance of Solibo's performance, then, we find the word was the thing; as our narrator, Chambizié, so cogently states: "The essential thing to see and hear was Papa's words: the things he *said*" (127/186; italics in the original). It was through this performative conflation of visibility and audibility that Solibo's significance to the community was signified; by communicating *with* and *for* the people, a Solibo could re-cite the rituals of survival by reminding the audience of its history of struggle and the continuity of its essential character: "For us, Solibo Magnificent was exactly that. A light on the horizon which breathes *Tjenbé rèd! Tjenbé rèd! (Hold on tight!)* and which helps you make it just by being there" (129/188; italics in the original). By incorporating and italicizing this indigenous rallying cry marking the identitarian spirit of the francophone Caribbean, a phrase that historically has signaled a commitment to an oppositional autonomy and cultural self-assertion in the face of unrelenting metropolitan domination, Solibo's discourse is metamorphosed into a mythical metaphor of endurance, mapping through his very existence a means of cultural survival that encompasses and empowers the community at large.

At the same time, however, these were the very same qualities that made Solibo into an elusive, undefinable presence, one in whom the combination of word and gesture, of past and present, of orality and discursivity created a cultural phenomenon whose common currency was the Caribbean experience of creolization. Since Solibo both inhabited and inscribed the immediacy and complexity of social exchange, he came to symbolize creolization itself, re-presenting a cultural totality that could be discerned but not categorized: "Solibo was like a reflection in a window, a sculpture with facets that allowed no angle to reflect the whole" (154/220). This intrinsic fragmentation and its corollary of difference inscribe Solibo within a framework of unrepresentability, one that shields his contentious subjectivity even as it necessarily imposes a signifying network of self-reflexivity upon the text. This perspective enables us to better understand the remarkable episodes of metamorphosis to which Solibo's body is subjected during the investigation; it is the impossibility of a *vision globale* informing his life that is necessarily revisited and recodified to undergird his shifting, intangible subjectivity, even in demise.

The efforts of the emergency personnel to transport the corpse following their preliminary examination are met with an arresting series of transformations, first rendering Solibo's body increasingly and impossibly heavier, then quickly accomplishing the reverse: "They couldn't lift him off the ground: Solibo weighed a ton all the sudden, like the corpses of those blackmen unwilling to leave this life" (91/137). As their added efforts against this incomprehensible phenomenon are successively met with increased weights of one and a half, then two, and then five tons (138), charms are consulted and precautions against obeah and sorcery are taken, but all is to no avail; Solibo remains immovable.

These developments effectively breach the boundaries of narrative credibility and verge on the magical; they can be read as an extension of Solibo's composite, discernible, yet indefinable personality. And as if to reinforce this scene of mythical transformation, we are soon confronted by its opposite; Solibo's body becomes light enough to be balanced on Bouaffesse's wrist and bounced from finger to finger, "a body lighter than sugar cane ashes. . . . Bouaffesse now passed the body to his middle finger, then his thumb, from the thumb to the index, from the index to the middle, spellbound by Solibo effortlessly floating in his loose ties" (103–4/153–54). Finally, if this is not enough, the conteur's body is quickly and mysteriously infested by a species of ant found on only two islands to the north in Guadeloupe: "They were manioc ants and not mad ants. . . . there were four ant species, the biting, the black, the mad, and the manioc. . . . All were gathered on Solibo. . . . He had barely articulated that thought when he realized the strangeness of what he had just said: *Good God! The manioc ant only lives in Guadeloupe!*" (101/150; italics in the original). Triply described by these scenes of impossibility, Solibo's demise appears to engender as much of an enigma in death as its subject did in life; indeed, inasmuch as these episodes border on the unimaginable, they appear to work, perhaps deliberately, to impede a fuller understanding of the insistent social immediacy of the conteur and the dissonance created by his disappearance.

Given that all these events are inscribed beyond the pale of possibility, sketching paradigms of a Caribbean marvellous realism, itself a sign of a creolized culture, which does not differentiate between the mythological and the

real and thus defies rational explanation, what role do they play in constructing a framework for our comprehension of Solibo?

It might be useful to begin at the level of the mystery surrounding his departure from this mortal coil; cut off in full voice after uttering the incomprehensible "Patat' sa!" Solibo experienced a death generated from within, an event
marking the end of an era that had placed him at its cultural and symbolic
center. Yet at bottom his death was not a suicide but rather a curious inability
to sustain the incremental metamorphoses of a society undergoing monumen-
tal if unconscious change. If the fundamental traditions and practices of this
society were no longer to have their basis in a subaltern subjectivity secured
and supported by oraliture, then not only was there no longer a place for a
Solibo, but his increasingly untenable subjective space was being progressively closed off by the very society in whose reciprocity with their storyteller
the dual hinge of their special relationship was founded: "the Magnificent had
beeen losing his listeners in his latter days. . . . he found himself submerged by
the reality he thought he could vanquish" (156–57/222–24). In this climate of
change, in which the role and place of the conteur were indeed becoming
increasingly incomprehensible and inchoate, only the ultimate sacrifice
would serve to transmit that final kernel of sociocultural signification. As
Walter Benjamin's "The Storyteller" tellingly reminds us, "It is, however, characteristic that not only a man's knowledge or wisdom, but above all his real
life — and this is the stuff that stories are made of — first assumes transmissible
form at the moment of his death" (1968:94). In these terms, it is Solibo himself
that attains transmissible discursive force, his unrepresentability effectively
eclipsed, his entire existence symbolically and retrospectively transformed
into a cultural palimpsest upon which can be read — and written — the fundamental framework of the Caribbean creole.

Thus it is that the end of Chamoiseau's plot leaves us literally at its beginning — in a place both the same and yet different, not having solved the mystery of Solibo's death but now in a position, perhaps, to comprehend the meaning of his life, the people through whom he lived it, and the events leading
toward his demise. Here, the double gesture enacted by the intersection of a
self-reflexive creole style with the subtle strategies of the detective fiction format works through these narrative transparencies of cultural transmission to
inscribe new parameters and possibilities for discursive form, in which spatial-
ity and temporality are both inverted and mestastasized into a moving medita-

tion on the Caribbean condition. We may find in these episodes traces of that mysticism that takes "the synthesis of heterogeneous elements as the basic characteristic of marvelous realism," as Barbara Webb puts it, generating through discourse "a new arrangement of elements, textures, juxtapositions, convolutions of form, and metaphor" that "attempts to capture the density and proportions of New World realities" (1992:19–20); at the same time, these enigmatic epiphenomena teach us the importance, in a colonial context, that the question holds over the answer, drawing on that conflation of history and culture that was perhaps the ultimate *lieu de mémoire* animated and transmitted by Solibo: "To learn to question, no more certainties or evidences. . . . That's what Solibo was about" (127/185). The questions posed all his life by Solibo's stories—the call-and-response that framed his cultural specificity, the "what" that makes the Caribbean people who they are, a tradition of physical resistance and spiritual and verbal opposition—these are the ones that assume the shape of mystery and enigma at the moment of his demise. Similarly, the double discourse that forms the essential framework of this novel stresses the striking simultaneity of its principal stories; by retracing the life of the victim through the account of the inquiry into his death, the author produces a complex act of performative narration that becomes an allegory of the act of writing itself. It is this consciously self-reflexive turn that, in continuously drawing attention to the status of this text as literary artifact, reiterates the ongoing role of discourse in the contestation of cultural hegemony and the construction of new patterns of identitarian possibility.

Establishing and maintaining tangible links with a recognizable past forged in resistance and opposition, and emphasizing the place of this cultural identity in the social identity of the present, has historically been the role of the conteur. His oral mastery mirrored and memorized the heritage of his essentially African ancestry: born on the slave plantation, valorized by visions of maroon resistance, enriched by ethnic admixture, and inscribed in the immediacy of cultural performance. Such a vibrant synthesis of creole invention and social subversion is summed up by Chamoiseau himself in the introduction to his *Caribbean Folktales* (originally *Au temps de l'antan*): "Our Storyteller speaks for a people enchained: starving, terrorized, living in the cramped postures of survival. . . . these tales provide . . . an apprenticeship in life—a life of survival in a colonized land. . . . the storyteller must take care to use language that is opaque, devious—its significance broken up into a thousand sybilline fragments . . . to help camouflage any dangerously subversive content. . . . the Storyteller's object is almost *to obscure as he reveals*" (xii–xiii; emphasis in the original).

Yet along with his awareness of the symbolic complexities bound up in his social role, and the composite layers of meaning communicated by his speech, the fleeting relevance of this relation was also supremely evident to Solibo, who recognized the subtle social transformations that marked the advent of modernity, and with it the painful passage from the oral to the written: "This transition between his epoch of memory passed down orally, of resistance in the curves of speech, and this new time, when things only survived through writing, ate him up" (156/223). Faced with the encroaching territoriality of "other pasts," with the disappearance of a resistance bred in the word and the inevitable progression of a future both unknown and unreliable, Solibo essentially succumbed to the internal machinations of cultural irrelevance. But, in the final analysis, his unique conflation of memory and performance stands guardian, in all its elusive unrepresentability, at the gates of alternative possibilities; as his discourse traces a path through the challenges of departmentalization and the allure of autonomy, the ironic parentheses that frame the discursive impressionism of his oral gesture signal a comprehension of geopolitical complexities constructed beyond, and in spite of, the hierarchies of history: "Solibo Magnificent used to tell me: 'Oh, Oiseau, you want Independence, but that idea weighs you down like handcuffs. First, be free before the idea. That's where it starts, that struggle of yours'" (87/133). As this oppositional praxis undergirding the maroon tradition is steadily transformed into a differential discourse of Caribbean heterogeneity, the corollaries and constants of Solibo's self-reflexive oralature do not die away but are progressively reiterated into performative patterns of infinite possibility.

Conclusion

Creolizing the Colonial Encounter

None of the people who now occupy the islands—black, brown, white, African, European, American, Spanish, French, East Indian, Chinese, Portuguese, Jew, Dutch—originally "belonged" there. It is the space where the creolisations and assimilations and syncretisms were negotiated. The New World is the third term—the primal scene—where the fateful/fatal encounter was staged between Africa and the West.

Stuart Hall, *Cultural Identity and Diaspora*

It would probably be foolhardy to attempt to provide any sort of definitive conclusion to the complex concatenation of history, politics, ethnicity, and discourse articulated here. This exercise in the exegesis of reading and writing began by inscribing the problematics of ambivalence posed for the peoples of the Caribbean by the arrival of Christopher Columbus, an explorer whose ambiguous accomplishments are perhaps best signified by the fact that a national holiday in his honor is celebrated in the United States despite his never having set foot on the North American continent. But the true significance of Columbus's arrival in the "New World" lies not in this act of "discovery" but in the ethnic and cultural synthesis that was produced in its wake for the five centuries that followed. As Herman J. Viola and Carolyn Margolis, the editors of the volume *Seeds of Change*, point out: "What Columbus had really discovered was, however, another old world, one long populated by numerous and diverse peoples with cultures as distinct, vibrant, and worthy as any to be found in Europe. Tragically, neither Columbus nor those who followed him recognized this truth. . . . Only recently, in fact, have we come to realize that what Columbus did in 1492 was to link two old worlds, thereby creating one new world" (12). The implicit interrogations of departmentalization and its corollaries of cultural identity that have informed these chapters reflect these intersections of the old and the new that subtend a creolization process driven, in its Caribbean context, by the forces of slavery, colonialism, racism, and ethnic and cultural admixture.

In analyzing these novels, I have set forth some of the themes and tensions that tend to shape the boundaries of such creolizing discourses. Because I have only touched the surface of this area of analysis, it is beyond question that further consideration of the implications raised by such intersections of relationality and re-presentation is both necessary and urgent. Indeed, I have argued that what is at stake is Caribbeanness as the summa of a larger phenomenon of creolization, stressing the polysemic character of this regional palimpsest in which, as Derek Walcott explains in "What the Twilight Said," these composite populations were compelled to create "a language that went beyond mimicry, a dialectic that had the force of revelation as it invented names for things, one which finally settled on its own mode of inflection, and which began to create an oral culture of chants, jokes, folksongs and fables" (17). It is the ways in which this language has interacted with and has been transformed by its corollaries of history, literature, and culture as it spawns new paradigms for discursive inscription, that I have attempted to elucidate here.

The performative gestures and linguistic and discursive creolization of such texts are grounded, as Antonio Benitez-Rojo explains in "Three Words toward Creolization," in an understanding of this phenomenon in its Caribbean context, one that frames "the unstable states that a Caribbean cultural object presents over time. In other words, creolization is not merely a process (a word that implies forward movement) but a discontinuous series of recurrences, of happenings, whose sole law is change"(55). This insistence on discontinuity, instability, and change works to debunk old, stereotypical ways of reading and writing, highlighting the slippage between what is bequeathed by the praxis of colonialism and departmentalization and the challenge of cultural and discursive reinvention, and produces multivalencies of transformation out of this conflation of creolization and intertextuality.

The principal question here has been how to approach these modes of reading and writing as differentially as their content implies, to find a way, as Jonathan Cu puts it, "to make sense of novels which thematize the difficulties of making sense and especially ridicule attempts to read life as if it were a novel, in accordance with those very operations which the reader is engaged in performing" (1985:212). The reading strategies employed here have been geared toward highlighting the deliberate dislocation between form and content that French Caribbean geopolitics demand, as well as the differential structural and organizational principles of language. As Françoise Lionnet puts it, "The otherness of the local vernacular produces hybridity, within the poetic text" (1998:76). It is to the conjunction of these phenomena that Benita Parry refers when, in her article "Resistance Theory," she writes, "Identity is now perceived as multi-located and polysemic—a situation that characterises postcoloniality and is at its most evident in the diasporic condition" (175). The ancient, metropolitan dialectic of self and Other, here and elsewhere, gives way to the creative slippages and strategies of hybridization and synthesis.

As a literary discourse that speaks for the many, French Caribbean literature distills from the experiences of exile, slavery, migration, marooning, ethnic and linguistic creolization, colonialism, slavery, departmentalization, and diaspora a narrative voice of creative coherence, of a compound cultural practice that revels in its own disjunctures. Its creative conjunctures of form and content seek, paradoxically, to embody the very discontinuities that make the Caribbean a site of specifically multiple identities. As Chamoiseau himself put it in a recent interview, "It's a question of constant tensions between competing identities, and that is what makes the Caribbean such a vital place" (1999:51). In this creative newness that marks its differential modernity, reflecting the paradoxical disjunctures both of its metropolitan diasporas and the complex discontinuities of ethnicity, language, and place that are the result of colonialism, departmentalization, and modern-day migration, Caribbean creolization stands poised to extend the boundaries of its discursive praxis, becoming as exuberantly polyvalent as the identities it re-presents.

Notes

Introduction. Conceptualizing Creoleness: French Caribbean "Postcolonial" Discourse

1. The further etymological and ethnocultural implications of the word "creole," as defined here, are discussed in detail in chapter 4; I have drawn on the 1992 edition of the OED here.

2. This discussion is laid out in detail in the opening sections of Edouard Glissant's *Caribbean Discourse*; see, in particular, 14–26.

3. See, for example, "The Gendering of *Créolité*," by A. James Arnold, in *Penser la créolité*, edited by Maryse Condé and Madeleine Cottenet-Hage, 21–40, and Maryse Condé's closing piece, "Chercher nos vérités," in the same volume, as well as her "Order, Disorder, Freedom, and the West Indian Writer," 121–35.

4. Indeed, attacking the créolistes on these and other grounds now appears to be de rigueur if not à la mode, as recent exchanges at such fora as the M/MLA, Chicago 1997, ALA, Austin 1998, ICCL, Bahamas 1998, and the MLA, San Francisco 1998 can readily attest. See also, for example, Richard Price and Sally Price's article "Shadowboxing in the Mangrove," 123–62, a piece whose unmitigatedly critical stance toward the approach taken by the créolistes and, indeed, toward Martinican society at large—this from critics who profess to spend half of each year there—begs the question of the very discursive legitimacy of créolité. The implications of their position, as well as that of Arnold, will be explored in chapter 5.

1. *La Lézarde*: Alienation and the Poetics of Antillanité

1. All page references for Edouard Glissant's *Le Discours antillais* will be made parenthetically in the text.

2. Homi Bhabha lays out the basis for this idea and the range of its implications in "The Commitment to Theory," *Questions of Third Cinema*, edited by Jim Pines and Paul Willemen, 111–32.

3. All page references for *La Lézarde* will be made parenthetically in the text. Translations are taken from the English version, *The Ripening*, translated by J. Michael Dash.

4. See, for example, Chris Bongie, *Islands and Exiles*, 46; see also Frederick I Case, *The Crisis of Identity*, 61. The latter's references to Glissant's insistence upon "the perfectibility of the human being and the possibilities of a deepening ideological consciousness" seem, given my own reading, particularly anachronistic.

5. "The Other is the locus in which is situated the chain of the signifier that governs whatever may be made present of the subject—it is the field of that living being in which the subject has to appear. . . . The signifier, producing itself in the field of the Other . . . functions as a signifier only to reduce the subject in question to being no more than a signifier, to petrify the subject in the same movement in which it calls the subject to function, to speak, as subject. . . . What we find once again here is the constitution of the subject in the field of the Other. . . . If he is apprehended at this birth in the field of the Other, the characteristic of the subject of the unconscious is that of being . . . at an indeterminate place." Jacques Lacan, *The Four Fundamental Concepts of Psycho-Analysis*, 203, 207, 208.

6. Both Wallace Martin's *Recent Theories of Narrative* and Dorrit Cohn's *Transparent Minds* offer the most thorough and far- reaching discussions of the implications of free indirect discourse for the construction of subjectivity. The function of this form in narrative discourse is also examined in Shlomith Rimmon-Kenan's *Narrative Fiction* and Seymour Chatman's *Story and Discourse*. It is the implications of these positionalities for postcolonial discourse and the alienation of its attendant subjectivities that I wish to emphasize in this reading.

7. See, for example, works by Paul Jay, and James Olney.

8. See also the introduction to White's *Metahistory*.

9. See *Larousse Greek and Roman Mythology*, edited by Joël Schmidt and Seth Benardete, 9.

2. *En attendant le bonheur*: Creole Conjunctions and Cultural Survival

1. Maryse Condé, *En attendant le bonheur (Hérémakhonon)*. All page references will be made parenthetically in the text. Translations are taken from the English version, titled *Heremakhonon*, translated by Richard Philcox.

2. In a striking anomaly, this protagonist has been given an anglicized first name, itself linked oppositionally to a French surname. While insisting that a perfectly adequate French equivalent for the former, Véronique, remains elided, this additional level of symbolic duality underlines the basic pattern of identitarian alienation by which she is framed. On the one hand, then, this form of nominalization may be read as a deliberate discursive attempt to stress her strangeness, to inscribe the deep-rooted pervasiveness of her alterity. But other, related issues are also at work: the French *véronique* also refers, on the one hand, to a flower whose symbolic language is related to virginity, virtue, and lack of desire; etymologically, its Greek root meaning is "authentic representation" or "true icon." On the other hand, Mercier, the other half of the protagonist's oxymoronic nomenclature, is drawn from the root word *mercerie*, conveying an inscription in the masculine through its meaning of haberdashery, or the purveying of men's notions. This symbolic chiasmus, whose opposing axes are drawn across the very body of the protagonist, inscribes her quest for the truth of herself precisely between a pure and virtuous womanhood and a desire of/for the masculine, and provides an interesting commentary on Véronica's paradoxical but compelling subjectivity. I owe these insights in part to a commentary made from the floor by Dr. Pascale de Souza of the University of Maryland,

during a session of the Carolina Conference on the Romance Literatures at the University of North Carolina-Chapel Hill, 20 March 1998.

3. This reading of Véronica's silent textual inscription was confirmed to the author by Maryse Condé herself during the discussion period at a panel devoted to her work at the African Literature Association Conference in Austin, Texas, 25–29 April 1998.

4. If desire plays a prominent role in the construction and resolution of the narrative of *En attendant le bonheur*, it is a desire for alterity, to be Other, to inscribe the subject into the field and discourse of the (cultural) counterpart. In Lacanian terms, desire determines the relationship of the subject to the Other in whom its alienation will always already be inscribed; it succeeds the essential lack experienced by the subject separated from the (m)Other, and marks the alienation of the subject. But, given that the subjectivity of this (m)Other is itself also based on a lack in being, it becomes impossible for it to respond fully to the *demand* for love made upon it by the alienated subject. Subjected to and alienated by the (m)Other, who cannot furnish what the subject lacks or has lost, the subject cannot resolve his or her lack in being. Desire comes to delineate what is barred to the subject, and is rendered as that which can never be satisfied. Ultimately, the subject must relinquish the attempt to fulfill the vagaries of desire, and address the inscription of alienation on its own terms: "That is why the question of the Other, which comes back to the subject from the place from which he expects an oracular reply . . . is the one that best leads him to the path of his own desire — providing he sets out . . . to reformulate it, even without knowing it, as 'What does he want of me?'" See Jacques Lacan, *Ecrits*, p. 312. See also the chapter titled "The Subversion of the Subject," in Bice Benvenuto and Roger Kennedy, *The Works of Jacques Lacan: An Introduction* (New York: St. Martin's, 1986), as well as chapters 13 and 14 in Anika Lemaire, *Jacques Lacan*, translated by David Macey (London: Routledge and Kegan Paul, 1977), for admirably clear expositions of Lacan's notoriously periphrastic prose.

5. See Mayotte Capécia, *Je suis martiniquaise* (Paris: Corréa, 1948) and Fanon's reading of its implicit theme of "lactification" in *Black Skin, White Masks*.

3. *L'Isolé Soleil/Soufrières*: Textual Creolization and Cultural Identity

1. Daniel Maximin, *L'Isolé Soleil*. Translations are taken from the English version *Lone Sun*, edited and translated by Clarisse Zimra.

2. Documentation of this sequence of events may be found in Robert Deville and Nicolas Georges, *Les Départements d'outre-mer: L'Autre Décolonisation* (Paris: Gallimard, 1996), 27–35. See also Germain St. Ruf, *L'Epopée Delgrès: La Guadeloupe sous la révolution française, 1789–1802* (Paris: L'Harmattan, 1988).

3. This symbolic rendering of the colonial undertaking is not without precedent. See Assia Djebar's *L'Amour, la fantasia* (Paris: J. C. Lattès, 1985) and Kateb Yacine's *Nedjma* (Paris: Seuil, 1956) for an inscription of Algeria as absent, nonspeaking female object of colonial desire, a reading which draws on the binaries of bilingualism and biculturalism produced by the colonial encounter. On Djebar, and the textual articulation of postcolonial heterogeneity, see also my "Rewriting Writing," *Yale French Studies* 83 (1992):71–92.

4. Michael Richardson, "Introduction," in *Refusal of the Shadow: Surrealism and the Caribbean*, translated by Michael Richardson and Krzysztof Fijalkowski (London: Verso, 1996), 8.

4. *L'Autre qui danse*: The Modalities and Multiplicities of Métissage

1. Suzanne Dracius-Pinalie, *L'Autre qui danse*.

2. This novel, published in 1948, has achieved a certain notoriety through its apparent insistence on Martinican women's duty to "whiten the race" by marrying white.

3. See Erik Erikson, *Childhood and Society* (New York: Norton, 1963). While Shelton's use of Erikson's work is linked to her subsequent reading of Lacrosil, I am attempting to juxtapose both readings in order to conflate the principle of rage against the self with Lacrosil's important confrontation of the feminine subject with her own mirror image. Such a double reading, I would argue, illuminates more precisely the specific issue of Caribbean feminine alienation.

4. For a detailed description and documentation of this process, the cardinal role played by the state agency BUMIDOM, and an evaluation of the integration of these immigrants into metropolitan society, see Alain Anselin, "West Indians in France," in *French and West Indian: Martinique, Guadeloupe and French Guiana Today*, edited by Richard D. E. Burton and Fred Reno (London: Macmillan Caribbean, 1995), chapter 8.

5. See, for example, Claude Lévi-Strauss, *Race et Histoire* (Paris: Gonthier, 1961), and Nancy Stepan, "Biological Degeneration: Races and Proper Places," in *Degeneration: The Dark Side of Progress*, edited by J. Edward Chamberlin and Sander Gilman (New York: Columbia University Press, 1985). See also K. Anthony Appiah, "The Uncompleted Argument," 21–37. Here Appiah discusses Du Bois's "The Conservation of Races," in *W.E.B. Du Bois Speaks: Speeches and Addresses,1890–1919*, edited by Philip S. Foner (1897; New York, 1970).

6. See Richard Allsopp, *Dictionary of Caribbean Usage* (New York: Oxford, 1996), for an effective definition and contextual examples of this verbal marker of Caribbean culture.

7. These references were confirmed to the author by Suzanne Dracius in a fax communication dated 27 February 1998, and in a personal interview conducted on 16 April, 1998.

5. *Solibo Magnifique*: Carnival, Opposition, and the Narration of the Caribbean Maroon

1. Patrick Chamoiseau, *Solibo Magnifique*. Translations are taken from the English version, *Solibo Magnificent*, translated by Rose-Myriam Réjouis and Val Vinokurov.

2. Accounts of the extent and effectiveness of Caribbean slave revolts are widespread and can be found not only in Michael Craton's *Testing the Chains* but also in David Barry Gaspar's *Bondmen and Rebels* (Baltimore: Johns Hopkins, 1985), Robin Blackburn's *The Overthrow of Colonial Slavery* (London: Verso, 1988), Eric Williams's *From Columbus to Castro*, and C. L. R. James's *The Black Jacobins* (New York: Vintage, 1963). Taken together or separately, the analyses in these texts provide overwhelming proof of the perva-

siveness of both large and small-scale resistance as a historical phenomenon across the region, from slavery's inception to the achievement of emancipation.

3. Despite claims to the contrary in some quarters, slaves were limited not so much perhaps by the topography but by the relative size of the islands of Guadeloupe and Martinique; marooning encompassed both the formation of large bands of escapees and single acts of petit marronnage. The slave populations of these islands found that their limited size was not necessarily a complete barrier to larger-scale acts of freedom; detailed and extended maroon activity was recorded as taking place in Antigua—an island which is both Guadeloupe's closest neighbor and one-third its size—and St. Vincent, itself also smaller than either Guadeloupe or Martinique. It stands to reason, then, that slaves in larger territories would have a proportionately greater chance of making good their escape. The flourishing communities of maroons on the smaller islands of the Grenadines and Grenada also convincingly attest to their widespread installation and success in the region. See, in particular, Craton, *Testing the Chains*, chapter 16, 195–210, and Gaspar, *Bondmen and Rebels*, chapter, 8, 171–84.

4. It has become almost de rigueur in some critical quarters to cite Glissant's textual rebuke of the créolistes concerning the latent risk of essentialism that lurks within their theoretical position. This critique, which appears in the *Poétique* and should perhaps be read more as a discursive act of distancing, is usually read as evidence of the irreversible epistemological break between their position and that of Glissant. He writes, "C'est ce qui fait notre départ d'avec le concept de 'créolité.' . . . Les créolisations introduisent à la Relation, mais ce n'est pas pour universaliser; la 'créolité,' dans son principe, régresserait vers des négritudes, des francités, des latinités, toutes généralisantes—plus ou moins innocemment" (103). However, in this regard, the following facts may perhaps speak for themselves: While Glissant did indeed critique the créoliste movement at the outset, its adherents have on more than one occasion acknowledged their debt to him, although such an act should by no means be assumed to imply approbation. Chamoiseau, in particular, speaks of this debt in "En témoignage d'une volupté," *Carbet* 10 (December 1990):143–52, tracing it back to his reading of Glissant's novel *Malemort* (Paris: Gallimard, 1975). Raphaël Confiant originally dedicated his novel *Le Nègre et l'amiral* (1988) to Glissant. Not uncoincidentally, the epigraph from Chamoiseau's first novel, *Chronique des sept misères* (Paris: Gallimard, 1986), is taken from Glissant's *Discours antillais*, and Glissant provided a four-page preface to the work titled, significantly, "Un Marqueur de paroles," precisely the term that Chamoiseau will use to define his own role as novelist, and which will come into self-referential play in *Solibo*. In this preface Glissant speaks of Chamoiseau as "d'une génération qui . . . a porté son attention sur le détail du réel antillais," and states unequivocally in this context that "La littérature antillaise de langue française qui avait beaucoup d'éclat prend désormais corps" (3). Chamoiseau also cites Glissant's *Discours antillais* a number of times in his preface to his *Au temps de l'antan*.

It is also worthy of note that one of the two epigraphs to Chamoiseau's *Solibo Magnifique* is taken from Glissant's oeuvre, as is one of the epigraphs to *Texaco*, a work which is also dedicated, *entre autres*, to Glissant. Besides the publication of the *Eloge* in 1989 (dedicated to Glissant, Césaire, and the Haitian writer Frank Etienne, and one of whose four epigraphs was also taken from Glissant), it should be noted that Chamoiseau's most recent literary work, *L'Esclave vieil homme et le molosse* (Paris: Gallimard, 1997), contains a multiparagraph *entre-dire* written by Glissant himself. In a recent interview with a U.S. magazine publication (*Islands*, January–February 1999, 26–30), Chamoiseau speaks candidly of "timidly" presenting Glissant with the manuscript of his first novel, *Chronique des sept misères*, at Le Diamant, in Martinique. Since that time, both families have taken their annual vacations together at Le Diamant.

5. See Michel de Certeau's "On the Oppositional Practices of Everyday Life," in *Social Text* 3 (1980):3–43. I use this distinction for the basis of the discursive definitions that inform several aspects of this chapter, drawing on the use Richard Burton makes of this distinction in his book *Afro-Creole*.

6. See Derek Walcott, "A Letter to Chamoiseau."

7. The role of the *makoumè* in the binary system that governs the gendered world of the créolistes is also discussed at length in A. James Arnold's "The Gendering of *Créolité*," several of whose parameters and implications have been analyzed in depth above. At the same time, it should be noted that both the historical influences on and the ritualistic aspects of this emphasis on forms and perceptions of masculinity are given short shrift in Arnold's argument. Alternative, more wide-ranging social analyses of Caribbean masculinity, including its attendant rites, cultural practices and prejudices, and historical heritage can be found, inter alia, in Roger D. Abraham's *The Man-of-Words in the West Indies*, Evelyn O'Callaghan's *Woman Version*, and Edith Clarke's *My Mother who Fathered Me*.

Selected Bibliography

Abrahams, Roger D. *The Man-of-Words in the West Indies: Performance and the Emergence of Creole Culture*. Baltimore: Johns Hopkins University Press, 1983.

Alleyne, Mervyn C. "A Linguistic Perspective on the Caribbean." In *Caribbean Contours*, edited by Sidney W. Mintz and Sally Price, 155–80. Baltimore: Johns Hopkins University Press, 1985.

Allsopp, Richard. *Dictionary of Caribbean English Usage*. New York: Oxford University Press, 1996.

Andrade, Susan Z. "The Nigger of the Narcissist: History, Sexuality, and Intertextuality in Maryse Condé's *Hérémakhonon*." *Callaloo* 16, no. 1 (winter 1993):213–26.

Anselin, Alain. *L'Emigration antillaise en France: La Troisième Ile*. Paris: Karthala, 1990.

Appiah, K. Anthony. "The Uncompleted Argument: Du Bois and the Illusion of Race." In *"Race," Writing, and Difference*, edited by Henry Louis Gates Jr., 21–37. Chicago: University of Chicago Press, 1986.

Armstrong Scarboro, Ann. "Afterword." In *I, Tituba, Black Witch of Salem*, translated by Richard Philcox. New York: Ballantine Books, 1992, 187–225.

Arnold, A. James. "The Gendering of *créolité*." In *Penser la créolité*, edited by Maryse Condé et Madeleine Cottenet-Hage, 21–40. Paris: Karthala, 1995.

Ashcroft, Bill, Gareth Griffiths, and Helen Tiffin. *The Empire Writes Back: Theory and Practice in Post-Colonial Literatures*. New York: Methuen, 1989.

Bakhtin, Mikhail. *Rabelais and His World*. Translated by Helen Iswolsky. Bloomington: Indiana University Press, 1984.

Balutansky, Kathleen M. and Marie-Agnès Sourieau. "Introduction." In *Caribbean Creolizations: Reflections on the Cultural Dynamics of Language, Literature, and Identity*, edited by Kathleen M. Balutansky and Marie-Agnès Sourieau, 1–11. Gainesville: University Press of Florida, 1998.

Baudelaire, Charles. *Les Fleurs du mal*. Paris, 1857; rpt. Garnier-Flammarion, 1964.

Benítez-Rojo, Antonio. *The Repeating Island: The Caribbean and the Postmodern Perspective*. Translated by James E. Maraniss. Durham: Duke University Press, 1992.

———. "Three Words toward Creolization." In *Caribbean Creolization: Reflections on the Cultural Dynamics of Language, Literature, and Identity*, edited by Kathleen M. Balutansky and Marie-Agnès Sourieau, 53–61. Gainesville: University Press of Florida, 1998.

Benjamin, Walter. *Illuminations*. Translated by Harry Zohn. Edited by Hannah Arendt. New York: Schocken Books, 1968.

Bernabé, Jean, Patrick Chamoiseau, and Raphaël Confiant. *Eloge de la Créolité/In Praise of Creoleness.* Bilingual edition. Translated by M. B. Taleb-Khyar. Paris: Gallimard, 1993.

———. Interview. "Créolité Bites," by Lucien Taylor. *Transition* 74, 124–161.

Bettelheim, Judith, John Nunley, and Barbara Bridges. "Caribbean Festival Arts: An Introduction." In *Caribbean Festival Arts,* edited by John W. Nunley and Judith Bettelheim, 31–37. Seattle: University of Washington Press, 1988.

Bhabha, Homi K. "The Commitment to Theory." In *Questions of Third Cinema,* edited by Jim Pines and Paul Willemen, 111–32. London: BFI, 1989.

———. *The Location of Culture.* London: Routledge, 1994.

———. "Signs Taken for Wonders: Questions of Ambivalence and Authority under a Tree outside Delhi, May 1917." In *"Race," Writing, and Difference,* edited by Henry Louis Gates Jr., 163–84. Chicago: University of Chicago Press, 1986.

———. "The Third Space." In *Identity: Community, Culture, Difference,* edited by Jonathan Rutherford, 207–21. London: Lawrence and Wishart, 1990.

Blau DuPlessis, Rachel. *Writing beyond the Ending: Narrative Strategies of Twentieth-Century Women Writers.* Bloomington: Indiana University Press, 1985.

Boehmer, Elleke. *Colonial and Postcolonial Literature.* Oxford: Oxford University Press, 1995.

Bolland, O. Nigel. "Creolization and Creole Societies: A Cultural Nationalist View of Caribbean Social History." In *Intellectuals in the 20th Century Caribbean,* vol. 1, *Spectre of the New Class: The Commonwealth Caribbean,* edited by Alistair Hennessy, 50–79. London: Macmillan Caribbean, 1992.

Bongie, Chris. *Islands and Exiles: The Creole Identities of Post/Colonial Literature.* Stanford, Calif.: Stanford University Press, 1998.

———. "The (Un)Exploded Volcano: Creolization and Intertextuality in the Novels of Daniel Maximin." *Callaloo* 17, no. 2 (1994):627–42.

Brathwaite, Edward Kamau. *The Development of Creole Society in Jamaica, 1770–1820.* Oxford: Oxford University Press, 1971.

Britton, Celia. *Edouard Glissant and Postcolonial Theory.* Charlottesville: University Press of Virginia, 1999.

Brooks, Jane. "Challenges to Writing Literature in Creole: The Cases of Guadeloupe and Martinique." In *An Introduction to Caribbean Francophone Writing: Guadeloupe and Martinique,* edited by Sam Haigh, 119–34. Oxford: Berg, 1999.

Brooks, Peter. *Reading for the Plot: Design and Intention in Narrative.* New York: Vintage, 1984.

Burton, Richard D. E. *Afro-Creole: Power, Opposition and Play in the Caribbean.* Ithaca: Cornell University Press, 1997a.

———. "Between the Particular and the Universal: Dilemmas of the Martinican Intellectual." In *Intellectuals in the 20th Century Caribbean,* vol. 2, *Unity in Variety: The Hispanic and Francophone Caribbean,* edited by Alistair Hennessy, 186–210. London: Macmillan Caribbean, 1992.

————. "Comment peut-on être martiniquais? The Recent Work of Edouard Glissant." *Modern Language Review* 79, no. 2 (April 1984).

————. "Maman-France doudou: Family Images in French West Indian Colonial Discourse." *Diacritics* 23, no. 3 (fall 1993): 69–90.

————. "Négritude, Antillanité and Créolité." In *French and West Indian: Martinique, Guadeloupe and French Guiana Today*, edited by Richard D. E. Burton and Fred Reno. London: Macmillan Caribbean, 1995.

————. *Le Roman marron: Etudes sur la littérature martiniquaise contemporaine*. Paris: L'Harmattan, 1997b.

Burton, Richard D. E., and Fred Reno, eds. *French and West Indian: Martinique, Guadeloupe and French Guiana Today*. London: Macmillan Caribbean, 1995.

Cailler, Bernadette. *Conquérants de la nuit nue: Edouard Glissant et L'histoire antillaise*. Tubingen: Gunter Narr Verlag, 1988.

Callois, Roger. "The Detective Novel as Game." Tr. William W. Stowe. In *The Poetics of Murder: Detective Fiction and Literary Theory*, edited by Glenn W. Most and William W. Stowe, 1–12. New York: Harcourt Brace Jovanovich, 1983.

Case, Frederick I. *The Crisis of Identity: Studies in the Guadeloupean and Martiniquan Novel*. Sherbrooke: Naaman, 1985.

Césaire, Aimé. *The Collected Poetry*. Translated and with an introduction by Clayton Eshleman and Annette Smith. Berkeley: University of California Press, 1983.

————. *Discourse on Colonialism*. Translated by Joan Pinkham. New York: Monthly Review Press, 1972.

Chamoiseau, Patrick. *Ecrire en pays dominé*. Paris: Gallimard, 1997.

————. *Martinique*. Paris: Editions Hoa-Qui, 1994.

————. *Solibo Magnifique*. Paris: Folio, 1988a. Translated as *Solibo Magnificent* by Rose-Myriam Réjouis and Val Vinokurov. New York: Pantheon Books, 1997.

————. *Au temps de l'antan: Contes du pays Martinique*. Paris: Hatier, 1988b. Translated as *Creole Folktales* by Linda Coverdale. New York: New Press, 1994.

————. Interview. "Return of the Creole: An Interview with Patrick Chamoiseau," by James Ferguson. *Caribbean Beat*, no. 39, Sept.-Oct. 1999, 48–52.

Chamoiseau, Patrick, and Raphaël Confiant. *Lettres Créoles: Tracées antillaises et continentales de la littérature, 1635–1975*. Paris: Hatier, 1991.

Chatman, Seymour. *Story and Discourse: Narrative Structure in Fiction and Film*. Ithaca: Cornell University Press, 1978.

Chow, Rey. *Writing Diaspora: Tactics of Intervention in Contemporary Cultural Studies*. Bloomington: Indiana University Press, 1993.

Clark, Katerina, and Michael Holquist. *Mikhail Bakhtin*. Cambridge: Harvard University Press, 1984.

Clarke, Edith. *My Mother Who Fathered Me*. London: George Allen and Unwin, 1957.

Cohn, Dorrit. *Transparent Minds: Narrative Modes for Presenting Consciousness in Fiction*. Princeton: Princeton University Press, 1978.

Condé, Maryse. *En attendant le bonheur (Hérémakhonon)*. Paris: Seghers, 1988. Translated as *Heremakhonon* by Richard Philcox. Washington, D.C.: Three Continents Press, 1982.

———. *Guadeloupe*. Paris: Editions Hoa-Qui, 1994.

———. Interview with Ina Césaire. In *La Parole des femmes: Essai sur des romancières des antilles de langue française*, 124–29. Paris: L'Harmattan, 1979.

———. Interview with VèVè Clark. *Callaloo* no. 38, 12, no. 1 (winter 1989):85–133.

———. "Order, Disorder, Freedom, and the West Indian Writer." *Yale French Studies*, 83 (1993): 121–35.

Confiant, Raphaël. *Aimé Césaire: Une Traversée paradoxale du siècle*. Paris: Stock, 1993.

Craton, Michael. *Testing the Chains: Opposition to Slavery in the British West Indies*. Ithaca: Cornell University Press, 1982.

Crosta, Suzanne. "Breaking the Silence: Cultural Identities and Narrative Configurations in the French Caribbean Novel." In *An Introduction to Caribbean Francophone Writing: Guadeloupe and Martinique*, edited by Sam Haigh, 159–76. Oxford: Berg, 1999.

Culler, Jonathan. *Flaubert: The Uses of Uncertainty*. Ithaca: Cornell University Press, 1985.

———. *On Deconstruction: Theory and Criticism after Structuralism*. Ithaca: Cornell University Press, 1982.

Dash, J. Michael. *Edouard Glissant*. New York: Cambridge University Press, 1995.

———. *The Other America: Caribbean Literature in a New World Context*. Charlottesville: University Press of Virginia, 1998.

———. "Writing the Body: Edouard Glissant's Poetics of Re-membering." In *L'Héritage de Caliban*, edited by Maryse Condé, 75–84. Paris: Editions Jasor, 1992.

Davis, Gregson. *Aimé Césaire*. London: Cambridge, 1997.

de Man, Paul. *Blindness and Insight: Essays in the Rhetoric of Contemporary Criticism*. Minneapolis: University of Minnesota Press, 1983.

Depestre, René. "Les Aspects créateurs du métissage culturel aux Caraïbes." *Notre Librairie* 74 (April–June 1984): 61–65.

Derrida, Jacques. *Of Grammatology*. Translated by Gayatri Chakravorty Spivak. Baltimore: Johns Hopkins University Press, 1974.

———. *Writing and Difference*. Translated by Alan Bass. Chicago: University of Chicago Press, 1978.

do Nascimento Oliveira Carneiro, Maria. "Le Symbolisme de l'eau dans *La Lézarde*." In *Horizons d'Edouard Glissant*, edited by Yves-Alain Favre and Antonio Ferreira de Brito, 411–21. Paris: J & D Editions, 1992.

Dracius-Pinalie, Suzanne. *L'Autre qui danse*. Paris: Seghers, 1989.

Edwards, Bryan. *The History, Civil and Commercial, of the British Colonies in the West Indies*. Vol. 2. London, 1819. (Quoted in Keith Warner, *Kaiso!*)

Erickson, John D. "*Maximin's* L'Isolé soleil *and Caliban's Curse*." *Callaloo* 15, no. 1 (winter 1992):119–30.

Fallope, Josette. "La Politique d'assimilation et ses résistances." In *Autrement* 28, 1994.

Guadeloupe 1875–1914: Les Soubresauts d'une société pluri-ethnique ou les ambiguïtés de l'assimilation, edited by Henriette Levillain, 34–47.

Fanon, Frantz. *Black Skin, White Masks.* Translated by Charles Lam Markham. London: MacGibbon and Kee, 1968.

———. *The Wretched of the Earth.* Translated by Constance Farrington. New York: Grove Press, 1968.

Favre, Yves-Alain, and Antonio Ferreira de Brito, eds. *Horizons d'Edouard Glissant.* Paris: J & D Editions, 1992.

Freud, Sigmund. "Negation." In *General Psychological Theory.* New York: Collier, 1963, 213–17.

Furman, Nelly. "The Politics of Language: Beyond the Gender Principle?" In *Making a Difference: Feminist Literary Criticism,* edited by Gayle Green and Coppelia Kahn, 59–79. New York: Methuen, 1985.

Gates, Henry Louis, Jr. "Criticism in the Jungle." In *Black Literature and Literary Theory,* edited by Henry Louis Gates Jr., 1–24. New York: Methuen, 1984.

———. *Figures in Black: Words, Signs, and the "Racial" Self.* New York: Oxford University Press, 1987.

Gikandi, Simon. *Writing in Limbo: Modernism and Caribbean Literature.* Ithaca: Cornell University Press, 1992.

Gilroy, Paul. *The Black Atlantic: Modernity and Double Consciousness.* Cambridge, Mass.: Harvard University Press, 1993.

———. *Small Acts: Thoughts on the Politics of Black Cultures.* London: Serpent's Tail, 1993.

Glissant, Edouard. *Le Discours antillais.* Paris: Seuil, 1981. Translated as *Caribbean Discourse: Selected Essays* by J. Michael Dash. Charlottesville: University of Virginia Press, 1989.

———. *L'Intention poétique.* Paris: Seuil, 1969.

———. *Introduction à une poétique du divers.* Paris: Gallimard, 1996.

———. *La Lézarde.* Paris: Seuil, 1958. Translated as *The Ripening* by J. Michael Dash. London: Heinemann, 1985.

———. *Poetics of Relation.* Translated by Betsy Wing. Ann Arbor: University of Michigan Press, 1997.

Hall, Stuart. "Cultural Identity and Diaspora." In *Colonial Discourse and Post-Colonial Theory: A Reader,* edited by Patrick Williams and Laura Chrisman, 392–403. New York: Columbia University Press, 1994.

———. "Introduction: Who Needs Identity?" In *Questions of Cultural Identity,* edited by Stuart Hall and Paul du Gay, 1–17. London: Sage, 1996.

———. "Minimal Selves." In *The Real Me: Post-Modernism and the Question of Identity,* 44–46. ICA Documents no. 6, 1987. London: Institute of Contemporary Arts.

———. "New Ethnicities." In *Stuart Hall: Critical Dialogues in Cultural Studies,* edited by David Morley and Kuan-Hsing Chen, 441–49. London: Routledge, 1996.

———. "When Was 'the Post-colonial'? Thinking at the Limit." In *The Post-Colonial*

Question: Common Skies, Divided Horizons, edited by Iain Chambers and Lidia Curti, 242–60. London: Routledge, 1996.

Harlow, Barbara. *Resistance Literature.* New York: Methuen, 1987.

Heissenbüttel, Helmut. "Rules of the Game of the Crime Novel." Translated by Glenn W. Most and William W. Stowe. In *The Poetics of Murder: Detective Fiction and Literary Theory,* edited by Glenn W. Most and William W. Stowe, 79–92. New York: Harcourt Brace Jovanovich, 1983.

Hewitt, Leah D. *Autobiographical Tightropes: Simone de Beauvoir, Nathalie Sarraute, Marguerite Duras, Monique Wittig, and Maryse Condé.* Lincoln: University of Nebraska Press, 1990.

JanMohamed, Abdul. "The Economy of Manichean Allegory: The Function of Racial Difference in Colonialist Literature." In *"Race," Writing, and Difference,* edited by Henry Louis Gates Jr., 78–106. Chicago: University of Chicago Press, 1985.

Kamuf, Peggy. *Signature Pieces: On the Institution of Authorship.* Ithaca: Cornell University Press, 1988.

———. "Writing like a Woman." In *Women and Language in Literature and Society,* edited by Sally McConnell-Ginet, Ruth Borker, and Nelly Furman, 284–99. New York: Praeger, 1980.

Kauffman, Linda S. *Discourses of Desire: Gender, Genre, and Epistolary Fictions.* Ithaca: Cornell University Press, 1986.

Khoury, Elias. "The World of Meanings in Palestinian Poetry." In *The Lost Memory.* Beirut: Institute for Arab Research, 1982. Translated and quoted in Barbara Harlow, *Resistance Literature.*

Lacan, Jacques. *Ecrits.* Translated by Alan Sheridan. New York: Norton, 1977.

———. *The Four Fundamental Concepts of Psycho-Analysis,* edited by Jacques-Alain Miller. Translated by Alan Sheridan. Paris: Seuil, 1973.

Lecloux, Dominique. "Le Jeu de la lumière et de l'eau dans *La Lézarde.* In *Horizons d'Edouard Glissant,* edited by Yves-Alain Favre and Antonio Ferreira de Brito, 401–10. Paris: J & D Editions, 1992.

Lewis, Gordon K. *Main Currents in Caribbean Thought: The Historical Evolution of Caribbean Society in its Ideological Aspects.* Baltimore: Johns Hopkins University Press, 1983.

Lionnet, Françoise. *Autobiographical Voices: Race, Gender, Self-Portraiture.* Ithaca: Cornell University Press, 1989.

———. "*Logiques métisses:* Cultural Appropriation and Postcolonial Representations." *College Literature* 19 and 20 (1992/1993):100–20.

———. "*Métissage,* Emancipation, and Female Textuality in Two Francophone Writers." In *Life/Lines: Theorizing Women's Autobigraphy,* edited by Bella Brodzki and Celeste Schenck, 260–78. Ithaca: Cornell University Press, 1988.

———. *Postcolonial Representations: Women, Literature, Identity.* Ithaca: Cornell University Press, 1995.

———. "Reframing Baudelaire: Literary History, Biography, Postcolonial Theory, and Vernacular Languages." *Diacritics* 28, no. 3 (1998):63–85.

Lowenthal, David. *West Indian Societies.* New York: Oxford University Press, 1972.

Makward, Christiane. "Cherchez la franco-femme." In *Postcolonial Subjects: Francophone Women Writers,* edited by Mary Jean Greene, Karen Gould, Micheline Rice-Maximin, Keith L. Walker, and Jack A. Yeager, 115–23. Minneapolis: University of Minnesota Press, 1996.

Martin, Wallace. *Recent Theories of Narrative.* Ithaca: Cornell University Press, 1986.

Maximin, Daniel. "Entretien." *Les Nouvelles du sud* 3 (1986):35–50.

———. *L'Isolé Soleil.* Paris: Points, 1981. Translated as *Lone Sun,* and with an introduction, by Clarisse Zimra. Charlottesville: University of Virginia Press, 1989.

———. *Soufrières.* Paris: Seuil, 1987.

Memmi, Albert. *The Colonizer and the Colonized.* Translated by Howard Greenfeld. Boston: Beacon Press, 1967.

Miller, Christopher L. "After Negation: Africa in Two Novels by Maryse Condé." In *Postcolonial Subjects: Francophone Women Writers,* edited by Mary Jean Greene, Karen Gould, Micheline Rice-Maximin, Keith L. Walker, and Jack A. Yeager, 173–85. Minneapolis: University of Minnesota Press, 1996.

Mimiko-Bestman, Ajoké. "Mère révée, mère réelle: Le Désarroi d'une rencontre." *Franzosisch Heute* 2 (1987):163–69.

Most, Glenn W., and William W. Stowe, eds. *The Poetics of Murder: Detective Fiction and Literary Theory.* New York: Harcourt Brace Jovanovich, 1983.

Musset, Alfred de. *On ne badine pas avec l'amour.* Paris, 1834; rpt. Bordas, 1963.

Nandy, Ashis. *The Intimate Enemy: Loss and Recovery of Self under Colonialism.* Delhi: Oxford University Press, 1983.

Nettleford, Rex. "Implications for Caribbean Development." In *Caribbean Festival Arts,* edited by John W. Nunley and Judith Bettelheim, 183–97. Seattle: University of Washington Press, 1988.

———. *Mirror, Mirror: Identity, Race and Protest in Jamaica.* Kingston: Collins and Sangster, 1970.

Nunley, John. "Masquerade Mix-Up in Trinidad Carnival: Live Once, Die Forever." In *Caribbean Festival Arts,* edited by John W. Nunley and Judith Bettelheim, 85–116. Seattle: University of Washington Press, 1988.

O'Callaghan, Evelyn. *Woman Version: Theoretical Approaches to West Indian Fiction by Women.* London: Macmillan, 1993.

Ormerod, Beverley. *An Introduction to the French Caribbean Novel.* London: Heinemann, 1985.

———. "The Representation of Women in French Caribbean Fiction." In *An Introduction to Caribbean Francophone Writing: Guadeloupe and Martinique,* edited by Sam Haigh, 101–18. Oxford: Berg, 1999.

Parry, Benita. "Problems in Current Theories of Colonial Discourse." *Oxford Literary Review* 9, nos. 1 and 2 (1987), 27–58.

———. "Resistance Theory/Theorising Resistance or Two Cheers for Nativism." In *Colonial Discourse/Postcolonial Theory,* edited by Francis Barker, Peter Hulme, and Margaret Iversen, 172–96. Manchester: Manchester University Press, 1994.

Pepin, Ernest and Raphaël Confiant. "The Stakes of *Créolité.*" In *Caribbean Creolizations: Reflections on the Cultural Dynamics of Language, Literature, and Identity,* edited by Kathleen M. Balutansky and Marie-Agnès Sourieau, 96–100. Gainesville: University Press of Florida, 1998.

Pfaff, Françoise. *Entretiens avec Maryse Condé.* Paris: Karthala, 1993.

Price, Richard, and Sally Price. "Shadowboxing in the Mangrove: The Politics of Identity in Postcolonial Martinique." In *Caribbean Romances: The Politics of Regional Representation,* edited by Belinda Edmondson, 123–62. Charlottesville: University Press of Virginia, 1999.

Radhakrishnan, R. *Diasporic Meditations: Between Home and Location.* Minneapolis: University of Minnesota Press, 1996.

Rimmon-Kenan, Shlomith. *Narrative Fiction: Contemporary Poetics.* New York: Methuen, 1983.

Roberts, Peter A. *West Indians and Their Language.* New York: Cambridge University Press, 1988.

Rosello, Mireille. *Littérature et identité créole aux Antilles.* Paris: Editions Karthala, 1992.

Said, Edward W. *Culture and Imperialism.* New York: Knopf, 1993.

Scharfman, Ronnie. "*Créolité* is/as Resistance: Raphaël Confiant's *Le Nègre et l'Amiral.*" In *Penser la créolité,* edited by Maryse Condé and Madeleine Cottenet-Hage, 125–34. Paris: Editions Karthala, 1995.

———. "Rewriting the Cesaires: Daniel Maximin's Caribbean Discourse." In *L'Héritage de Caliban,* edited by Maryse Condé, 233–45. Paris: Editions Jasor, 1992.

Schmidt, Joël, and Seth Bernardete, eds. *Larousse Greek and Roman Mythology.* New York: McGraw-Hill, 1980.

Schwarz-Bart, Simone. *Pluie et vent sur Télumée Miracle.* Paris: Seuil, 1972.

Sekyi-Otu, Ato. *Fanon's Dialectic of Experience.* Cambridge: Harvard University Press, 1996.

Shelton, Marie-Denise. "Women Writers of the French-Speaking Caribbean-An Overview." In *Caribbean Women Writers: Essays from the First International Conference,* edited by Selwyn Cudjoe, 346–56. Wellesley, Mass.: Calaloux, 1990.

Silverman, Kaja. *The Subject of Semiotics.* New York: Oxford University Press, 1983.

Slemon, Stephen. "Postcolonial Critical Theory." In *New National and Post-colonial Literatures: An Introduction,* edited by Bruce King, 178–97. New York: Oxford University Press, 1996.

Sourieau, Marie-Agnès. "Patrick Chamoiseau, *Solibo Magnifique:* From the Escheat of Speech to the Emergence of Language." *Callaloo* 15, no. 1 (winter 1992): 131–37.

Spillers, Hortense. "Notes on an Alternative Model: Neither/Nor." In *The Year Left 2: Toward a Rainbow Socialism. Essays on Race, Ethnicity, Class and Gender,* edited by Mike Davis, Manning Marable, Fred Pfeil, and Michael Sprinker, 176–94. London: Verso, 1987.

Spivak, Gayatri C. "Woman in Difference: Mahasweta Devi's 'Douloti the Beautiful.'" *Nationalisms and Sexualities.* Andrew Parker, Mary Russo, Doris Sommer, and Patricia Yaeger, eds., 96–117. New York: Routledge, 1992.

Todorov, Tzvetan. *The Conquest of America: The Question of the Other.* Translated by Richard Howard. New York: Harper and Row, 1984.

———. *Introduction to Poetics.* Translated by Richard Howard. Minneapolis: University of Minnesota Press, 1981.

———. *The Poetics of Prose.* Translated by Richard Howard. Ithaca: Cornell University Press, 1977.

Viola, Herman J. "Seeds of Change." In *Seeds of Change: Five Hundred Years since Columbus,* edited by Herman J. Viola and Carolyn Margolis, 11–15. Washington, D.C.: Smithsonian Institution, 1991.

Walcott, Derek. "A Letter to Chamoiseau." *New York Review of Books,* August 14, 1997, 45–48.

———. "The Muse of History: An Essay." In *Is Massa Day Dead? Black Moods in the Caribbean,* edited by Orde Coombs, 1–29. New York: Anchor Press, 1974.

———. "What the Twilight Says: An Overture." In *Dream on Monkey Mountain and Other Plays,* 3–40. New York: Farrar, Straus and Giroux, 1970.

Warner, Keith Q. *Kaiso!: The Trinidad Calypso. A Study of the Calypso as Oral Literature.* Washington, D.C.: Three Continents Press, 1982.

Waugh, Patricia. *Metafiction: The Theory and Practice of Self-Conscious Fiction.* New York: Methuen, 1984.

Webb, Barbara J. *Myth and History in Caribbean Fiction.* Amherst: University of Massachusetts Press, 1992.

White, Hayden. *Metahistory.* Baltimore: Johns Hopkins University Press, 1973.

———. "The Value of Narrativity in the Representation of Reality." In *On Narrative,* edited by W. J. T. Mitchell, 1–23. Chicago: University of Chicago Press, 1981.

Williams, Eric. *From Columbus to Castro: The History of the Caribbean 1492–1969.* New York: Vintage, 1970.

Young, Robert. *White Mythologies: Writing History and the West.* London: Routledge, 1990.

Zimra, Clarisse. "Daughters of Mayotte, Sons of Frantz: The Unrequited Self in Caribbean Literature." In *An Introduction to Caribbean Francophone Writing: Guadeloupe and Martinique,* edited by Sam Haigh, 177–94. Oxford: Berg, 1999.

———. "Je(ux) d'histoire chez Daniel Maximin et Vincent Placoly." In *L'Héritage de Caliban,* edited by Maryse Condé, 265–85. Paris: Editions Jasor, 1992.

Index

H. Adlai Murdoch, associate professor of French and Francophone studies at the University of Illinois at Urbana-Champaign, is the author of articles in *Callaloo, Research in African Literatures,* and *Yale French Studies.*